ALGORITHMIC TRADING WITH INTERACTIVE BROKERS (PYTHON AND C++)

MATTHEW SCARPINO

Algorithmic Trading with Interactive Brokers (Python and C++)

Matthew Scarpino

© 2019 by Matthew Scarpino. All rights reserved.

DISCLAIMER

The content of this book does not constitute financial advice. Like all financial trading, algorithmic trading carries a signficant amount of risk and may not be suitable for all investors. Past performance is not indicative of future results.

A computer error can produce a significant loss of funds, even beyond a client's available funds. Therefore, you should not write algorithmic trading applications until you've acquired a great deal of experience with programming and debugging applications. Seek advice from a professional advisor if you have concerns.

No part of this publication may be reproduced, distributed, or transmitted in any form or by any means, including photocopying, recording, or other electronic or mechanical methods, without the prior written permission of the publisher, except in the case of brief quotations embodied in critical reviews and certain other noncommercial uses permitted by copyright law.

Printed in the United States of America

Publisher's Cataloging-in-Publication data

Author: Scarpino, Matthew

Title: Algorithmic Trading with Interactive Brokers (Python and C++)

Description: Guide to writing algorithmic trading applications using Python and C++

ISBN: 978-0-9973037-3-5

p. cm.

Table of Contents

Chapter 1 – Introducing Algorithmic Trading and Interactive Brokers 1

    1.1 Interactive Brokers 2

    1.2 Trader Workstation and the TWS API 7

    1.3 Organization of this Book 10

    1.4 More Information 12

    1.5 Summary 13

Chapter 2 – Stocks, Bonds, and Trader Workstation (TWS) 15

    2.1 Overview of Trader Workstation 15

    2.2 Buying Stock with TWS 19

    2.3 Buying Bonds with TWS 29

    2.4 IB Gateway 35

    2.5 Summary 36

Chapter 3 – Stock Options 37

　3.1　A Gentle Introduction to Stock Options 38

　3.2　Calls and Puts 40

　3.3　Option Expiration 46

　3.4　Trading Options in TWS 48

　3.5　Moneyness 50

　3.6　Option Value 50

　3.7　Greeks 52

　3.8　Summary 55

Chapter 4 – Option Trading Strategies 57

　4.1　Stock and Option Strategies 57

　4.2　Spreads 60

　4.3　Delta Neutral Strategies 66

　4.4　Advanced Strategies 68

　4.5　Building Strategies in TWS 73

　4.6　Summary 75

Chapter 5 – Trading Futures Contracts 77

　5.1　Overview of Futures Contracts 78

　5.2　Ordering Futures Contracts in TWS 83

　5.3　Index and Security Futures 84

　5.4　Futures Spreads 85

　5.5　Summary 88

Chapter 6 – Fundamental Classes of the TWS API 91

    6.1 Overview of TWS API Applications 92

    6.2 Fundamental Classes in Python 95

    6.3 Fundamental Classes in C++ 99

    6.4 Summary 108

Chapter 7 – Contracts and Orders 111

    7.1 Contracts 112

    7.2 Orders 128

    7.3 Placing Orders 139

    7.4 Requesting Order Data 142

    7.5 Submitting Orders in Code 147

    7.6 Summary 154

Chapter 8 – Accessing Financial Data 157

    8.1 Technical Data 157

    8.2 Fundamental Data 176

    8.3 Accessing News 178

    8.4 Accessing Financial Data in Code 181

    8.5 Summary 187

Chapter 9 – Scanning for Securities 189

    9.1 Creating a Scanner Subscription 190

    9.2 Requesting the Subscription 194

9.3 Security Scanning in Code..199

9.4 Summary..203

Chapter 10 – Advanced Order Configuration..........................205

10.1 Parent-Child Orders..206

10.2 Submitting Large Orders..209

10.3 Order Submission Algorithms...211

10.4 Dynamic Conditions...215

10.5 Submitting Advanced Orders..221

10.6 Summary..227

Chapter 11 – Technical Indicators..229

11.1 Trend Indicators...230

11.2 Momentum Indicators..236

11.3 Volume Indicators..245

11.4 Volatility Indicators...251

11.5 Summary..257

Chapter 12 – Implementing Option Combinations...................259

12.1 Option-Specific Functions..260

12.2 Constructing Vertical Spreads...271

12.3 Constructing Delta Neutral Strategies...........................284

12.4 Summary..293

Chapter 13 – The Turtle Trading and Bollinger-MFI Systems **295**

    13.1   Obtaining Test Data 296

    13.2   The Turtle System 303

    13.3   The Bollinger-MFI System 315

    13.4   Summary 326

Chapter 14 – Practical Algorithmic Trading **329**

    14.1   Introducing SimpleAlgo 330

    14.2   Evaluating Investor Sentiment 331

    14.3   Selecting Candidate Stocks 336

    14.4   Implementing a Breakout Strategy 340

    14.5   Selecting the Target Stock 344

    14.6   Placing the Order 353

    14.7   Summary 358

Appendix A – The FIX Protocol **359**

    A.1   Overview of FIX 360

    A.2   QuickFIX 364

    A.3   Common Messages 372

    A.4   Summary 388

Appendix B – The Kelly Criterion **391**

    B.1 Using the Kelly Criterion 392

    B.2 Derivation 392

    B.3 Criticism and Alternatives 396

    B.4 Summary 397

Index **399**

Chapter 1

Introducing Algorithmic Trading and Interactive Brokers

Michael Lewis has written several books on finance and politics, but one of his most fascinating books involves baseball. His 2003 book *Moneyball* covers the Oakland Athletics and their revolutionary method of recruiting players. Instead of relying on agents and scouts, the Athletics developed an algorithm that focused primarily on a player's ability to get on base.

As a result of this approach, the Athletics recruited players overlooked by teams with deeper pockets. These players succeeded beyond anyone's expectations, and the Athletics reached the Major League playoffs in 2002 and 2003—a feat that stunned the world of baseball. Inspired by the Athletics, the Boston Red Sox adopted a similar recruiting method and won the World Series in 2013.

As I read *Moneyball*, I thought of how I could improve my investing by following a similar method. *What if I picked stocks using statistics instead of rumors and recommendations? What if I focused on undervalued companies that get on base instead of overvalued companies that hit home runs? And what if I programmed a computer to select securities and submit orders?*

The idea of using a computer to place trades is called *algorithmic trading*, and I'm far from the first to consider it. One of the first instances of algorithmic trading took place in 1987, when Thomas Peterffy programmed a computer to read NASDAQ prices and place trades. Horrified, the exchange promptly banned the program, but Peterffy won in the end—he started Interactive Brokers, the first brokerage firm devoted solely to electronic trading.

Interactive Brokers is also one of the first brokerages to provide free access to algorithmic trading. This makes it possible to toss aside human biases and psychological issues and take advantage of the speed and memory of modern computers.

In writing this book, my goal is to teach you how to implement algorithms using the tools provided by Interactive Brokers. To be precise, I'll show you how to write applications in Python and C++ capable of scanning securities, reading financial data, and submitting orders automatically. I can't promise that you'll be as successful as Thomas Peterffy, but your success will be limited only by the shrewdness of your algorithm and the quality of your programming.

The goal of this chapter is far less ambitious. I'll start by describing Interactive Brokers and the process of opening an account. Then I'll present a non-technical overview of their programming tools and the content of this book.

1.1 Interactive Brokers

When I first became interested in algorithmic trading, I looked at a number of programming interfaces, including those provided by Fidelity, TD Ameritrade, E*Trade, and LightSpeed. Most were focused on simplicity and ease of development, but in the end, I chose Interactive Brokers (or IB) because of three factors:

- IB's API is mature, flexible, and intended for high-speed data acquisition and order execution.
- IB provides access to a wide variety of financial instruments, including IPOs, corporate bonds, and international securities.
- IB's commissions are significantly lower than those of other trading firms.

This section discusses the process of starting an account with IB and the fees it charges. But first, I'd like to provide a brief history of IB as a company.

1.1.1 Brief History

While most brokerage firms are founded by bankers, traders, and financiers, Interactive Brokers was started by a programmer. In 1987, Thomas Peterffy coded one of the very first algorithmic trading programs, which read NASDAQ prices and placed orders automatically. NASDAQ banned Peterffy's program but only strengthened his belief in the importance of computers in trading.

In 1993, Peterffy incorporated Interactive Brokers to provide high-speed electronic trading. In 1995, IB released the first version of its Trader Workstation (TWS) platform for trading. The company grew rapidly, and in 2001, IB handled more than 200,000 trades daily.

Today, IB is the largest electronic brokerage firm in the U.S., with more than 600,000 client accounts. Barron's has rated it the #1 online broker in 2018 and 2019, and it has won several awards from Investopedia and StockBroker.com.

1.1.2 Starting an Account

If you want to use IB's tools for automatic trading, you'll need to become a client of the brokerage. Thankfully, IB makes it easy to open an account and the brokerage doesn't require any initial minimum balance.

IB supports many different types of accounts, including accounts for institutions, small businesses, and individuals. Applying for an individual account requires ten steps:

1. Visit the web page https://www.interactivebrokers.com/en/index.php?f=4695.
2. Click the red button labeled **INDIVIDUAL INVESTOR OR TRADER**.
3. Fill out the Application page, which requires an email address, username, and password. Then click the **SAVE & CONTINUE** button in the lower right.
4. IB will send a message to your listed email account. To confirm your email address, click the message's **Verify Account** button. Then enter your username and password.
5. The following page asks for your place of residence and account type (Individual). Fill in the information and click **SAVE & CONTINUE** in the lower right.
6. Now the real application starts. The first page asks for personal information, such as addresses and contact information. When finished, click **SAVE & CONTINUE**.
7. The second page asks for regulatory information, such as your annual income and investment objectives. It also asks for your experience investing in stocks, bonds, options, futures, mutual funds, and so on.
8. The third page presents all the agreements and disclosures that brokerage firms are required to provide. To continue, you need to agree to each item and sign your name electronically at the bottom of the form.
9. The fourth page presents two optional features for your account: a debit card and a stock lending program.
10. After the fourth page, IB will give you a chance to look over the current application information. Once you click **SAVE & CONTINUE**, the application will be submitted to IB for processing.

If all goes well, you'll receive a welcome email message and a link to log into your new account. But you can't access market data or submit orders until you transfer funds to your account.

1.1.3 Fees

A trading algorithm may submit hundreds or thousands of trades in a day, so brokerage fees play a significant role in determining its profit. Thankfully, IB charges lower fees than almost every other online broker. This is a central reason why it wins awards year after year.

The bad news about IB's fees is that they can be difficult to understand. In the following discussion, I'll do my best to explain how IB arrives at fees for stocks, warrants, ETFs, options, and futures.

Stocks, Warrants, and ETFs

The second page of the account application asks whether you'd prefer tiered pricing or fixed pricing. This determines how commissions and fees are computed for stocks, warrants, and ETFs. Tiered pricing bases trading fees on average monthly volume, and Table 1.1 presents the fee structure for tiered pricing in the United States.

Table 1.1
Tiered Pricing Fees — Stocks, Warrants, and ETFs (in USD)

Monthly Volume	Commission Per Share	Minimum Per Order	Maximum Per Order
Less than/equal 300,000 shares	0.0035	0.35	1% of trade
300,001 - 3,000,000 shares	0.002	0.35	1% of trade
3,000,001 - 20,000,000 shares	0.0015	0.35	1% of trade
20,000,001 - 100,000,000 shares	0.001	0.35	1% of trade
Greater than 100,000,000 shares	0.0005	0.35	1% of trade

These figures are current as of July 2019 and apply only to clients in the United States. To see the fee structures for different countries, visit https://www.interactivebrokers.com/en/index.php?f=1590.

If an applicant chooses a fixed pricing structure, commissions for stocks, warrants, and ETFs will be determined as follows:

- **Base fee** — 0.005 USD per share
- **Minimum fee per order** — 1.00 USD
- **Maximum fee per order** — 1% of trade

To understand the difference between the tiered and fixed pricing structures, suppose you buy 400 shares of BGCR at 10 USD/share. If you trade fewer than 300,000 shares per month, tiered pricing sets the commission to 1.40 USD (400 * 0.0035 = 1.40). The fixed pricing option sets the fee to 2.00 USD (400 * 0.005 = 2.00).

The preceding discussion doesn't take into account the trading activity fee (TAF) charged by FINRA (Financial Industry Regulatory Authority). In the United States, this is computed by multiplying the quantity sold by 0.000119 USD.

Options

Fees for trading options are more complicated than those for trading stocks. This is because the fee depends on three factors: monthly trading volume, the option's premium, and whether the order is submitted to IB's SMART routing system or sent directly to a specific exchange (I'll discuss exchanges and order routing in Chapter 2).

Table 1.2 lists the fees for options orders sent to IB's SMART routing feature.

Table 1.2

Option Trading Fees for SMART Routing (in USD)

Monthly Volume	Option Premium	Commission	Minimum Per Order
Less than/equal 10,000	less than/equal 0.05	0.25/contract	1.00
	greater than 0.05, less than 0.10	0.50/contract	1.00
	greater than/equal 0.10	0.70/contract	1.00
10,001 - 50,000	less than 0.05	0.25/contract	1.00
	greater than/equal 0.05	0.70/contract	1.00
50,001 - 100,000	all premiums	0.25/contract	1.00
Greater than 100,000	all premiums	0.15/contract	1.00

If you direct an option trade to a specific exchange, IB charges 1.00 USD per contract with a minimum fee of 1.00.

In addition to the fee structure presented above, the exchange that receives the contract charges its own fee for options trading. You can view exchange-specific fees by visiting https://www.interactivebrokers.com/en/index.php?f=1590&p=options1 and clicking the link for the desired exchange.

In the United States, every trade also has an options regulatory fee required by the Options Clearing Corporation (0.0388 USD per contract). As with stocks, FINRA charges a trading activity fee (0.002 USD * quantity sold).

Futures

As with stocks, ETFs, and warrants, fees for futures contracts are determined by whether tiered pricing or fixed pricing was selected in the application. Table 1.3 lists the fees for futures contracts in USD when the tiered pricing option is selected. As shown in the last two columns, IB may charge contract-specific fees.

Table 1.3
Tiered Pricing Fees — Futures Contracts (USD)

Monthly Volume	Commission	E-mini FX Futures	E-micro FX Futures
Less than/equal to 1,000	0.85	0.5	0.15
1,001 - 10,000	0.65	0.4	0.12
10,001 - 20,000	0.45	0.3	0.08
Greater than 20,000	0.25	0.15	0.05

Table 1.4 lists the fees associated with futures contracts when the fixed pricing option is selected. Note that these figures only apply to clients in the United States. For a full list of fees, visit https://www.interactivebrokers.com/en/index.php?f=1590&p=futures1.

Table 1.4
Fixed Pricing Fees — Futures Contracts (USD)

Contract Type	Commission
US Future/Future Options	0.85
NYBOT Russell 1000/2000 Index	0.45
GLOBEX E-mini Futures	0.50
GLOBEX E-micro Futures	0.50
CFE Bitcoin (GXBT)	5.00
CME Bitcoin (BRR)	10.00

The majority of futures contracts make use of leverage. On top of the fees listed, IB charges extra fees depending on the level of funding relative to margin requirements. Chapter 5 discusses futures contracts and margin requirements in greater depth.

In addition to the fees discussed in this section, IB sets fee structures for bonds, mutual funds, metals, and foreign exchange trading. For up-to-date fee schedules, visit the main page at https://www.interactivebrokers.com/en/index.php?f=1590.

1.2 Trader Workstation and the TWS API

Every IB programmer should be familiar with Trader Workstation (TWS), IB's application for reading financial data and submitting orders. There are two reasons for this:

1. Applications send messages to IB's servers through TWS or the IB Gateway, so developers must have one of the two applications running on their system.

2. IB's programming API automates the operations that can be performed in TWS. Therefore, the better you understand TWS, the better you'll understand the capabilities of the programming API.

This section provides a brief overview of TWS and its capabilities. Then I'll introduce the programming interface, whose full name is Trader Workstation Application Programming Interface (TWS API). The last part of the section explains how to obtain and execute the example source code for this book.

1.2.1 Introducing Trader Workstation

Most individual clients submit orders through Trader Workstation (TWS). Anyone can download this from https://www.interactivebrokers.com/en/index.php?f=16042, but only users with IB accounts can access financial data and place trades. Figure 1.1 shows what the main window of TWS looks like.

Figure 1.1 The Main Window of IB's Trader Workstation

Chapters 2 through 5 discuss Trader Workstation and its many features in detail. For now, all you need to know about TWS is that you can automate its operation by writing applications with the Trader Workstation API.

1.2.2 The Trader Workstation API (TWS API)

While it's helpful to understand how to use TWS manually, this book focuses on automating TWS operations in code. To accomplish this, you need to obtain the TWS API, which requires the following steps:

1. Visit the web site https://www.interactivebrokers.com/en/index.php?f=5041.
2. Scroll down and click the red button entitled **GET API SOFTWARE**.
3. Agree to the non-commercial license. This forbids selling the API to others or giving it to others for financial benefit.

After you agree to the license, the next page illustrates the different versions available for download. Figure 1.2 shows what this looks like on my system.

Windows

IB API Stable for Windows

Version: API 9.72
Release Date: Sep 14 2016
RELEASE NOTES

IB API Latest for Windows

Version: API 9.76
Release Date: May 08 2019
RELEASE NOTES

Mac / Unix

IB API Stable for Mac/Unix

Version: API 9.72
Release Date: Sep 14 2016
RELEASE NOTES

IB API Latest for Mac / Unix

Version: API 9.76
Release Date: May 08 2019
RELEASE NOTES

IB API Beta

Figure 1.2 Versions of the Trader Workstation API

No matter what operating system you use, I recommend downloading the latest API. That is, if your development system runs Windows, I recommend clicking on **IB API Latest for Windows**. If you develop applications on Linux or Mac OS, I recommend clicking on **IB API Latest for Mac/Unix**.

After you choose an API version, the browser will download an archive to your system. If you decompress the archive for Windows systems, you'll find the following folders:

- **source** — contains source code for C++, C#, Java, and Python
- **samples** — contains sample code for C++, C#, Excel, Java, Python, and VB
- **test** — contains a Visual Studio project for C# development

If you decompress the archive for Mac OS and Linux systems, you'll find a directory named IBJts. Inside IBJts, you'll find two folders:

- **samples** — contains sample code for C++, Java, and Python
- **source** — contains source code for C++, Java, and Python

It's important to see that IB doesn't provide any libraries or precompiled modules. The API contains all of the source code needed to develop TWS applications. The good news is that these files provide complete visibility into the operation of TWS applications. The bad news is that compiling all the source files with each build takes a significant amount of time.

For this reason, I recommend compiling IB's source code into a library before developing applications. This means creating a dynamic-linked library (*.dll) on Windows, a shared object library (*.so) on Mac OS/Linux systems, or a Java archive (*.jar) for Java development.

If you choose not to precompile the API source code, be sure to identify the location of the API's source files. For Python developers, this means setting the `PYTHONPATH` environment variable to the location of the source\pythonclient\ibapi directory. For Java developers, this means setting `CLASSPATH` to the location of the source\JavaClient folder. For C++ developers, this means telling the compiler that source files and header files are in the source\cppclient\client directory.

1.2.3 Example Code

This book touches on many financial concepts, but in essence, this is a book on programming. Most of the book's content deals with the classes and functions in the TWS API. To demonstrate how these classes and functions can be used in practice, I've provided example code on the www.algo-book.com web site.

If you visit this site, you can freely download three archives, all named algobook.zip. Two of them contain C++ code (one for Visual Studio users, one for GCC users). The third archive contains Python code.

As the title makes clear, this book is concerned with developing trading applications in Python and C++. I chose these languages because I feel that C++ is the best language when speed is a priority and Python is the best language to use in (nearly) all other circumstances.

In the Python archive, the example code is split into directories named after chapters. That is, the ch7 folder contains the modules discussed in Chapter 7, the ch8 folder contains the modules discussed in Chapter 8, and so on. Remember to set the `PYTHONPATH` variable to point to the TWS API directory containing Python modules.

For Linux and Mac OS users, the C++ archive contains one folder per project. For example, the Ch07_SubmitOrder contains the C++ code for the SubmitOrder project discussed in Chapter 7. The Ch11_MovingAverage folder contains the code for the MovingAverage project discussed in Chapter 11. Each folder has a Makefile that uses the `TWS_DIR` macro to set the location of TWS API files.

For Visual Studio users, the example C++ code is contained in a single solution named AlgoBook. If you open this in Visual Studio, you'll see that it contains several projects with names like Ch07_SubmitOrder and Ch11_MovingAverage. In each project, I've configured the compiler settings to look for files in a folder relative to `TWS_DIR`. If you'll set the `TWS_DIR` environment variable to point to the location of the TWS API installation, you shouldn't have trouble compiling the code.

On a personal note, I do all my initial development in Python and run tests against my paper-trading account. When I'm satisfied, I rewrite the algorithm in C++ and test it again using my paper-trading account. If that works, I copy the application to my Linux system and use it to submit orders for my brokerage account. The performance gain of C++ over Python probably isn't worth all the effort, but I sleep better knowing that my application runs as quickly as possible.

1.3 Organization of this Book

This book is primarily intended for readers familiar with Python and C++ who want to develop trading applications based on the TWS API. I'm not going to walk through the basics of Python and C++, but I will provide a thorough introduction to TWS and many of the financial instruments that it can access.

Financially-astute readers may find it odd that a programming book spends an entire chapter discussing options strategies and another chapter discussing futures. I've included these chapters because many programmers don't have a solid grasp of this material. Also, these chapters introduce the terminology that I'll rely on later in the book.

With this in mind, I've split the fourteen chapters of this book into three parts:
- Part 1 — Introduces TWS and financial instruments such as stocks, bonds, options, and futures
- Part 2 — Discusses the classes and functions in the TWS API
- Part 3 — Demonstrates how the TWS API classes/functions can be used in practice

Following Chapter 14, I've provided two appendices that discuss topics outside of the TWS API that may be of interest to readers. Appendix A explores the Financial Information eXchange (FIX) protocol and explains how to develop FIX-based applications using the open-source QuickFIX toolset. Then Appendix B introduces and derives the Kelly Criterion, which mathematically determines how much an investor should risk on an event of a given probability.

Part 1: Preliminary Topics

Before you start developing applications with the TWS API, you should have a solid familiarity with TWS and the different types of securities available for trading. Chapter 2 provides an in-depth introduction to Trader Workstation and explains how it can be used to research and trade stocks and bonds.

Chapter 3 explains what options are and how they can be ordered with TWS, and Chapter 4 discusses the fascinating topic of options strategies. Chapter 5 provides an overview of futures contracts.

Part 2: Exploring the TWS API

The next four chapters focus on the classes and functions that make up the TWS API. Chapter 6 introduces the fundamental classes that every developer (C++ or Python) should know. It also provides a simple application that demonstrates how these fundamental classes work together.

Chapter 7 discusses the all-important `Contract` and `Order` structures, and explains how to obtain contract information and place orders. Chapter 8 introduces the many functions available for obtaining financial data, including technical data and fundamental data. Chapter 9 explains how to search for contracts using scanners and Chapter 10 discusses many advanced features for placing orders, such as the different algorithms available for filling orders.

Part 3: Putting the TWS API to Work

At the end of Chapter 10, you should have a solid grasp of the TWS API and its capabilities. Starting with Chapter 11, the discussion shifts away from exploring the API and concentrates on using it to code practical applications. Specifically, Chapter 11 explains how to implement many of the indicators used to analyze securities, such as moving averages, moving average convergence/divergence (MACD), and the relative strength index (RSI).

Chapter 12 presents trading applications that select options strategies. Chapter 13 walks through the implementation of two popular trading systems: the Turtle Trading System and the Bollinger Band System. The final chapter presents a framework for developing practical algotrading applications in Python and C++.

1.4 More Information

The TWS API is a vast topic, and though I've done my best to provide a comprehensive and up-to-date guide, there are still parts that I haven't touched on. Also, Interactive Brokers updates the API on a regular basis, so it won't be long before much of the material in this book becomes obsolete.

For this reason, I strongly recommend looking at the official documentation for the TWS API, which can be found at https://interactivebrokers.github.io/tws-api. At the top of the page, you can choose which programming language you're interested in. In the left-hand menu, the Classes option lists the API classes available for the chosen language.

If you can't find an answer to your question in the documentation, the next place to look is the TWS API forum on groups.io. The web address is groups.io/g/twsapi/topics, and the Search button at the top makes it easy to search through the posts to see if someone has encountered an issue similar to yours. If not, simply register for an account and submit a post of your own.

If you have questions related to trading contracts with Trader Workstation, Interactive Brokers developed the Trading Academy at www.interactivebrokers.com/en/index.php?f=1322. This site provides webinars and a vast number of courses on general trading and trading with TWS.

1.5 Summary

There are many books available on algorithmic trading, and they all discuss the topic in broad terms. That is, they introduce equations, indicators, and testing methods, but they don't present any real code. They offer theories and guidelines, but nothing readers can actually use to start trading.

To the best of my knowledge, this is the first book that delves into the nuts and bolts of algotrading. This book emphasizes practice, not theory. By the time you finish reading Chapter 14, you'll have a practical understanding of how to code and deploy algorithmic trading applications.

The downside of writing a book on real-world algotrading is that I have to make choices that alienate potential readers. This book covers only the tools and API provided by Interactive Brokers, and other brokerages won't be mentioned. Similarly, the only programming languages used in this book are Python and C++. Other languages won't be considered.

If you know Python or C++ but you're not well acquainted with financial concepts and Trader Workstation, you'll find the next four chapters helpful. If you're already familiar with these topics, feel free to skip to Chapter 6. If you don't know Python or C++, I recommend reading *Head First Python* or *A First Book of C++*.

Chapter 2

Stocks, Bonds, and Trader Workstation (TWS)

The goal of this book is to teach you how to code applications that create and submit orders through Interactive Brokers. These applications can't run by themselves—you need to have Trader Workstation (TWS) or Interactive Brokers Gateway (IB Gateway) executing on your system. Once you have one of these running, your trading application will be able to execute orders by sending and receiving messages.

Many readers will prefer to run applications through Trader Workstation, so this chapter starts by describing the TWS user interface and its many capabilities. If you're an experienced IB trader, you'll probably be familiar with this material. If you're new to Interactive Brokers, you can obtain TWS by visiting https://www.interactivebrokers.com/en/index.php?f=16042 and clicking the red box labeled **DOWNLOAD**.

IB Gateway is smaller and simpler than TWS, and doesn't enable manual trading. Its sole purpose is to transfer data between your applications and IB's servers. At the end of this chapter, I'll explain how to download and use IB Gateway.

2.1 Overview of Trader Workstation (TWS)

TWS is the primary application for interacting with IB, and it provides an incredible wealth of features. When I used TWS for the first time, I found its user interface overwhelming. But as I became better acquainted, I came to appreciate its intuitive layout. Figure 2.1 shows what the TWS window looks like when you launch it for the first time.

Chapter 2 Stocks, Bonds, and Trader Workstation (TWS)

Figure 2.1 Main Window of the Trader Workstation (TWS)

In this figure, I've opened TWS in *paper-trading mode*, which means trades won't affect my real account. The alternative is the *brokerage mode*, in which trades are made using real money. As you proceed through this book, I strongly recommend that you use paper-trading mode until you're absolutely certain that you're ready to execute applications in brokerage mode.

The user interface in paper-trading mode is nearly identical to that of brokerage mode. The difference is the message displayed at the top of the window: **THIS IS NOT A BROKERAGE ACCOUNT. THIS IS A PAPER TRADING ACCOUNT FOR SIMULATED TRADING.**

To describe TWS, I've split the main window into five sections:

- **Main Menu/Toolbar** — Menu/toolbar items that affect the entire application
- **Order Entry** — Controls for executing orders and viewing securities
- **Activity** — Lists submitted orders and trades
- **Monitor** — Presents data related to the user's portfolio and securities of interest
- **News** — List of news articles related to finance and the user's portfolio

As you proceed through this discussion, keep in mind that you can automate most of TWS's operations in your applications. The better you understand TWS, the easier it will be to write programs that communicate with it.

2.1.1 The Main Menu/Toolbar

If you look toward the top of the window, you'll find TWS's main menu in the upper left. This has three entries:

- **File** — Configure aspects of TWS including its appearance, load and save data
- **Account** — Account management, access TWS reports and logs
- **Help** — Documentation, customer service, status monitoring

For this book, the most important item in the main menu is **File > Global Configuration**. This opens a window that makes it possible to update a number of TWS settings. Figure 2.2 shows what it looks like.

Figure 2.2 Global Configuration Settings Dialog

The left portion of the window lists a series of configuration categories, and many of the categories have subcategories. The figure displays the options available when the **API > Settings** option is selected. The settings available include the following:

- Enable ActiveX and socket clients
- Read-only API
- Download open orders on connection
- Socket port
- Create API message log file
- Include market data in API log file

I'll provide a proper introduction to these settings in Chapter 6. For now, all you need to know is that the API settings of TWS can be accessed by selecting the **File** > **Global Configuration** menu option and the **API** > **Settings** category.

Beneath the main menu, you'll find three links named **New Window**, **IBot**, and **FYI**. The first link lets you configure which views are displayed in TWS, the second accesses technical support and documentation, and the third provides notifications from IB. These links won't be needed in this book.

In the upper-right corner of the window, you'll find common entries for minimizing, maximizing, and closing the window. You'll also see a link (hopefully green) entitled **DATA**. If you click this, a dialog box will appear and tell you about TWS's connections to data sources, or farms. Figure 2.3 shows what it looks like.

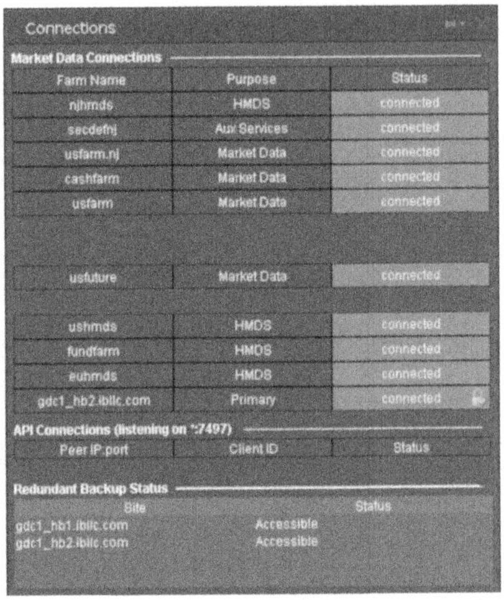

Figure 2.3 Data Connections Dialog

The dialog lists the different farms that can be accessed, the purpose served by each, and the connection status. IB doesn't provide many details about its farms, such as what "Aux Services" refers to. But we know that HMDS stands for Historical Market Data Service.

In the figure, ndc1.ibllc.com is listed as the Primary farm. I assume this is the main server that TWS connects to for executing orders. This explains why the connection has a lock, which implies that the communication uses Secure Sockets Layer (SSL).

Toward the bottom of the dialog, you can see a listing of API connections listening on Port 7497. In the figure, this list is empty. But as you start writing code, this list will be populated with the names of your applications.

Returning to the upper-right of the window, you'll find links for changing the font size, searching for help or a ticker symbol, and contacting IB. You'll also find a clock that displays the time for your time zone.

2.1.2 The Order Placement Process

In my opinion, the best way to learn the TWS interface is to create and place orders. For this reason, the rest of the chapter walks through the process of placing two orders. The first will purchase 100 shares of Tesla stock and the second will purchase a corporate bond that was selected through the TWS scanner.

In both cases, the general process of placing trades with TWS is similar. There are five main steps to follow:

1. Add a ticker to the watchlist in the Monitor pane.
2. Select a contract in the Order Entry box.
3. Analyze the financial instrument.
4. Place an order.
5. Monitor the order in the Activity section.

In the following discussion, I'll explain how to use these steps to buy 100 shares of Tesla stock. If you'd like to follow along, be sure to open TWS in paper-trading mode.

2.2 Buying Stock with TWS

If you're reading this book, you're probably familiar with stocks and stock trading. A share of stock represents partial ownership of a corporation. If you own a significant amount of stock in a company, you're a *shareholder* and you can vote in corporate elections. If you own the majority of the company's stock, you're a *majority shareholder* and you can influence the officers who run the company.

Most owners of stock are interested in making money, not influencing the company's operations. The two most popular ways of making money are:

1. Sell the shares for more than they were purchased for.
2. Hold the shares and receive portions of the company's earnings (*dividends*) if the company offers dividends.

This section explains how to buy Tesla stock with TWS. Once you understand this, the process of selling the stock is trivially easy. At the end of this section, I'll discuss the process of short selling, which involves borrowing shares and buying them later.

2.2.1 Watchlist

If you listen to music on a computer or smartphone, you're probably familiar with the idea of a playlist, which contains songs you're interested in hearing. TWS provides similar lists called *watchlists*, which contain financial instruments you're interested in trading.

To create a watchlist, go to the Monitor panel and click the plus sign in the upper right. TWS refers to this as the *new page icon*, and Figure 2.4 shows where it's located.

Figure 2.4 The Monitor Panel

When you click the new page icon, a window will appear and allow you to add new pages to the Monitor panel. If you click **Watchlist**, a dialog box will ask you to enter a ticker symbol. This discussion focuses on Tesla stock, so enter **TSLA** and press Enter.

The next dialog will ask you to select a financial instrument related to the TSLA ticker. Depending on your account permissions, you can choose stocks, futures, options, warrants, structured products, CFDs (contracts for differences), or bonds. Figure 2.5 shows what this looks like.

This book doesn't discuss warrants or structured products, but Chapters 3 and 4 discuss options and Chapter 5 covers futures contracts. This discussion focuses on stocks, so choose the **Stock** option and press Enter.

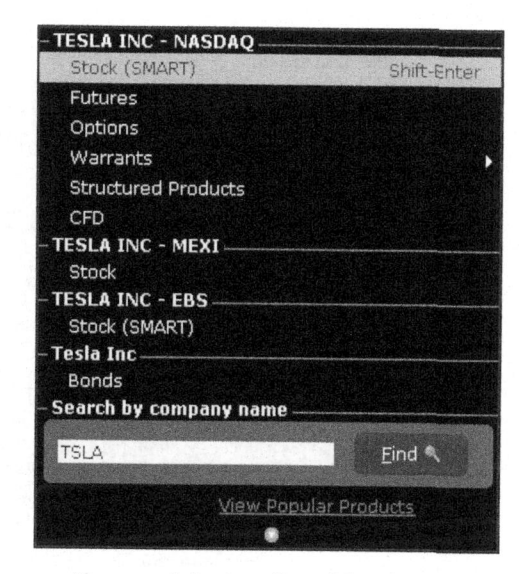

Figure 2.5 Selecting a Financial Instrument

After you've selected a financial instrument, you can assign a name to the watchlist. Then a new page will appear in the Monitor panel with the desired name. This new watchlist contains the TSLA stock and identifies its last price and the percentage change.

To add more instruments to the watchlist, double-click one of the empty bars in the Monitor panel. Then type the ticker symbol in the white text box, press Enter, and choose the instrument associated with the ticker.

In the upper-left of the Monitor panel, you'll see a chain immediately left of the maximize button. The color of this chain identifies the group to which the panel belongs. By default, all panels in TWS belong to the same group.

If you hover the mouse pointer over the chain in the Monitor panel, you'll see a tooltip that reads **Source**. Because this panel is a source, every panel in the group will respond when the user selects a financial instrument in the Monitor panel.

2.2.2 Order Entry

By default, the Order Entry receives selection information from source panels in its group. Therefore, when you select an instrument to the Monitor panel, you'll see its ticker symbol displayed in the Order Entry box in the upper-left of TWS. Figure 2.6 shows what the Order Entry region looks like when the TSLA stock is selected.

Figure 2.6 The Order Entry Region

Below the Order Entry area, you can see two sources of information about the stock. To the left, you can read a series of statistics related to the stock's price and the Tesla corporation. To the right, a candlestick chart illustrates the trends in Tesla's stock price.

The following discussion introduces the statistics on the left and the candlestick chart. Then I'll walk through the process of placing an order for Tesla stock.

Stock Statistics

Below the Order Entry box and to the left of the graph, TWS lists eleven statistics:

Table 2.1
Order Entry Statistics for Stocks

Name	Description
Last Size	Number of contracts traded at the last price
Last Exch	Last price at which the stock was sold
Bid/Ask	Best price at which the market will buy the stock (bid) and the best price at which the market will sell the stock (ask)
Bid Size	Number of contracts offered at the bid price
Ask Size	Number of contracts offered at the asking price
Hi/Lo	High and low prices of the day

52 H/L	High and low prices of the preceding 52-week period
EPS (Earnings Per Share)	Corporate earnings (minus dividends) divided by the number of shares
P/E (Price to Earnings Ratio)	Price of a share of stock divided by the earnings per share
MCap (Market Capitalization)	Price of a share of stock divided by the number of outstanding shares
Pr/Bk (Price to Book Ratio)	Market capitalization divided by Tesla's total book value

These statistics provide an overview of Tesla's stock prices and the Tesla corporation in general. Like all financial instruments, the stock has two prices displayed: the bid and the asking price. The bid (305.22) is always less than the asking price (305.99) because the market is never willing to buy a stock for more than it's willing to sell. The difference between them is called the *spread*. The size of a spread is determined in large part by the number of interested traders, and Tesla's narrow spread ($0.77) indicates that its stock is very popular.

The recent high of the Tesla stock (307.45) is near the middle of the 52-week range (244.59 – 387.46). This gives an idea of how wildly the stock has been moving over the last year.

The price-to-earnings ratio is commonly employed to determine whether a stock is overpriced or underpriced. At the time of this writing, the average P/E ratio is between 25 and 30. Analysts prefer low positive values over high positive values.

In the case of Tesla, the EPS and P/E ratio are negative because the company has lost money. For a normal company, this would dissuade investors from purchasing the stock. Tesla has never been a normal company.

Candlestick Charts

If you look closely at the graph of Tesla's stock price, you'll notice that it doesn't connect prices with straight lines. Instead, each trading period is represented by a rectangle with straight lines extending from its top and bottom. These symbols are called *candlesticks*, and each candlestick identifies the high, opening, closing, and low prices of its trading period.

The default trading period is ten minutes, but you can change this using the drop-down menu above the graph. Figure 2.7 illustrates how the shape of a candlestick identifies the security's prices.

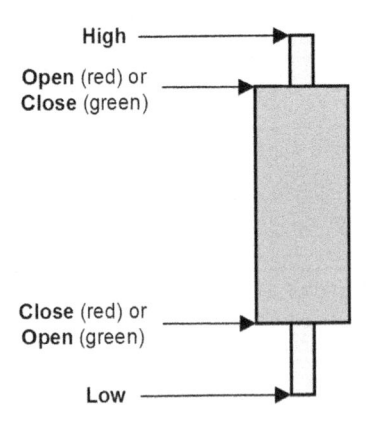

Figure 2.7 Candlestick Geometry

Analysts refer to the main rectangle as the candle and the extending lines as the upper and lower wicks. The top of the upper wick identifies the highest price of the period and the bottom of the lower wick identifies the lowest price of the period.

The body of the candle is more complicated. If body of the candle is green, the price rose during the period. In this case, the top of the candle is the close and the bottom of the candle is the open. If the body of the candle is red, the price fell during the period. In this case, the top of the candle is the open and the bottom is the close.

The process of monitoring prices with candlestick charts hearkens back to 18th century Japan, and they're still widely used. A long candle and wicks indicate that the price varied widely during the period. If the candle and the wicks are short, the price stayed within a tight range.

Placing an Order

After you've analyzed a security's statistics and price history, you can place an order using the Order Entry box at the top of Figure 2.6. When you select a security in the Monitor panel, this box will automatically display the selected ticker symbol.

Below the Order Entry box, TWS presents two adjacent buttons: **BUY** and **SELL**. Click **BUY** if you want to buy shares of the chosen instrument or **SELL** if you'd like to sell. When you choose one, the panel's background will be set to blue (buy) or red (sell).

To the right of the Order Entry box, a series of controls allow you to configure the order. If you click the **QTY** button, you can specify how many shares you'd like to buy or sell. If you want to purchase a different number of shares than the options listed, simply type in the desired number.

To the right of the **QTY** button, a drop-down menu allows you to select the order's type. If you're using a paper-trading account, some order types will be grayed out. Table 2.2 lists the full set of codes and order types.

Table 2.2
Types of Orders

Code	Order Type	Description
LMT	Limit	Trade at the limit price or better
MKT	Market	Trade immediately at the market price
MTL	Market-to-Limit	Market order which creates a limit order if not completely filled
STP	Stop	Submit a market order if the stop price is reached or penetrated
STP LMT	Stop Limit	Submit a limit order if the stop price is reached or penetrated
TRAIL	Trailing Stop	A sell stop order whose stop price changes with the current price
TRAIL LMT	Trailing Stop with Limit	A trailing stop order that submits a limit order when the stop price is reached or penetrated
REL	Relative/Pegged to Primary	A limit order whose limit price is computed using an offset from the current price
RPI	Retail Price Improvement	Relative order that takes advantage of NYSE's price improvement process
SNAP MKT	Snap to Market	Relative order whose offset doesn't change
SNAP MID	Snap to Midpoint	Relative order computed using the midpoint of the bid and asking prices
SNAP PRIM	Snap to Primary	Relative order computed using offsets from the bid and asking prices
MOC	Market on Close	Market order to execute as close to the closing price as possible
LOC	Limit on Close	Limit order to execute as close to the closing price as possible
Adaptive (IBALGO)	Adaptive	Market or limit order that takes advantage of IB's smart routing capabilities
IBALGO	--	Select IB's algorithm that waits for optimal prices for placing orders

Beginning investors frequently confuse limit orders and stop orders. Both types wait to place an order until a given price is reached, but traders place limit orders because they hope to execute the trade at a favorable price. For example, when the trader sets a limit price for a sell limit order, the order will execute if the market price rises to the limit price or higher. When the trader sets a limit price for a buy limit order, the order will execute if the market price falls to the limit price or lower.

Stop orders are more straightforward than limit orders—if the security's price reaches the stop price, a market order is placed whether the price is favorable or not. The most popular type of stop order is the *sell stop*, which submits a sell order as soon as the security's price reaches the stop price. Sell stop orders are frequently used to limit the loss associated with a trade.

Similarly, a buy stop order submits a buy order as soon as the security's price reaches the stop price. Traders may submit a buy stop order if they're waiting to see whether a security's upward movement will exceed a given price.

Trailing stop orders are like regular stop orders, but the stop price changes with the security's price. For sell stop orders, the stop price rises when the security's price rises, but never drops below the initial value. With TWS, traders can specify whether the stop price should trail the security's price using a fixed offset or a percentage.

I'll discuss order types further in Chapter 7, which explains how to create and submit orders programmatically. Chapter 10 presents many of the different algorithms that can be used to submit orders.

If you select an order that involves a limit order (**LMT**, **STP LMT**, **TRAIL LMT**, and so on), you need to identify a limit price. There are two different ways to do this:

- Type the price to the right of the type-selection box
- Click the box to the right of the type-selection box and choose the limit price relative to the bid price, ask price, or the midpoint between the two.

Many order types, such as limit orders, don't execute immediately. For this reason, TWS makes it possible to specify how long the order should remain active. This is called the order's *time in force*, and you can set this to one of three options:

- **DAY** — The order remains in force until the end of the day
- **GTC** — The order remains in force until it's canceled (Good Till Canceled)
- **OPG** — The order should be executed at the day's opening price

To the immediate right, the **advanced** button makes it possible to configure advanced orders such as bracket orders and one cancels all (OCA) orders. A full description of advanced orders will have to wait until later chapters.

After you've configured an order, you can press the **SUBMIT** button in the lower right. This tells TWS to open the Order Confirmation dialog, which displays information about the order, the security, and the user's account. If you press the **Transmit** button, TWS will submit the order to IB.

Monitoring Order Status

After you've submitted an order, it's a good idea to check its status. If the order executed successfully, it's important to check the trade price.

In TWS, this information is provided in the Activity panel in the lower left. Figure 2.8 shows what it looks like when you select the Orders view.

Figure 2.8 Monitoring Order Activity

As illustrated in this figure, two orders have been submitted. The first was a market order to buy 100 shares of TSLA. The second was a limit order for 200 shares of TSLA at a limit price of 340.

Short Sales and Margin

Going back to Figure 2.6, you can see the **Shortable** label displayed beneath the Order Entry box. This indicates that traders can short sell (or just *short*) the stock. The process of shorting a stock consists of two steps:

1. The trader tells IB to borrow shares of stock.
2. At a later time, the trader buys shares to repay the debt. This is referred to as covering the short.

A short seller's goal is to make money when the stock's price falls between the borrowing and repayment. In TWS, a trader can submit a short sale order by simply selling a security that the trader doesn't own. TWS doesn't allow traders to have long and short positions in a security at the same time, so if a trader attempts to sell an unowned security, TWS will interpret the order as a short sale.

Before TWS can submit a short sale order, two conditions must be met:
1. The equity in the trader's account must exceed the margin requirement.
2. IB must be able to locate a sufficient number of shares for borrowing.

This first point is important to understand. IB allows traders to borrow funds needed to execute an order, but the trader's account must have equity to serve as collateral. This reserve equity is called *margin*, and if the account's equity doesn't meet the requirement, the order won't be executed.

IB's margin requirements depend on many factors, including the trader's location, the location of the exchange executing the order, and the type of security being traded. You can check the full list of margin requirements by visiting https://www.interactivebrokers.com/en/index.php?f=24176 in a browser.

When determining how much equity needs to be in a trader's account, IB applies (at least) three requirements:

- **initial margin** — Equity that must be present in the trader's account when the trade is submitted
- **maintenance margin** — Equity that must be present in the trader's account after the trade is submitted
- **Reg T end of day margin** — Equity that must be present in the trader's account at the end of each trading day after the trade is submitted

An example will clarify how margin requirements work. For trades involving U.S. stocks, IB has separate requirements for long positions (stock purchases) and short positions (short sales). The requirements for long positions are:

- **initial margin** — 25% of the stock value (minimum of $2,000 or 100% of the purchase price, whichever is less)
- **maintenance margin** — same as initial margin
- **Reg T end of day margin** — 50% of the stock value

For short sales, the margin requirements are as follows:

- **initial margin** — 30% of the stock value for share price greater than $16.67, $5.00 per share if share price less than $16.67 and greater than $5.00, otherwise 100% of stock value
- **maintenance margin** — same as initial margin
- **Reg T end of day margin** — 50% of the stock value

Requirements like these are common for stock trades, but trades involving futures follow an entirely different set of rules. Chapter 5 discusses futures contracts and the different margin requirements that apply.

If you're concerned with meeting margin requirements, you can get a risk report in TWS by opening **Account** in the main menu and selecting the **Risk Report > Margin Report** entry. This opens a web page that displays your available funds and the requirements for initial and maintenance margin.

2.3 Buying Bonds with TWS

Anyone can buy Treasury bonds on www.treasurydirect.com or municipal bonds on www.municipalbonds.com. But unlike other brokers, IB allows individual investors to purchase *corporate bonds*. These provide a higher return than other bonds and carry a higher risk of default. In this section, I'll explain how to purchase them with TWS.

The preceding discussion walked through the process of purchasing a specific stock. But what if you don't know which security you're interested in? You could tell IB what types of securities you're interested in and let IB make suggestions. This requires the market scanner, and I'll discuss this next.

2.3.1 Market Scanners

If you don't have a specific security in mind, you can ask a market scanner to select securities for you. TWS provides scanners for many different types of securities, and there are two main ways to create them:

- In the Monitor panel, click the plus sign and select **Mosaic Market Scanner**.
- In the upper left of TWS, click **New Window** and select an option in the **Scanners** submenu.

This discussion focuses on using a scanner to choose bonds. To create a bond scanner, click **New Window** and select the **Scanners > Bond Scanner** option. Figure 2.9 shows what the resulting window looks like.

This dialog has two main parts. The top part defines criteria for selecting bonds and the bottom part lists the bonds that meet the given criteria.

To set the scanner's criteria, you need to have a basic familiarity with corporate bonds. Therefore, before I explain how to use this dialog, I'd like to present a quick overview of bond trading.

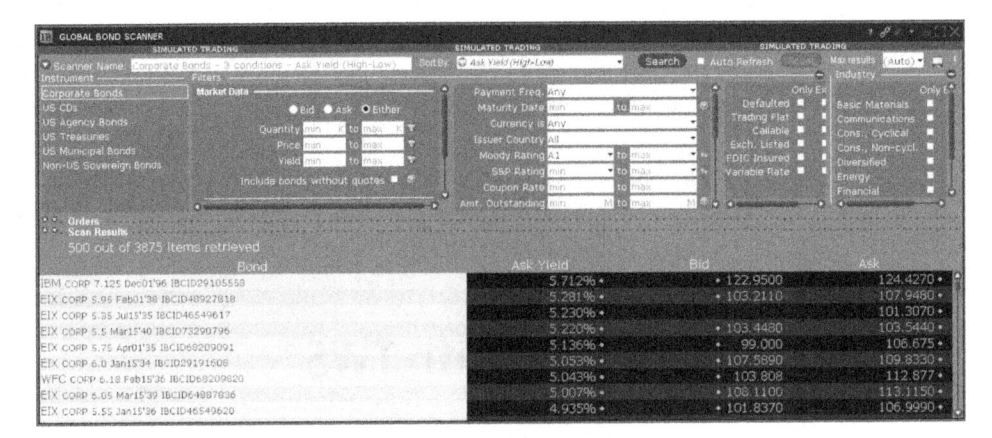

Figure 2.9 The Bond Scanner

Fundamentals of Corporate Bonds

If a corporation needs to raise money, it may issue shares of stock or borrow money by selling debt instruments. These debt instruments are called bonds and they function like IOUs. That is, the corporation receives money upfront and promises to pay back more money over time.

To be precise, the issuer promises to pay a fixed amount at the end of a time period called the bond's *maturity*, which must be at least one year. The amount to be paid is called the bond's *face value*, also known as a *par value* or *par*. For example, if you purchase a $1,000 bond from BigCorp with a maturity of two years, BigCorp promises to pay you $1,000 when the two years have elapsed.

A bond's discount is the difference between the face value and its price. If the price is less than its face value, the bond is said to be trading at a *discount*. If the price is greater than the face value, the bond is said to be trading at a *premium*. If the price equals the face value, the bond is said to be trading at *par*.

In addition to paying face value at maturity, many bonds pay interest at fixed intervals up to maturity. U.S. bonds generally pay interest twice a year. A bond's interest payments are called *coupon payments*, and the *coupon rate* is the ratio of the sum of the coupons paid per year to the face value.

An example will clarify how the coupon rate is determined. Suppose a $1,000 bond pays 3% interest twice a year until maturity. Each coupon payment equals $1,000 * 0.03, which equals $30. The sum of the coupons paid per year is $60, so the coupon rate is $60/$1,000, or 6%.

When comparing bonds, it's important to be familiar with the concepts of *current yield* and *yield to maturity*. A bond's current yield is its coupon rate divided by its current price, expressed as a percentage. Yield to maturity (YTM) is more complex, and identifies the total return received by the holder if he/she holds the bond to maturity. YTM takes into account the bond's price, coupon rate, face value, and the years remaining until maturity.

Risks and Ratings

Corporate bonds have significantly higher returns than government bonds, but this higher return comes with greater risk. If a corporation can't meet its financial obligations, bonds will default and bankruptcy may follow. If this occurs, the corporation may only pay a portion of its debt to bondholders or it may issue new bonds.

Due to the possibility of default, bond investors are deeply interested in the likelihood of a corporation fulfilling its obligations. This likelihood is referred to as the corporation's *credit quality*, which is similar in principle to an individual's credit history.

When it comes to credit ratings for corporations, the world pays attention to three agencies: Moody's, Standard & Poor's, and Fitch. Their opinions exert a great deal of influence, and for this reason, they're referred to as The Big Three. Bonds are frequently categorized according to The Big Three's ratings, and Table 2.3 lists each of the categories.

Table 2.3
Bond Categories and Ratings

Bond Category	Moody's Rating	S&P Rating	Fitch Rating
Prime	Aaa	AAA	AAA
High grade	Aa1	AA+	AA+
High grade	Aa2	AA	AA
High grade	Aa3	AA-	AA-
Upper medium grade	A1	A+	A+
Upper medium grade	A2	A	A
Upper medium grade	A3	A-	A-
Lower medium grade	Baa1	BBB+	BBB+
Lower medium grade	Baa2	BBB	BBB
Lower medium grade	Baa3	BBB-	BBB-
Non-investment grade speculative	Ba1	BB+	BB+
Non-investment grade speculative	Ba2	BB	BB

Non-investment grade speculative	Ba3	BB-	BB-
Highly speculative	B1	B+	B+
Highly speculative	B2	B	B
Highly speculative	B3	B-	B-
Substantial risks	Caa1	CCC+	CCC
Extremely speculative	Caa2	CCC	CCC
Default imminent	Caa3	CCC-	CCC
Default imminent	Ca	CC	CCC
Default imminent	Ca	C	CCC
In default	C	D	DDD
In default	/	D	DD
In default	/	D	D

At a high level, corporate bonds are divided into two categories: investment grade and non-investment grade. Investment grade bonds have ratings from Aaa to Baa3 from Moody's, AAA to BBB- from Standard and Poor's, and AAA to BBB- from Fitch. Bonds with lower ratings fall into the non-investment grade (junk bond) category.

Special Bonds

The vast majority of bonds are boring and provide fixed, regular payments until maturity. But some bonds have characteristics that make them noteworthy. This discussion touches on three special types of bonds:

1. **convertible** — the holder can convert the bond into shares of stock
2. **callable** — the issuer can redeem the bond before maturity
3. **putable** — the holder can sell the bond back at a specified price

Early-stage companies with high growth potential frequently issue convertible bonds. This gives holders the ability to convert bonds into shares of stock. The number of shares is determined by the conversion ratio. Convertible bonds have lower yields than regular bonds, but holders can take advantage of increases in the price of the issuer's shares.

Just as corporations can buy back shares of stock, they can repurchase (or *call*) callable bonds. Corporations may redeem a callable bond if they find loans at a lower interest rate. When calling a bond, the issuer pays more than the bond's par value, and the earlier the call, the more the issuer pays. Callable bonds have higher coupon rates to offset the possibility of being called.

The next chapter introduces put options, which give the owner the right to sell an asset at a specific price. A putable bond is a bond with an embedded put, which allows the holder to sell the bond back to the issuer at a specific price on one or more specific dates. This frees the holder from having to wait for income, but because of this freedom, putable bonds have higher prices and lower yields than regular bonds.

Selecting a Bond

Now that you understand the fundamental characteristics of bonds, let's return to the scanner. For this demonstration, the goal is to find bonds that meet four criteria:

- Quantity between 1 and 2
- Price between 80 and 100 basis points
- Traded in USD
- Standard and Poor's rating between BBB– and AAA

Entering criteria into the bond scanner is simple, and proceeds from left to right. On the far left, make sure the **Corporate Bond** option is selected. Moving right, look for the **Quantity** entry and set the minimum value to 1 and the maximum value to 2. Next, find the **Price** entry and set the minimum value to 70 and the maximum value to 90.

It's important to note that price values are given in *basis points*, which represent hundredths of a percentage of the face value. If the price is less than 100 basis points, the bond is selling at a discount. If the price is greater than 100 basis points, the bond is selling at a premium. If the face value is $2,000 and the price is 90 basis points, the price in dollars is $2,000 * 90/100 = $1,800.

Moving further right, find the **Currency** option, click the combo box, and select USD. Then find the **S&P Rating** label and set the min value to BBB– and the max value to AAA. This limits the search to investment grade bonds.

After you've set the scanner's criteria, click the **Search** button at the top of the scanner dialog. This searches through all the corporate bonds that IB can access. When the search is complete, you'll find a listing of suitable candidates at the bottom of the dialog.

For each entry in the list, the scanner displays the bond's ask yield, bid price, and asking price. By clicking on a column name, you can sort the bonds in ascending or descending order. Figure 2.10 shows what the scanner looks like on my system when I sort bonds by ask yield.

Of the bonds listed, the one with the highest ask yield is issued by PSEC (Prospect Capital Corp.). This bond has a coupon rate of 6.0 and a maturity date of April 15, 2043. The bond's CUSIP is IBCID125389154.

Figure 2.10 Bond Scanner Results

CUSIP stands for Committee on Uniform Security Identification Procedures and a CUSIP code is a nine-character identifier for North American securities. CUSIP codes are assigned to many types of securities, but in my experience, they're primarily used to identify bonds. The first six characters identify the issuer, the 7th and 8th digits identify the security, and the last character is used for error-checking.

If you select a row in the bond scanner, a dialog will appear and provide additional information. One interesting piece of information is that the PCEG bond is callable, which means the issuer may repurchase it before the maturity date.

2.3.2 Purchasing a Bond

After you've decided on a bond offering, TWS makes it easy to create and submit the order. First, you need to open the bond offering in the Open Entry box. For this example, this can be accomplished with three steps.

1. In the Monitor panel, add the PCEG ticker to the watch list.
2. When the dialog asks for a specific financial instrument, select Bonds.
3. In the PCEG bond listing, choose the bond with the CUSIP listed in the scanner (125389154).

After you've selected the bond, its name will appear in the Order Entry box. On the following page, Figure 2.11 shows what this looks like.

Figure 2.11 Creating a Bond Order

Once the bond is displayed, you can place the order. The process of ordering bonds is nearly identical to that of ordering stocks:

1. Select **BUY** to create a buy order.
2. Choose the desired quantity as a multiple of the face value (a quantity of 2,000 means two bonds with a face value of 1,000).
3. Click **SUBMIT** to initiate order submission.
4. In the order confirmation box, click **Transmit** to send the order to IB.

After you've submitted the order, you can check its status in the Activity panel.

2.4 IB Gateway

As I'll explain more fully in Chapter 6, trading programs can't send or receive data unless Trader Workstation (TWS) or IB Gateway is running on the development system. These applications serve as translators between your application and IB's servers.

Like TWS, IB Gateway is an application that you can download freely from Interactive Brokers. The main difference between the two is that IB Gateway doesn't provide any capabilities for manual trading. Its sole purpose is to receive requests from your trading program and transmit data to and from IB's servers. As a result, IB Gateway consumes approximately 40% fewer computing resources than TWS.

To obtain IB Gateway, visit www.interactivebrokers.com/en/index.php?f=16457 and click the red box labeled **DOWNLOAD**. Once the download is complete, you can install and run the application.

One reason I like to use IB Gateway is that it makes it easy to view API messages as an algotrading application runs. To illustrate this, Figure 2.12 shows what the IB Gateway application looks like.

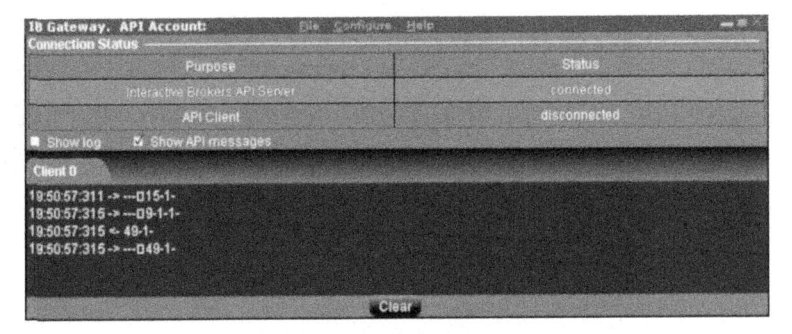

Figure 2.12 The IB Gateway Application

If you choose to use IB Gateway with your algotrading applications instead of TWS, remember to change the port number. TWS listens to Port 7497 while IB Gateway listens for Port 4002. This will make more sense in Chapter 6, which explains how trading applications communicate with TWS and IB Gateway.

2.5 Summary

Most individual clients of Interactive Brokers do their trading through Trader Workstation. They add contracts to a watchlist, study the candlestick graphs, and submit orders through TWS. Then they monitor the order's status to ensure that it executed successfully.

The goal of this book is to explain how to perform these operations programmatically. I'll present classes like `Contract` and `Order`, and then show how to read financial data with functions like `reqMktData` and submit orders with `placeOrder`. These produce the same results as traditional TWS usage, but you can automate them.

TWS makes it possible to trade several types of securities, but this chapter has focused on the two most traditional assets: stocks and bonds. The process of placing an order is similar for both. If you know which security you want to trade, you can add its symbol to the watchlist. If not, you can use TWS's scanner to get a list of candidates.

The last part of the chapter discussed a second IB application named IB Gateway. This is useless for manual traders, but it provides two benefits for algorithmic traders. First, it uses less resources than TWS, allowing your computer to crunch more numbers and sort more database records. Second, it makes it easier to read API messages as they're received.

Chapter 3

Stock Options

The preceding chapter discussed assets, which are securities that represent real property. This chapter looks at securities whose value are based on assets, but are not themselves assets. These securities are called *derivatives*, and the four most popular types of derivatives are:

- **forward contracts** — private agreements to buy/sell something at a given date
- **futures contracts** — exchange-traded obligations to buy/sell something at a given date
- **options** — exchange-traded rights to buy/sell before or on a given date
- **swaps** — private agreements to exchange cash flows from financial instruments

IB provides access to many different types of derivatives, but this chapter focuses on options, specifically stock options. Stock option trading has grown incredibly popular over the last few years, and IB provides many capabilities for this type of trading. As I'll demonstrate in this chapter, a large part of the TWS user interface is geared toward stock option trading.

Despite their popularity, I'm going to assume that you've never heard of stock options. This may annoy some readers, but it gives me an opportunity to introduce terms that I'll use throughout this book. If you already have a sound knowledge of puts and calls, feel free to skip this chapter. Otherwise, I'll begin this chapter with a gentle introduction to the wonderful world of stock options.

3.1 A Gentle Introduction to Stock Options

Options can be hard to understand because they don't constitute property. When you purchase an option, you don't own part of a company (stock) or a legal contract to be repaid (bond). Instead, you have the right to take action on or before a specific time.

To introduce this topic, I'll present an analogy that compares options with lottery tickets. Then I'll compare options to limit orders.

3.1.1 Options and Lottery Tickets

At a high level, options are like lottery tickets. When you buy an option, you receive the right to take action if favorable circumstances occur. But buyers are never, ever *obligated* to do anything. Whether circumstances turn out favorably or unfavorably, a buyer can do nothing and the option will be as worthless as a losing lottery ticket.

Lotteries vary from place to place, but let's suppose that all lottery tickets have the same five qualities:

1. The buyer pays money up front and hopes to make money later.
2. The seller receives money up front and hopes not to lose money later.
3. The ticket is potentially valuable for a limited time.
4. If the ticket wins, the buyer has the right to take action (redeem the ticket for money). But the buyer isn't obligated to take action.
5. If a ticket wins and the buyer redeems the ticket, the seller is *obligated* to pay. If the buyer doesn't take action, the seller has no obligation.

These qualities apply to options as well as lottery tickets. But this analogy has major flaws and I'll discuss them in just a moment. Right now, I'd like to introduce four important terms in the context of a lottery:

- A ticket's price is called its *premium*.
- If a buyer takes action, such as redeeming the ticket, we say that the buyer is *exercising* the ticket.
- The time after which the buyer can no longer exercise the ticket is called the ticket's *expiration*.
- If the seller is obligated to take action as a result of the buyer exercising the ticket, the resulting arrangement is called *assignment*.

It's worth spending a couple minutes making sure you're comfortable with the terms premium, exercise, expiration, and assignment. As you'll see, these terms apply to options as they do to lottery tickets.

When dealing with options and lotteries, it's helpful to visualize profit and loss using special charts called *risk graphs*. A simple example will demonstrate how they're used. Suppose you purchase a two-dollar lottery ticket that consists of a single number between 1 and 500. If the selected number is k, you win 1000 dollars.

Figure 3.1 presents the risk graphs for the buyer and seller. In both cases, the x-axis identifies the ticket number and the y-axis represents the amount of money made or lost.

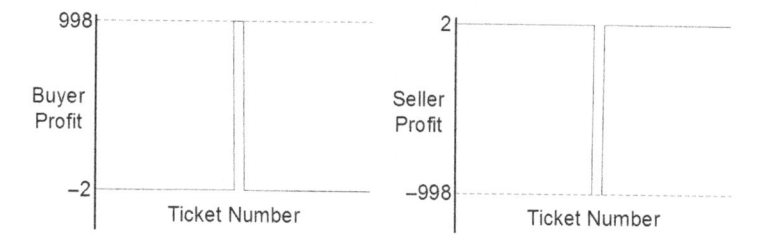

Figure 3.1 Risk Graphs for Buying and Selling a Lottery Ticket

On the left, you make a profit of 998 if the ticket's number is k, and you lose 2 if the number isn't k. For the seller, this is reversed. As shown on the right, the seller makes 2 if the ticket's number isn't k and loses 998 if it is. It's important to see that the graphs for the buyer and seller are always vertical mirror images of each other. What's good for the buyer is bad for the seller, and vice-versa.

3.1.2 Options and Limit Orders

A stock option is like a limit order on steroids. As discussed in Chapter 2, a limit order allows you to set a specific price at which you want to buy or sell a stock. If the stock never reaches your desired price, the order won't be executed.

But let's say you *really* want to buy or sell a stock at a specific price, regardless of its current price or future price. If you want it badly enough, you can buy a stock option. The option's price is called its *premium* and your desired price is called its *strike price*.

One major difference between options and limit orders involves duration. You can submit limit orders that are good for a day or good until canceled. But every stock option has a specific date after which the owner can no longer execute the desired transaction. This is the *expiration*.

Another major difference involves rights versus obligations. When you send a limit order to a broker, you are obligated to buy/sell when the condition is reached. But when you buy an option, you can buy/sell the stock at the strike price at any time up to the expiration. If you'd rather not buy/sell the stock, you don't have to. The term for using an option to buy/sell a stock at the strike price is called *exercising* the option.

If an options buyer chooses to exercise an option, the seller is obligated to respond. If the option involves buying stock, the seller must sell stock to the buyer at the strike price. If the option involves selling stock, the seller must sell the buyer's stock at the strike price. This obligation is called *assignment*.

The terms premium, expiration, exercise, and assignment apply to stock options as well as lottery tickets. But there are at least four major flaws in my analogy.

1. Lotteries are run by organizations that sell vast numbers of tickets. Options can be bought or sold by individuals or small firms.
2. In a lottery, a seller is obligated to provide only one buyer with a prize. In options trading, a seller has the same obligations to every buyer.
3. In a lottery, buyers generally don't sell tickets after the original purchase. But options traders can buy and sell options after the initial purchase.
4. In a lottery, sellers can't buy back tickets from buyers. In an options trade, the seller can buy back an option from the buyer without getting the buyer's permission.

The third and fourth points are important to understand. After a buyer pays a premium to purchase an option, the value of the option will change. This change in value is determined by a number of factors, including the change in the price of the underlying stock and the time left until expiration.

Personally, I've always found the fourth point to be somewhat unfair. In a fair lottery, ticket sellers can't buy back tickets to avoid giving out the prize. But matters are different in options trading. If circumstances go badly for the seller, he or she can simply buy back the option to avoid assignment.

3.2 Calls and Puts

At this point, you should have a hazy understanding of what stock options are about. If you buy a stock option, you have the right to buy/sell a stock at the strike price at any time up to the option's expiration. Taking advantage of this right is called exercising the option.

All option orders can be divided into *calls* and *puts*. A call gives you the right to buy a stock at the strike price. A put gives you the right to sell a stock at the strike price. This section explores these categories in depth, and I'll start by explaining the process of buying a call.

3.2.1 Buying Calls

If you're confident that a stock's price is going to rise and you have the money to buy shares, you should buy the shares. But what if you're only mostly certain that the price is going to rise and you don't have the funds to purchase the shares. What then?

In this case, you can buy a *call option*, which gives you the right to purchase the shares at a strike price. Buying calls provides (at least) two advantages over buying shares:

1. **Lower price** — Like all stock options, calls are (almost always) much less expensive than the underlying shares.
2. **Less risk** — If the stock drops in value, you won't lose as much as investors who own the stock. The most you can lose is the premium you paid for the option.

There are also important disadvantages, including the following:

1. **Lower profit** — If the stock rises, owners of shares will make more money than owners of a call. Also, the seller of the call may buy back the option, limiting the buyer's earnings.
2. **Expiration** — Like all options, calls are worthless after expiration. In contrast, stock ownership never expires.
3. **No dividend** — Owners of shares receive dividends. Owners of calls don't.

An example will clarify how this works. Suppose your analysis tells you that the price of BigCorp (BGCR) shares is about to skyrocket. Shares are currently trading at 150, and you expect the price to reach 180-190. Unfortunately, you can't afford to buy enough shares at 150 to take advantage of this.

Instead, you spend 500 to buy a call (5/share * 100 = 500). This gives you the right to buy 100 shares of BGCR at a strike price of 155. You can't afford to buy 100 shares at 155, but if the stock price rises, the value of your call will rise with it. That is, as the stock's price rises above 155, investors will be more interested in buying your call, which gives them the right to buy shares at 155. Instead of exercising the call, you're going to sell it.

This raises an important point. An option's value may change, but *the strike price never changes*. When you purchase an option to buy/sell a stock for 155, the strike price will remain at 155 throughout the life of the option.

Chapter 3 Stock Options

The following risk graph illustrates the profit/loss after purchasing a call for 100 shares of BGCR at a strike price of 155. Keep in mind that the graph only applies to time before expiration. After expiration, options are always worthless.

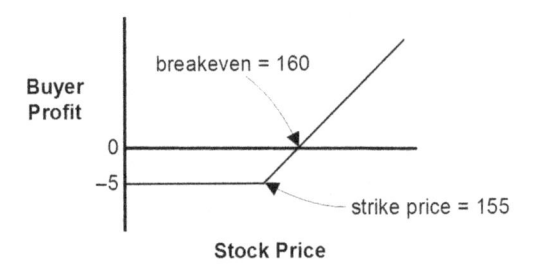

Figure 3.2 Risk Graph for Buying a Call (Premium = 5/share, Strike Price = 155)

As shown, the buyer's profit is −5 per share until the stock price rises above the strike price. If the stock continues rising, it will reach the breakeven point. If the option buyer exercises the call at the breakeven point, he or she can sell the stock and recoup the cost of the option, ending up with a profit of 0. If the stock price exceeds the breakeven point, exercising the option and selling the stock will result in a positive profit.

The equations for a call buyer's profit and breakeven point can be computed with the following equations:

$$profit = (sell\ price - strike\ price) - premium$$
$$breakeven = strike\ price + premium$$

To demonstrate this, let's return to the BigCorp example. If the strike price is 155 and the call premium is 5, the breakeven point is 160. To see why this is the case, consider what happens when the buyer exercises the option at 160. That is, suppose the buyer obtains shares at 155 each and sells them at 160. The profit is given as (160 − 155) − 5, which equals 0. At this point, the buyer has broken even.

Of course, the buyer doesn't have to exercise the option. If the stock price increases, the buyer can sell the option if a buyer is available. If the stock price increases very highly, the call seller may choose to buy back the option, thereby limiting the buyer's profit.

Now let's compare the profit of a call owner to that of a stock owner. Figure 3.3 presents the same risk graph as in Figure 3.2, but in this case, the dashed line identifies the profit realized by an owner of the stock.

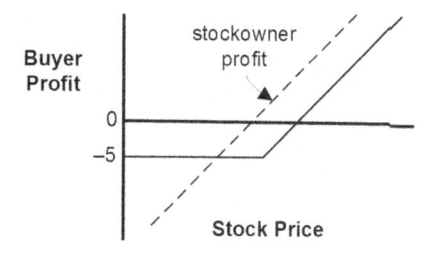

Figure 3.3 Risk Graph for Buying Calls versus Stocks

This graph illustrates two points:

1. If a stock's price exceeds the strike price, the stock owner will realize greater profit than the call owner. This is because the call owner paid a premium for the call.
2. If a stock performs poorly, the stock owner can lose the entire value of the stock. The call owner's loss is limited to the premium.

These points are important to consider when you're deciding whether to buy a call or buy the underlying stock.

3.2.2 Selling Calls

When I first learned about options trading, I found the idea of selling options unsettling. How can I sell something I don't own and haven't borrowed? Unsettling or not, anyone can sell stock options, regardless of whether they own stock. But it's crucial to understand the risks.

A call buyer makes money when the stock price rises above the strike price. Similarly, a call seller loses money when the price exceeds the strike price. This is illustrated in Figure 3.4, which depicts the risk graph associated with selling a call at a premium of 5. Note that this can be obtained by flipping the buyer's graph vertically.

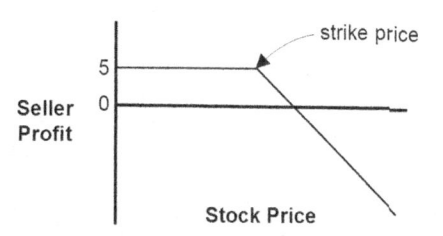

Figure 3.4 Risk Graph for Selling a Call (Premium = 5/share)

As shown, the seller receives the premium up front, and this is the only profit he or she can make. If the stock price rises above the strike price *and* the buyer exercises the option, the seller's profit will fall. If the stock price rises significantly, the seller can lose a great deal of money.

The option seller's mentality is similar to that of a lottery ticket seller. He or she receives money initially, but bears the risk of losing a significant amount of money later. To mitigate this risk, successful call sellers perform three tasks:

1. Ensure that the strike price is high enough that the stock is unlikely to rise above it.
2. Set the premium high enough to offset the risk of losing money if the stock rises.
3. Plan to buy back the option if the stock price soars.

The last point is critical. Sellers of options have unlimited risk, so it's important to monitor the stock and buy back the option if circumstances become unfavorable.

3.2.3 Buying Puts

Just as a call gives its owner the right to buy shares at a strike price, a put gives its owner the right to sell shares at a strike price. If the stock price falls below the strike price, the put owner can buy shares at the current price and sell the shares at the strike price by exercising the option.

Newcomers to options find puts more confusing than calls, so I'll present a simple example. Suppose your research tells you that BigCorp (BGCR) stock is about to plunge from its current price, 150, to around 110–120. You could short the stock, but it's less risky and less expensive to buy a put.

You spend 500 to buy a put on 100 shares of BGCR (5/share * 100 = 500) at a strike price of 140. Figure 3.5 shows what the associated risk graph looks like. Its overall shape is the same as the call buyer's graph, but flipped horizontally.

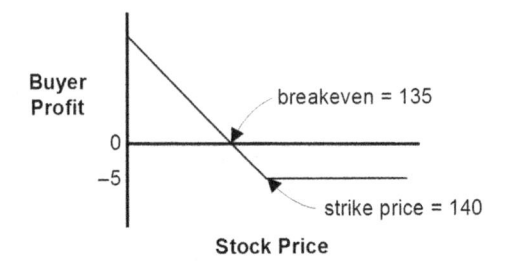

Figure 3.5 Risk Graph for Buying a Put (Premium = 5/share)

The buyer's profit is −5 per share until the stock price falls below the strike price. If the stock continues falling, it will reach a point where the buyer's profit is 0. This is the breakeven point. If the stock falls below the breakeven point, buying the stock and exercising the option will result in a positive profit.

The equations for a put buyer's profit and breakeven point can be computed in the following way:

$$profit = (strike\ price - buy\ price) - premium$$
$$breakeven = strike\ price - premium$$

Returning to the BigCorp example, if the strike price is 140 and the put premium is 5, the breakeven point is 135. To see why, think about what happens when the buyer exercises the option at 135. The buyer will buy shares at 135 each and then sell them at 140 each. The buyer's profit is (140 − 135) − 5 = 0.

It's instructive to compare the risks/rewards of buying a put versus those of short selling a stock. As discussed in Chapter 2, a short sale involves borrowing shares, selling them at the current price, and then covering the short later by buying shares at a (hopefully) lower price. Short selling is similar to buying a put in that profit increases when the stock's price decreases. Figure 3.6 makes this clear.

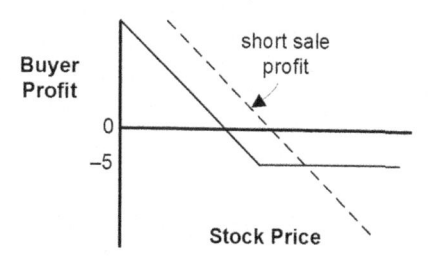

Figure 3.6 Risk Graph for Buying Puts versus Stocks

As illustrated, the short seller makes more money than the put buyer when the price of the stock falls below the strike price. This is because the put buyer paid a premium for the stock option.

But the added reward of the short sale carries greater risk. If the stock's price rises significantly, the short seller will lose more money than the put buyer. The put buyer's loss is limited to the price of the option.

3.2.4 Selling Puts

If you're confident that a stock isn't going to fall below a certain price, you can sell puts at a strike price of your choosing. The good news is that you'll receive profit as soon as someone buys a put. The bad news is that, if the stock price falls below the strike price before expiration, you can lose a significant amount of money.

Figure 3.7 depicts the profit and loss associated with selling a put at a premium of 5. The graph's shape can be obtained by vertically flipping the graph of the put buyer or horizontally flipping the graph of a call seller.

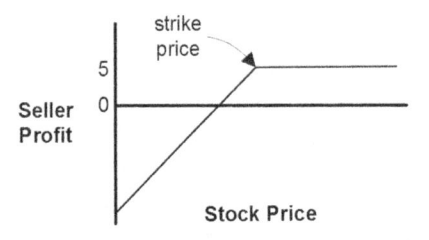

Figure 3.7 Risk Graph for Selling a Put (Premium = 5/share)

If the stock stays at the strike price or above, the put seller will keep the premium and incur no loss. But if the stock falls below the stock price and the buyer exercises the option, the seller can incur significant loss.

Given the risk exposure, option sellers need to carefully monitor stock prices. If a stock falls, a put seller needs to buy back the put to limit the loss.

3.3 Option Expiration

Every stock option has an expiration date beyond which it can no longer be exercised. No matter how the stock price changes, the option is worthless beyond expiration.

In the United States, expiration dates are set according to a regular but confusing system. Every option is assigned to one of three monthly cycles:

- **January** — January, April, July, and October
- **February** — February, May, August, and November
- **March** — March, June, September, and December

An option's cycle partly determines the months in which it can expire. There are two rules that determine an option's expiration month:

1. If an option is sold in a given month, it can expire in that month or the following month.
2. If an option is sold in a given month, it can expire in the next two months belonging to its cycle.

These rules can be confusing, so here are some examples:

- If an option belonging to the March cycle is sold in July, its possible expiration months are July, August, September, or December.
- If an option belonging to the January cycle is sold in March, its possible expiration months are March, April, May, or August.
- If an option belonging to the February cycle is sold in June, its possible expiration months are June, July, August, and November.

When you know an American option's expiration month, it's easy to determine the expiration date and time. All options expire at 4:00 PM Eastern Time on the third Friday of the expiration month. If this Friday is a holiday, the option will expire on the preceding Thursday.

The preceding discussion holds true for the majority of options traded in America. But there are two types of options that follow a different set of rules. The first are weekly options and the second are LEAPS.

3.3.1 Weekly Options

Most options are monthly, and expire on the third Friday in a month. But weekly options are released on Thursday and expire the following Friday. The short lifetime makes this type of option much riskier than other types, but weeklies have become very popular for two main reasons:

1. Because of the added risk, premiums on weekly options are smaller than those for regular options.
2. Traders don't need to predict events three months in advance. They can make decisions based on recent news and analysis.

Sellers are particularly happy with weekly options. This is because they can receive premium payments 52 times a year instead of 12.

3.3.2 LEAPS

Just as weeklies expire much sooner than regular options, long-term equity anticipation securities (LEAPS) expire much later. LEAPS are like regular options, but they remain active longer than one year. The majority of LEAPS have expiration dates two years in the future.

Because LEAPS last for such a long term, their prices are more closely aligned with the underlying stock price than other options. In fact, many investors think of LEAPS as less-risky, less-expensive stock substitutes.

This decrease in risk and expense comes with a higher premium. Also, LEAPS buyers never receive the benefits of owning actual stock, such as voting rights and dividends.

3.4 Trading Options in TWS

Chapter 2 explained how to order stocks and bonds in TWS, and the process of trading options is similar. This section walks through the process of buying calls for Starbucks (SBUX) stock.

The first step is to add the ticker of the underlying stock to the watchlist. For this example, you can do this by right-clicking in the Monitor panel and typing SBUX. When you press Enter, a dialog will appear and allow you to select a financial instrument. For this example, select the **Options** entry.

Next, TWS will open a dialog that displays different dates and strike prices for SBUX options. This is called an option chain, and Figure 3.8 shows what it looks like.

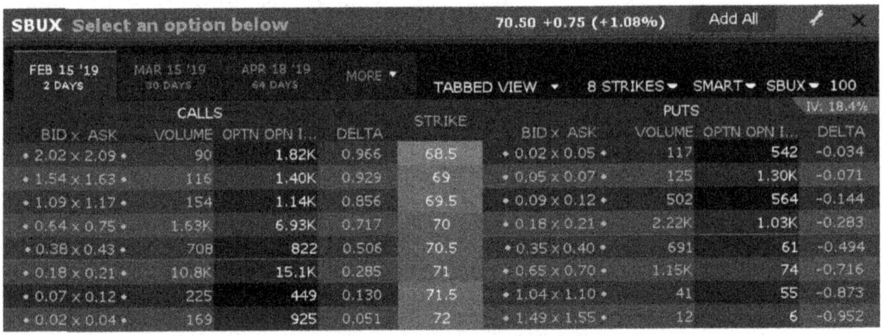

Figure 3.8 SBUX Option Chain

This dialog provides a great deal information, and I'd like to call your attention to four points:

1. The tabs in the upper left make it possible to select different expirations of SBUX options. In this case, you can select expirations in February, March, or April.
2. Below the tabs, the dialog displays two sets of columns: call-related columns under the **CALLS** heading, put-related columns under the **PUTS** heading.
3. The middle column lists strike prices in ascending order (low strike prices above high prices).
4. For each option type and strike price, the chain lists the market's buying price (bid) and selling price (ask).

Before proceeding further, I'd like to walk through two demonstrations of how this option chain can be used to find option premiums:

- Suppose you want to buy a February SBUX call with a strike price of 71. You'd find the row whose strike price is 71 and look for the bid/ask price (0.18/0.21) in the **CALLS** section. In this case, the asking price is 0.21/share, or 21 for a call representing 100 shares.
- Suppose you want to buy a March SBUX put with a strike price of 75. You'd click the tab for the March option chain, find the row whose strike price is 75, and look for the bid/ask price (4.50/4.60) in the **PUTS** section. In this case, the asking price is 4.50/share, or 450 for a put representing 100 shares.

As illustrated, an option chain provides more information than just the bid, ask, and strike price. The available data includes the following values:

- **volume** — number of contracts sold over the last day
- **open interest** — the number of options of the given type that haven't expired, haven't been exercised, and haven't been closed by the seller
- **delta** — change in the option's price with each dollar increase of SBUX stock (discussed further in a later section)

To add an option to the watchlist, find the row containing the strike price you're interested in. Then click the bid price or the ask price. TWS will automatically add the option to the watchlist.

When you add an option to the watchlist, it will appear in the Order Entry box. At this point, you can select **BUY** or **SELL** and configure the order as if it was a regular stock order. Then click **SUBMIT** to submit the order for execution.

3.5 Moneyness

If you look closely at Figure 3.8, you'll see that call premiums always decrease as strike price increases. This should make sense, since the call buyer's profit depends on the stock price exceeding the strike price. For a similar reason, put premiums always increase as the strike price increases.

An option's *moneyness* is determined by an option's type (call or put) and how its strike price relates to the stock's current price. There are three categories of moneyness:

- **out of the money** (OTM) — a call whose strike price is higher than the stock price or a put whose strike price is lower than the strike price
- **at the money** (ATM) — an option whose strike price equals the stock price
- **in the money** (ITM) — a call whose strike price is less than the stock price or a put whose strike price is greater than the strike price

These designations may seem arbitrary, but it's worth spending some time until you're comfortable with them. It should be clear that if you buy an ITM option, you can immediately exercise it for money.

For example, suppose you buy a call whose strike price, 180, exceeds the stock price of 170. After purchasing the option, you can exercise it and buy shares at 170. Then you can sell the shares at 180. This makes you 10 per share, but this won't be sufficient to offset the price you paid for the option.

From a buyer's perspective, ITM options are safe but expensive, ATM options are reasonably safe and moderately expensive, and OTM options are cheap but unsafe. From a seller's perspective, these judgements are reversed.

3.6 Option Value

One major difference between options and lottery tickets is that an option's value changes before its expiration. As a result, options buyers can sell their options at market before the expiration date.

This raises an important question: How is an option's value determined? Earlier, I mentioned that an option's price is related to the profit received when the option is exercised. Now it's time to discuss this subject further.

According to current theory, an option's value is found by computing the sum of two components: *intrinsic value* and *time value*. This section provides a basic discussion of both components.

3.6.1 Intrinsic Value

Of the two components of an option's value, intrinsic value is the easier to compute and understand. This is simply the owner's payoff if he or she immediately exercises the option. For calls, the intrinsic value equals the stock price minus the strike price. For puts, the intrinsic value equals the strike price minus the stock price.

In essence, intrinsic value measures how in-the-money an option is. If an option isn't in the money, its intrinsic value is zero.

3.6.2 Time Value

Time value is more complicated. An option with a longer time to maturity is considered more valuable than an option with a shorter time to maturity. This is because the longer-term option has a greater chance of rising or falling sufficiently to increase the option's value.

What makes time value complicated is the influence of *volatility*, which measures how much the underlying stock changes over time. If a stock's price changes dramatically on a daily basis, it has high volatility and a stock option is likely to gain in intrinsic value at some point. If a stock's price changes very little, it has low volatility and a stock option is unlikely to gain in intrinsic value at some point. Therefore, an option's time value is determined by the time to maturity and its volatility.

When describing an option's volatility, investors employ two terms: historical volatility (HV) and implied volatility (IV). Historical volatility is the standard deviation of a stock's price over the course of a year. This isn't directional. That is, it doesn't measure how far the price rises or falls, but only how dramatically it changes over a year.

For example, if the vector x_i contains the N prices of IBM stock over the past year and the average stock price is x_{avg}, the historical volatility can be computed with the following equation:

$$HV = \sqrt{\frac{\sum_i (x_i - x_{avg})^2}{N}}$$

An option's time value is affected by the stock's volatility in the future, not the past. For this reason, investors focus on *implied volatility* (IV) instead of historical volatility. No one can reliably predict the future, but if you look in the upper right of Figure 3.8, you can see that TWS computed the IV of SBUX to be 18.4%. How did TWS arrive at this value?

There are a few different ways to obtain IV values, and the most popular method is to apply the Black-Scholes equation. This famous equation is too complex for this book, but it computes implied volatility using five variables:

1. Market price of the option
2. Price of the underlying stock
3. Time to maturity
4. Option's strike price
5. Risk-free interest rate

If you'd like to see how the Black-Scholes equation works in practice, you can find many "Black-Scholes calculator" sites on the Internet. If you want to compute the implied volatility, you'll find the calculator at http://www.option-price.com/implied-volatility.php to be very helpful.

3.7 Greeks

In Figure 3.8, the **CALLS** and **PUTS** sections both contain a column named *delta*. Delta is one of a set of statistics that measure how the option's value changes in response to external factors. These statistics are called *Greeks* because most of their names are Greek in origin.

Financial sources disagree on the full list of Greeks, but the four most common are as follows:

- **delta** — how the option's price changes when the stock price changes
- **gamma** — how delta changes when the stock price changes
- **vega** — how the option's price changes due to volatility
- **theta** — how the option's price changes over time

In TWS, you can view the Greeks for an option by clicking the **New Window** button in the upper left. Then go to **Option Analysis > Interactive Analytics > Greeks**. Figure 3.9 shows what this looks like for SBUX options.

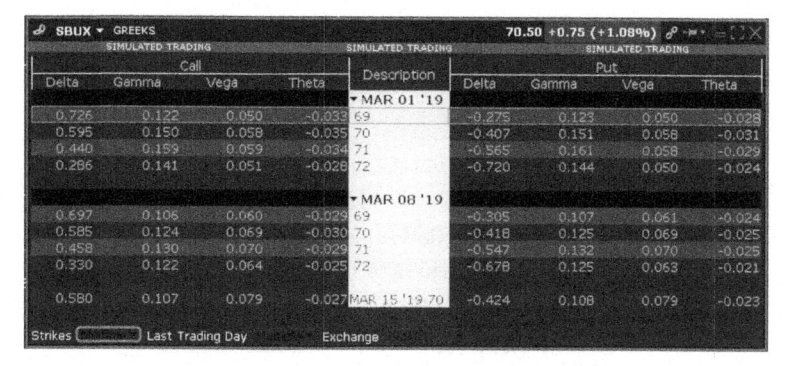

Figure 3.9 Example Values for Greeks

By paying attention to Greeks, investors hope to predict how the option's price will change. The goal of this section is to explain precisely what these statistics represent.

3.7.1 Delta

Delta relates the price of an option to the price of its underlying security. To be specific, delta measures how much the option changes every time the price of the underlying security changes by 1. For stock options, the value of a call option increases when the stock price rises, so delta is always positive for calls. The value of a put option decreases when the stock price falls, so delta is always negative for puts.

According to the figure, a SBUX call expiring on 3/1/19 with a strike price of 69 has a delta of 0.726. This means the option's price is expected to increase by 0.726 every time the price of SBUX goes up by 1.

Similarly, a SBUX put expiring on 3/8/19 with a strike price of 72 has a delta equal to −0.678. This indicates that the option's price is expected to drop by 0.678 every time the price of SBUX rises by 1.

Delta increases as options become further in the money, and approaches 1 for options deep in the money. At-the-money options usually have deltas of 0.5 (calls) or −0.5 (puts). You can see this in Figure 3.9 by checking the deltas for calls and puts with strike prices at 70 and 71 (which are close to being at the money).

Many investors use delta to estimate the likelihood of an option expiring in the money. If the option is already deep in the money, its high delta implies that it's likely to remain in the money. If an option is out of the money, its low delta implies that it's unlikely to become in the money.

Many sources discuss portfolio delta, which is the delta value associated with a group of securities. Portfolio delta can be computed by adding the delta of each individual security. A portfolio is delta-neutral if the deltas of its securities add to zero.

3.7.2 Gamma

If an analyst relies on delta alone, he or she is assuming that a linear relationship exists between the option price and the stock price. But there's more to the relationship than just a straight line. For this reason, analysts take both delta and gamma into account.

Gamma identifies how much delta changes in response to a change in the price of the underlying security. For example, if gamma equals 0.2 and the stock price changes by 4, delta is expected to increase by 0.2 * 4 = 0.4.

Gamma is always positive for both calls and puts. This should be obvious for calls, where an increase in stock price produces an increase in delta. But it's not obvious for puts. To understand why gamma values for puts is positive, remember that any increase in a stock's price moves a put out of the money. This means that, for puts, delta approaches zero (becomes less negative) as the stock's price increases. Therefore, gamma is positive.

To see how this works, consider the 3/1/19 SBUX put with a strike price of 72, which is illustrated in Figure 3.9. In this case, delta equals −0.720 and gamma equals 0.144. If the stock price rises by 1, the put's price is expected to decrease by −0.72 and then the delta value will approach zero. More precisely, the new value of delta will be delta + gamma = −0.720 + 0.144, which equals −0.576.

Delta is more sensitive to stock price changes for at-the-money options than for in-the-money options or out-of-the-money options. Therefore, gamma grows larger as an option's strike price approaches the stock price. You can verify this in Figure 3.9 by comparing gamma values of ATM options to those of ITM and OTM options.

If you're familiar with calculus, then you can think of delta as the derivative of the option's price with respect to the stock's price. Gamma is the second derivative of the option's price with respect to the stock's price, or the slope of the first derivative.

3.7.3 Vega

Delta and gamma are fine for basic analysis, but they don't take volatility into account. It should be clear that a highly volatile stock will be more likely to enter in-the-money territory before expiration than a stock whose price remains flat over time. All other things being equal, a highly-volatile option will be more likely to make money than an option with low volatility.

Vega measures the relationship between an option's price and the implied volatility (IV). As discussed earlier, IV is the estimated volatility of a security based on the Black-Scholes equation. Vega measures how much an option's price increases when the IV increases by 1%.

As volatility increases, calls and puts both become more likely to reach in-the-money prices. For this reason, vega is positive for both calls and puts. In fact, the values of vega for puts and calls with the same strike price are nearly equal.

An example will clarify how vega is used. As shown in the figure, the value of vega for the 3/1/19 SBUX call at a strike price of 71 is 0.058. This implies that, if the IV of SBUX rises to 5%, the price of the option will rise by 5 * 0.058 = 0.29.

3.7.4 Theta

As mentioned earlier, an option's value can be split into two parts: intrinsic value and time value. As time approaches the option's expiration, the option's time value decreases. The statistic that takes this into account is *theta*.

To be specific, theta tells us how much the value of an option changes with each approaching day. The value always decreases, so it should be clear that theta is always negative.

As an example, consider the 3/8/19 SBUX put with a strike price of 69. In this case, theta equals −0.024. This means that the option's value is expected to decrease by 0.024 during the course of the day. Keep in mind that theta isn't linear, so the time decay could be quite different the day after tomorrow.

3.8 Summary

This chapter has explored the topic of options—what they are, how they work, and how to trade them in TWS. In particular, the discussion has focused on stock options, whose value is based on the price of the underlying stock. A call option grants the right to buy shares of stock at a strike price and a put option grants the right to sell shares of stock at a strike price. Every stock option has a price (its premium) and a date after which the rights are no longer available (its expiration).

To configure options orders in TWS, you need to know how to read an option chain. An option chain lists the premiums associated with calls and puts with the same expiration at different strike prices. For calls, premiums are higher when the strike price is less than the stock price (in-the-money) than when the strike price is greater than the stock price (out-of-the-money). For puts, premiums are higher when the stock price is less than the strike price (in-the-money) than when the stock price is greater than the strike price (out-of-the-money).

The last part of this chapter presented four statistics that analysts use to predict option prices. Delta relates the option's price to the price of the underlying stock. Gamma identifies how much delta changes when the price of the underlying stock changes. Vega relates the change in an option's price to an increase in the option's implied volatility. Theta identifies how much the option's value drops as the date approaches the option's expiration date.

Chapter 4

Option Trading Strategies

The preceding chapter discussed the fundamentals of options and option trading. But instead of submitting an order for a single call or a single put, many professionals combine their options order with a stock order, or execute multiple options transactions in a single order. The goal of these combinations is to increase the profit or reduce the risk associated with single-option orders.

Throughout this book, I'll refer to these combinations as strategies. Over the years, traders have devised many types of strategies with whimsical names like butterfly spread and iron condor. This chapter doesn't present every strategy ever conceived, but I'll discuss all the popular strategies that I've encountered.

With so many strategies, it's easy to get overwhelmed. Personally, I keep track of them by associating each with its risk graph. For example, when I think about a bull call spread, I think about its risk graph instead of the strategy's individual transactions. You may find this helpful as well, so I strongly recommend reviewing Chapter 3 until you're comfortable with the risk graphs for buying calls, selling calls, buying puts, and selling puts.

4.1 Stock and Option Strategies

There are many ways to classify options orders, such as type (put or call), position (long or short), and moneyness (OTM, ATM, or ITM). Another way to classify an options trade depends on whether the buyer of the option owns shares of the underlying stock. If a buyer already owns stock, the option is referred to as *covered*. If the buyer doesn't own any stock, the option is referred to as *naked*.

If you're selling options, covered options are safer than naked options. This is because, if the option buyer executes the option, the seller will have shares ready to buy or sell.

With this in mind, the first of the strategies discussed in this chapter is the covered call, which involves selling calls for stock that the seller owns.

4.1.1 Covered Calls

One of the simplest options strategies is the covered call. This involves selling a call on shares of stock that are owned by the seller. Investors who want to hold on to their shares over a long term like this strategy because it allows them to receive the call's premium without losing their shares (hopefully).

Like every strategy, writing a covered call has its risks:

1. If the stock price falls, the investor will take a loss due to the decrease in share value.
2. If the stock price rises above the strike price, the buyer of the call may exercise the call and purchase the seller's shares.

Given these risks, covered calls are ideal only if the seller expects the stock price to remain below the call's strike price.

This second point is particularly important to understand. Call buyers make a profit when the stock price rises above the strike price. Therefore, if the stock price surges, buyers may exercise the option and buy the seller's shares at the strike price.

Of course, long-term stock owners want to avoid this. Therefore, writers of covered calls need to carefully monitor the stock price. If it rises to a point where the buyer might consider exercising the option, they should buy back the option. Also, writers should sell the call at a high strike price (OTM) to reduce the likelihood that the stock's price will exceed it.

To understand covered calls, you need to understand the associated risk graph. As with all strategies, you can obtain the risk graph by combining (adding) the graphs of each individual transaction.

On the following page, Figure 4.1 depicts the risk graph for covered calls. The graph on the left depicts the risk of selling calls—the seller receives the premium and takes a loss if the shares rise in value.

The graph in the middle displays the risk of owning shares of stock—the owner makes a profit if the price increases and takes a loss if it decreases. The graph on the right adds the values from the preceding two graphs to illustrate the risk associated with selling a covered call.

As shown, the covered call doesn't prevent the seller from taking a loss if the price falls, but the loss is offset by the receipt of the call's premium. If the price remains below the strike price, the seller keeps the premium and doesn't need to worry about losing the shares.

Figure 4.1 Risk Graph for Selling a Covered Call

If the stock price rises above the strike price, the call seller won't make a profit if the call buyer exercises their option. Therefore, the seller needs to buy back the option before this becomes a serious possibility.

4.1.2 Protected Puts

Unlike a covered call, a protective put (also called a married put) isn't a money-making strategy. Instead, it helps investors who are nervous about their shares losing value. A protective put involves buying a put for shares of stock while owning the same number of shares. The investor makes a profit if the shares rise in value, and the loss is reduced if the price falls below the strike price.

Figure 4.2 illustrates the profit and loss associated with a protective put. The left graph illustrates the risk of buying a put, the middle graph illustrates the risk of buying stock, and the last graph illustrates the risk of combining the two in a protective put.

Figure 4.2 Risk Graph for Buying a Protective Put

If the stock price falls below the strike price, the investor can exercise the put and sell the shares at the strike price. In a way, protective puts serve as stock insurance, guaranteeing that the owner's loss won't be too terrible.

At a high level, the profit and loss of a protective put is similar to that of buying a call. You can see this by comparing the right graph in Figure 4.2 to the graph of buying a call.

4.2 Spreads

In general, the term *spread* refers to the difference between what the market is willing to pay for a security (bid) and what the market is willing to take for it (ask). But in the world of options strategies, spread refers to buying and selling equal numbers of options for the same stock, but with different strike prices or expiration dates.

Options spreads can be divided into three groups:

1. **Vertical spreads** — Buy/sell the same type of option on the same stock with the same expiration dates, but with different strike prices
2. **Horizontal (calendar) spreads** — Buy/sell the same type of option on the same stock with the same strike prices, but with different expiration dates
3. **Diagonal spreads** — Buy/sell the same type of option on the same stock with different strike prices and expiration dates

This discussion presents each of these types of spreads. In each case, I'll present the risk graph that illustrates the strategy's profit and loss.

4.2.1 Vertical Spreads

There are two categories of vertical spreads: debit spreads and credit spreads. Each appeals to a different type of trader:

- Debit spreads are for option buyers who are willing to receive a potentially reduced profit in return for paying a reduced premium.
- Credit spreads are for options sellers who are willing to receive a smaller premium in return for a limited potential loss.

Once an investor has chosen a category, the next step is to pick the specific type of vertical spread. Debit spreads are divided into bull call spreads and bear put spreads. Credit spreads are divided into bull put spreads and bear call spreads.

The distinction between specific types involves the investor's expectation for the stock (bullish or bearish). On the following page, Figure 4.3 presents the general thought process for choosing a vertical spread.

If you find it hard to distinguish debit spreads and credit spreads, keep in mind that traders *pay* a smaller premium for a debit spread because debit spreads are intended for buyers. Traders *receive* a smaller premium for a credit spread because credit spreads are intended for sellers.

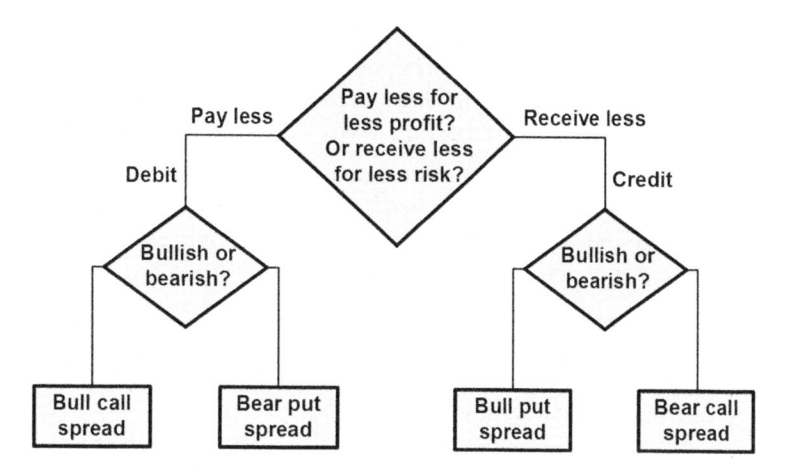

Figure 4.3 Vertical Spread Selection Process

Debit Spreads: Bull Call and Bear Put

As discussed in Chapter 3, buying an option is like buying a lottery ticket. Buyers pay a premium for the opportunity to make a large profit if circumstances turn out well. Buyers don't have to worry about major loss, but some may be willing to sacrifice potential profit in return for a lower premium.

These buyers should consider debit spreads. More specifically, traders should consider bull call spreads if they think a stock is increasing and bear put spreads if they think the stock is decreasing.

In a bull call spread, a buyer reduces the cost of buying a call by selling a second call for the same stock at a higher strike price. This is a good strategy for optimistic traders who don't want to pay the full premium for buying a call.

Suppose a trader buys a call with strike price K1 for a premium of P1. The trader also sells a call with strike price K2 for a premium of P2. If K1 < K2, this is a bull call spread and Figure 4.4 illustrates the risk.

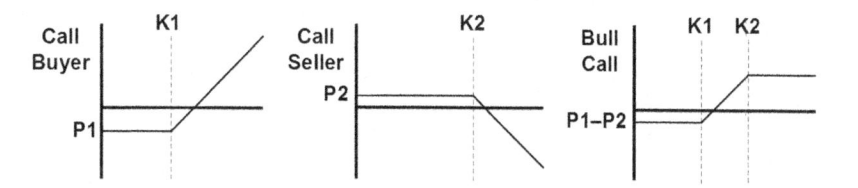

Figure 4.4 Risk Graph for a Bull Call Spread

Chapter 4 Option Trading Strategies

This graph can be divided into three regions. If the stock price is below both strike prices, the trader loses the difference of the two premiums, P1 − P2. If the stock price is between K1 and K2, the investor's return is (S − K1) − (P1 − P2), where S is the price of the stock. If the stock price exceeds K2, the return is (K2 − K1) − (P1 − P2).

If a trader is pessimistic about a stock's price but doesn't want to pay the full premium for a put, he or she can execute a bear put spread. This involves buying a put at one strike price and selling a put at a lower strike price. As a result of the sale, the investor receives a small premium but sacrifices profit if the price declines dramatically.

To see how bear put spreads work, consider the risk graph in Figure 4.5. In this case, the investor buys a put with strike price K1 for a premium of P1. The investor also sells a put with strike price K2 for a premium of P2. As a result of the purchase and sale, the net premium equals P1 − P2.

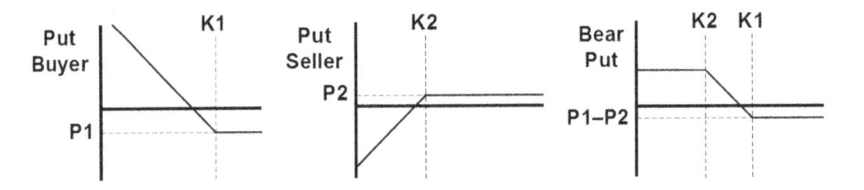

Figure 4.5 Risk Graph for a Bear Put Spread

As with bull call spreads, the risk graph of a bear put spread can be divided into three regions. If the stock price rises above K1, the investor's loss is limited to the net premium, P1 − P2. If the stock price (S) is greater than K2 but less than K1, the investor's profit is (S − K2) − (P1 − P2). If the stock price exceeds K1, the profit increases to the maximum, (K1 − K2) − (P1 − P2).

Credit Spreads: Bull Put and Bear Call

In a credit spread, an option seller sacrifices part of the received premium to limit the risk of the sale. If the investor is bullish, he or she should consider a bull put spread. If bearish, he or she should consider a bear call spread.

In a bull put spread, the investor sells a put at one strike price and buys another put for the same stock at a lower strike price. The purchased put limits the potential loss of the sold put, but also reduces the premium received from the sale. The investor hopes that the stock will rise above both strike prices, as this provides the full premium.

For example, suppose an investor sells a put for a premium of P1 and a strike price of K1. Then the investor buys a put for a premium of P2 and a strike price of K2. Figure 4.6 shows what the investor's profit and loss look like.

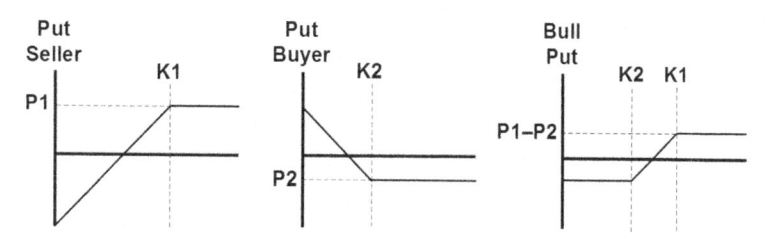

Figure 4.6 Risk Graph for a Bull Put Spread

Credit spreads are intended for sellers, so the investor wants the premium to be as large as possible and the loss to be as small as possible. As shown in the figure, if the stock price falls below K2, loss is limited to (K1 − K2) − (P1 − P2). If the price is greater than K2 but less than K1, the spread's value is (S − K2) − (P1 − P2). Ideally, the price will rise above K1, and the investor will receive the full net premium of P1 − P2.

If the investor thinks the stock's value is about to fall, he or she may prefer to execute a bear call spread. This involves selling a call at one strike price and selling a second call at a higher strike price. For the investor to receive the full net premium as profit, the stock price must fall below both strike prices.

For example, suppose an investor sells a call for a premium of P1 and a strike price of K1. Then the investor buys a call for a premium of P2 and a strike price of K2, which is greater than K1. Figure 4.7 shows what the investor's profit and loss look like.

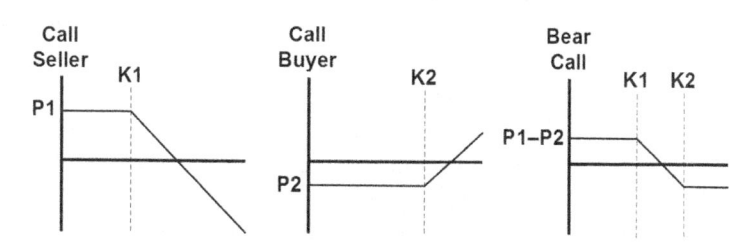

Figure 4.7 Risk Graph for a Bear Call Spread

If the stock price falls below K1, the investor receives the full net premium, P1 − P2. If the price, S, rises above K1 but stays below K2, the spread's value is (S − K1) − (P1 − P2). If the stock price exceeds K2, the investor's loss is (K2 − K1) − (P1 − P2).

If you find it hard to distinguish between debit and credit spreads, keep two points in mind. In a debit spread, the maximum profit is determined by the difference in strike prices and the maximum loss is determined by the difference in premiums. For a credit spread, the situation is reversed—the maximum profit is determined by the difference in premiums and the maximum loss is determined by the difference in strike prices.

4.2.2 Horizontal Spreads

Chapter 3 discussed the time value of options and explained how implied volatility (IV) affects an option's value. It should be clear that long-term options are more valuable (have higher premiums) than short-term options.

The goal of a horizontal spread (also called a calendar spread) is to take advantage of time decay. To be specific, a horizontal spread involves buying/selling a short-term option and selling/buying a long-term option. In both transactions, the options are for the same stock and have the same strike price.

As with vertical spreads, horizontal spreads come in two categories that can be further split into four types. The two categories are:

1. **long horizontal spreads** — sell short-term options, buy long-term options
2. **short horizontal spreads** — sell long-term options, buy short-term options

Like debit spreads, long horizontal spreads are intended for buyers willing to sacrifice profit in return for a lower premium. Like credit spreads, short horizontal spreads are intended for sellers willing to accept a lower premium in return for a lower risk.

Long Horizontal Spreads

If an investor believes that a stock is going to approach the strike price over time or stay near the strike price, he or she may want to consider a long horizontal spread, also called a time spread. This can be implemented with calls or puts. In both cases, the trader sells a short-term option and buys a long-term option.

To implement a long horizontal spread with calls, an investor sells a short-term call and buys a long-term call with the same strike price. If the stock's price equals the strike price at the earlier expiration date, the sold call will expire worthless. The bought call will continue to have value because of its longer term.

If the stock's price isn't close to the strike price at the earlier expiration date, the investor's loss is the net premium. If the price falls significantly below the strike price, the bought option will (probably) be worthless. If the price rises significantly above the strike price, the sold option will be exercised and the investor will execute the purchased option to obtain shares.

Figure 4.8 illustrates the risk graph associated with long horizontal spreads at the time of the earlier expiration date. Note that the maximum profit can't be determined in advance—it depends on the value of the long-term purchased call.

Figure 4.8 Risk Graph for a Long Horizontal Spread

Long horizontal spreads can also be implemented with puts. In this case, the trader sells a short-term put and buys a long-term put with the same strike price. As in the preceding discussion, the trader makes a profit if the stock price stays close to the strike price and loses if the stock price moves significantly away.

The risk graph of a long horizontal spread with puts is similar to that of a long horizontal spread with calls. If this seems strange, remember that the graphs of puts and calls are horizontal mirror images of one another. The graph in Figure 4.8 is symmetric, so it applies to horizontal spreads with calls and puts.

Short Horizontal Spreads

If a trader believes a stock's price is going to move away from the strike price, he or she should consider a short horizontal spread, also called a reverse time spread. This involves selling a long-term option and buying a short-term option. As in a credit spread, the goal is to keep the net premium and minimize the potential loss.

To implement a short horizontal spread with calls, a trader sells a long-term call and buys a short-term call at the same strike price. If the stock price is below the strike price at the earlier expiration date, both options will (probably) be worthless, and the trader will keep the net premium. If the stock price is above the strike price, the trader will exercise the long-term option to receive shares for when the sold call is exercised.

If the stock's price equals the strike price at the earlier expiration date, the bought call will expire worthless. The investor's loss could be significant because the sold call still has time value. Figure 4.9 illustrates the risk chart for a short horizontal spread at the earlier expiration date.

Figure 4.9 Risk Graph for a Short Horizontal Spread

This chart also applies to short horizontal spreads with puts. In this case, the investor sells a long-term put and buys a short-term put with the same strike price.

4.2.3 Diagonal Spreads

A diagonal spread involves buying and selling options of the same type and for the same stock, but with different strike prices and different expiration dates. Many different types of diagonal spreads are available, but the two most common types are:

1. **long diagonal spreads** — buy long-term, in-the-money options, sell short-term, out-of-the-money options
2. **short diagonal spreads** — sell long-term, in-the-money options, buy short-term, out-of-the-money options

These strategies are like the similarly-named horizontal spreads, but allow more flexibility with regard to strike price. In a long diagonal spread, the investor buys an option and reduces the net premium by selling a less expensive option. In a short diagonal spread, the investor sells an option and buys a less expensive option, thereby reducing the received premium in exchange for lower risk.

4.3 Delta Neutral Strategies

Many types of options trades are based on an assumption that the price of the underlying security will move in a particular direction. These types of trades are called *directional*.

The directionality is reflected by the delta value of the securities. As discussed in Chapter 3, delta is the change in a security's price when the underlying security's price increases by 1. Calls always have positive delta, puts always have a negative delta, and stock ownership always has a delta of 1.

Delta can be computed for a group of securities by adding the individual delta values. If the delta values add to 0.5, the securities' value will be expected to increase by half every time the underlying securities increase by 1. If the delta values add to −0.5, the securities' value will be expected to increase by half every time the underlying securities decrease by 1.

If the delta values of a set of securities add to 0, we say that the position is *delta neutral*. If a strategy involves buying securities that add to 0, the strategy is referred to as delta neutral. This section looks at two of the simplest delta neutral strategies: straddles and strangles.

- **straddle** — buy ATM puts and calls with the same expiration
- **strangle** — buy OTM puts and calls with the same expiration

In both cases, the goal is to obtain a position whose total delta value is 0. This means the position will potentially make money if the price of the stock increases or decreases.

4.3.1 Straddles

As discussed in Chapter 3, at-the-money (ATM) calls have a delta value of 0.5 and ATM puts have a delta of −0.5. If a trader buys an equal number of ATM calls and puts for the same stock, the position will be delta neutral.

The calls make money if the stock price rises above the strike price and puts make money if the stock price falls below the strike price. The more the stock moves away from the strike price, the more profit the trader receives.

This type of strategy is called a *straddle*. As an example, suppose a stock is selling for K and a trader believes that the price will either rise or fall dramatically. The trader can establish a straddle by purchasing a call (premium: P1) and a put (premium: P2). Both options have a strike price of K, and Figure 4.10 presents the risk graph.

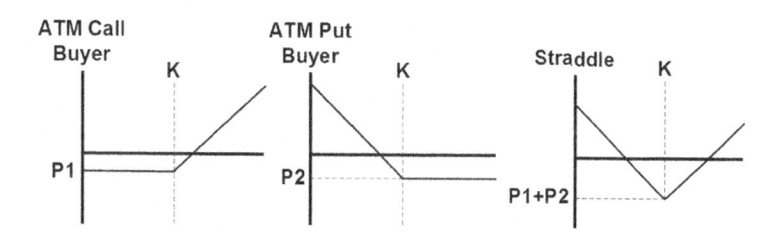

Figure 4.10 Risk Graph of a Straddle

As with a regular put or call, the straddle's potential for profit is unbounded. This makes many traders overoptimistic if they're certain that a major event is about to occur. In practice, the effect of the event has driven the high premiums of the put and call. Therefore, the stock's price needs to move very significantly to offset the cost of the two premiums.

If an investor is confident that a stock's price won't change dramatically, he or she may consider a short straddle, which involves selling a put and a call with the same expiration and strike price. In this strategy, the seller receives two premiums but risks significant loss if the stock price moves up or down. The risk graph for a short straddle can be found by vertically flipping the graph in Figure 4.10.

4.3.2 Strangles

ATM options can be expensive, so many investors reduce the cost by buying OTM calls and puts with opposite delta values. A straddle based on OTM options is called a *strangle*.

For example, suppose a trader is confident that a stock's price is going to move away from its current price of K. Rather than spend the premiums for a straddle, he or she buys a strangle consisting of an OTM call (strike price K1) and an OTM put (strike price K2). Figure 4.11 depicts the risk graph for this strategy.

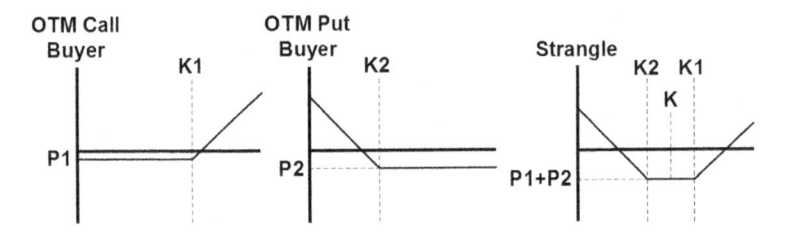

Figure 4.11 Risk Graph of a Strangle

As illustrated, the difference between the strike prices K1 and K2 creates a gap around K. If the stock price stays in this gap, the trader doesn't make a profit. Therefore, some traders position the gap hoping that the stock price won't move in that direction. These types of strangles are partially directional and not delta neutral.

If an investor doesn't think the stock price will move out of the gap, he or she may be interested in a short strangle. This involves selling a put and call at different strike prices. The investor receives two premiums, but if the stock price moves dramatically, the investor's loss will be unlimited.

4.4 Advanced Spreads

So far, all the of the strategies discussed in this chapter can be implemented with two transactions, also called legs. But investors have devised more complicated spreads that involve more legs than just two. This section looks at six of them:

1. **butterfly** — bull and bear spread of the same type with a common strike price
2. **iron butterfly** — butterfly spread with transactions of different types
3. **condor** — bull and bear spread of the same type and uncommon strike prices
4. **iron condor** — condor with transactions of different types

5. **box** — combines a bull call spread with a bear put spread to obtain constant profit
6. **ratio** — similar to a vertical spread, different number of puts and calls

Many of these names may seem whimsical, but they identify the shape of the strategy's risk graph. As you proceed through this section, be sure to see the relationship between the strategies' names and their graphs.

4.4.1 Butterfly Spreads

Like straddles, butterfly spreads are delta neutral and are intended for investors who feel that a stock's price won't move away from a strike price. While a straddle combines a put and a call, a butterfly spread combines two vertical spreads: a bull spread (bull call or bull put) and a bear spread (bear call or bear put).

As a quick review, bull spreads and bear spreads both involve two transactions:

- **bull spread** — Buy and sell options of the same type but different strike prices hoping that the stock price will rise
- **bear spread** — Buy and sell options of the same type but different strike prices hoping that the stock price will fall

In a butterfly spread, the higher strike price of the bull spread is equal to the lower price of the bear spread. Therefore, a butterfly consists of four transactions: two option purchases at a low strike price and a high strike price, and two option sales at the same strike price at the central strike price.

Figure 4.12 shows how the bull and bear spread combine to form a butterfly spread.

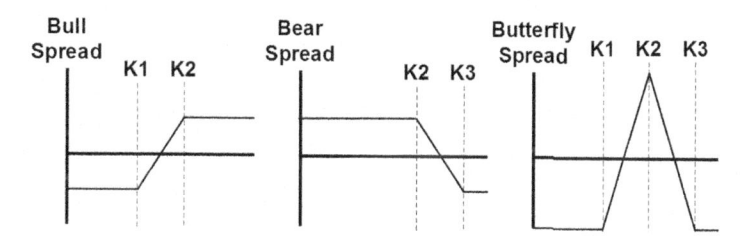

Figure 4.12 Risk Graph of a Butterfly Spread

As illustrated, the trader receives maximum profit if the stock price stays at K2. If the stock price falls below K1 or rises above K3, the trader loses the net premium paid for the option purchases.

4.4.2 Iron Butterfly Spreads

In a butterfly spread, all four transactions involve options of the same type: four calls or four puts. One of the options must be purchased in the money, so butterfly spreads can be expensive.

The risk graph of an iron butterfly spread is similar to that of a butterfly spread, but the four transactions involve options of different types:

1. Purchase one OTM put
2. Sell one ATM put
3. Sell one ATM call
4. Purchase one OTM call

The first two transactions form a bull put spread and the second two form a bear call spread. Figure 4.13 makes this clear.

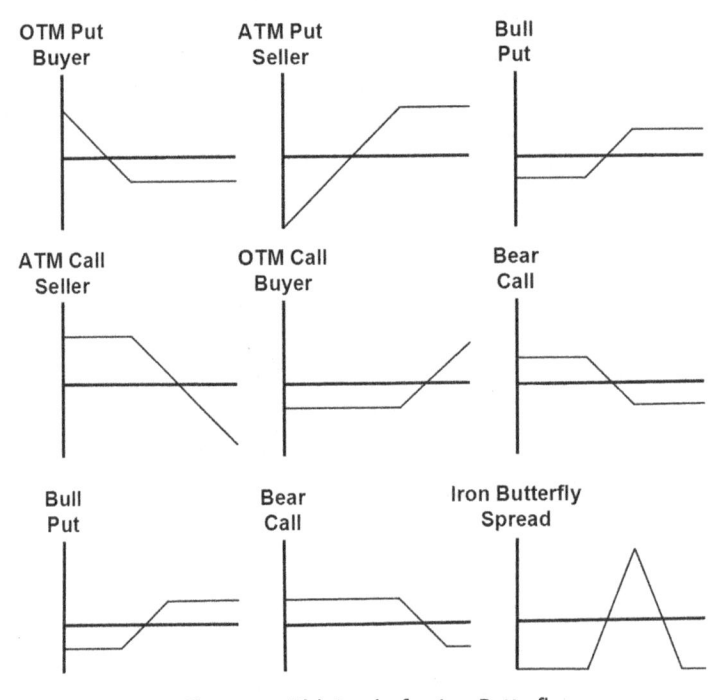

Figure 4.13 Risk Graph of an Iron Butterfly

4.4.3 Condor Spreads and Iron Condor Spreads

Condor spreads are similar to butterfly spreads in many respects:

1. Both require (at least) four transactions — two option purchases, two option sales.
2. All of the transactions have the same time — all puts or all calls.
3. Both combine a bull spread and a bear spread.
4. The trader's intention is to profit if the stock price moves dramatically away from the current price.

The main difference between condor spreads and butterfly spreads involves the options' strike prices. In a butterfly spread, the bull spread and bear spread have a common central strike price. This is why the graph of a butterfly spread comes to a point at the stock's current price.

In contrast, the bull spread and bear spread that make up a condor spread don't have a common strike price. As a result, the risk graph of the condor spread is wider at the top, allowing the trader to make a profit if the stock price stays in this region. Figure 4.14 shows what the graph looks like.

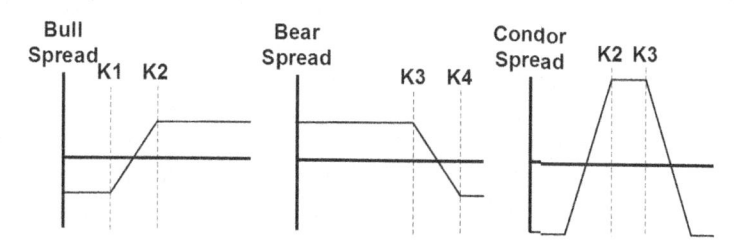

Figure 4.14 Risk Graph of a Condor Spread

In this example, the higher strike price of the bull spread is K2 and the lower strike price of the bear spread is K3. As a result of this combination, a trader makes profit if the stock price remains between K2 and K3.

At least one option in a condor spread must be purchased in the money, and this makes condor spreads expensive. To reduce the cost, many traders prefer *iron condors*. The transactions in an iron condor aren't all the same type—one buy/call pair involves calls and one buy/call pair involves puts.

The risk graph of an iron condor is essentially similar to that displayed in Figure 4.14. The advantage of iron condors is that the ITM option purchase is replaced with an OTM option purchase.

4.4.4 Box Spreads

Box spreads are unique among the strategies discussed in this chapter because the trader makes no assumptions about the price of the underlying security. Instead, the trader's goal is to take advantage of inexpensive options to receive a small but (theoretically) riskless profit.

Like the butterfly and condor spreads, a box spread combines two vertical spreads. To be precise, a box spread is made up of a bull call spread with a bear put spread whose strike prices are chosen to ensure constant, positive profit for all values of the underlying stock. Figure 4.15 shows what this looks like.

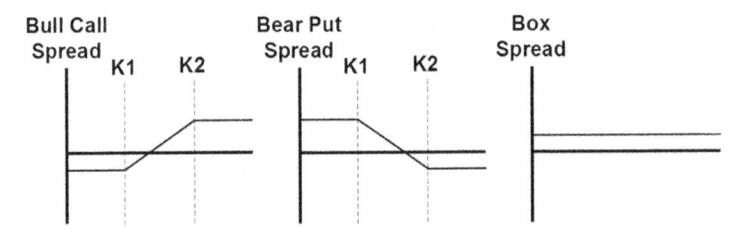

Figure 4.15 Risk Graph of a Box Spread

It may seem odd that this combination of a bull spread and bear spread can produce a constant graph instead of the graph of a butterfly or condor. But keep in mind that both spreads have identical strike prices. This is illustrated in the figure, which depicts the bull spread and the bear spread as having strike prices K1 and K2.

In a box spread, the two options purchases are in the money (high premium) and the two sales are out of the money (low premium). Therefore, a box spread trader needs to choose the options carefully to ensure that the profit exceeds the net premium.

The cost of commissions and premium make it difficult for traders to make reliable profit from box spreads. For this reason, these spreads are frequently employed by market makers, who have less fees to contend with.

4.4.5 Ratio Spreads

A ratio spread is similar to a vertical spread in that it combines buying and selling options with the same expiration date for the same underlying security. The difference is that the trader buys a different number of options than he or she sells. Ratio spreads are commonly identified by $x:y$, where x is the number of options sold for every y options bought. All of the options have the same type (calls or puts).

In general, the options purchased are in the money and the options sold are out of the money. Therefore, the ratio spread is a form of debit spread, which uses option sales to reduce the premium of an option purchase.

Figure 4.16 gives an idea of how this kind of ratio spread works. The leftmost graph illustrates a bull call spread, which involves selling a call to reduce the premium associated with buying a call. The middle graph illustrates selling a second call at the same premium and strike price as in the bull call spread. The rightmost graph illustrates the risk associated with this 2:1 ratio spread.

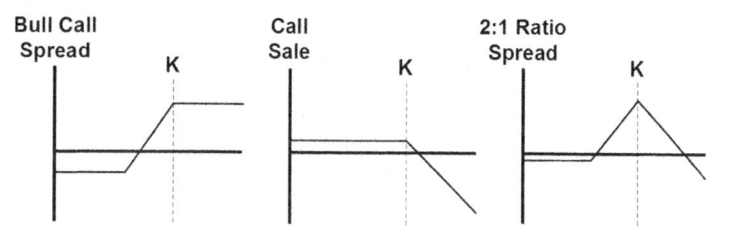

Figure 4.16 Risk Graph of a 2:1 Ratio Spread

The premium received from the second sale brings the net premium to nearly zero. However, the second sale exposes the trader to significant loss if the stock price rises higher than the common strike price (denoted K in the figure). For this reason, the ratios in ratio spreads rarely exceed 2:1.

4.5 Building Strategies in TWS

Chapter 3 explained how to submit TWS orders for individual options, but if you'd like to submit orders involving combinations, you'll find it easier to use the Strategy Builder. To access this in TWS, you need to follow four steps:

1. Make sure the underlying security is displayed in the **Order Entry** box.
2. Click the **New Window** button in the upper left of TWS.
3. Select the **Advanced Option Tools** submenu.
4. In the submenu, select the **Strategy Builder** option

The Strategy Builder dialog has two parts. The upper part presents the option chain discussed in Chapter 3. The lower part makes it possible to build a strategy from option trades. Figure 4.17 shows what the dialog looks like.

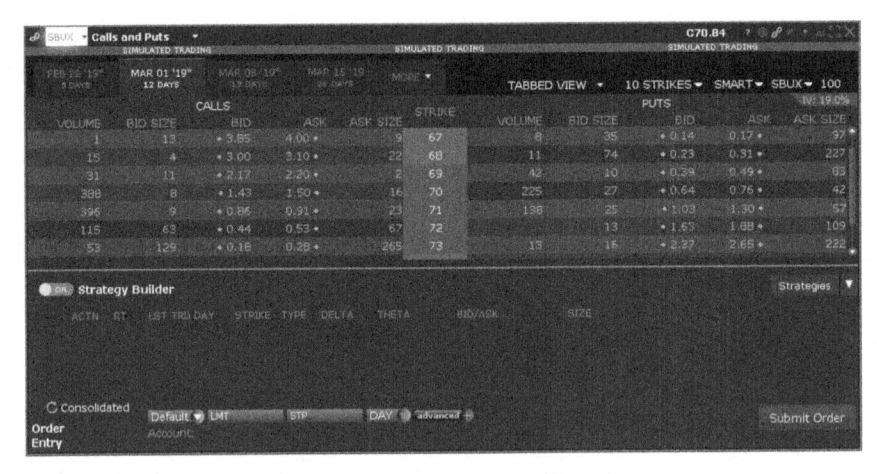

Figure 4.17 The Strategy Builder

There are two main ways to build strategies from options trades, or *legs*. The first method is to manually add legs by clicking the bid or ask price of each option you're interested in. As you select options, they'll appear in a list toward the bottom of the window.

The second method involves using the **Strategies** drop-down menu to the right of the dialog. This provides a list of strategies, such as vertical spreads, butterfly spreads, straddles, and strangles. When you choose a strategy, the dialog will ask you to select a leg. When you select a leg, the dialog will automatically add that leg and all other legs required to implement the strategy.

An example will clarify how this works. Suppose you want to create a strangle, which involves buying an out-of-the-money put and call. If you select Strangle in the Strategies drop-down and click on an OTM call, the builder will automatically add the corresponding OTM put to the list of legs that make up the strategy.

As you add legs to a strategy, the dialog will draw a diagram that displays the strategy's risk graph. For more information, you can click the **PROFILE** button. This plots a much more detailed risk graph, and it also displays helpful statistics such as the maximum return, maximum loss, and the probability of profit.

After you've created a strategy, you can add it to the watchlist by clicking the **Add to Watchlists** button. If you're ready to place the order, you can use the Order Entry buttons on the bottom of the dialog. This allows you to set the order's type, such as market or limit, and the time in force, such as day or good-till-canceled. Then you can submit the order by pressing the **Submit Order** button in the lower right.

4.6 Summary

This chapter builds on Chapter 3 by showing how option trades can be combined into strategies. Most of the chapter has been concerned with vertical spreads, which combine a purchase and sale of options with different strike prices but similar expirations. A credit spread is a vertical spread that reduces a seller's risk in return for a lower premium. A debit spread reduces the premium a buyer pays in return for a lower potential profit.

Vertical spreads are bullish or bearish, but delta-neutral strategies can make a profit if the asset's price moves in either direction. To set up a straddle, an investor needs to buy a call and put with the same strike price. The trader makes a profit if the asset's price moves away from the strike price in either direction. Strangles are less expensive than straddles, but require a more significant price move to make a profit.

The last part of this chapter explains how to set legs of a strategy in Trader Workstation. The Strategy Builder provides a graphical means of constructing a spread and submitting the order. In Chapter 12, I'll explain how to set up similar trades programmatically.

Before I end this chapter, I'd like to extend a word of warning. The Series 3 examination always asks whether spreads are inherently less risky than individual option trades. The answer is always *no*. Both legs can move against the trader, leading to a greater loss than if the trader had chosen a single direction. Keep this in mind when you read an investment guru's assurances to the contrary.

Chapter 5

Trading Futures Contracts

From what I've seen, most investors are familiar with stocks, bonds, and options, but have very little experience with the exotic world of futures contracts. This is a shame, because futures trading provides low margins, expanded trading hours, and the opportunity to make a great deal of money in a short time. Unfortunately, there are many new concepts and rules to be aware of, and it's easy to lose your shirt if you don't know what you're doing.

A futures contract is an obligation to trade an underlying asset on a future date called the settlement date. The contract's buyer is obligated to buy an asset on the settlement date and the seller is obligated to sell an asset on the settlement date.

Futures contracts are commonly categorized according to the nature of the underlying asset, which includes commodities and financial instruments. Futures contracts can also be divided into two groups depending on the nature of the obligation on the settlement date: some types of contracts require physical delivery and others require cash settlement.

For example, futures contracts based on soybeans require physical delivery. If a trader buys and holds a soybeans futures contract, he or she is obligated to buy 5,000 bushels of soybeans when the contract expires. If a trader sells a soybeans contract, he or she is obligated to sell 5,000 bushels of soybeans when the contract expires.

In contrast, cotton contracts are cash-settled. If a buyer buys a cotton futures contract and holds it until the settlement date, he or she is obligated to pay the difference between the current price of cotton (the spot price) and the price of the futures contract if the difference is positive. But if the spot price exceeds the futures price at expiration, the seller pays the difference.

In practice, the vast majority of futures traders don't deal with the underlying assets, and offset their positions before settlement. This chapter provides an overview of futures contracts and then explains how to create and submit orders in Trader Workstation.

5.1 Overview of Futures Contracts

A futures contract is an obligation to buy/sell an asset at a given time. At first glance, this may seem similar to an option, which gives the *right* to buy/sell an asset before a given time. But futures trading and options trading are as different as night and day.

Therefore, before I explain how to buy and sell futures with TWS, I'd like to explain what futures contracts are. I'll start by comparing them to options, and then I'll discuss some of the qualities that make futures trading unique.

5.1.1 Comparing Futures Contracts and Options

Futures contracts and options are both derivatives, which means their value depends on the value of an underlying asset. But there are several differences between the two:

1. An option gives the owner the *right* to buy/sell an asset by an expiration date. A futures contract *obligates* the owner to buy/sell an asset at an expiration date (unless the contract is sold to another party).
2. Futures contracts can be based on many different types of assets than options. These include soft commodities (grain, sugar, pork), hard commodities (gold, oil, ethanol), and financial instruments.
3. An option buyer pays a premium in addition to the broker's commission. A futures contract has no premium—buyers and sellers only pay the commission.
4. For stocks, traders have to apply for margin and common margin rates approach 40–50%. When trading futures, traders don't need to apply for margin and margin rates typically range from 10–20%.
5. If the daily price of a futures contract rises or falls by more than the daily trading limit, the exchange will prevent the price from rising or falling further.
6. Option premiums and strike prices are given in terms of currency. Prices of futures contracts are given in terms of points, which have to be converted into currency.

To clarify these differences, the following discussion presents the assets underlying futures contracts, daily trading limits, and margin requirements.

5.1.2 Assets Underlying Futures Contracts

The first futures contracts sold in America involved grain. Farmers needed to sell their grain without having to store and carry it, and futures contracts enabled farmers to create contracts for future delivery.

Today, futures contracts are available for a vast range of assets. At a high level, these assets can be divided into two categories—commodities and financial instruments.

Commodities are raw, physical goods that benefit society. These can be divided into soft commodities, which can be grown at a farm, and hard commodities, which need to be mined or extracted. Soft commodities include sugar, corn, wheat, and pork. Hard commodities include gold, oil, copper, and natural gas.

The second type of futures contracts are based on financial instruments. Currency futures are common, as are futures based on stocks in an index, such as the S&P 500. Interest rate futures are based on assets that bear interest, and popular futures are based on U.S. Treasury bonds and Eurodollars.

One confusing aspect of futures trading is knowing what quantity of an asset is controlled by a contract. This quantity changes from asset to asset, as does the minimum change in a contract's price. To clarify this, Table 5.1 lists eleven different assets and their contract codes. The fourth column identifies the minimum change in the price and the last column identifies the exchange.

Table 5.1

Assets Underlying Futures Contracts (All Figures in USD)

Asset	Code	Point Value	Min. Change	Exchange
Eurodollar	GE	2,500	12.50/6.25	CME
10-Year T-note	TY	1,000	15.625	CBOT
S&P 500 E-Mini	ES	50	2.50	CME
Japanese yen	JY	125,000	6.50	CME
Light crude oil	CL	1,000	10.00	NYMEX
Gold	GC	100	10.00	NYMEX
Natural Gas	NG	10,000	10.00	NYMEX
Wheat	W	50	12.50	CBOT
Soybeans	S	50	12.50	CBOT
Lumber	LB	110	11.00	CME
Coffee	KC	375	18.25	ICE

The first entry in the table, the Eurodollar, is the most popular asset for futures contracts. According to the Chicago Mercantile Exchange (CME), the average daily volume (ADV) for Eurodollars in the third quarter of 2018 was 2,185,519 contracts. A Eurodollar contract controls a million-dollar deposit in a foreign bank, where interest may be higher and restrictions may be lessened.

Another popular contract is the S&P 500 E-Mini, which represents 50 USD invested in each corporation in the S&P 500 Index. The term "Mini" indicates that this is a reduced version of another contract. In this case, the S&P 500 E-Mini is 1/5 of an S&P 500 contract, which controls 250 USD invested in each S&P 500 company.

The third column of the table is important to understand. Prices of futures contracts are given in *points*, not currency. The value of a point changes from contract to contract, and vary widely (50 USD for wheat contracts, 125,000 USD for Japanese yen contracts). As an example, if you buy a soybeans contract and the price rises ten points, you've made 500 USD because each point has a value of 50.

The fourth column identifies the minimum change in the contract's price, also known as the minimum tick or *mintick*. For example, the smallest change for wheat contracts is 12.50 USD. If the price of wheat rises 0.02, the price of each wheat contract rises by 25.

5.1.3 Expiration

Futures contracts expire just as options do. The expiration date depends on the asset and the exchange, but every futures contract has a known expiration month. Many contracts traded in the U.S. expire quarterly, and have expiration months of March, June, September or December. Outside the U.S., futures contracts generally don't expire quarterly.

When identifying a contract's expiration month, traders need to use a special letter designation. Table 5.2 presents the designations for the different months. These codes become important when you need to identify which futures contract you're interested in.

Table 5.2
Codes for Expiration Months

Month	Code	Month	Code
January	F	July	N
February	G	August	Q
March	H	September	U
April	J	October	V
May	K	November	X
June	M	December	Z

If a contract expires in a succession of months, the month that is nearest is called the front month or the spot month. Contracts in the front month attract the most investor interest and have the highest volumes.

Interactive Brokers makes it possible to buy or sell futures contracts that *don't* expire in a particular month. These are called *continuous futures contracts*. A continuous contract is a combination of monthly and quarterly contracts, and if one contract in the combination expires, IB will add the new lead month contract and remove the old one.

After purchasing a non-continuous futures contract, a trader can take one of three actions:

- **offset** — exit the position by buying or selling
- **rollover** — roll the contract to a future expiration date
- **allow expiration** — take no action before expiration

If a trader allows a futures contract to expire, one of two results will (theoretically) occur. For contracts like the E-Mini S&P 500, the result is *cash settlement*, in which the contract holder pays or receives the difference between the purchase price and the final settlement. For many contracts based on currency and grains, the result is *physical delivery*, in which the contract owner receives the asset on which the contract is based.

IB permits physical delivery of currency, but for other assets, "IB does not have the facilities necessary to accommodate physical delivery." To prevent delivery, IB may liquidate the contract. Therefore, traders should offset their position or roll over the contract before the close-out deadline. This deadline depends on the contract's asset, and you'll find the full list of IB's deadlines at https://ibkr.info/node/992.

Offsetting a futures contract simply involves executing the purchase or sale needed to close the contract. To roll over a contract in TWS, traders need to create a suitable futures spread. I'll discuss futures spreads later in the chapter.

5.1.4 Margin Requirements

As mentioned earlier, the prices of futures contracts are given in *points*, not in currency. This means that the assets underlying futures contracts are usually very expensive. For example, if you buy a Eurodollar contract priced at 98 points, the real price in USD is 98 times 2,500 = 245,000 USD.

Most investors don't have enough funds to trade these kinds of contracts. Thankfully, traders can take advantage of margin, which makes it possible to place an order for an expensive contract while only having a fraction of the full price available for trading in the account.

Margin for futures contracts works differently than margin for stocks. When a trader buys stocks on margin, the paid margin serves as a down payment. In contrast, futures traders don't pay margin. That is, the margin stays in the trader's account and serves as an assurance that the trader will be able to cover the position if the trade goes badly.

Chapter 2 introduced the topic of margin and described the laws that regulate margin requirements for stocks. Those requirements don't apply to futures contracts, but IB defines its own set of margin requirements:

- **intraday initial margin** — required equity when the trade takes place
- **intraday maintenance margin** — required equity during regular trading hours
- **overnight initial margin** — required equity at the close of the trading day
- **overnight maintenance margin** — required equity outside regular trading hours

An example will help make this clear. Suppose a trader submits an order to buy a platinum contract. If the initial margin is 4,000 USD, the trader must have at least 4,000 USD of equity in his/her account when the order is submitted. If the maintenance margin is 2,500 USD, the trader must make sure the account's equity never falls below 2,500.

If account equity falls below the maintenance margin limit, IB will send the trader a notice called a margin call. At this point, the trader must deposit enough funds into the account to reach the *initial margin limit*, not the maintenance margin limit.

If the contract's price moves unfavorably, the amount of equity in the trader's account will fall, but the debt doesn't change. If the contract's price moves unfavorably enough that the trader's account equity falls below the maintenance margin limit, the trader will have to deposit enough funds to raise the equity above the initial margin limit.

5.1.5 Trading and Position Limits

To reduce volatility, exchanges set daily trading limits for futures contracts. These limits identify how far a contract's price can change during a day. For example, the price of a gold contract can't rise more than 75 USD per ounce above the preceding day's price or fall more than 75 USD per ounce below the preceding day's price.

A contract is said to be *limit up* if the upper limit is reached and *limit down* if the lower limit is reached. If a contract's price reaches either extreme, it's likely that the next day's price will change dramatically. Because of the heightened risk, exchanges may increase margin requirements.

In addition to trading limits, exchanges set position limits that limit the number of positions that a trader can take. This prevents any individual from manipulating a market with a low volume of trades.

5.2 Ordering Futures Contracts in TWS

The process of ordering a futures contract is essentially similar to that of ordering stocks and bonds. To add a futures contract to the watchlist, there are three main steps:

1. In the TWS watchlist, click in an empty box and enter the code for the underlying asset. Table 5.1 lists eleven of these codes, such as GE for Globex Eurodollar and GC for gold.
2. A box lists the financial instruments associated with the ticker symbol. Find the instrument corresponding to the futures asset and click the **Futures** link.
3. In the next box, choose the contract's expiration. You can choose the contract's expiration month or the continuous contract.

Figure 5.1 displays the box containing available expirations for gold futures contracts sold through NYMEX. The first three options identify contracts expiring in February, March, and April. The fourth option identifies the continuous futures contract, whose name is followed by the infinity symbol.

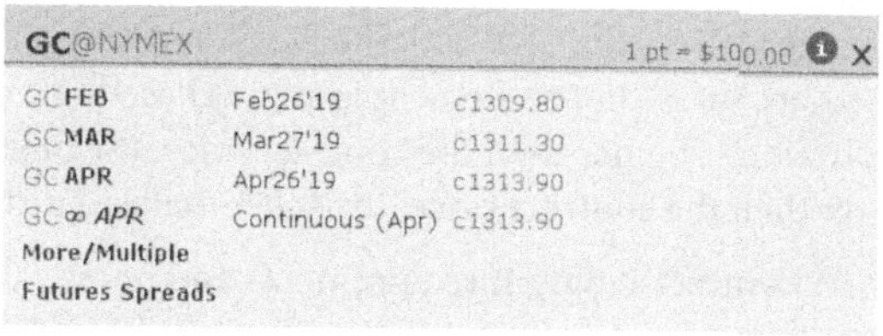

Figure 5.1 Selecting a Contract Expiration

This dialog also has an entry named **More/Multiple**. This lists a wide range of contracts for the asset, and you can select multiple contracts by pressing Shift and clicking on different contracts.

If you'd like to avoid these selection boxes, you can identify the futures contract by providing an identifier that combines the asset code, expiration month code, and the last digit of the year. For example, if you want to identify the Eurodollar contract that expires in April 2019, you'd enter GEJ9. GE specifies the Eurodollar futures contract, J specifies April, and 9 specifies the year 2019.

After you've selected a futures contract, you can view the margin requirements by right-clicking on the watchlist entry, expanding the context menu, and selecting **Financial Instrument Info > Details**. This opens a web page that provides a great deal of information, including the requirements for the intraday initial margin, intraday maintenance margin, overnight initial margin, and overnight maintenance margin.

When you add a futures contract to the watchlist, TWS updates the **Order Entry** box. At this point, you can order the futures contract as though it involved a stock or bond. Click **BUY** or **SELL**, set the order type and the time in force, and then click **SUBMIT**.

5.3 Index and Security Futures

Two popular types of futures contracts are based on stock indexes and individual securities. Many investors use these contracts to hedge against price risk. For example, if a corporate shareholder is concerned about falling share prices but doesn't want to lose voting rights, he or she can limit the potential risk by selling futures contracts. If a mutual fund manager is going to buy securities in the future and is concerned about rising prices, he or she can reduce price risk by buying futures contracts.

5.3.1 Stock Index Futures

Traders can buy futures contracts based on several indexes like the Dow Jones Industrial Average (DJIA), the S&P 500, the NASDAQ 100, and the Russell 2000. The underlying assets are stocks but settlement is always based on cash. Therefore, if the index price at expiration is higher than the contract price, the buyer makes a profit. If the index price is lower than the contract price, the seller makes a profit.

A contract's margin requirements and point value depend on the exchange and the type of contract. On the CME, the E-mini S&P 500 has a maintenance margin of 3,758.10 USD and a point value of 50 per contract. On the CBOT, the Dow Futures E-mini has a maintenance margin of 2,750 USD and a point value of 5.

5.3.2 Single-Stock Futures

In addition to index futures, traders can buy or sell futures contracts based on individual stocks. These are called single-stock futures (SSFs), and they behave very differently from other futures contracts. Here are five notable differences:

- Most SSFs are based on round lots (sets of 100 shares), though some are based on 1,000 shares.
- SSFs require physical delivery. That is, the seller is obligated to sell the stocks at the contract price and the buyer is obligated to buy them.
- The nature of the contract changes due to corporate actions, such as stock splits, reverse splits, mergers, spin-offs, and stock dividends.

- The only exchange that offers SSFs is OneChicago, which is partially owned by Interactive Brokers.
- SSFs are considered security futures, which means they're regulated by both the CFTC and the SEC.

This last point is important to understand. Because SSFs are regulated by the SEC, margin requirements are more standard. At minimum, the margin requirement is 20% of the underlying value of the contract. IB's margin requirement is likely to be larger.

There's one last point to know about single-stock futures. If a trader has a long or short position in a stock, IB makes it possible to replace this position with an equivalent SSF. This replacement is called an *exchange for physical*, or EFP. Traders can accomplish this by creating and submitting a suitable futures spread. I'll explain this in the next section.

5.4 Futures Spreads

Chapter 3 introduced the topic of options and Chapter 4 presented a number of strategies that combine options trades. The preceding discussion focused on stock options, but IB also supports options and strategies based on futures. You can execute straddles, strangles, and iron condors based on soybeans just as easily as you can execute strategies based on Tesla stock.

As discussed in Chapter 4, an options spread involves buying two options of the same type with the same asset. A futures spread is similar, but involves buying two futures contracts with the same asset. These spreads become important in two instances:

1. Rolling over a futures position requires a horizontal (calendar) spread.
2. The process of converting a stock position into an SSF (exchange for physical, or EFP) requires a spread.

This discussion explains how to roll over positions using calendar spreads and how to create EFP orders.

5.4.1 Creating Futures Spreads in TWS

When you enter a symbol of a futures contract, TWS provides an option for creating a futures spread (if you expand the selection box). Figure 5.2 shows what this looks like.

Chapter 5 Trading Futures Contracts

Figure 5.2 Selecting the Futures Spread Entry

If you select **Combinations > Futures Spreads**, TWS will open a dialog that allows you to configure a calendar spread. Figure 5.3 shows what this looks like.

In the upper left, the text boxes identify the underlying asset (GE for Eurodollar) and the strategy. The default strategy is always **Calendar Spread** and the only alternative is the **Reverse Calendar Spread**.

The boxes on the left allow you to select expiration dates of the futures contracts that make up the spread. The front month is the expiration month of the nearer contract and the back month is the expiration month of the further contract.

When you select a front month and back month, TWS will configure a spread that sells a contract in the front month and purchases a contract in the back month. This is the most common type of spread needed for rollovers, which usually involve selling long positions in the front month. If you're rolling over a short position in the front month, you'll need to sell the spread order instead of buying it.

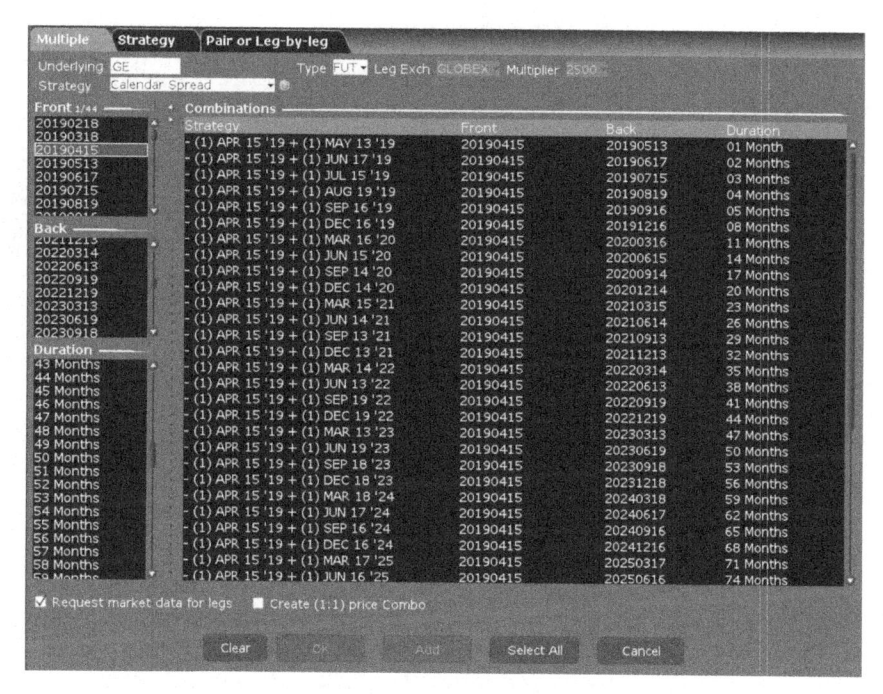

Figure 5.3 Configuring a Futures Spread

After you've configured the futures spread, click the **OK** button at the bottom. This tells TWS to add the futures spread to the watchlist. When this is available, you can access the spread in the **Order Entry** box and submit an order.

5.4.2 Creating EFP Orders in TWS

Creating an exchange-for-physical (EFP) order is similar to creating a calendar spread, but instead of clicking on a futures contract, you need to click on a new stock contract. Expand the list of financial instruments and select the Combinations submenu. This lists a number of combinations involving the stock, including **EFP (SMART)** and **EFP (Directed)**.

Clicking either EFP link opens a dialog that allows you to configure the exchange for physical contract. Figure 5.4 shows what this looks like for exchanging shares in Starbucks (SBUX) for single stock futures (SSFs).

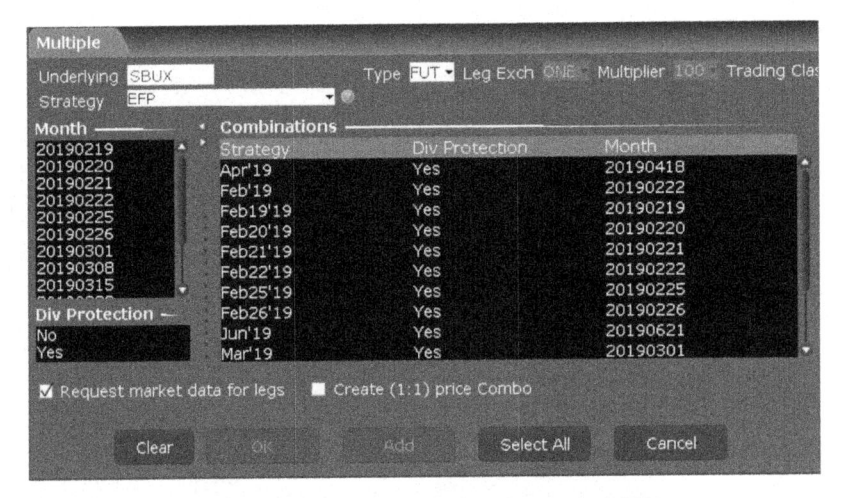

Figure 5.4 Configuring an Exchange for Physical (EFP)

To the left, the dialog allows you to choose the expiration month of the SSF contract. You can also set **Div Protection** to **No** or **Yes**. If you set this to **Yes**, TWS will take advantage of dividend protection if it's available. This treats ordinary dividends as corporate events, and adjusts the previous day's price by the dividend amount on the morning of the expiration date.

After you've configured the EFP contract, press the **OK** button at the bottom of the dialog. This adds an entry to the watchlist that identifies the configured EFP contract. When you select this, the contract will appear in the **Order Entry** box and you can submit the order using the normal process.

5.5 Summary

This chapter has explored the fascinating world of futures trading, which allows traders to trade derivatives based on soft commodities, hard commodities, and financial instruments. When trading futures, it's important to remember that the underlying assets are generally very expensive. For most, the low margin requirement isn't just a luxury but a necessity.

When buying and selling futures, traders need to be very conscious of IB's margin requirements. The initial margin requirement identifies how much equity must be in the account when the order is submitted. The maintenance margin requirement identifies how much equity must remain in the account while the order is active.

Single-stock futures (SSFs) have a number of characteristics that make them unique, such as the requirement of physical delivery at settlement and a minimum margin requirement of 20%. In addition, IB makes it possible to convert a long/short stock position into an equivalent SSF position using exchange-for-physical (EFP) conversion.

With Trader Workstation, it's just as easy to trade futures contracts as it is to trade stocks. TWS also provides special capabilities for creating futures spreads. These become useful if you want to roll over a futures position or convert a stock position into an SSF position.

Chapter 6

Fundamental Classes of the TWS API

Now that you understand how to use TWS, it's time to start writing applications that interact with TWS through the TWS API. In essence, the classes and functions in the TWS API are focused on one goal: asking IB's servers to provide information (such as stock prices) or to perform an action (such as executing an order).

With this in mind, the general operation of a TWS API application can be split into five steps:

1. Establish a connection to IB's servers.
2. Request information from IB's servers or the execution of an action.
3. If a response is provided, receive and process the response.
4. Repeat Steps 2 and 3 until all desired information has been received and all operations have been executed.
5. Terminate the connection.

To implement this in code, you need to be familiar with two fundamental classes: `EClient` and `EWrapper`. An `EClient` manages communication with IB's servers and sends requests for information or actions to be taken. An `EWrapper` contains the functions that are invoked when a response from IB's servers has been received. Once you understand how these classes work together, you'll find the TWS API easy to work with.

This chapter introduces the central classes of the TWS API and then presents a simple application that asks IB's servers for the time. But before we delve into the classes and functions, I'd like to provide a more in-depth discussion of how TWS API applications work.

6.1 Overview of TWS API Applications

Chapter 2 introduced two important applications provided by Interactive Brokers: Trader Workstation (TWS) and the IB Gateway. When you execute code based on the TWS API, your code must be able to access one of these two applications. These applications receive messages from your code and send them to IB's servers.

From what I've seen, most developers prefer to use TWS instead of the IB Gateway. In the interest of brevity, the rest of this book refers to Trader Workstation/IB Gateway as simply *TWS*. With this in mind, the communication process consists of three steps:

1. Connect to TWS by creating a socket
2. Send messages (requests) to TWS through the socket
3. Receive messages (responses) from TWS through the socket

The first step isn't difficult to code, but before you write an application that interacts with TWS, you should have a basic understanding of sockets. This section presents a quick overview of sockets and then introduces the Secure Sockets Layer (SSL).

6.1.1 Sockets

Socket communication is like telephone communication, but it relies on Internet Protocol (IP) addresses and port numbers instead of telephone numbers. When an application sends a socket-based request to a specific IP address and port number, the receiving application can reply with a response.

The most popular usage of sockets is the HyperText Transfer Protocol, or HTTP. When you enter a URL in a browser and press Enter, the browser sends an HTTP request to the IP address corresponding to the URL. Different protocols have different port numbers, and in the case of HTTP, the port number of the request is 80.

When an application at the given IP address receives a message on Port 80, it examines the HTTP request and responds with an HTTP response. This response tells the browser how to display the web page corresponding to the URL.

Communicating with TWS follows a similar process. If an application sends a message to the IP address of a system running TWS and sets the port number to 7497 (4002 for the IB Gateway), TWS will receive the message, authenticate the source, and send an appropriate response.

To be specific, TWS will send a message to one of IB's servers. Figure 6.1 illustrates the process that trading applications use to communicate.

Figure 6.1 Executing Orders Programmatically

Each arrow in the figure identifies a step in the socket communication process:

1. The application (client) sends a message to the IP address of a system running TWS. The message's port number is 7497.
2. TWS receives the message, authenticates it, and sends another message to the Interactive Brokers (IB) server.
3. The IB server receives the message, processes it, and sends a response to TWS.
4. TWS forwards the message to the client.

As developers, we're only concerned with Steps 1 and 4. That is, our goal is to write code that sends requests to TWS and receives responses. This chapter presents the basic classes and functions that make this possible.

In many cases, the client application and TWS run on the same system. In this case, the IP address is simply 127.0.0.1. If TWS is running on a remote system, you must know the system's address before you can send messages.

6.1.2 Secure Sockets Layer (SSL)

Basic sockets execute quickly, but they're not secure. This means an eavesdropping application can read the socket's messages as they're sent and received.

The Secure Sockets Layer (SSL) makes it possible to secure socket communication to prevent eavesdropping. This involves cryptographic encryption and handshaking protocols that authenticate the sender. Many online sources describe SSL in detail.

SSL protection adds delay to the communication, and many traders may find this unacceptable. Further, if you're running your application on the same computer as TWS, you may find SSL unnecessary. This chapter explains how to set up communication using basic sockets and SSL-protected sockets, but I'm not going to recommend one over the other.

6.1.3 Threads and Messages

At this point, you should know that applications communicate with IB using sockets. An application writes data to the socket and reads data from the socket. Packages of received data are called *messages*, and applications store messages in first-in, first-out data structures called *message queues*.

Applications can't control when new data will be available, so they create a separate execution thread to read from the socket and write to the message queue. For this reason, most applications perform their processing in two threads:

- **client thread** — send data to the socket, read messages from the queue
- **reader thread** — read data from the socket, write messages to the queue

In many applications, these threads work together in a four-step process:

1. The application starts the client thread, which sends requests to TWS.
2. The client thread goes to sleep while TWS transfers data to its socket.
3. While the client thread sleeps, the reader thread reads data from the socket and writes a message to the message queue.
4. As messages enter the queue, a decoder processes each of them and invokes the corresponding callback function of the client's wrapper.

It's not important to know how applications work at a low level, and you'll probably never write code that interacts directly with the reader thread, message queue, or decoder. But as you develop applications, you'll find it helpful to understand how a client's requests result in wrapper functions being invoked.

6.1.4 Basic Classes of the TWS API

Whether you program in Python or C++, the fundamental classes to know are `EClient` and `EWrapper`. The primary class of your application will be a subclass of `EClient`, which manages the overall operation of the application. I'll refer to it as the *client class*.

Every client class has a handful of member variables, and one of them is an instance of the `EWrapper` class. This contains the callback functions that are invoked in response to messages in the message queue. I'll refer to this instance as the *wrapper*. Most of your development time will be spent writing code for the client class and its wrapper.

As I'll explain shortly, `EClient` provides a wide range of functions that send requests to TWS, and most have names like `reqXYZ(...)`. For example, `reqCurrentTime` requests the time and `reqContractDetails` requests details about a contract.

After TWS sends a response, the decoder translates the message and invokes the appropriate `EWrapper` callback function. The name of this function is usually similar to the client's function. For example, the `currentTime` callback provides the application with IB's response to the `reqCurrentTime` function. Similarly, the `contractDetails` callback provides the application with IB's response to `reqContractDetails`.

6.2 Fundamental Classes in Python

If you open the TWS API directory, you'll find a folder named source that contains a subfolder named pythonClient. This has two subdirectories: ibapi and tests. The ibapi folder is very important because it contains the source files for the Python API. Therefore, when you run an application, you'll need to set the `sys.path` or `PYTHONPATH` variable to the location of ibapi.

If you've configured your path correctly, you'll be able to import classes using statements like the following:

```
from ibapi.client import EClient
from ibapi.wrapper import EWrapper
```

These `import` statements provide access to the two most important classes in IB's Python API: `EClient` (ibapi/client.py) and `EWrapper` (ibapi/wrapper.py). This section discusses both and shows how they can be used.

6.2.1 The EClient Class

The client.py module is the largest module in the IB API, and it's no surprise. This contains the code of the `EClient` class, whose functions manage the socket connection to TWS and send requests over the socket.

The `EClient` constructor accepts one argument—an `EWrapper` that provides the application's callback functions. I'll discuss the `EWrapper` class in the next section.

It will take the next four chapters to present the majority of the `EClient` functions. For now, I just want to provide a small sample of the different functions you can call. Table 6.1 lists the signatures of five representative functions of the `EClient` class.

Table 6.1
Representative Functions of the EClient Class

Function	Description
`connect(host, port, clientId)`	Attempts to connect to TWS
`disconnect()`	Sever the connection to TWS
`run()`	Read a message from the queue
`placeOrder(orderId, contract, order)`	Places an order through the IB server
`reqCurrentTime()`	Requests current time

The first function, `connect`, establishes the connection to TWS. It accepts three parameters: a string identifying the IP address of the system running TWS, a port number, and a number that identifies which client is connecting. TWS supports up to 32 simultaneous client connections.

If your application is running on the same system as TWS, you can set the IP address to 127.0.0.1, also known as localhost. The following code creates an `EClientSocket` and calls `connect` to create a socket to TWS running on localhost.

```
client = EClient(wrapper)
client.connect("127.0.0.1", 7497, 0)
```

In addition to connecting to the socket, the connect function creates a `Decoder` and an `EReader`. `EReader` is a subclass of `Thread`, and when the client creates an `EReader` instance, it launches the reader thread. As discussed earlier, this waits for data on the socket and writes it to the client's message queue when available. The `EReader` repeats this operation so long as the client is connected.

After establishing the connection, an application can send messages to TWS by calling functions like `placeOrder`, which I'll discuss in Chapter 7. Then the application can check to see if a response is in the queue by calling the client's `run` function. If the queue isn't empty, `run` will read every message and pass it to the decoder.

The `run` function executes in a loop that repeats as long as the client is connected. For this reason, applications frequently execute the client's `run` function in a separate thread using code like the following:

```
thread = Thread(target=self.run)
thread.start()
```

If `run` passes a recognizable message to the decoder, the decoder will invoke a callback method of the client's `EWrapper` instance. I'll discuss the `EWrapper` class next.

6.2.2 The EWrapper Class

The wrapper.py module defines the `EWrapper` class, which contains over one hundred methods. But if you look through these methods, you'll see that most of them simply write a message to the log. To understand how these functions can be used, consider the following code, which prints the argument received by the `currentTime` method:

```
def currentTime(self, cur_time):
    t = datetime.fromtimestamp(cur_time)
    print('Current time: {}'.format(t))
```

This may not look exciting, but if the client calls `reqCurrentTime` and the response is stored in the message queue, the decoder will access the client's wrapper and call `currentTime`. These response methods of the `EWrapper` class are called *callbacks*, and I'll discuss them fully in this and later chapters.

As application developers, our job is to create a custom subclass of `EWrapper` and override the callbacks we're interested in. For example, if the client is going to request open orders by calling `reqOpenOrders`, the custom wrapper should provide code in the `openOrder` callback, which the decoder will call when it receives order data from an IB server.

It can be hard to distinguish `EWrapper` methods from other methods, so I find it helpful to precede callback methods with the `iswrapper` annotation. This is declared in utils.py, so an application can import the annotation with the following `import` statement:

```
from ibapi.utils import iswrapper
```

Different applications provide code for different callbacks, but every application should provide code for the `error` callback. When a TWS API error occurs, this callback provides the ID of the request that produced the error, the error code, and the error message. The following code shows how this can be used.

```
@iswrapper
def error(self, req_id, code, msg):
    print('Error {}: {}'.format(code, msg))
```

Communication errors crop up occasionally in TWS API applications. Therefore, it's important to handle errors in a way that doesn't disrupt your algorithm.

6.2.3 Simple Client Example (Python)

It's critical to understand the relationship between the client's request functions (such as `reqCurrentTime`) and the wrapper's callbacks (such as `currentTime`). To clarify how these functions work together, Listing 6.1 demonstrates how a client can connect to TWS and request the current time.

Listing 6.1: ch6/simple_client.py

```
class SimpleClient(EWrapper, EClient):
    ''' Serves as the client and the wrapper '''

    def __init__(self, addr, port, client_id):
        EWrapper.__init__(self)
        EClient.__init__(self, self)

        # Connect to TWS
        self.connect(addr, port, client_id)

        # Launch the client thread
        thread = Thread(target=self.run)
        thread.start()

    @iswrapper
    def currentTime(self, cur_time):
        t = datetime.fromtimestamp(cur_time)
        print('Current time: {}'.format(t))

    @iswrapper
    def error(self, req_id, code, msg):
        print('Error {}: {}'.format(code, msg))

def main():

    # Create the client and connect to TWS
    client = SimpleClient('127.0.0.1', 7497, 0)

    # Request the current time
    client.reqCurrentTime()

    # Sleep while the request is processed
    time.sleep(0.5)

    # Disconnect from TWS
    client.disconnect()
```

This code defines the `SimpleClient` class, which extends both `EClient` and `EWrapper`. The constructor calls the `EWrapper` and `EClient` constructors, and then connects to TWS. The `connect` method sets the IP address to `127.0.0.1`, which indicates that TWS is running on the same system as the application.

After connecting to TWS, the constructor launches a thread to execute the client's `run` method. This client thread reads data from the message queue and passes it to the decoder. This operation executes in a loop as long as the client is connected.

The `main` function creates a `SimpleClient` instance and calls its `reqCurrentTime` method. This accesses the connection socket and sends a request to TWS. In this case, the request asks for the current time.

TWS responds by sending data to the application's socket. Inside the reader thread, the `EReader` created by the client reads this data and stores it to the client's message queue. Inside the client thread, the `EClient` checks the message queue to see if it's empty. If it's not, the client will read the message and pass it to the client's decoder.

The decoder determines what kind of message was received and invokes the appropriate callback of the wrapper class. In this case, the appropriate callback is `currentTime`, so the decoder calls this method. The parameter, `cur_time`, identifies how many seconds have elapsed since Jan 1, 1970.

In this application, `SimpleClient` is its own `EWrapper` instance. As a result, the decoder calls `SimpleClient`'s `currentTime` method, which overrides the `currentTime` method in the `EWrapper` class. This method converts the time value into a date and time, and prints the result to the console.

I'll use this general structure for most of the Python examples in this book. That is, the application defines a class that inherits from `EWrapper` and `EClient`. The `main` function creates an instance of the class and calls its request methods.

6.3 Fundamental Classes in C++

On Windows systems, the top-level TWS API folder holds its C++ source files in the source/CppClient/client folder. On Mac OS/Linux systems, C++ source files are stored in the IBJts/source/cppclient/client folder.

As discussed in Chapter 1, the www.algo-book.com site provides two archives containing C++ code. The first contains code for Mac OS/Linux users, and is intended to be compiled with GNU tools like g++. The second contains code for Windows users and is intended to be compiled with Microsoft Visual Studio. In each case, the compiler relies on the `TWS_DIR` variable to locate the files in the TWS API folder.

6.3.1 The Client Classes

To code a C++ application that interacts with TWS, you need to create an instance of a subclass of `EClient`. The two subclasses are `ESocketClient` and `ESocketClientSSL`. Figure 6.2 illustrates the inheritance hierarchy.

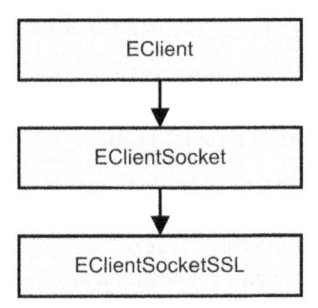

Figure 6.2 Inheritance Hierarchy of the Client Classes

These three classes provide hundreds of functions, and it will take several chapters to present the majority of them. This section provides a brief overview of the client classes, explaining what they accomplish and presenting their fundamental functions.

The EClient Class

The `EClient` class represents a general client application, regardless of how the client communicates with TWS. Some of its functions are pure virtual, which means you can't create an `EClient` instance directly.

For developers, the `EClient` class is important because it provides the functions that execute orders and request information. Table 6.2 lists seven representative functions of the `EClient` class.

Table 6.2
Representative Functions of the EClient Class

Function	Description

`placeOrder(OrderId id,`
`    const Contract& contract,`
`    const Order& order)`
	Places an order through the IB server

`cancelOrder(OrderId id)`	Cancels the given order
`reqOpenOrders()`	Requests data about open orders

`reqContractDetails(int reqId, const Contract& contract)`	Request details regarding a contract
`reqPositions()`	Request open positions
`serverVersion()`	Returns the version of the server
`TwsConnectionTime()`	Returns the time needed for communication

The first three functions are very important, and Chapter 7 discusses orders and contracts in detail. Similarly, Chapter 8 discusses the functions that request financial data from IB. Request functions start with the `req-` prefix, such as `reqOpenOrders`. At the end of this section, I'll present a simple application that demonstrates how `reqCurrentTime` can be used to request the current time.

All of the `EClient` functions return void except for the last two listed in the table. `serverVersion` returns an integer that identifies the version of the IB server and `TwsConnectionTime` returns a string that tells you how long it took the application to connect to TWS.

In addition to functions, the `EClient` class provides member variables that provide access to the client's state. Table 6.3 lists six of them and provides a description of each.

Table 6.3
Member Variables of the EClient Class (Abridged)

Name	Type	Description
`m_pEWrapper`	`EWrapper*`	Used to receive data back from TWS
`connState`	`ConnState`	Identifies the state of the client's connection
`m_connectOptions`	`std::string`	Settings used for the connection
`m_clientId`	`int`	Uniquely identifies the client
`m_host`	`std::string`	The host (IP address) of the communication target
`m_port`	`int`	The port number of the communication target

The first variable is particularly important. The `EWrapper*` enables the client to receive data from TWS. I'll discuss the `EWrapper` class later in this section.

`connState` identifies the current connection state, and can take one of four values:

- `CS_CONNECTING` — The client is in the process of connecting to TWS
- `CS_CONNECTED` — The client has connected to TWS
- `CS_DISCONNECTED` — The client has disconnected from TWS
- `CS_REDIRECT` — TWS redirected the client to another address

In addition to checking `connState`, you can determine if the client is connected by calling the `isConnected()` function. This returns a boolean that identifies if the client has connected to TWS.

The EClientSocket Class

The `EClientSocket` class represents a client that connects to TWS using sockets. Unlike the `EClient` class, `EClientSocket` doesn't have any pure virtual functions. This means you can create instances of an `EClientSocket` by calling its constructor:

```
EClientSocket(EWrapper *ptr, EReaderSignal *pSignal = 0)
```

The first argument points to the `EWrapper` that will be used to receive data back from TWS. The second argument defines low-level details of the client-TWS communication. I'll provide a proper introduction to the `EWrapper` and `EReaderSignal` classes shortly.

After you've created an `EClientSocket`, the next step is to connect to TWS. Table 6.4 lists the three functions that manage connections.

Table 6.4
EClientSocket Communication Functions

Name	Description
`eConnect(const char *host, int port, int clientId = 0, bool extraAuth = false)`	Creates socket connection
`eDisconnect(bool resetState = true)`	Closes the socket connection
`redirect(string host)`	Redirect connection to a different host

The most important function to know is `eConnect`, which establishes the connection to TWS. This accepts a string identifying the IP address and the port number. The third argument, `clientId`, identifies which client is connecting. TWS supports up to 32 simultaneous connections.

If the application is running on the same system as TWS, the socket's IP address can be set to `127.0.0.1`, also known as localhost. The following code creates an `EClientSocket` and calls `eConnect` to connect to TWS, which is running on the same system (localhost).

```
socket = new EClientSocket(&wrapper, &reader)
socket->eConnect("127.0.0.1", 7497, 0);
...
socket->eDisconnect();
```

`eConnect` returns void, but you can check the connection status by calling the `isConnected` function provided by `EClient`. You can terminate the connection by calling `eDisconnect`.

The EClientSocketSSL Class

Earlier in the chapter, I explained how the Secure Sockets Layer (SSL) makes it possible to cryptographically secure socket communication. If you'd like to use SSL in your application, you need to create an instance of `EClientSocketSSL` to serve as your client. From a coding perspective, this class is nearly identical to the `EClientSocket` class. The constructor is exactly similar:

```
EClientSocketSSL(EWrapper *ptr, EReaderSignal *pSignal = 0)
```

The `eConnect` and `eDisconnect` functions are also identical to that of the `ESocketClient`. Therefore, the following code creates an SSL-based socket to the TWS instance on the local system:

```
socket = new EClientSocketSSL(&wrapper, &reader)
socket->eConnect("127.0.0.1", 7497, 0);
...
socket->eDisconnect();
```

SSL-based sockets provide greater security than regular sockets, and this explains why HTTPS has supplanted HTTP as the fundamental protocol of the Internet. But this increased security comes with increased time delay, which means your orders may not be placed as quickly as you'd like.

6.3.2 The EWrapper Class (C++)

Of the fundamental classes in the C++ API, the `EWrapper` class is one of the most important and one of the most confusing. It's important because its functions make it possible for applications to receive data from TWS. It's confusing because the class definition barely contains any code:

104   Chapter 6 Fundamental Classes

```
class EWrapper
{
public:
   virtual ~EWrapper() {};

   #define EWRAPPER_VIRTUAL_IMPL = 0
   #include "EWrapper_prototypes.h"
};
```

The `EWrapper` class doesn't define any constructors, but it includes the content of the header file, EWrapper_prototypes.h. This contains nearly one hundred function prototypes, such as the following:

```
virtual void openOrder(OrderId orderId, const Contract&,
   const Order&, const OrderState&) EWRAPPER_VIRTUAL_IMPL;

virtual void contractDetails(int reqId,
   const ContractDetails& contractDetails) EWRAPPER_VIRTUAL_IMPL;
```

The prototypes in EWrapper_prototypes.h define the standard functions that TWS uses to pass data to an application. I'll refer to them as IB's *callback functions*, or just *callbacks*. When you create an `EClientSocket` with an `EWrapper` reference, you're identifying the functions that should be called in response to requests.

For example, suppose you place an order by calling a client's `placeOrder` function. After IB executes the order, TWS will call the `EWrapper`'s `orderStatus` callback.

Similarly, if you call the client's `reqHistoricalData` function, TWS will provide data by calling the `EWrapper`'s `historicalData` function. In general, for every req*XYZ* function of `EClient`, the corresponding callback in `EWrapper` is named *XYZ*.

Callback functions always return void and they're all virtual. As given in the example, each prototype is followed by EWRAPPER_VIRTUAL_IMPL, which is defined as =0. This means these functions are pure virtual and `EWrapper` is abstract. To create a subclass of `EWrapper`, you have to provide code for every callback function.

6.3.3 The EReader and EReaderSignal Classes (C++)

In the preceding discussion, I said that the `EClientSocket` sends requests to TWS and the `EWrapper` processes the response. Between these operations, an `EReader` handles read and write operations involving the message queue. An application can create an `EReader` instance through its constructor:

```
EReader(EClient Socket *client Socket, EReaderSignal *signal)
```

After creating the `EReader`, an application needs to call two of its functions: `start` and `processMsgs`. The first is responsible for reading data from the socket and storing messages into the message queue. The second reads messages from the message queue and invokes the appropriate functions of the `EWrapper`.

Reading Socket Data

Once the `EReader` instance is available, most applications immediately call its `start` function. `start` launches a thread that repeatedly checks the socket for data. If the reader finds data, it performs three important operations:

1. It creates an `EDecoder` and uses it to parse the data.
2. It creates an `EMessage` from the parsed data and pushes it onto the message queue.
3. It accesses the `EReaderSignal` and calls its `issueSignal` function.

As a result of the first step, the `EDecoder` receives the socket data and checks to see whether the data corresponds to a TWS message. If so, the reader creates an `EMessage` from the data and pushes the message onto the message queue. The message queue is declared in EReader.h with the following code:

```
std::deque<std::shared_ptr<EMessage>> m_msgQueue;
```

In the third step, the `EReader` calls the `issueSignal` function of the `EReaderSignal` that was passed as the second argument in the `EReader` constructor. This function frees access to the message queue, thereby allowing the application to read messages.

Reading from the Message Queue

Before an application can read from the message queue, it needs to wait until the queue is available. This is accomplished by calling the `waitForSignal` function of the `ReaderSignal` passed to the `EReader`.

The `EReaderSignal` class is abstract, so applications create an instance of its concrete subclass, `EReaderOSSignal`. The constructor accepts an optional timeout value that determines how long the application should wait for `waitForSignal` to return. If this value isn't set, the function may block indefinitely.

If the `waitForSignal` function returns, it means that the message queue is available for reading or that the timeout was reached. If the message queue is available, the application can process its messages by calling the second important function of the `EReader`: `processMsgs`.

processMsgs reads each message in the message queue and passes it to the EDecoder. The decoder determines what type of data is contained in the message and invokes the appropriate function of the EWrapper. For example, if the decoder decides that the message contains the server's response to placeOrder, it will invoke the openOrder callback of the client's wrapper.

6.3.4 Simple Client Example (C++)

The interaction of the EClientSocket, EWrapper, EReader, and EReaderSignal classes can be confusing, so it helps to look at a simple example. If you open the Ch06_SimpleClient project, you'll find the SimpleClient.cpp source file. This defines a class named SimpleClient, which is a subclass of both EWrapper and EClientSocket. Listing 6.2 presents its code.

Listing 6.2: Ch06_SimpleClient/SimpleClient.cpp

```
SimpleClient::SimpleClient(const char *host, int port,
    int clientId) : signal(1000), EClientSocket(this, &signal) {

  // Connect to TWS
  bool conn = eConnect(host, port, clientId, false);
  if (conn) {
    reader = new EReader(this, &signal);
    reader->start();
  }
  else
    std::cout << "Failed to connect" << std::endl;
}

SimpleClient::~SimpleClient() { delete reader; }

// Receive and display the current time
void SimpleClient::currentTime(long curTime) {
  time_t epoch = curTime;
  std::cout << "Current time: " << asctime(localtime(&epoch))
    << std::endl;
}

// Respond to errors
void SimpleClient::error(int id, int code,
    const std::string& msg) {
  std::cout << "Error: " << code << ": " << msg << std::endl;
}
```

The `SimpleClient` constructor creates an `EReaderOSSignal` with a timeout of one second, and passes this to the `EClientSocket` constructor. Then it performs three operations:

1. It connects to TWS.
2. It creates an instance of `EReader` and passes it the `EReaderOSSignal`.
3. It calls the `EReader`'s `start` function, which launches the thread that waits for data on the socket.

`SimpleClient` is a subclass of `EWrapper`, so it needs to provide code for the callback functions of interest. In this example, the application requests the current time by calling the client's `reqCurrentTime` function. The corresponding callback function is `currentTime`, and this explains why `SimpleClient` provides code for it.

To be specific, the `EDecoder` calls `currentTime` when it finds a message in the queue containing a response from TWS to `reqCurrentTime`. This callback function converts the time into a string and prints it to the console.

The last callback in SimpleClient.cpp is the `error` function. If a communication error occurs, this will provide the request ID, error code, and error message.

Listing 6.3 presents the code in the Main.cpp source file. This code creates the `SimpleClient` instance and calls `reqCurrentTime` to ask TWS for the current time.

Listing 6.3: Main.cpp

```cpp
int main() {

  // Connect to TWS or IB Gateway
  SimpleClient sc("127.0.0.1", 7497, 0);

  // Request the current time
  sc.reqCurrentTime();

  // Sleep while the message is received
  std::this_thread::sleep_for(std::chrono::seconds(1));

  // Read the message
  sc.signal.waitForSignal();
  sc.reader->processMsgs();

  // Disconnect
  sc.eDisconnect();
  return 0;
}
```

The `main` function in Main.cpp manages communication through the `EReader` and `EReaderSignal` fields of the `SimpleClient`. Making these fields public is bad programming practice, but it helps to clarify the process involved in sending requests and receiving responses:

1. Call a client function that sends a request to TWS. These functions include `reqCurrentTime`, `reqContractDetails`, and `placeOrder`.
2. Put the main thread to sleep while the reader thread reads socket data and stores it to the message queue.
3. Call the `EReaderSignal`'s `waitForSignal` function to halt processing until the message queue is free for reading.
4. Call the `EReader`'s `processMsgs` function to have the message sent to the `EDecoder`, which will invoke the appropriate callback function.

When you code applications in C++, it's critical to understand these steps. If you forget a step or perform steps out of order, your application may hang or disconnect. I've spent many hours riddling out communication errors and they're much more frustrating than regular syntax errors.

6.4 Summary

The TWS API provides a great deal of power and flexibility, but it's not particularly easy to learn. To have a deep understanding of TWS API applications, you need to have a solid grasp of network sockets, multithreading, and interthread communication.

Thankfully, you don't really need to understand these details in day-to-day programming. Once you have a working application, you can copy and paste much of its content to other applications. The portions of code that require updating are the request functions in the client class and the callbacks in the wrapper class.

The client class initiates communication and invokes functions that send requests to TWS. As examples, `reqCurrentTime` requests the current time and `reqHistoricalData` requests historical data. These request functions always return void and always accept a numeric ID as their first parameter.

For each request function in the client class, the wrapper class provides at least one callback function. When the application receives a response from IB, its decoder invokes the appropriate callback. For example, the `currentTime` callback is called when the response to `reqCurrentTime` is received. The `historicalData` callback is called when the response to `reqHistoricalData` is received.

To code TWS API applications, you don't need to understand all the details involving readers, decoders, and threads. But you should be comfortable with the general structure of the example code presented in this chapter. Most of the example code in later chapters will resemble the code shown here.

Chapter 7

Contracts and Orders

Algorithmic trading applications analyze financial data and submit orders automatically. To write these applications, you need to understand how to create and place orders in code. The goal of this chapter is to show how this is done with the TWS API.

Before you can place orders, you need to be familiar with contracts. In IB jargon, *contract* is synonymous with *financial instrument*. In other words, a contract is anything that can be traded through IB. Stocks, bonds, and derivatives are all contracts. The purpose of an order is to trade (buy or sell) contracts.

In the TWS API, contracts are represented by `Contract` structures and orders are represented by `Order` structures. Both are essentially data objects. That is, each contains several fields and few methods/functions. The fields have the same names whether you use Python or C++.

When working with `Contract`s and `Order`s, it's critical to understand what their fields represent and what values are appropriate. A contract representing a bond will need a different set of fields than a contract representing a futures option. This chapter discusses both structures in depth and provides several examples of creating them in code.

Contracts and orders become complex when you intend to trade combinations of options. These combinations may have multiple legs, and the `Contract` and `Order` structures provide fields and routines specifically for these trades.

After explaining what contracts and orders are, this chapter explains how to execute orders. I'll also present the functions that make it possible to obtain information about contracts and orders. This requires understanding methods/functions in the API's client and wrapper class.

7.1 Contracts

Contract is a general term for a financial instrument, and in the TWS API, contracts are represented by instances of the `Contract` structure. If you look through the contract.py module (Python) or the contract.h header file (C++), you'll see that this structure contains a considerable number of fields.

To describe these fields, this discussion splits them into three categories:

1. **four fundamental fields** — needed for (almost) all contracts
2. **optional fields** — apply to different types of securities, but aren't always necessary
3. **derivative-specific fields** — fields only used when placing derivative orders

After discussing the fields of the `Contract` structure, this section discusses functions that access information about contracts. At the end of the section, I'll provide example code that demonstrates how to access contract information programmatically.

7.1.1 Fundamental Fields

When you place an order using the TWS API, you need to create one or more `Contract`s. For example, if you want to purchase shares of IBM, your application will need to create a `Contract` that represents IBM stock. In Python, the code might look like this:

```
con = Contract()
con.symbol = "IBM"
con.secType = "STK"
con.currency = "USD"
con.exchange = "SMART"
```

In C++, the code might look like this:

```
Contract con;
con.symbol = "IBM";
con.secType = "STK";
con.currency = "USD";
con.exchange = "SMART";
```

As shown, the code is nearly identical for both languages. That is, the `Contract` structure has the same fields in both languages and the fields can be set to similar values.

This code presents the four fields that I consider fundamental for `Contracts`. These are all strings and they're almost always necessary to identify a contract. Table 7.1 lists each of them and provides a description.

Table 7.1

Fundamental Fields of a Contract

Field	Description
`symbol`	The contract's ticker symbol
`secType`	Identifier for the contract's type (stock, bond, etc.)
`currency`	Currency in which the contract is traded
`exchange`	Exchange through which the contract can be accessed

The `symbol` and `currency` fields are the easiest to understand. `symbol` identifies the ticker symbol of the asset or underlying asset. `currency` identifies the asset's currency code. This identifies how the asset is priced, not what you're intending to pay with. Common currency codes include `USD` (US Dollar), `EUR` (Euro), `JPY` (Japanese Yen), `CNY` (Chinese Yuan Renminbi), `GBP` (British Pound), `INR` (Indian Rupee), `CAD` (Canadian Dollar), `AUD` (Australian Dollar), and `CHF` (Swiss Franc).

The `secType` field identifies the contract's type. An application can set this to one of twelve values:

- **STK** — stock or exchange-traded fund (ETF)
- **BOND** — bond
- **IND** — index
- **FUND** — mutual fund
- **OPT** — option
- **FUT** — future
- **WAR** — warrant
- **FOP** — futures option
- **CASH** — forex pair
- **CMDTY** — commodity
- **NEWS** — news
- **BAG** — combo

Of the fundamental fields, `exchange` is the most complicated. Just as you'd visit a store to buy merchandise, you need to specify an exchange to trade contracts. On many trading platforms, you need to know in advance which exchange lists a given contract. For example, to trade shares of Microsoft, you'd need to know that its stock is listed on the NASDAQ exchange.

To make life easier, IB provides a free service called SMART routing. This router scans exchanges and directs orders to the best exchange for the given contract. For this reason, most of the code presented in this book sets the `exchange` field to SMART.

If SMART routing won't be sufficient, you can set the `exchange` field to the IB code for a specific exchange. IB provides access to hundreds of different exchanges throughout the world. Table 7.2 lists fifteen of them and their codes.

Table 7.2
Supported Exchanges (Abridged)

Code	Name	Types of Contracts
ISLAND	NASDAQ	Stocks, warrants
NYSE	New York Stock Exchange	Indices, stocks, warrants
IDEALPRO	IB's exchange for forex trading	Forex
IEX	Investor's Exchange	Stocks
CBOE C2	CBOE Options Exchange	Options (equity)
CFE	CBOE Futures Exchange	Futures, indices
BOX	Boston Options Exchange	Options (equity)
BondDesk	Tradeweb Direct	Fixed Income
DTB	EUREX	Options, indices, futures, futures options
SEHK	Hong Kong Stock Exchange	Stocks, options, fixed income, ETFs, warrants, structured products
ASX	Australian Stock Exchange	Stocks, options, indices, ETFs, warrants
BATS	Better Alternative Trading System	Stocks, options, warrants
ISE	International Securities Exchange	Indices, options, warrants
SBF	Euronext France	Stocks, ETFs, warrants, structured products
GLOBEX	CME Globex	Fixed income, indices, futures, futures options

You can view the full list of supported exchanges at https://www.interactivebrokers.com/en/index.php?f=1562. Keep in mind that different exchanges require different amounts of time to access.

The Boston Options Exchange (BOX) provides options trading capabilities that aren't available elsewhere. The most important capability involves Price Improvement Period (PIP) auctions, which allow brokers to gradually improve the orders of their clients. According to BOX, PIP has saved investors an average of one dollar per options contract.

7.1.2 Optional Fields

Many applications need more information than the four fields listed in Table 7.1. Table 7.3 lists six optional fields of the `Contract` structure.

Table 7.3
Optional Contract Fields

Field	Type	Description
`conId`	`int`	Identifies contracts in an application
`primaryExchange`	`string`	Exchange identified to prevent ambiguity
`localSymbol`	`string`	Contract symbol on its local exchange
`tradingClass`	`string`	IB-specific designation for a contract
`secIdType`	`string`	Type of specific security identification
`secId`	`string`	Specific security identification value

`conId` is an integer that uniquely identifies a contract. This is determined by IB, and I'll explain how to access a contract's identifier shortly.

SMART routing is a powerful capability, but it can't always distinguish between similarly-named contracts in different exchanges. If you encounter ambiguity errors, you can direct SMART to a particular exchange by setting the `primaryExchange` field. For example, if the contract is listed in the Boston Options Exchange, the application should set `primaryExchange` to `BOX`.

In rare cases, a contract may have a different symbol in its primary exchange. In this case, you should set `localSymbol` to the appropriate symbol.

The idea of a contract's trading class is specific to Interactive Brokers, and you can view a contract's class in TWS by opening the contract description window. If you can't fix ambiguity errors by setting `symbol`, `localSymbol`, or `primaryExchange`, you can set `tradingClass` to an appropriate value.

When creating contracts that represent bonds, it's not enough to identify the ticker of the corporation issuing the security. An application should further identify the bond using the `secIdType` and `secId` fields. `secIdType` can be set to one of four strings:

1. `ISIN` — International Securities Identification Number (ISIN)
2. `CUSIP` — Committee on Uniform Securities Identification Procedure (CUSIP) identifier
3. `SEDOL` — Stock Exchange Daily Official List (SEDOL) identifier
4. `RIC` — Reuters Instrument Code

If an application assigns `secIdType` to one of these values, it should set `secId` to the appropriate identifier. For example, if you want to identify a bond by its CUSIP, you should set `secIdType` to `CUSIP` and set `secId` to the appropriate value.

> **NOTE**
>
> When creating a `Contract` for a Dutch warrant or a structured product, applications must set the `conId` or `localSymbol` field.

7.1.3 Derivative-Specific Fields

Many fields of the `Contract` structure are only relevant for contracts involving derivatives. Table 7.4 lists eight of these fields and provides a description of each.

Table 7.4
Derivative-Specific Contract Fields

Field	Type	Description
`strike`	`double`	Strike price of an option
`right`	`string`	The type of an option (put or call)
`multiplier`	`string`	The number of assets controlled by the derivative
`includeExpired`	`bool`	Whether data should be provided for expired futures contracts
`lastTradeDateOrContractMonth`	`string`	Last trading day or contract month (options and futures)
`deltaNeutralContract`	`Delta Neutral Contract*`	Delta and underlying price for delta neutral options and futures contracts

comboLegs	ComboLeg ListSPtr	Trades that make up an options combination
comboLeg Description	string	Description of the trades that make up an options combination

The `strike` field identifies an option's strike price, which is the price at which the option holder can buy or sell the underlying asset. The type of option is specified with the `right` field. For put options, this can be set to `P` or `PUT`. For call options, this can be set to `C` or `CALL`.

IB doesn't provide historical data for options contracts. By default, applications can't access historical data related to expired futures contracts either. But if `includeExpired` is set to `TRUE`, applications can obtain information related to expired futures contracts.

The last three fields relate to combo `Contract`s, denoted by the `BAG` type. A combo contains multiple trades, or *legs*. Chapter 4 discussed delta neutral combinations, in which the sum of the legs' delta values equals 0. In code, an application can define a delta neutral combination by setting `deltaNeutralContract`, which has three fields:

- **conId** — the identifier of the underlying asset
- **delta** — the delta of the underlying asset
- **price** — price of the underlying asset

The `comboLegs` field contains one or more `ComboLeg` instances, and each represents a different trade in the combination. Table 7.5 lists six fields of the `ComboLeg` structure and provides a description of each.

Table 7.5
Fields of a ComboLeg Structure

Field	Type	Description
conId	int	Unique contract identifier
ratio	int	Relative number of contracts
action	string	Side of the leg (buy or sell)
exchange	string	Exchange to which an order should be routed
shortSaleSlot	int	Configures short sale
designated Location	string	The location for handling the short sale (if applicable)

An example will clarify how legs of a combination can be defined. In Python, the `comboLegs` field is a list of `ComboLeg` structures. The following code defines a `Contract` for a ratio spread (two sell orders, one buy order) based on Starbucks (SBUX) stock.

```
# Define the combo contract
contract = Contract()
contract.symbol = "SBUX"
contract.secType = "BAG"
contract.currency = "USD"
contract.exchange = "SMART"

# First leg of the combo
leg1 = ComboLeg()
leg1.conId = ...
leg1.ratio = 2
leg1.action = "SELL"

# Second leg of the combo
leg2 = ComboLeg()
leg2.conId = ...
leg2.ratio = 1
leg2.action = "BUY"

# Add the legs to the combo
contract.comboLegs = []
contract.comboLegs.append(leg1)
contract.comboLegs.append(leg2)
```

This code creates a `Contract` of type `BAG`, which identifies it as a combo contract. The combination consists of two legs, and the first identifies a sale of two options. The second leg identifies the purchase of one option.

The details of the combo's options are specified by their identifiers, given by the `conId` field. Unlike request identifiers, contract identifiers are *not* chosen by the developer. To determine a contract's ID, you need to call `reqContractDetails`, which I'll discuss next.

7.1.4 Accessing Contract Data

The `EClient` class provides two helpful functions that request information related to `Contracts`. The first, `reqContractDetails`, requests data about a contract beyond that defined in the `Contract` structure. The second function, `reqMatchingSymbols`, is helpful when you know part of a contract's symbol but are unsure of the complete string.

Requesting Contract Details

To obtain background information about a `Contract`, applications can call `reqContractDetails`. The signature is identical in Python and C++:

```
reqContractDetails(int reqId, Contract contract)
```

In this function, `reqId` is a unique identifier for the request and `contract` is a `Contract`. The application receives the response through the wrapper's `contractDetails` callback function:

```
contractDetails(int reqId, ContractDetails contractDetails)
```

The first argument, `reqId`, has the same value as the ID set in `reqContractDetails`. The second argument provides current information about the contract. This `ContractDetails` structure has a wide range of fields and Table 7.6 lists the fields that apply to many types of contracts.

> **NOTE**
>
> A `ContractDetails` structure provides a great deal of information, but it doesn't provide current or past prices. Chapter 8 explains how to read financial data.

Table 7.6
ContractDetails Fields (General-Purpose)

Field	Type	Description
`contract`	`Contract`	Fully-defined contract
`longName`	`string`	Descriptive name
`secIdList`	`List/TagValueListsPtr`	List of contract identifiers
`orderTypes`	`string`	Supported order types for the product
`validExchanges`	`string`	Valid exchange fields when placing an order for the contract
`marketName`	`string`	Market on which the contract is traded
`lastTradeTime`	`string`	Last trade time
`tradingHours`	`string`	Trading hours of the current day and the next's
`liquidHours`	`string`	Regular trading hours of the contract

`timeZoneId`	`string`	Time zone for the contract's trading hours
`industry`	`string`	Industry classification of the contract or underlying asset
`category`	`string`	Industry category of the contract or underlying asset
`subcategory`	`string`	Industry subcategory of the contract or underlying asset
`evRule`	`string`	The economic value rule name
`evMultiplier`	`double`	How much the market value would change if the price changed by 1
`mdSizeMultiplier`	`int`	Market data size multiplier
`aggGroup`	`int`	SMART routing group

An application can provide a partially-defined `Contract` in `reqContractDetails`. But the `contract` field of the `ContractDetails` will be completely defined. This means that an application can access the contract's ID through the `Contract`'s `conId` field. In fact, this is the only way I know of to obtain a contract's unique ID.

An example will demonstrate how an application can request and receive data. The following code creates a `Contract` representing Intel stock and asks the server for details.

```
Contract con;
con.symbol = "INTC";
con.secType = "STK";
con.currency = "USD";
con.exchange = "SMART";
reqContractDetails(0, con);
```

After TWS receives the request, the application will receive the response through the `contractDetails` callback. This provides a request `ContractDetails` structure containing information about the stock. The following code accesses this structure to obtain the contract's long name, market name, and contract ID:

```
// Defined in the wrapper class
void contractDetails(int id, const ContractDetails& cd) {
  std::cout << "Long name: " << cd.longName << std::endl;
  std::cout << "Market name: " << cd.marketName << std::endl;
  std::cout << "Contract ID: "
    << cd.contract.conId << std::endl;
}
```

Table 7.7 lists fields of the `ContractDetails` structure that relate to bonds. These fields identify many characteristics about bond contracts, including the bond's type and the coupon rate.

Table 7.7

ContractDetails Fields (Bond-Related)

Field	Type	Description
`bondType`	`string`	Type of the bond
`coupon`	`double`	Coupon rate
`issueDate`	`string`	Date the bond was issued
`maturity`	`string`	Date the issuer pays the principal
`cusip`	`string`	The bond's CUSIP identifier
`convertible`	`bool`	Whether the bond is convertible
`callable`	`bool`	Whether the bond is callable
`putable`	`bool`	Whether the bond is putable
`notes`	`string`	Additional bond information
`descAppend`	`string`	Description string

Chapter 2 discussed the types and characteristics of bonds. The `bondType` field identifies the nature of the organization that issued the bond. For corporate bonds, this will be set to `CORP`.

A bond's coupon rate, given by the `coupon` field, is the sum of the interest payments paid to the bond holder each year. The `issueDate` field identifies when the bond was issued and the `maturity` field identifies when the issuer must pay the holder the bond's face value.

The `cusip` field identifies the bond's CUSIP (Committee on Uniform Security Identification Procedures) identifier. This is a nine-character string whose first six characters identify the issuer and whose seventh and eighth characters identify the exact security. The ninth character is used for error checking.

If the `convertible` field is true, the holder can convert the bond into shares of stock. If the `callable` field is true, the issuer can purchase (or call) the bond after issue. If `putable` is true, the holder has the right to receive repayment of the bond's face value on specified dates.

In addition to bond-specific fields, the `ContractDetails` structure provides fields specifically related to derivatives. Table 7.8 lists seven of these fields and provides a description of each.

Table 7.8
ContractDetails Fields (Derivative-Related)

Field	Type	Description
`underConId`	`int`	Identifier of the underlying contract
`underSymbol`	`string`	Symbol of the underlying contract
`underSecType`	`string`	Security type of the underlying contract
`contractMonth`	`string`	Expiration month of the derivative
`realExpirationDate`	`string`	Expiration date of the derivative
`minTick`	`double`	Minimum tick for a futures contract
`priceMagnifier`	`long`	Used to define prices of futures options

The value of a derivative is based on the value of an underlying asset. The first three fields in Table 7.8 provide information about the underlying asset, such as its identifier (`underConId`), symbol (`underSymbol`), and security type (`underSecType`).

The `contractMonth` field identifies the month in which the derivative expires. `realExpirationDate` provides the day of expiration.

The last two fields in the table relate to futures contracts, which were discussed at length in Chapter 5. `minTick` identifies the smallest variation in the price of a futures contract.

`priceMagnifier` is more involved, and its value depends on the TWS version. Prior to version 972 of TWS, applications could multiply the price of a futures option by setting the `priceMagnifier` field. Later versions don't apply price magnifiers when computing strike prices of futures options. Every time I check `priceMagnifier`, it equals 1.

Requesting Contract Symbols

If you can't remember a contract's symbol, you can request possible symbols by calling the client's `reqMatchingSymbols` function:

`reqMatchingSymbols(int reqId, string pattern)`

The second argument doesn't accept a formal pattern, such as those used in regular expressions. Instead, an application can set this to the start of a ticker symbol or the name of a company. For example, if you can't remember that the symbol of DMC Global is BOOM, you can call `reqMatchingSymbols` and set the `pattern` argument to `DMC Global`.

After an application calls `reqMatchingSymbols`, it can obtain the server's response through the `symbolSamples` callback. The second argument is an array of `ContractDescriptions` whose symbols correspond to the suggested candidate symbols.

Like the `ContractDetails` structure discussed earlier, the `ContractDescription` structure has a `contract` field that identifies a `Contract`. But this `Contract` structure isn't fully populated with data. The only information that can be reliably accessed is the `symbol` field.

7.1.5 Obtaining Contract Data in Code

At this point, you should have a solid understanding of what `Contract`s are and the functions that make it possible to access contract data. In this discussion, I'll demonstrate how these functions can be used in Python and C++.

In both cases, the code calls `reqMatchingSymbols` to obtain ticker symbols for contracts whose name contains the pattern `Cheesecake`. Then it calls `reqContractDetails` to obtain information about the stock with the first ticker symbol.

Obtaining Contract Data in Python

The code in Listing 7.1 demonstrates how the `reqMatchingSymbols` and `reqContractDetails` functions can be called in Python. It starts by defining a class named `ContractReader` and then uses the class to make requests.

Listing 7.1: ch7/contract_details.py

```python
class ContractReader(EWrapper, EClient):
    ''' Serves as the client and the wrapper '''

    def __init__(self, addr, port, client_id):
        EWrapper.__init__(self)
        EClient.__init__(self, self)

        # Connect to TWS
        self.connect(addr, port, client_id)

        # Launch the client thread
        thread = Thread(target=self.run)
        thread.start()
```

Listing 7.1: ch7/contract_details.py (Continued)

```python
    @iswrapper
    def symbolSamples(self, reqId, descs):

        # Print the symbols in the returned results
        print('Number of descriptions: {}'.format(len(descs)))
        for desc in descs:
            print('Symbol: {}'.format(desc.contract.symbol))

        # Choose the first symbol
        self.symbol = descs[0].contract.symbol

    @iswrapper
    def contractDetails(self, reqId, details):
        print('Long name: {}'.format(details.longName))
        print('Category: {}'.format(details.category))
        print('Subcategory: {}'.format(details.subcategory))
        print('Contract ID: {}\n'.format(details.contract.conId))

    @iswrapper
    def contractDetailsEnd(self, reqId):
        print('The End')

    def error(self, reqId, code, msg):
        print('Error {}: {}'.format(code, msg))

def main():
    # Create the client and connect to TWS
    client = ContractReader('127.0.0.1', 7497, 0)
    time.sleep(0.5)

    # Request descriptions of contracts related to cheesecake
    client.reqMatchingSymbols(0, 'Cheesecake')
    time.sleep(3)

    # Request details for the stock
    contract = Contract()
    contract.symbol = client.symbol
    contract.secType = "OPT"
    contract.exchange = "SMART"
    contract.currency = "USD"
    client.reqContractDetails(1, contract)

    time.sleep(3)
    client.disconnect()
```

The `main` function starts by creating a `ContractReader` instance and calling its `reqMatchingSymbols` function with the second argument set to `Cheesecake`. This requests symbols for securities related to `Cheesecake`, and the application accesses the server's response through the `symbolSamples` callback.

`symbolSamples` provides a series of `ContractDescriptions` and prints the symbol of each one. The first symbol serves to identify the security of interest.

After determining the symbol, the `ContractReader` creates a `Contract` for an option whose underlying security is given by the symbol. Then it calls `reqContractDetails` to obtain information about the option.

The `ContractReader` receives contract information through the `contractDetails` callback, which provides a `ContractDetails` structure. This callback prints the contract's long name, category, subcategory, and ID. Keep in mind that this is the only way to reliably access contract IDs.

Obtaining Contract Data in C++

The code in the Ch07_ContractReader project demonstrates how contracts can be created and accessed in C++. The Main.cpp source file provides the `main` function and Listing 7.2 presents its code.

Listing 7.2: Ch07_ContractReader/Main.cpp

```
int main() {

  // Connect to TWS or IB Gateway
  ContractReader client("127.0.0.1", 7497, 0);

  // Request symbols associated with cheesecake
  client.reqMatchingSymbols(0, "Cheesecake");
  std::this_thread::sleep_for(std::chrono::seconds(3));
  client.signal.waitForSignal();
  client.reader->processMsgs();

  // Define a contract
  Contract con = Contract();
  con.symbol = client.symbol;
  con.secType = "OPT";
  con.exchange = "SMART";
  con.currency = "USD";
```

Listing 7.2: Ch07_ContractReader/Main.cpp (continued)

```cpp
  // Read the message
  client.reqContractDetails(1, con);
  std::this_thread::sleep_for(std::chrono::seconds(3));
  client.signal.waitForSignal();
  client.reader->processMsgs();

  // Disconnect
  client.eDisconnect();
  return 0;
}
```

The `main` function performs three main tasks:

1. It creates an instance of the `ContractReader` class.
2. It calls the `ContractReader`'s `reqMatchingSymbols` function with the second argument set to Cheesecake.
3. It creates a `Contract` and calls the `ContractReader`'s `reqContractDetails` function to obtain information about the `Contract`.

After the request functions are called, the `ContractReader` accesses the response data through its callback functions. Listing 7.3 presents the code for these callbacks.

Listing 7.3: Ch07_ContractReader/ContractReader.cpp

```cpp
ContractReader::ContractReader(const char *host, int port,
  int clientId) : signal(1000), EClientSocket(this, &signal) {

  // Connect to TWS
  bool conn = eConnect(host, port, clientId, false);
  if (conn) {

    // Launch the reader thread
    reader = new EReader(this, &signal);
    reader->start();
  }
  else
    std::cout << "Failed to connect" << std::endl;
}

ContractReader::~ContractReader() { delete reader; }
```

Listing 7.3: Ch07_ContractReader/ContractReader.cpp (continued)

```cpp
// Receives symbols for contracts related to the given string
void ContractReader::symbolSamples(int reqId,
  const std::vector<ContractDescription> &descs) {

  std::cout << "Number of descriptions: " << descs.size()
    << std::endl;

  for (ContractDescription desc: descs) {
    std::cout << "Symbol: " << desc.contract.symbol
      << std::endl;
  }

  // Choose the first symbol
  symbol = descs[0].contract.symbol;
}

// Receives details related to the contract of interest
void ContractReader::contractDetails(int reqId, const
ContractDetails& details) {
  std::cout << "Long name: " << details.longName << std::endl;
  std::cout << "Category: " << details.category << std::endl;
  std::cout << "Subcategory: " << details.subcategory
    << std::endl;
  std::cout << "Contract ID: " << details.contract.conId
    << std::endl;
}

// Called when all contract data has been received
void ContractReader::contractDetailsEnd(int reqId) {
  std::cout << "The end." << std::endl;
}

void ContractReader::error(int id, int code,
  const std::string& msg) {
  std::cout << "Error: " << code << ": " << msg << std::endl;
}
```

After the `reqMatchingSymbols` function is called, the `symbolSamples` callback provides a `ContractDescription` for each related contract. This callback prints the symbols from each description and sets the first symbol as the security of interest.

`contractDetails` provides the data requested by the `reqContractDetails` function. Then it prints the contract's long name, category, subcategory, and ID.

7.2 Orders

Chapter 2 explained how to create and submit orders using Trader Workstation. It also discussed many of the different types of orders that can be submitted. To create and execute orders programmatically, you need to be familiar with the `Order` data structure.

The `Order` structure provides a bewildering number of data fields, but most applications will only require a small subset. This section presents the basic fields of the `Order` structure and discusses many of the order types available.

7.2.1 Basic Fields

Every order requires at least three pieces of information: the action (`BUY` or `SELL`), a quantity to be bought or sold, and the order's type. Table 7.9 lists these fundamental fields and their data types.

Table 7.9

Basic Order Fields

Field	Type	Description
`action`	string	Nature of the order: BUY or SELL
`totalQuantity`	double	The quantity to be bought or sold
`orderType`	string	The type of order to be executed

For example, the following code configures an `Order` to buy a quantity of 100:

```
order = Order()
order.action = "BUY"
order.totalQuantity = 100
order.orderType = "MKT"
```

This code creates the same order in C++:

```
Order order;
order.action = action;
order.orderType = "MKT";
order.totalQuantity = quantity;
```

Both examples set `orderType` to `MKT`. This type code tells IB that the order should be placed as a *market order*. I'll discuss order types shortly.

When you create an `Order`, you don't mention the `Contract` to be bought or sold. You'll provide this information in the `placeOrder` function that I'll discuss later. By keeping `Order`s and `Contract`s separate, the TWS API makes it possible to reuse `Order`s and `Contract`s as needed.

7.2.2 Order Types

When you create an `Order` structure, you need to set `orderType` to a string that identifies the nature of the order. These different types of orders can be divided into six categories:

1. **market order** — orders executed at the current market price
2. **limit order** — orders executed at the limit price or better
3. **stop order** — orders executed at the stop price
4. **trailing stop order** — stop orders whose stop prices may change with the market
5. **pegged** — orders executed at a price related to another price
6. **volatility** — orders that don't fall into any of the preceding categories

As you look through the order types, keep in mind that some may not be available for particular products. In addition, some can only be submitted for specific exchanges. That is, some orders are only available when using SMART routing and others are only available when accessing the Boston Options Exchange (BOX).

Some types of orders require special configuration fields, such as a limit price, trailing percentage, or benchmark contract ID. To provide this information, you need to set additional fields of the `Order` structure. Table 7.10 lists fourteen type-dependent fields and their data types.

Table 7.10

Type-Dependent Data Fields

Field	Type	Description
`lmtPrice`	`double`	The desired order price for limit orders
`auxPrice`	`double`	Additional price used in many order types (example: stop order price in stop orders)
`trailingPercent`	`double`	Percentage difference between the market price and order price in trailing stop orders
`trailStopPrice`	`double`	Constant offset between the market price and order price in trailing stop orders

`referenceContractId`	int	Identifier of the benchmark contract used in Pegged to Benchmark orders
`referenceExchangeId`	string	Exchange of the benchmark contract used in Pegged to Benchmark orders
`referenceChangeAmount`	double	Minimum change of the benchmark price used in Pegged to Benchmark orders
`peggedChangeAmount`	double	Amount of change in the order price used in pegged orders
`isPeggedChangeAmountDecrease`	bool	Whether the pegged change amount represents a decrease in the order price
`stockRefPrice`	double	Price that must be reached for monitoring to start (pegged orders)
`stockRangeLower`	double	Minimum price for monitoring (pegged orders)
`stockRangeUpper`	double	Maximum price for monitoring (pegged orders)
`volatilityType`	int	Type of volatility used in volatility orders
`volatility`	double	Percentage of volatility used to compute prices of volatility orders

I'll provide a proper introduction to these fields as they're encountered in the following discussion of IB's order types.

Market Orders

The simplest orders are market orders. These execute as quickly as possible and perform trades at the current market price. IB supports a handful of different types of market orders and Table 7.11 presents their type codes.

Table 7.11

Types of Market Orders

Code	Type	Description
MKT	Market	Trade at the current market price
MOC	Market on Close	Market order submitted to execute as close to the closing price as possible
MIT	Market if Touched	Trade when the market price changes (high or low)
MKT PRT	Market with Protection	Market order that will be canceled if it doesn't execute completely at market price

MTL	Market to Limit	If market order fails to fully execute, the remainder is canceled and resubmitted as a limit order
BOX TOP	Box Top	If market order executes partially, the remainder is canceled and resubmitted as a limit order (BOX only)

Setting `orderType` to `MKT` identifies the order as a market order, and IB will execute it as soon as it's placed. If `orderType` is set to `MOC`, IB will wait until closing and execute the order as close to the closing price as possible.

Similarly, if you set `orderType` to `MIT`, IB will delay executing the order until the market price reaches the trigger price identified by the `auxPrice` field. For example, the following code creates an `Order` and sets its `orderType` field to `MIT` and the `auxPrice` to 75. As a result, IB will wait until the market price touches 75 before submitting the market order.

```
order = Order()

// Set the order's type to Market if Touched (MIT)
order.orderType = "MIT"

// Set the trigger price to 75
order.auxPrice = 75
```

If IB can only fill part of an order at the market price, it will fill the rest of the order at a different (possibly worse) price. But if `orderType` is set to `MKT PRT`, IB will cancel the order if it isn't completely filled. If you set `orderType` to `MTL`, IB will submit an order for the remainder as a limit order whose limit price is the price at which the initial order was filled. The last market order type, `BOX TOP`, is similar to `MTL`, but it's only available for options contracts on the BOX exchange.

Limit Orders

Limit orders are safer than market orders because you set the price (the *limit price*) at which the order should be executed. IB will execute the order if it can trade at the limit price *or better*. For example, if you submit a sell order at a limit price of 100, IB will execute the order at any price greater than or equal to 100.

I know many investors who only submit limit orders, and they make a profit if the limit price is reached. Of course, if the limit price isn't reached, no trade will be submitted at all.

The TWS API supports three different types of limit orders. Table 7.12 lists their codes and provides a description of each.

Table 7.12
Types of Limit Orders

Code	Type	Description
LMT	Limit	Trade at a specified price or better
LOC	Limit on Close	Limit order submitted at the close, will execute if the closing price is at or better than the submitted price
LIT	Limit if Touched	Trade when the price rises above or below the limit price

Setting `orderType` to `LMT` identifies the order as a traditional limit order. When you create a limit order, you should set the `lmtPrice` field to the worst price you're willing to accept. If you set `orderType` to `LOC`, IB will submit the order at the close of day if the closing price is equal to or better than `lmtPrice`.

If you set `orderType` to `LIT`, IB won't submit the limit order until the market price reaches the trigger price given by `auxPrice`. For example, if you submit an `Order` whose `orderType` is `LIT`, `lmtPrice` is 90, and `auxPrice` is 110, IB won't execute the limit order until the market price reaches 110.

Stop Orders

Like a limit order, a stop order has a price at which the investor wants the order to be filled. But while limit orders are executed at the given price or better, stop orders are always executed as soon as the stop price is reached.

In general, traders submit stop orders to limit loss after purchasing a contract. Put simply, limit orders are motivated by hope, stop orders are motivated by fear. Table 7.13 lists three codes that identify stop orders in the TWS API.

Table 7.13
Types of Stop Orders

Code	Type	Description
STP	Stop	Submit a market order if the trigger price is reached
STP LMT	Stop Limit	Submit a limit order if the trigger price is reached
STP PRT	Stop with Protection	Regular stop order unless partially filled, then the remainder is canceled and resubmitted as a limit order

When you create a stop order, you need to set the `auxPrice` field to your desired trigger price. Then, if you set `orderType` to `STP`, IB will submit a market order when the market price reaches `auxPrice`. If you set `orderType` to `STP LMT`, IB will submit a limit order when the market price penetrates `auxPrice`. In this case, you need to set the `lmtPrice` field to the desired limit price.

The following code demonstrates how to create a stop limit order. In this case, the stop price is 60 and the limit price is 58.

```
order = Order()
...
order.orderType = "STP LMT"
order.auxPrice = 60
order.lmtPrice = 58
```

A atop-with-protection order (`STP PRT`) is similar to the stop limit order (`STP LMT`). The difference is that, if IB fails to completely fill the stop order, the remainder will be submitted as part of a limit order.

Trailing Stop Orders

Trailing stop orders are like stop orders, but if the market price rises, the stop price rises with it. But if the market price drops, the stop price won't drop below its initial setting. You can set the stop price with the `trailStopPrice` field of the `Order` structure.

There are two ways to control how the stop price changes with the market price. If you set `auxPrice` to a value, IB will interpret this value as a constant offset from the market price. If you set the `trailingPercent` field to a value, IB will set the trailing amount to the given percentage of the market price. The TWS API supports four types of trailing stop orders and Table 7.14 lists each of them.

Table 7.14
Types of Trailing Stop Orders

Code	Type	Description
TRAIL	Trailing Stop	Stop order whose stop price rises with the market price
TRAIL LIMIT	Trailing Stop Limit	Stop order that submits a limit order when the market price reaches the stop price
TRAIL LIT	Trailing Stop Limit if Touched	Stop order that submits a limit-if-touched order when the market price reaches the stop price
TRAIL MIT	Trailing Stop Market if Touched	Stop order that submits a market-if-touched order when the market price reaches the stop price

Setting `orderType` to `TRAIL` configures the order as a trailing stop order whose stop price is given by the `trailStopPrice` field. If `orderType` is set to `TRAIL LIMIT`, IB will submit a limit order if the market price reaches or penetrates the stop price. In this case, an application will need to set the limit price using the `lmtPrice` field.

For example, the following code creates a trailing stop order whose trailing stop price is ten percent less than the market price. The final stop price is 85.

```
Order order;
...
order.orderType = "TRAIL";
order.trailStopPrice = 85;
order.trailingPercent = 10;
```

An earlier discussion introduced the limit-if-touched (LIT) and market-if-touched (MIT) orders. If you set `orderType` to `TRAIL LIT` or `TRAIL MIT`, TWS will execute the corrresponding order if the market price reaches or penetrates the stop price.

Pegged Orders

Pegged orders, or relative orders, are similar to limit orders. The difference is that the limit price is determined by another price. Table 7.15 lists six types of pegged orders.

Table 7.15
Types of Pegged Orders

Code	Type	Description
`PEG MKT`	Pegged To Market	Order price relative to national best offer/bid
`PEG MID`	Pegged To Midpoint	Order price relative to the average of the national best offer/bid
`PEG BENCH`	Pegged To Benchmark	Order price relative to another security
`PEG STK`	Pegged To Stock	Order price relative to a stock price (BOX only)
`REL`	Pegged To Primary	Order price more aggressive than the NBBO
`PASSV REL`	Passive Relative	Order price less aggressive than the NBBO

When purchasing stocks, you may want to place a limit order whose limit price changes with the stock's price. To accomplish this, you'll need to set `orderType` to `PEG MKT` and `auxPrice` to an offset value. IB will update the order's purchase price according to the lowest possible ask price and the highest possible bid price.

These bid and ask prices are determined by the National Best Bid and Offer (NBBO). For sell orders, the price will be the national best bid + `auxPrice`. For buy orders, the price will be the national best offer − `auxPrice`.

A pegged-to-midpoint order is like a pegged-to-market order in that it's only available for stocks. The difference is that a pegged-to-midpoint order finds the buy/sell price relative to the midpoint of the national best offer and national best bid.

In a pegged-to-benchmark order, IB updates the order price of stocks and options when the price of another contract changes by a given amount. You can configure this type of order using several fields:

- `startingPrice` — The initial order price
- `referenceContractId` — The identifier (`conId`) of the benchmark contract
- `referenceExchangeId` — The name of the benchmark contract's exchange
- `referenceChangeAmount` — Amount by which the benchmark contract's price needs to change
- `peggedChangeAmount` — The amount by which the order price changes when the benchmark contract's change exceeds `referenceChangeAmount`
- `isPeggedChangeAmountDecrease` — Identifies whether the pegged change amount represents an increase or a decrease
- `stockRefPrice` — If the reference asset is a stock, it must reach this price before monitoring starts
- `stockRangeLower` — If the reference asset is a stock, its price must exceed this value for monitoring to continue
- `stockRangeUpper` — If the reference asset is a stock, its price must stay below this value for monitoring to continue

For example, the following code creates an order whose price is pegged to the price of a contract named `con`, which is listed on the exchange `conExch`. If the price of `con` changes by `refAmt` or more, the order price should decrease by `orderAmt`.

```
order = Order()
...
order.orderType = "PEG BENCH"
order.referenceContractId = con
order.referenceExchangeId = conExch
order.referenceChangeAmount = refAmt
order.peggedChangeAmount = orderAmt
order.isPeggedChangeAmountDecrease = True
```

Pegged-to-stock orders are similar to pegged-to-benchmark orders, but they're specific to options orders based on the underlying stocks. Further, they're only available on the Boston Options Exchange (BOX) exchange.

When you create a pegged-to-stock order, you don't identify the reference contract because the order price will always be pegged to the price of the option's underlying stock. You also don't identify the pegged change amount. Instead, the order's price is computed by adding `startingPrice` to `delta` times the change in the stock's price. `delta` is assumed to be positive for calls and negative for puts.

A relative order, also called a pegged-to-primary order, seeks more aggressive pricing than that provided by the NBBO. In this order, the `auxPrice` field identifies an offset that should be added to or subtracted from the NBBO when computing the order price. If set, the `lmtPrice` field identifies the maximum acceptable offset.

A passive relative order is similar to a passive order, except that it seeks a less aggressive price than that provided by the NBBO. The fields work in the same way, but the offset is subtracted from the NBBO for buy orders and added to the NBBO for sell orders.

Volatility Order

For U.S. options and futures options, you can create a volatility order by setting `orderType` to `VOL`. In a volatility order, the limit price is based on the implied volatility (IV) of the underlying asset. Chapter 3 discussed volatility and implied volatility.

Volatility orders accept two additional fields:

- `volatilityType` — whether the daily IV value (1) or annual IV value (2) should be taken into account
- `volatility` — the percentage of the volatility that should be used to compute the order price

Volatility orders must use SMART routing, all legs must be based on the same underlying asset, and orders must be configured as `DAY` orders. I'll explain what `DAY` orders are in the following discussion.

7.2.3 Order Timing and Visibility

All of the orders discussed so far either execute immediately, when a market condition occurs, or at the close (`MOC` and `LOC`). But the `Order` class provides fields that allow you to control when the order executes and how long it remains active. Table 7.16 lists nine of these fields.

Table 7.16
Order Timing Fields

Field	Type	Description
`goodAfterTime`	`string`	Date/time when the order will be active
`tif`	`string`	Order's time in force
`activeStartTime`	`string`	The order's start time (if tif is set to GTC)
`activeStopTime`	`string`	The order's stop time (if tif is set to GTC)
`goodTillDate`	`string`	Date/time when the order will stop being active
`outsideRth`	`bool`	Whether the order can be placed outside regular trading hours
`sweepToFill`	`bool`	Whether to immediately execute at best possible prices (SMART only)
`allOrNone`	`bool`	Whether the order has to be fully completed or canceled
`whatIf`	`bool`	Whether TWS should provide commission/margin information for a trade instead of transmitting it
`notHeld`	`bool`	Whether TWS should be held in IB's order book
`transmit`	`bool`	Whether TWS should submit the order

The `goodAfterTime` field makes it possible to delay when an order becomes active. This accepts a string in the format `yyyymmdd hh:mm`, where `yyyymmdd` is the activity date and `hh:mm` is the activity time.

After an order becomes active, the duration of its activity is determined by the `tif` field, which stands for "time in force." This field can be set to one of seven values:

- `DAY` — the order is active for the day only
- `DTC` — the order is deactivated after one day, but not canceled
- `IOC` — any portion of the order that isn't filled immediately is canceled
- `FOK` — if the entire order isn't filled immediately, the entire order is canceled
- `GTC` — the order is active until it's canceled
- `GTD` — the duration is determined by the order's `goodTillDate` field
- `OPG` — the order should execute at opening

It's important to see the difference between the `DAY` and `DTC` settings. If you set `tif` to `DAY`, the order will be canceled if it's not executed within the same day it became active. If you set `tif` to `DTC`, the order will be deactivated if it doesn't execute within the day, but not canceled.

The `IOC` and `FOK` values can also be confusing. If you set `tif` to `IOC` (immediate or canceled), any part of the order that isn't filled immediately will be canceled. If you set tif to `FOK` (fill or kill), the entire order will be canceled if any part of it isn't filled as soon as it becomes available.

If `tif` is set to `GTC`, the order will remain in force until one of five events occur:

- An application calls `cancelOrder` (which I'll present later).
- A corporate action causes a stock split, exchange for shares, or distribution of shares.
- The time given by `activeStopTime` is reached.
- You fail to log into your IB account for more than 90 days.
- The end of the calendar quarter following the current quarter.

If you set `tif` to `GTD`, the order will remain in force until the date and time given by the order's `goodTillDate` field. This field accepts a string in the format `yyyymmdd hh:mm`, where `yyyymmdd` is the last activity date and `hh:mm` is the last activity time.

If you want an order to be executed at the day's opening price, set `tif` to `OPG`. If you want the order to be executable outside regular trading hours, set the `outsideRth` date to a true value.

If speed is important and you're using SMART routing, you can create a market order (`MTK`) and set the `sweepToFill` field to a true value. This tells the SMART algorithm to find the best price and the quantity available at that price, and transmit the corresponding portion of the order for immediate execution. At the same time, it finds the next best price and quantity, and submits a matching quantity for execution.

The last three fields are boolean and determine whether the order will be transmitted. If `whatIf` is true, TWS will provide information about the order's effect on commission and margin, but it won't transmit the order. If `notHeld` is true, the order will be tagged as "post only" and will be held in IB's order book without execution. The last field, `transmit`, identifies whether the order should be created and transmitted or just created.

7.2.4 One Cancels All (OCA) Groups

A one-cancels-all (OCA) group consists of multiple orders and only the fastest of them will execute. Orders in an OCA group are like runners in a running race where only the fastest can cross the finish line.

To configure an order as part of an OCA group, you need to set two fields: `ocaGroup` and `ocaType`. The first is a string that uniquely identifies the group. Every order with the same value for `ocaGroup` will be considered a member of the same OCA group.

The `ocaType` field identifies what happens to the orders after one is partially filled. This can be set to one of three values:

- `1` — Other orders are canceled with overfill protection
- `2` — Other orders are reduced in size with overfill protection
- `3` — Other orders are reduced in size with no overfill protection

Orders in an OCA group may be transmitted to multiple exchanges, and it's conceivable that more than one order in the group will be processed. This excessive execution is called *overfill*. If `ocaType` is set to `1` or `2`, orders will be submitted one at a time to prevent overfill. If `ocaType` is set to `3`, the orders will be executed faster but the danger of overfill becomes a concern.

7.3 Placing Orders

Once you've created a `Contract` and `Order`, IB makes it easy to execute the order. All you need is the client's `placeOrder` function. This accepts three parameters: a unique identifier, a `Contract`, and an `Order`.

After an application places an order, IB will provide the order's status by calling the `openOrder` function of the client's `EWrapper`. This section explains how to code the `placeOrder` and `openOrder` functions. But first, I'll explain how an application can obtain a unique identifier for the order.

7.3.1 Obtaining an Order ID

When coding applications, it's important to provide a unique identifier for each order. This is because the IB server uses the order ID when providing status and other related information. Also, if you're concerned about orders for tech support or tax reasons, you'll need to identify it by number.

Rather than keep track of order IDs yourself, you can ask the IB server to give you a suitable value. You can request this value by calling the client's `reqIds` function, which doesn't accept any arguments.

If an application calls `reqIds`, the server will respond by calling the `EWrapper`'s `nextValidId` function. This provides the next valid ID as a parameter. Later in the chapter, I'll provide code that demonstrates how `reqIds` and `nextValidId` work together in practice.

7.3.2 Placing Orders

To place orders, applications need to call the `placeOrder` function:

`placeOrder(orderId, contract, order)`

The first parameter, `orderId`, serves as a unique identifier for the order. `contract` identifies the `Contract` to be traded and `order` is the `Order` that performs the trade.

After the server receives and executes an order, it will provide the client with status information by invoking two callback functions: `openOrder` and `orderStatus`. The signature of `openOrder` is given as follows:

`openOrder(orderId, contract, order, orderState)`

The last argument, `orderState`, contains status about the order and the account that placed it. This is an instance of `OrderState`, whose fields are listed in Table 7.17.

Table 7.17

Fields of the OrderState Class

Field	Type	Description
status	string	Current status of the order
warningText	string	Warning message
initMarginBefore	string	Current initial margin of the account
initMarginChange	string	Change of the account's initial margin
initMarginAfter	string	Impact on the account's initial -margin
maintMarginBefore	string	Current maintenance margin of the account
maintMarginChange	string	Change of the account's maintenance margin
maintMarginAfter	string	Impact on the account's maintenance margin
equityWithLoanBefore	string	Account's current equity with loan
equityWithLoanChange	string	Change of the account's equity with loan
equityWithLoanAfter	string	Impact on the account's equity with loan
commission	double	Commission generated for the order
minCommission	double	Minimum commission for the order's execution
maxCommission	double	Maximum commission for the order's execution
commissionCurrency	string	Currency for the generated commission

Most of these fields relate to the commission spent for the order or the margin requirements. As discussed in earlier chapters, initial margin is the equity that must be present when the order is placed. Maintenance margin is the equity that must be present during each trading day following the order.

The second callback invoked after order placement is `orderStatus`:

```
orderStatus(int orderId, string status, double filled,
   double remaining, double avgFillPrice, int permId, int parentId,
   double lastFillPrice, int clientId, string whyHeld,
   double mktCapPrice)
```

The `status` argument tells the application what has happened to the order. This can take one of the values listed in Table 7.18.

Table 7.18
Values of Order Status

Value	Description
`PendingSubmit`	Order transmitted but not accepted
`PendingCancel`	Order cancellation request sent but not confirmed
`PreSubmitted`	Simulated order accepted but not submitted
`Submitted`	Order accepted by IB
`ApiCanceled`	Order cancellation requested by API client but not confirmed
`Canceled`	Order canceled
`Filled`	Order completely filled
`Inactive`	Order received but not active because of rejection or cancellation

If the order was filled, the `filled` argument identifies the number of filled positions. If the order was only partially filled, `remaining` identifies the number of positions that weren't filled.

Regarding the purchase/sale price, `avgFillPrice` tells you the average price for the order and `lastFillPrice` tells you the price at which the last positions were filled. If the order was capped, `mktCapPrice` identifies the current capped price.

It's important to distinguish between the different IDs provided by `orderStatus`. `orderId` is the ID of the order whose status is being provided and `permId` is the ID used by TWS. `parentID` is the ID of the order's parent, and I'll discuss parent orders in Chapter 10. `clientId` is the ID of the API client that submitted the order.

7.4 Requesting Order Data

The TWS API provides many functions related to orders, and they can be frustrating to use because of the relationship between request functions and their callbacks. For most operations, there's a one-to-one relationship—every request function has one callback and every callback is invoked as a result of one request function. But the situation is different for orders. Many request functions have multiple callbacks and some callbacks are invoked in response to multiple request functions.

The left column of Table 7.19 lists six functions that request information related to orders, positions, and accounts. The right column lists the callbacks that are invoked to provide response data from IB.

Table 7.19

Requesting Order Data

EClient Request Functions	EWrapper Callback Functions

`reqOpenOrders()/`
`reqAllOpenOrders()/`
`reqAutoOpenOrders(bool bind)`
	`openOrder(int orderId,`
	`    Contract contract, Order order,`
	`    OrderState orderState)/`
	`orderStatus(int orderId,`
	`    string status, double filled,`
	`    double remaining,`
	`    double avgFillPrice,`
	`    int permId, int parentId,`
	`    double lastFillPrice,`
	`    int clientId, string whyHeld,`
	`    double mktCapPrice)`

`reqExecutions(int reqid,`
`    ExecutionFilter filter)`
	`execDetails(int reqId,`
	`    Contract contract,`
	`    Execution execution)/`
	`commissionReport(`
	`    CommissionReport report)`

`reqPositions()`	`position(string account,`
	`    Contract contract, double pos,`
	`    double avgCost)`

`reqAccountSummary(int reqId,`
`    string group, string tags)`
	`accountSummary(int reqId,`
	`    string account, string tag,`
	`    string value, string currency)`

The `reqOpenOrders` and `reqAllOpenOrders` functions have a lot in common. Neither accepts an argument, and the `openOrder` and `orderStatus` callbacks are invoked in response to both. These are the same callbacks invoked when an application places an order with `placeOrder`.

The difference between `reqOpenOrders` and `reqAllOpenOrders` involves the clients responsible for the orders. If an application calls `reqOpenOrders`, it will only receive data about the orders submitted by the client that called `reqOpenOrders`. If an application calls `reqAllOpenOrders`, it will receive the state of all open orders for each client transmitting orders to the target TWS.

`reqAutoOpenOrders` requests status of future orders placed by TWS. This is only available for the master client (Client 0). If its argument is set to true, future orders will be assigned IDs associated with the client calling `reqAutoOpenOrders`.

The `reqExecutions` function requests information about orders that were successfully executed since midnight. This accepts an `ExecutionFilter` that identifies which executed orders should be identified. Table 7.20 lists the different fields of the `ExecutionFilter` structure.

Table 7.20
ExecutionFilter Fields

Value	Type	Description
clientId	int	ID of the client that submitted the order
acctCode	string	Account to which the order was allocated
time	string	Time at which the order was executed
symbol	string	Symbol of the security involved in the order
secType	string	Type of security involved in the order
exchange	string	Exchange that executed the order
side	string	Nature of the order (BUY or SELL)

After an application calls `reqExecutions`, two callback functions are invoked in response: `execDetails` and `commissionReport`. `execDetails` contains information about the executed order and `commissionReport` identifies the order's commission, profit, loss, and yield.

`execDetails` is invoked once for every order executed in the last 24 hours that meet the criteria set by the `ExecutionFilter`. The last argument of `execDetails` is an instance of the `Execution` structure. The fields of the `Execution` structure provide a great deal of information about the executed order, and Table 7.21 lists each of them.

Table 7.21
Execution Fields

Value	Type	Description
orderId	int	ID of the order that was executed
clientId	int	ID of the client that submitted the order
execId	string	ID of the executed order
time	string	Time at which the order was executed
acctNumber	string	Account to which the order was allocated
exchange	string	Exchange that executed the order
side	string	Nature of the order (BOT for purchase, SLD for sale)
shares	double	Number of shares filled by the order
price	double	Execution price excluding commissions
permID	int	ID for the order used by TWS
liquidation	int	Whether the execution occurred because of IB-initiated liquidation
cumQty	double	Cumulative quantity
avgPrice	double	Average price at which the order was filled
orderRef	string	User-specified string associated with the order
evRule	string	Economic Value Rule name and optional argument
evMultiplier	double	How much the market price changes when the contract price changes by 1
modelCode	string	Model code
lastLiquidity	Liquidity	Liquidity type of the execution

The `execId` field provides an identifier for the executed order. If an order was partially filled, each partial execution has its own `execId`. Therefore, one `orderId` might be associated with multiple `execId`s.

IB liquidates orders if margin requirements aren't met or if a derivative's expiration deadline passes. The value of the `liquidation` field identifies whether IB has liquidated an order.

The `price` field of an `Execution` identifies the price of the executed order before commission. To obtain information about an order's commission, an application needs to access `commissionReport`, which is the second callback associated with `reqExecutions`. This provides a single argument, which is an instance of the `ComisssionReport` structure.

Each `CommissionReport` instance has six fields. Table 7.22 lists them and provides a description of each.

Table 7.22

CommissionReport Fields

Value	Type	Description
`execId`	string	ID of the execution that produced the report
`commission`	double	Total commission cost
`currency`	string	Currency in which the order was executed
`realizedPnL`	string	Realized profit and loss
`yield`	double	Income return
`yieldRedemptionDate`	string	Date of yield redemption

In addition to providing the commission cost, a `CommissionReport` also identifies the profit and loss through the `realizedPnL` field. It also identifies the income returned by the order through the `yield` field.

If an executed order establishes a position, an application can request position data by calling `reqPositions`. Keep in mind that an *open order* is an order that hasn't executed yet and an *open position* is a completed trade that hasn't been closed by an opposing trade. This is an important distinction.

After calling `reqPositions`, the application receives data through the `position` callback, which is called once for each open position. This provides four pieces of information: the account holding the position, the contract, the number of positions held, and the average cost of each position.

For general information related to an account, applications can call `reqAccountSummary`. This requires two strings: one identifying a group and one identifying a tag. For financial advisors, the `group` parameter identifies the group whose account information is being sought. Most developers should set `group` to `All` to obtain information for all accounts associated with TWS.

The `tag` parameter of `reqAccountSummary` identifies the nature of the information desired by the application. An application can set this to one or more of the fields listed in the left column of Table 7.23 (on the following page).

Applications must combine tag values in a string separated by commas. For example, suppose you're interested in the leverage and funds available for your account. In this case, you'd set the `tag` parameter of `reqAccountSummary` to `"Leverage,AvailableFunds"`.

Table 7.23
Account Summary Information Tags

Tag	Information Provided
`AccountType`	The IB account structure
`NetLiquidation`	Basis for determining the price of assets in the account
`TotalCashValue`	Cash balance plus futures profit-and-loss
`SettledCash`	Cash recognized at time of settlement
`AccruedCash`	Accrued cash value of stock, commodities, and securities
`BuyingPower`	Value of securities that can be purchased
`EquityWithLoanValue`	Sum of cash, stocks, bonds, and mutual funds
`PreviousEquityWithLoanValue`	Marginable value of equity with loan as of 4:00 PM EST the preceding day
`GrossPositionValue`	Sum of the absolute value of all stock and equity option positions
`RegTEquity`	Regulation T equity for universal account
`RegTMargin`	Regulation T margin for universal account
`SMA`	Special Memorandum Account - line of credit created when Reg T securities increase in value
`InitMarginReq`	Iniital margin requirement of the portfolio
`MaintMarginReq`	Maintenance margin requirement of the portfolio
`AvailableFunds`	Funds available for trading
`ExcessLiquidity`	Excess liquidity as a percentage of the net liquidation value
`Cushion`	Margin cushion before liquidation
`FullInitMarginReq`	Initial margin requirement with no discounts or intraday credits
`FullMaintMarginReq`	Maintenance margin requirement with no discounts or intraday credits
`FullAvailableFunds`	Funds available with no discounts or intraday credits
`FullExcessLiquidity`	Margin cushion before liquidation with no discounts or intraday credits
`LookAheadNextChange`	Time when look-ahead values take effect
`LookAheadInitMarginReq`	Initial margin requirement as of the next period's margin change
`LookAheadMaintMarginReq`	Maintenance margin requirement as of the next period's margin change
`LookAheadAvailableFunds`	Funds available as of the next period's margin change

`LookAhead ExcessLiquidity`	Margin cushion before liquidation as of the next period's margin change
`HighestSeverity`	How close the account is to liquidation
`DayTradesRemaining`	Number of trades before Pattern Day Trading is detected
`Leverage`	Ratio of the gross position value to net liquidation
`$LEDGER`	Access all flags related to cash balance
`$LEDGER:CURRENCY`	Access all flags related to cash balance in the given currency
`$LEDGER:ALL`	Access all flags related to cash balance in all currencies

Most of these are straightforward to understand. Chapter 2 discussed the importance of initial margin requirements and maintenance margin requirements. It mentioned Regulation T, which places legal requirements on margin requirements.

Regulation T defines a new type of account called special memorandum accounts, or *SMAs*. An SMA is a line of credit extended by the broker that increases when a portfolio's securities increase in value. SMAs provide traders with unrealized gains with greater buying power.

An application can request all account information related to an account's cash balance by setting the `tag` parameter of `reqAccountSummary` to `$LEDGER`. By default, the values will be provided in the default currency associated with the account.

7.5 Submitting Orders in Code

To demonstrate how orders can be submitted, the applications presented in this section perform six steps:

1. Create a contract representing shares of Apple stock and an order to buy 200 shares.
2. Get a suitable order ID by calling `reqIds`.
3. Submit the order by calling `placeOrder`.
4. Print order information provided in the `openOrder` and `orderStatus` callbacks.
5. Obtain information about current positions by calling `reqPositions`.
6. Obtain information about the account by calling `reqAccountSummary`.

This discussion explains how these steps can be implemented in Python and C++. In both cases, I've set the order's `transmit` field to a false value. This ensures that readers won't execute orders by mistake.

7.5.1 Submitting Orders in Python

The code in the ch7/submit_order.py module demonstrates how the `reqIds`, `placeOrder`, `reqPositions`, and `reqAccountSummary` functions and their callbacks can be used in a Python script. Listing 7.4 presents the code.

Listing 7.4: ch7/submit_order.py

```
class SubmitOrder(EWrapper, EClient):
    ''' Serves as the client and the wrapper '''

    def __init__(self, addr, port, client_id):
        EWrapper.__init__(self)
        EClient.__init__(self, self)
        self.order_id = None

        # Connect to TWS
        self.connect(addr, port, client_id)

        # Launch the client thread
        thread = Thread(target=self.run)
        thread.start()

    @iswrapper
    def nextValidId(self, order_id):
        ''' Provides the next order ID '''
        self.order_id = order_id
        print('Order ID: '.format(order_id))

    @iswrapper
    def openOrder(self, order_id, contract, order, state):
        ''' Called in response to the submitted order '''
        print('Order status: '.format(state.status))
        print('Commission charged: '.format(state.commission))

    @iswrapper
    def orderStatus(self, order_id, status, filled, remaining,
        avgFillPrice, permId, parentId, lastFillPrice, clientId,
        whyHeld, mktCapPrice):
        ''' Check the status of the submitted order '''
        print('Number of filled positions: {}'.format(filled))
        print('Average fill price: {}'.format(avgFillPrice))
```

Listing 7.4: ch7/submit_order.py (continued)

```python
    @iswrapper
    def position(self, account, contract, pos, avgCost):
        ''' Read information about open positions '''
        print('Position in {}: {}'.format(contract.symbol, pos))

    @iswrapper
    def accountSummary(self, req_id, account, tag, value,
        currency):
        ''' Read information about the account '''
        print('Account {}: {} = {}'.format(account, tag, value))

    def error(self, req_id, code, msg):
        print('Error {}: {}'.format(code, msg))

def main():
    # Create the client and connect to TWS
    client = SubmitOrder('127.0.0.1', 7497, 0)

    # Define a contract for Apple stock
    contract = Contract()
    contract.symbol = 'AAPL'
    contract.secType = 'STK'
    contract.exchange = 'SMART'
    contract.currency = 'USD'

    # Define the limit order
    order = Order()
    order.action = 'BUY'
    order.totalQuantity = 200
    order.orderType = 'LMT'
    order.lmtPrice = 150
    order.transmit = False

    # Obtain a valid ID for the order
    client.req_ids(1)
    time.sleep(2)

    # Place the order
    if client.order_id:
        client.placeOrder(client.order_id, contract, order)
        time.sleep(3)
    else:
        print('Order ID not received. Ending application.')
        sys.exit()
```

Listing 7.4: ch7/submit_order.py (continued)

```python
    # Obtain information about open positions
    client.reqPositions()
    time.sleep(2)

    # Obtain information about account
    client.reqAccountSummary(0, 'All',
        'AccountType,AvailableFunds')
    time.sleep(2)

    # Disconnect from TWS
    client.disconnect()

if __name__ == '__main__':
    main()
```

The `main` function starts by creating an instance of the `SubmitOrder` class, whose constructor establishes a connection to TWS. Next, `main` creates a `Contract` that represents Apple stock and an `Order` that represents a limit order for 200 securities at a price of 150. The `transmit` field is set to `False`, so the order won't actually be submitted when the application is run.

Next, `main` calls `reqIds` to obtain a valid ID for the next order. When the ID becomes available, main calls `placeOrder` with the `Contract` structure, `Order` structure, and ID.

As a result of the `placeOrder` call, two callbacks are invoked. The first, `openOrder`, prints the status of the order and the commission charged. The second, `orderStatus`, prints the number of filled positions and the average price at which the positions were filled.

After submitting the order, main calls `reqPositions` to request information related to the account's open positions and `reqAccountSummary` to request information related to the account. The application accesses the requested data through the `position` and `accountSummary` callbacks.

7.5.2 Submitting Orders in C++

The Ch07_SubmitOrder project demonstrates how to submit orders in C++. The code in Main.cpp creates an instance of the `SubmitOrder` class and calls its functions to place a limit order for 200 shares of Apple at a price of 150. Listing 7.5 presents its code.

Listing 7.5: Ch07_SubmitOrder/Main.cpp

```cpp
int main() {

    // Connect to TWS
    SubmitOrder client("127.0.0.1", 7497, 0);

    // Define a contract
    Contract con = Contract();
    con.symbol = "AAPL";
    con.secType = "STK";
    con.exchange = "SMART";
    con.currency = "USD";

    // Define the limit order
    Order order = Order();
    order.action = "BUY";
    order.totalQuantity = 200;
    order.orderType = "LMT";
    order.lmtPrice = 150;

    // Prevent the order from being executed
    order.transmit = FALSE;

    // Obtain a valid ID for the order
    client.reqIds(1);
    std::this_thread::sleep_for(std::chrono::seconds(2));
    client.signal.waitForSignal();
    client.reader->processMsgs();

    // Place the order
    if (client.orderId != -1) {
        client.placeOrder(client.orderId, con, order);
        std::this_thread::sleep_for(std::chrono::seconds(2));
        client.signal.waitForSignal();
        client.reader->processMsgs();
    }
    else {

        // Exit the application
        std::cout << "Order ID not received. Ending application."
            << std::endl;
        exit(-1);
    }
```

Listing 7.5: Ch07_SubmitOrder/Main.cpp (continued)

```cpp
    // Obtain information about open positions
    client.reqPositions();
    std::this_thread::sleep_for(std::chrono::seconds(2));
    client.signal.waitForSignal();
    client.reader->processMsgs();

    // Obtain information about account
    client.reqAccountSummary(0, "All",
        "AccountType,AvailableFunds");
    std::this_thread::sleep_for(std::chrono::seconds(2));
    client.signal.waitForSignal();
    client.reader->processMsgs();

    // Disconnect
    client.eDisconnect();
    return 0;
}
```

This code calls four central functions of the client: `reqIds`, `placeOrder`, `reqPositions`, and `reqAccountSummary`. In each case, the application receives data through callback functions of the `SubmitOrder` class. Listing 7.6 presents the code for this class.

Listing 7.6: Ch07_SubmitOrder/SubmitOrder.cpp

```cpp
SubmitOrder::SubmitOrder(const char *host, int port,
    int clientId) :

    signal(1000),
    orderId(-1),
    EClientSocket(this, &signal) {

    // Connect to TWS
    bool conn = eConnect(host, port, clientId, false);
    if (conn) {

        // Launch the reader thread
        reader = new EReader(this, &signal);
        reader->start();
    }
    else
        std::cout << "Failed to connect" << std::endl;
}
```

Listing 7.6: Ch07_SubmitOrder/SubmitOrder.cpp (continued)

```cpp
// Provide the ID of the next order
void SubmitOrder::nextValidId(OrderId id) {
    orderId = id;
    std::cout << "Order ID: " << id << std::endl;
}

// Respond when the order is placed
void SubmitOrder::openOrder(OrderId orderId,
    const Contract& contract, const Order& order,
    const OrderState& state) {
    std::cout << "Order status: " << state.status << std::endl;
    std::cout << "Commission charged: " << state.commission
        << std::endl;
}

// Provide the order's status
void SubmitOrder::orderStatus(OrderId orderId,
    const std::string& status, double filled,
    double remaining, double avgFillPrice,
    int permId, int parentId, double lastFillPrice,
    int clientId, const std::string& whyHeld,
    double mktCapPrice) {

    std::cout << "Number of filled positions: "
        << filled << std::endl;
    std::cout << "Average fill price: " << avgFillPrice
        << std::endl;
}

// Provide data related to the account's open positions
void SubmitOrder::position(const std::string& account,
    const Contract& contract, double pos, double avgCost) {
    std::cout << "Position in << " << contract.symbol
        << ": " << pos << std::endl;
}

// Provide data related to the account
void SubmitOrder::accountSummary(int reqId,
    const std::string& account, const std::string& tag,
    const std::string& value, const std::string& currency) {

    std::cout << "Account << " << account << ": "
        << tag << " = " << value << std::endl;
}
```

The `SubmitOrder` constructor creates a connection to TWS, which is expected to be running on the same system as the application. If the connection is successfully established, the constructor creates an `EReader` and launches the reader thread to check for incoming messages.

The first `SubmitOrder` callback, `nextValidId`, is invoked to provide the response to the client's `reqIds` function. The response consists of an integer that the application can use as the ID of its next order.

The next two callbacks, `openOrder` and `orderStatus`, provide the response to the client's `placeOrder` function. `openOrder` prints a string containing the order's status and the commission charged by the broker. `orderStatus` provides more information about the state of the order, and its body prints the number of filled positions and the average price at which the positions were filled.

The `position` callback is invoked once for each open position associated with the current account. The callback's body prints the symbol of the position's security and the position. Note that this callback only provides information about orders that have been successfully executed.

The last callback, `accountSummary`, provides the response to the client's `reqAccountSummary` function. This callback can provide a great deal of information, such as the account's funding level, margin, and buying power. But in this example, the `reqAccountSummary` set its tags to `"AccountType, AvailableFunds"`. As a result, `accountSummary` only provides the account's type and available funds.

7.6 Summary

Applications use `Contract` structures to represent financial instruments and `Order` structures to store data needed to trade contracts. `Contract`s and `Order`s are easy to understand, but it can be hard to keep track of all of their configuration fields.

The fields of the `Contract` class make it possible to precisely identify the financial instrument. For many applications, the only fields you need to set are `symbol`, `secType`, `exchange`, and `currency`. But when trading options and futures contracts, you may need to set additional fields such as `lastTradeDateOrContractMonth` and `primaryExchange`.

If you want non-financial information about a contract, the function to call is `reqContractDetails`. The callback provides a `ContractDetails` structure that holds a great deal of information. `reqContractDetails` is particularly important because it allows applications to obtain a contract's unique ID (`conId`).

The fields of the `Order` structure determine how and when/if the order will be executed. This makes them important to understand—an `Order` whose `orderType` field is set to `MKT` (market) will be submitted immediately while an `Order` whose `orderType` field is set to `LMT` (limit) will only be submitted if the asset's price reaches the limit price or better.

The `tif` field is also important to be familiar with. By default, orders become inactive if not executed within the same day. But you can change this behavior by setting `tif` to values such as `GTC` (good until canceled) or `FOK` (fill or kill).

After discussing the `Order` structure, this chapter explained how to submit orders by calling the `placeOrder` function. This requires a `Contract`, an `Order`, and a unique order ID that can be obtained by calling `nextValidId`. After the client thread calls `placeOrder`, the `openOrder` callback provides information about the order's status.

The last part of this chapter presented functions that request information about orders and the client's account. Of these, the two most helpful are `reqAccountSummary`, which provides account information such as the account's available funds, and `reqPositions`, which provides a list of the account's positions.

Chapter 8

Accessing Financial Data

To be successful in algorithmic trading, you need up-to-date information about the financial instruments you're interested in. The good news is that IB provides many capabilities for obtaining financial data. The bad news is that the functions are complex, there are timing issues to deal with, and many of the data sources aren't free.

At a high level, IB provides access to three types of financial information:

- **technical data** — data for technical analysis
- **fundamental data** — data for fundamental analysis
- **news** — sources of financial news

This chapter discusses each of these types, with most of the discussion focusing on technical data. I'll discuss the functions that make it possible to access data in an application, and toward the end, I'll provide working examples.

8.1 Technical Data

Security analysis is divided into two main camps. Technical analysts monitor a security's prices and volumes, hoping to find patterns that identify when to make trades. Fundamental analysts pay attention to corporate behavior and management. Many savvy investors employ a combination of both. As I've heard it, fundamental analysis tells you which securities to trade and technical analysis tells you when to trade them.

This is a book on algorithmic trading, so it's safe to assume that readers lean more toward technical analysis than fundamental analysis. This is reflected in the TWS API, which provides many functions for technical data and only one for fundamental data.

To present the functions that access technical data, this discussion splits them into two categories depending on how current the data is:

- **market data** — real-time/recent technical data
- **historical data** — technical data from a specific time interval

This section introduces the functions in both categories. First, I'll explain how to access market data.

8.1.1 Market Data

IB refers to current technical data as *market data* and the TWS API provides four functions that access market data. Each has a different delay between updates and each supports a different number of simultaneous requests. Table 8.1 lists the different functions and their characteristics.

Table 8.1

Functions for Accessing Market Data

Function	Update Delay	Data Provided
`reqTickByTickData`	Real-Time	Level I data (ticks)
`reqMktData`	100 ms/200 ms	Level I data
`reqRealTimeBars`	5 sec	Level I data (OHLC)
`reqMarketDepth`	Real-Time	Level II data

Each of these functions accepts a `Contract` that identifies a financial instrument of interest. If you don't know which `Contract` you're interested in, you can search for securities using a market scanner, which I'll discuss in the next chapter.

The callbacks associated with these functions provide market data in one of two forms: *ticks* or *bars*. Ticks are provided at real-time or close to real-time, and can contain any type of technical data. Ticks usually contain small amounts of data to ensure rapid transmission.

Bars are provided at a slower rate than ticks. At minimum, a bar provides a contract's open-high-low-close (OHLC) prices over an interval. Bars are conceptually identical to the candlesticks used in candlestick charts (discussed in Chapter 2).

Market Data Subscriptions

Before you can access technical data through the TWS API, you need to subscribe to data sources. To obtain a subscription, the first step is to open TWS in brokerage mode and go to **Account > Subscribe to Market Data/Research**. This opens a web page that lists the account's subscriptions. Figure 8.1 presents the current subscriptions for my account.

Current Subscriptions

North America

| NYSE (Network A/CTA) Billed by Broker - Trader Workstation | USD 45.00 Month |
| OPRA (US Options Exchanges) - Trader Workstation | USD 32.75 Month |

Global

Global Snapshot Pro and NP - Trader Workstation	Fee Waived
IDEAL FX - Trader Workstation	Fee Waived
US and EU Bond Quotes - Trader Workstation	Fee Waived
US Consolidated Snapshot - Trader Workstation	Fee Waived

Figure 8.1 Current Subscriptions to Market Data

As shown, my account has six subscriptions. The four on the bottom are free and are enabled for all users. The two on top, NYSE and OPRA, are not free.

I subscribed to these data sources so that I could access their data through the TWS API. To be specific, I subscribed to NYSE (New York Stock Exchange) so that I could access technical data related to the securities listed on its exchange. I subscribed to OPRA (Options Price Reporting Authority) so that I could access data related to options.

To configure new subscriptions, click the cog in the upper right of the **Current Subscriptions** box. This opens a second web page labeled **Configure Your Market Data Subscriptions**. As shown in Figure 8.2, TWS recognizes seven types of subscriptions:

1. **Quote bundles** — Package subscriptions for U.S. equities and options
2. **Indexes** — Quotes for different market indices and index funds
3. **Level I (NBBO)** — Simple prices and volumes for securities
4. **Level II (Deep Book)** — All prices and volumes for securities
5. **Fixed income** — Bond ratings and prices
6. **Mutual funds** — U.S. mutual bonds
7. **Other** — Order imbalances and academic research

Figure 8.2 Types of Market Data Subscriptions

The most important categories of technical data are Level I (NBBO) and Level II (Deep Book). Level I market data contains basic information about a security's trades, such as its bid price/size, ask price/size, and last price/size. NBBO stands for *National Best Bid and Offer*, which is the best trading price for a given security. Brokers are required to set their prices according to the NBBO, and Level I data consists of NBBO prices and sales throughout the day.

Level II market data contains all of the prices and sizes available for a given security, not just the NBBO prices. Because all of a security's orders are provided, this type of data is referred to as order book data, deep book data, market depth, or top of book data. Remember that Level II entries represent submitted orders, not executed orders. Savvy traders may submit orders and then adjust or cancel them to influence other traders.

Level II subscriptions are usually much more expensive than Level I subscriptions. For example, a Level I subscription to OTC Markets data costs $30/month and a Level II subscription to OTC Markets data costs $80/month.

Market Data Lines

When you call one of the functions in Table 8.1, you don't just get one message in response. Instead, you create a subscription that provides a stream of several messages separated by a time delay. Each subscription occupies a *market data line*.

At minimum, every client can access up to 100 concurrent lines of market data. After the first month, market data lines are allocated using the greater value of:

- Monthly commissions divided by 8 (USD)
- Equity multiplied by 100 divided by $1,000,000
- 100 (the regular minimum)

For example, if your monthly commissions reach 900 USD, you'll be able to access 112 market data lines because 900/8 = 112.5, which is rounded down to 112.

There's one more point to keep in mind. No matter how many market data lines are available, the TWS API supports a maximum of fifty messages per second. This is important to remember if you intend to access high-speed data for many securities.

The reqTickByTickData Function

reqTickByTickData is one of the newest additions to the API, and it provides market data faster than any other function. It streams ticks in *real-time*, which means it provides updates as each new tick becomes available.

While reqTickByTickData is a powerful function, it has important limitations that need to be remembered:

- Applications can't receive data indefinitely—you must identify how many ticks you want in advance.
- An application must wait 15 seconds before making successive requests for a given instrument.
- It doesn't provide real-time updates for options trades.
- It only provides real-time data for indexes if they're listed on the Chicago Mercantile Exchange (CME).
- It doesn't provide data for combination orders (combos).

The maximum number of streams an application can receive depends on the number of market lines being accessed. If you're reading less than 400 market lines, you can submit requests for three different contracts. You can submit four requests if you're reading between 400 and 500 lines, five requests if you're reading between 500 and 600 lines, and so on.

In both Python and C++, reqTickByTickData accepts five arguments:

1. **reqid** — the request's ID
2. **contract** — the contract of interest
3. **tickType** — the type of tick to be provided
4. **numberOfTicks** — the number of ticks to be provided
5. **ignoreSize** — whether the size (volume) should be provided

By default, reqTickByTickData always provides prices and sizes of reported orders. If ignoreSize is set to true, it will only provide pricing data.

The `numberOfTicks` argument identifies how many ticks should be provided. If this is set to 0, ticks will be provided indefinitely. The `tickType` argument tells IB which prices you're interested in. You can set this to one of four strings:

- **`Last` or `AllLast`** — Last price and size
- **`BidAsk`** — Bid/Ask prices and sizes
- **`MidPoint`** — Average of the bid/ask prices and sizes

`tickType` determines which callback the decoder invokes when it receives a message in response to `reqTickByTickData`. The three possible callbacks are `tickByTickAllLast`, `tickByTickBidAsk`, and `tickByTickMidpoint`.

If an application sets `tickType` to `Last` or `AllLast`, the decoder will invoke the `tickByTickAllLast` callback every time the server sends a response. This callback provides the arguments listed in Table 8.2.

Table 8.2
Parameters of the TickByTickAllLast Callback

Field	Description
`reqId`	Request identifier
`tickType`	Tick type: Last or AllLast
`time`	Timestamp
`price`	Last price
`size`	Last size
`tickAttribLast`	Tick attributes (bit 0 - past limit, 1 - unreported)
`exchange`	Reporting exchange
`specialConditions`	Special conditions

If an application sets `tickType` to `BidAsk`, the decoder will call the wrapper's `tickByTickBidAsk` function every time the server responds. This callback provides seven arguments and Table 8.3 lists them all.

Table 8.3
Parameters of the TickByTickBidAsk Callback

Field	Description
`reqId`	Request identifier
`time`	Timestamp

`bidPrice`	Bid price
`askPrice`	Ask price
`bidSize`	Bid size
`askSize`	Ask size
`tickAttribBidAsk`	Attributes (Bit 0 - bid past low, Bit 1 - ask past high)

The last value of `tickType` is `MidPoint`. If this is set, the decoder will call the wrapper's `tickByTickMidpoint` function with each response from the server. Table 8.4 lists the three arguments provided by `tickByTickMidpoint`.

Table 8.4
Parameters of the TickByTickMidpoint Callback

Field	Description
`reqId`	Request identifier
`time`	Timestamp
`midPoint`	Midpoint (average) of the bid and ask prices

If an application needs data as quickly as possible, setting `tickType` to `tickByTickMidpoint` is a good idea because the callback has the fewest arguments. To demonstrate this, the following code calls `reqTickByTickData` to request ten ticks containing midpoint data for the contract identified by `con`:

```
reqTickByTickData(0, con, "MidPoint", 10, True);
```

As each response is received from TWS, the application's `tickByTickMidpoint` callback will be called. The following code shows how it can be used to print each midpoint and its time:

```
def tickByTickMidPoint(self, reqId, time, midpoint):
    print('Midpoint at time {} is {}'.format(time, midpoint))
```

After requesting ticks, applications can cancel the subscription by calling the client's `cancelTickByTickData` function. The only argument required by this function is the same request ID used for `reqTickByTickData`.

The reqMktData Function

`reqMktData` doesn't provide data as quickly as `reqTickByTickData`. The delay between updates depends on the type of contract:

- **FX pairs** — 5 ms
- **US options** — 100 ms
- **Stocks, futures, and other** — 250 ms

Despite the delay, `reqMktData` has many advantages. First, you can request data for more contracts at a time and you can ask for many types of data with each request. The maximum number of requests is limited by the market data lines and the 50 messages per second limit.

The `reqMktData` function accepts six parameters:

1. `reqid` — the request's ID
2. `contract` — the `Contract` of interest
3. `genericTickList` — the nature of the data to be provided
4. `snapshot` — whether data should be provided as a snapshot
5. `regulatory` — whether snapshots should be provided as regulatory snapshots
6. `mktDataOptions` — list of configuration options (not used)

The data provided by `reqMktData` depends on the security type. For example, if an application requests data for a stock, the response will provide data including the stock's open, high, low, close, volume, bid size, bid price, ask size, ask price, last size, and last price. If an application searches for information about an option, the response will contain more information, including the Greeks discussed in Chapter 3.

The third argument, `genericTickList`, makes it possible to request data in addition to the default data of the security type. It accepts a string containing zero or more codes (also called *generic ticks*) that identify types of data. Table 8.5 lists the different generic ticks available.

Table 8.5

Generic Ticks for Market Data

Code	Description
108	Option volume (stocks)
101	Option open interest (stocks)

184	Historical volatility (stocks)
185	Average option volume (stocks)
186	Option implied volatility
162	Index future premium
165	Miscellaneous
221	Market price
225	Auction values (volume, price, and imbalance)
233	RTVolume (last trade price, last trade size, last trade time, total volume, VWAP, single trade flag)
236	Shortable
256	Inventory
258	Fundamental ratios
411	Real-time historical volatility
456	IBDividends

For example, suppose you want to access the open interest for an option represented by a contract named `con`. The code for open interest is `101`, so you can request the data with the following function call:

```
client.reqMktData(1, con, '101', False, False, [])
```

If an account has a subscription to an exchange, such as NYSE or NASDAQ, an application can request a snapshot of the market's state instead of a stream of ticks. This is accomplished by setting the fourth argument of `reqMktData` to a true value.

If the fifth argument of `reqMktData` is set to true and the account has subscribed to the U.S. Securities Snapshot Bundle, the returned snapshot will contain NBBO prices of U.S. stocks. These snapshots are called *regulatory snapshots*. Each request for a regulatory snapshot costs $0.01, regardless of whether TWS is running in brokerage mode or paper-trading mode.

At this point, `reqMktData` may seem fairly complicated. But the most difficult aspect of using this function is receiving data from its callback functions. The TWS API provides six different callbacks for `reqMktData`, and each provides a different type of data.

Table 8.6 lists the six different callback functions that may be called in response to `reqMktData`.

Table 8.6
Callbacks Associated with reqMktData

Callback	Description
`tickSize(reqId, field, size)`	Provides size-related tick data
`tickPrice(reqId, field, price, attribs)`	Provides price-related tick data
`tickString(reqId, field, value)`	Provides tick data that can be expressed as strings
`tickOptionComputation(reqId, field, impliedVolatility, delta, optPrice, pvDividend, gamma, vega, theta, undPrice)`	Provides data and statistics related to options
`tickEFP(reqId, field, basisPoints, formattedBasisPoints, impliedFuture, holdDays, futureLastTradeDate, dividendImpact, dividendsToLastTradeDate)`	Provides data for exhange-for-physical contracts
`tickGeneric(reqId, field, value)`	Provides generic tick data requested in reqMktData

`tickSize` provides size-related data, such as a security's ask sizes, bid sizes, and volumes. `tickPrice` provides price-related data, such as a security's ask price and bid price. `tickString` provides all string-based tick data. `tickOptionComputation` provides data related to options and `tickEFP` provides data related to exchange-for-physical contracts (discussed in Chapter 5). `tickGeneric` provides access to many of the additional data items listed in Table 8.5.

All of these callbacks provide an integer parameter named `field`. This identifies the nature of the value provided in the following parameter. The `field` parameter takes one of the values listed in Table 8.7.

Table 8.7
Tick Types

Field	Description	Callback	Tick
0	Bid size	`tickSize`	--
1	Bid price	`tickPrice`	--
2	Ask price	`tickPrice`	--

Chapter 8 Accessing Financial Data

3	Ask size	`tickSize`	--
4	Last price	`tickPrice`	--
5	Last size	`tickSize`	--
6	Highest price of the day	`tickPrice`	--
7	Lowest price of the day	`tickPrice`	--
8	Trading volume for the day	`tickSize`	--
9	Closing price for the previous day	`tickPrice`	--
10	Bid option computation	`tickOptionComputation`	--
11	Ask option computation	`tickOptionComputation`	--
12	Last option computation	`tickOptionComputation`	--
13	Model option computation	`tickOptionComputation`	--
14	Current session's opening price	`tickPrice`	--
15	13-week low	`tickPrice`	165
16	13-week high	`tickPrice`	165
17	26-week low	`tickPrice`	165
18	26-week high	`tickPrice`	165
19	52-week low	`tickPrice`	165
20	52-week high	`tickPrice`	165
21	Average volume over 90 days	`tickSize`	165
22	Deprecated	`tickSize`	--
23	30-day historical volatility	`tickGeneric`	104
24	Option implied volatility	`tickGeneric`	106
25	Not used	`tickString`	--
26	Not used	`tickString`	--
27	Call option open interest	`tickSize`	101
28	Put option open interest	`tickSize`	101
29	Call option volume	`tickSize`	100
30	Put option volume	`tickSize`	100
31	Number of points that the index is over the cash index	`tickGeneric`	162
32	Bid exchange	`tickString`	--
33	Ask exchange	`tickString`	--

34	Number of shares that would trade if no new orders were received and the auction was held now	`tickSize`	225
35	Price at which the auction would occur if no new orders were received and the auction was held now	`tickPrice`	225
36	Number of unmatched shares for the next auction	`tickSize`	225
37	Current theoretical calculated value	`tickPrice`	221/232
38	Computed EFP bid price	`tickEFP`	--
39	Computed EFP ask price	`tickEFP`	--
40	Computed EFP last price	`tickEFP`	--
41	Computed EFP open price	`tickEFP`	--
42	Computed high EFP price for the day	`tickEFP`	--
43	Computed low EFP price for the day	`tickEFP`	--
44	Computed closing EFP price for the day	`tickEFP`	--
45	Time of the last trade	`tickString`	--
46	Level of difficulty of short-selling	`tickGeneric`	236
47	Fundamental ratios	`tickString`	258
48	Details of the last trade	`tickString`	233
49	Identifies if a contract is halted	`tickGeneric`	--
50	Implied yield of a bond if purchased at the current bid	`tickPrice`	--
51	Implied yield of a bond if purchased at the current ask	`tickPrice`	--
52	Implied yield of a bond if purchased at the last price	`tickPrice`	--
53	Greek values	`tickOptionComputation`	--
54	Trade count for the day	`tickGeneric`	293
55	Trade count per minute	`tickGeneric`	294
56	Volume per minute	`tickGeneric`	295
57	Last price during regular trading hours	`tickPrice`	318
58	30-day real time historical volatility	`tickGeneric`	411
59	Contract's dividends	`tickString`	456

60	Not currently implemented	`tickString`	--
61	Regulatory imbalance	`tickSize`	--
62	Contract's news feed	`tickString`	292
63	Volume during the last three minutes	`tickSize`	595
64	Volume during the last five minutes	`tickSize`	595
65	Volume during the last ten minutes	`tickSize`	595
66	Delayed bid price	`tickPrice`	--
67	Delayed ask price	`tickPrice`	--
68	Delayed last traded price	`tickPrice`	--
69	Delayed bid size	`tickSize`	--
70	Delayed ask size	`tickSize`	--
71	Delayed last size	`tickSize`	--
72	Delayed highest price of the day	`tickPrice`	--
73	Delayed lowest price of the day	`tickPrice`	--
74	Delayed traded volume of the day	`tickSize`	--
75	The prior day's closing price	`tickPrice`	--
76	Not available	`tickPrice`	--
77	Last trade details excluding unreportable trades	`tickString`	375
78	Not available	`tickPrice`	--
79	Slower mark price update used in system calculations	`tickPrice`	619
80	Greeks based on delayed bid price	`tickPrice`	--
81	Greeks based on delayed ask price	`tickPrice`	--
82	Greeks based on delayed last price	`tickPrice`	--
83	Computed Greeks and model's implied volatility based on delayed prices	`tickPrice`	--
84	Exchange of last traded price	`tickString`	--
85	Timestamp of last trade	`tickString`	--
86	Total number of outstanding futures contracts	`tickSize`	588
87	Average volume of the corresponding option contracts	`tickSize`	105
88	Delayed time of the last trade	`tickString`	--
89	Number of shares available to short	`tickSize`	236

An example will clarify how the `field` parameter can be used. If an application calls `reqMktData` for a stock, the stock's ask price (0), bid price (2), and close price (9) will be provided by the `tickPrice` callback. The following Python code uses the `field` parameter to determine which price is being provided:

```
def tickPrice(reqId, field, price, attribs):
    if field == 0:
        self.ask_price = price
    elif field == 2:
        self.bid_price = price
    elif field == 9:
        self.close_price = price
```

The fourth column of the table identifies the generic tick that needs to be inserted into `reqMktData`. For example, if you want to determine how difficult it is to short-sell a security (tick type 46), you need to insert the code `236` into the third parameter of `reqMktData`.

The reqRealTimeBars Function

Chapter 2 explained how candlestick charts work and how each candlestick identifies a security's opening, low, high, and closing (OHLC) prices. In code, you can request this information by calling `reqRealTimeBars`. This provides data every five seconds and an application can submit up to 60 requests every 10 minutes.

`reqRealTimeBars` accepts six parameters:

- `reqId` — request identifier
- `contract` — the `Contract` of interest
- `barSize` — always set to 5
- `whatToShow` — type of desired data
- `useRTH` — whether to access data outside of regular trading hours
- `realTimeBarsOptions` — configuration options (not used)

The `whatToShow` parameter tells TWS about the prices you're interested in. You can set this to `BID` for the current buying price, `ASK` for the current selling price, or `MIDPOINT` for the average of the two. You can also set it to `TRADES` to get information about recent transactions. If an application sets `whatToShow` to `TRADES`, it can access more information.

The `useRTH` parameter looks simple, but the values are the reverse of what you'd expect. Setting `useRTH` to 0 tells TWS to access data inside and outside of regular trading hours. Setting the value to 1 tells TWS to restrict data to that generated within regular trading hours.

For example, the following code requests bid prices for the contract identified by `con`. The fifth argument tells TWS to access data inside and outside of regular trading hours.

```
reqRealTimeBars(id, con, 5, 'BID', True, [])
```

After an application calls `reqRealTimeBars`, the response will be provided in the callback function `realtimeBar`:

```
realtimeBar(reqId, time, open, high, low, close,
    volume, WAP, count)
```

`volume` is the daily volume, `WAP` is the Weighted Average Price, and `count` is the number of trades in the last five seconds. These three values are only available if the `whatToShow` parameter was set to TRADES.

After making the initial request with `reqRealTimeBars`, an application can cancel the subscription with `cancelRealTimeBars`. This accepts the ID of the original request.

The reqMktDepth Function

Earlier, I explained that Level II data contains all of the bid/ask prices for a security instead of just the NBBO prices. If an account has a subscription to a Level II data source, an application can request this data by calling `reqMktDepth`. This function accepts five arguments:

1. `reqId` — request identifier
2. `contract` — the Contract of interest
3. `numRows` — number of trades to provide data for
4. `isSmartDepth` — identifies whether this is a SMART depth request
5. `mktDepthOptions` — configures the request

In earlier versions of the TWS API, requests for Level II data had to be routed directly to the security's exchange. But in the current version, an application can set `isSmartDepth` to a true value, which tells the SMART router to access aggregated depth of market data.

If an application routes the request directly to the exchange, the response will be provided by the `updateMktDepth` callback, whose signature is given as:

```
updateMktDepth(reqId, position, operation, side, price, size)
```

If the exchange isn't specified, the response data will be provided through the `updateMktDepth2` callback. Its signature is given as follows:

```
updateMktDepthL2(reqId, position, marketMaker, operation,
    side, price, size, isSmartDepth)
```

The `position` argument is important in both callbacks. The first time the callback is invoked, it provides all requested rows to the client. After that, the callback will provide updates, and in some cases, the updates will modify rows provided earlier.

At the start, the application will receive all available rows. As the row data changes over time, TWS will provide updates that specify which rows should be updated and the operations to be performed. This is given by the `operation` parameter, which will be set to 0 for insertion, 1 for updating, or 2 for removal.

8.1.2 Historical Data

If you're interested in a contract's past technical data, such as for backtesting or statistical analysis, you can call one of the historical data functions of the TWS API. This discussion focuses on three of them:

- **`reqHistoricalData`** — Provides bars from a specified time interval
- **`reqHistoricalTicks`** — Provides ticks from a specified time interval
- **`reqHistogramData`** — Provides a histogram containing data from a given period

This discussion will explain what these functions accomplish and how to access them in code. I'll also present the callback functions that provide data in response.

The reqHistoricalData Function

`reqHistoricalData` is like `reqRealTimeBars`, and it accepts similar parameters and returns data in the form of bars. But `reqHistoricalData` provides bars for any time interval in IB's storage and you can configure how the bars are provided.

`reqHistoricalData` accepts nine parameters:

1. `reqId` — request identifier
2. `contract` — the `Contract` of interest
3. `endDateTime` — The last date/time of interest (`yyyyMMdd HH:mm:ss`)
4. `durationString` — The length of time to be measured
5. `barSizeSetting` — The time interval for each bar
6. `whatToShow` — type of desired data
7. `useRTH` — whether to access data outside of regular trading hours
8. `formatDate` — desired format for time/date data
9. `keepUpToDate` — whether to provide continuous updates

When you request historical data through `reqHistoricalData`, you don't set the starting and ending times. Instead, you set the ending time (`endDateTime`) and the interval preceding the ending time (`durationString`). When setting `durationString`, it's important to use the right units (`S` for seconds, `D` for days, `W` for weeks, `M` for months, and `Y` for years).

For example, suppose you want historical data for two weeks preceding February 7, 2019. In this case, you'd set `endDateTime` to `20190202` and `durationString` to `"2 W"`.

The `barSizeSetting` specifies the interval for which each bar provides data. An application can set this to one of twelve strings: `1 sec`, `5 secs`, `15 secs`, `30 secs`, `1 min`, `2 mins`, `3 mins`, `5 mins`, `15 mins`, `30 mins`, `1 hour`, or `1 day`.

The `whatToShow` parameter of `reqHistoricalData` is similar to that of `reqRealTimeBars` in that you can set its value to `BID`, `ASK`, `MIDPOINT`, and `TRADES`. But in `reqHistoricalData`, there are five more settings available: `BID_ASK`, `HISTORICAL_VOLATILITY`, `OPTION_IMPLIED_VOLATILITY`, `FEE_RATE`, and `REBATE_RATE`.

Each historical bar identifies its time using a format determined by the `formatDate` parameter. If `formatDate` is set to `1`, a bar's time will be given in the `yyyyMMdd HH:mm:ss` format. If `formatDate` is set to `2`, the time will be given as the number of seconds from the epoch (January 1, 1970).

By default, `reqHistoricalData` only provides bars up to the date/time set by the `endDateTime` parameter. But if an application sets `keepUpToDate` to true and doesn't set a value for `endDateTime`, the function will provide bars up to the current time. Current bars are provided through the `historicalDataUpdate` callback instead of the `historicalData` callback. Both have the same signature and provide the same data.

As with `reqRealTimeBars`, the data provided in response to `reqHistoricalData` is given in bars. But the bars provided by `historicalData` are given as instances of the `BarData` class. This contains eight fields:

- `date` — date/time represented by the bar
- `high` — the highest price during the interval
- `low` — the lowest price during the interval
- `open` — the price at the start of the interval
- `close` — the price at the end of the interval
- `barCount` — the bar count
- `volume` — the average daily volume
- `count` — the number of trades during the interval

After an application has requested historical data, it can cancel the subscription by calling `cancelHistoricalData`. The only required argument is the ID of the original request.

The reqHistoricalTicks Function

`reqHistoricalTicks` is similar to `reqHistoricalData`, but provides less information. In fact, each tick only provides the price and size for each requested time. This function accepts nine arguments:

1. `reqId` — request ID
2. `contract` — the `Contract` of interest
3. `startDateTime` — The first date/time of interest (`yyyyMMdd HH:mm:ss`)
4. `endDateTime` — The last date/time of interest (`yyyyMMdd HH:mm:ss`)
5. `numberOfTicks` — The number of ticks during the interval
6. `whatToShow` — type of desired data (`Bid_Ask`, `Midpoint`, or `Trades`)
7. `useRTH` — whether to access data outside of regular trading hours
8. `ignoreSize` — whether to remove the `size` field from the output
9. `miscOptions` — reserved for future use

Unlike `reqHistoricalData`, `reqHistoricalTicks` requires the starting date and time and the ending date and time. Instead of setting the time interval for each bar, an application needs to provide the number of ticks between the starting time and end time.

Another difference between `reqHistoricalTicks` and `reqHistoricalData` is that `reqHistoricalTicks` can't be configured to provide current data. This means the callback usually executes once and provides a collection containing multiple ticks of interest.

If an application sets the `whatToShow` parameter to `Bid_Ask`, the `historicalTicksBidAsk` callback will provide the response data. Its signature is given as follows:

```
historicalTicksBidAsk(int reqId, HistoricalTickBidAsk[] ticks,
    bool done)
```

If `whatToShow` is set to a value other than `Bid_Ask`, the response data will be provided in the `historicalTicks` callback:

```
historicalTicks(int reqId, HistoricalTick[] ticks, bool done)
```

The `historicalTicks` callback structures its data in `HistoricalTick` structures. Each `HistoricalTick` has three fields:

- **time** — seconds since January 1, 1970
- **price** — tick price
- **size** — tick size

In contrast, the `historicalTicksBidAsk` callback provides its data in `HistoricalTiskBidAsk` structures. Each structure contains the following fields:

- **time** — seconds since January 1, 1970
- **tickAttribBidAsk** — tick attributes
- **priceBid** — bid price
- **sizeBid** — bid size
- **priceAsk** — ask price
- **sizeAsk** — ask size

After an application calls `reqHistoricalData`, it can cancel the operation by calling `cancelHistoricalData`. The only parameter for the function is the ID of the original request.

The reqHistogram Function

`reqHistogram` is similar to `reqHistoricalData`, but instead of providing prices at different times, it provides the number of trades at different prices. This function accepts four arguments:

1. `reqId` — the request ID
2. `contract` — the contract of interest
3. `useRTH` — whether to use regular trading hours
4. `timePeriod` — the time period of interest

The `timePeriod` argument sets the duration of the analysis, ending with the present. This duration needs to be fully spelled out, as in `"3 days"` or `"1 week"`.

After requesting histogram data, an application can access the results through the `histogramData` callback:

```
histogramData(reqId, HistogramData[])
```

The second parameter contains a series of `HistogramData` structures. Each `HistogramData` has two fields: `count` and `price`. `count` identifies how many securities were traded when the security's price equaled `price`.

8.2 Fundamental Data

Up to this point, all of the functions discussed in this chapter have focused on technical data, which includes information like opening prices, closing prices, and volumes. But if you want a thorough view of a corporation, you need to examine its fundamental data, which includes information like revenue, earnings, debt, and analyst's estimates.

If an account has the right subscriptions, applications can access fundamental data by calling `reqFundamentalData`. This makes it possible to access reports containing fundamental data. It accepts four arguments:

1. `reqId` — request identifier
2. `contract` — the `Contract` of interest
3. `reportType` — identifier of the report of interest
4. `fundamentalDataOptions` — reserved for future use

The `reportType` parameter is particularly important, and it can be set to one of six values. Table 8.8 lists the different identifiers and their corresponding reports.

Table 8.8
Reports Available through reqFundamentalData

Report Identifier	Subscription	Description
`ReportsFinSummary`	Fundamentals	Financial summary
`ReportsOwnership`	Fundamentals	Company's ownership (large)
`ReportSnapshot`	Fundamentals	Company's financial overview
`ReportsFinStatements`	Fundamentals	Financial statements
`RESC`	Fundamentals	Analyst estimates
`CalendarReport`	Wall Street Horizon	Corporate calendar

The middle column identifies the subscription needed to access the report. For the first five reports, the user needs a Fundamentals subscription, which is available by default. To access calendar reports, the account needs to be subscribed to Wall Street Horizon (WTH).

When the decoder receives a response to `reqFundamentalData`, it invokes `fundamentalData`, whose parameters are the request ID and a string containing the report data.

As an example, suppose you want to access an overview of the DMC Group corporation (BOOM). The following Python code creates a contract and calls `reqFundamentalData` to obtain a report snapshot.

```
con = Contract()
con.symbol = 'BOOM'
con.secType = 'STK'
con.exchange = 'SMART'
con.currency = 'USD'
reqFundamentalData(0, con, 'ReportSnapshot', [])
```

After the server responds, the application can access the report through the second argument of the `fundamentalData` callback.

```
fundamentalData(reqId, data)
```

The `data` argument is a string whose text is formatted according to the extensible markup language (XML) format.

8.3 Accessing News

TWS makes it easy to set up news subscriptions. You can access and modify account subscriptions in the main menu by going to **File > Global Configuration...** and opening the **Information Tools** entry. Then select **News Configuration** and then **Settings**, and you can see the news sources that have been subscribed to.

In code, applications can check the account's news subscriptions by calling `reqNewsProviders`. When a response is received, the `newsProviders` callback will be called. This provides a list/array of `NewsProvider` structures, and each `NewsProvider` has a code field that provides its identifier and a name field that stores its full name.

Table 8.9 lists the codes and names associated with seven different news sources. The first three are automatically available through the API. The last four need to be specifically enabled in TWS.

Table 8.9

News Sources

Code	Name
BREG	Briefing.com General Market Columns
BRFUPDN	Briefing.com Analyst Actions
DJNL	Dow Jones Newsletters
BRF	Briefing Trader
BZ	Benzinga Pro
FLY	Fly on the Wall
MT	Midnight Trader

At the time of this writing, the API doesn't allow applications to add or remove subscriptions. But applications can access three types of news:

1. **bulletins** — Updates from Interactive Brokers
2. **news feeds** — Current news
3. **historical news articles** — Articles from a specific time

For the last two options, the application receives headlines. Then it can access the articles corresponding to headlines of interest.

8.3.1 Bulletins

IB provides news bulletins related to topics like system concerns and exchange issues. Applications can access these bulletins by calling reqNewsBulletins with a boolean that identifies whether all of the day's bulletins should be provided or just the latest.

Applications can access bulletin data through the updateNewsBulletin callback, which provides four parameters:

- **msgid** — Unique identifier for the bulletin
- **msgType** — Nature of the bulletin
- **message** — Bulletin content
- **origExchange** — Name of exchange that produced the issue (if applicable)

msgType will be set to 2 if an exchange is no longer available for trading and 3 if an exchange is available for trading. For regular news bulletins, msgType will be set to 1.

8.3.2 News Feeds

Applications can access news feeds by calling the reqMktData function discussed earlier in the chapter. This requires two steps:

1. Create a Contract representing the news provider using its code
2. Call reqMktData and add "mdoff, 292" to the genericTickList parameters

For example, the following Python code creates a contract representing the BriefingTrader news provider. Then it calls reqMktData to obtain headlines.

```
contract = Contract()
contract.symbol = "BRFG:BRFG_ALL"
contract.secType = "NEWS"
contract.exchange = "BRFG"
self.reqMktData(123, contract, "mdoff, 292", False, False, [])
```

This code accomplishes the same result in C++:

```
Contract contract;
contract.symbol = "BRF: BRF_ALL";
contract.secType = "NEWS";
contract.exchange = "BRF";
client->reqMktData(123, contract, "mdoff, 292",
    false, false, tags);
```

After the server receives the request, it will provide headlines through the `tickNews` callback. This has six arguments:

1. `reqId` — request identifier
2. `timeStamp` — time
3. `providerCode` — code of the news provider
4. `articleId` — unique ID for the article corresponding to the headline
5. `headline` — current headline
6. `extraData` — additional information

If a headline looks interesting, an application can access the content of the article by calling `reqNewsArticle` with the following parameters:

- `reqId` — request identifier
- `providerCode` — code of the news provider
- `articleId` — ID of the article
- `newsArticleOptions` — reserved for internal use

After the server receives the request and provides a message, the `newsArticle` callback will be invoked. This provides the ID of the corresponding request (`requestId`), the type of article (`articleType`), and the text of the article (`articleText`).

If `articleType` is 0, the text will be in plain text or HTML. If `articleType` is 1, text is provided in binary form, or PDF.

8.3.3 Historical News

If you're interested in past news about a specific contract, you can call `reqHistoricalNews`. This accepts seven arguments:

1. `reqId` — request identifier
2. `conId` — unique ID of the contract
3. `providerCodes` — codes of the news providers
4. `startDateTime` — initial date/time of interest
5. `endDateTime` — final date/time of interest
6. `totalResults` — maximum number of headlines to read
7. `historicalNewsOptions` — reserved for internal use

This tells the server to search through the headlines from `startDateTime` to `endDateTime` for the news sources identified in `providerCodes`. These are the same codes listed in Table 8.9, and if multiple news sources are requested, the codes can be separated with plus (+) signs. The last argument, `totalResults`, identifies the maximum number of headlines to fetch, and can be set to a value between 1 and 300.

After making the request, an application can access the response data through the `historicalNews` callback:

```
historicalNews(reqId, time, providerCode, articleId, headline)
```

The last two arguments are the most important. `headline` contains the headline of a news article, and `articleId` can be used in `reqNewsArticle` to obtain the article's content.

8.4 Accessing Financial Data in Code

To demonstrate how to access financial data, the application presented in this section performs six steps:

1. Creates a `Contract` representing shares of IBM stock.
2. Obtains real-time ticks by calling `reqTickByTickData`.
3. Requests near-real-time market data by calling `reqMktData`.
4. Requests bars containing OHLC (open-high-low-close) data every five seconds by calling `reqRealTimeBars`.
5. Requests two weeks of historical data by calling `reqHistoricalData`.
6. Requests a report snapshot of IBM stock by calling `reqFundamentalData`.

The `reqTickByTickData`, `reqRealTimeBars`, and `reqHistoricalData` functions accept an argument that identifies which type of price data should be provided. In each case, the argument is set to `MIDPOINT`. This means that the prices returned by the callbacks will equal the average of the bid and ask prices for the IBM stock.

The third argument of `reqFundamentalData` is set to `ReportSnapshot`. As a result, the callback will return XML text containing data from IBM's financial reports.

The following sections explain how these operations can be performed in Python and C++. The functions have the same name in both languages, but in some cases, their arguments have different data types.

8.4.1 Accessing Financial Data in Python

The code in the ch8/market_reader.py module demonstrates how an application can read financial data by calling `reqTickByTickData`, `reqMktData`, `reqRealTimeBars`, `reqHistoricalData`, and `reqFundamentalData`. Listing 8.1 presents the code.

Listing 8.1: ch8/market_reader.py

```python
class MarketReader(EWrapper, EClient):
    ''' Serves as the client and the wrapper '''

    def __init__(self, addr, port, client_id):
        EWrapper.__init__(self)
        EClient.__init__(self, self)

        # Connect to TWS
        self.connect(addr, port, client_id)

        # Launch the client thread
        thread = Thread(target=self.run)
        thread.start()

    @iswrapper
    def tickByTickMidPoint(self, reqId, tick_time, midpoint):
        ''' Called in response to reqTickByTickData '''
        print('tickByTickMidPoint - Midpoint tick: {}'.
            format(midpoint))

    @iswrapper
    def tickPrice(self, reqId, field, price, attribs):
        ''' Called in response to reqMktData '''
        print('tickPrice - field: {}, price: {}'.format(field,
            price))

    @iswrapper
    def tickSize(self, reqId, field, size):
        ''' Called in response to reqMktData '''
        print('tickSize - field: {}, size: {}'.format(field,
            size))

    @iswrapper
    def realtimeBar(self, reqId, time, open, high, low,
        close, volume, WAP, count):
        ''' Called in response to reqRealTimeBars '''
        print('realtimeBar - Opening price: {}'.format(open))
```

Listing 8.1: ch8/market_reader.py (Continued)

```python
        @iswrapper
        def historicalData(self, reqId, bar):
            ''' Called in response to reqHistoricalData '''
            print('historicalData - Close price: {}'
                .format(bar.close))

        @iswrapper
        def fundamentalData(self, reqId, data):
            ''' Called in response to reqFundamentalData '''
            print('Fundamental data: ' + data)

        def error(self, reqId, code, msg):
            print('Error {}: {}'.format(code, msg))

def main():
    # Create the client and connect to TWS
    client = MarketReader('127.0.0.1', 7497, 0)

    # Request the current time
    con = Contract()
    con.symbol = 'IBM'
    con.secType = 'STK'
    con.exchange = 'SMART'
    con.currency = 'USD'

    # Request ten ticks containing midpoint data
    client.reqTickByTickData(0, con, 'MidPoint', 10, True)

    # Request market data
    client.reqMktData(1, con, '', False, False, [])

    # Request current bars
    client.reqRealTimeBars(2, con, 5, 'MIDPOINT', True, [])

    # Request historical bars
    now = datetime.now().strftime("%Y%m%d, %H:%M:%S")
    client.reqHistoricalData(3, con, now, '2 w', '1 day',
        'MIDPOINT', False, 1, False, [])

    # Request fundamental data
    client.reqFundamentalData(4, con, 'ReportSnapshot', [])

    time.sleep(5)
    client.disconnect()
```

When calling `reqTickByTickData`, remember that the callback function depends on the type of price data. In this case, the third argument of `reqTickByTickData` is `Midpoint`, so the callback that provides data is `tickByTickMidpoint`.

In contrast, one call to `reqMktData` may require multiple callbacks. In Listing 8.1, the `tickPrice` callback prints floating-point values and `tickSize` prints integer values. Keep in mind that not all values printed in `tickPrice` are prices and not all values printed in `tickSize` are sizes.

`reqRealTimeBars` only has one associated callback, `realTimeBar`, but this can be tricky to work with. The callback has ten arguments, but the last three are only available if the sixth argument of `reqRealTimeBars` is set to `TRADES`. Otherwise, the application can only access the callback's `time`, `open`, `high`, `low`, and `close` values.

8.4.2 Accessing Financial Data in C++

The code in the Ch08_MarketReader project shows how financial data can be accessed in C++. Listing 8.2 presents the code of the `main` function, which creates an instance of the `MarketReader` class and a `Contract` for IBM stock. Then it calls `reqTickByTickData`, `reqMktData`, `reqRealTimeBars`, `reqHistoricalData`, and `reqFundamentalData` to obtain financial information about the contract.

Listing 8.2: Ch08_MarketReader/Main.cpp

```cpp
// Connect to TWS or IB Gateway
MarketReader client("127.0.0.1", 7497, 0);

// Request ten ticks containing midpoint data
Contract con = Contract();
con.symbol = "IBM";
con.secType = "STK";
con.exchange = "SMART";
con.currency = "USD";
client.reqTickByTickData(0, con, "MidPoint", 10, TRUE);
std::this_thread::sleep_for(std::chrono::seconds(2));
client.signal.waitForSignal();
client.reader->processMsgs();

// Request market data
client.reqMktData(1, con, "", FALSE, FALSE,
  TagValueListSPtr());
std::this_thread::sleep_for(std::chrono::seconds(2));
client.signal.waitForSignal();
client.reader->processMsgs();
```

Listing 8.2: Ch08_MarketReader/main.cpp (Continued)

```cpp
// Request current bars
client.reqRealTimeBars(2, con, 5, "MIDPOINT", TRUE,
    TagValueListSPtr());
std::this_thread::sleep_for(std::chrono::seconds(2));
client.signal.waitForSignal();
client.reader->processMsgs();

// Request historical bars
time_t tm = std::time(nullptr);
std::tm loc_tm = *std::localtime(&tm);
std::ostringstream ostr;
ostr << std::put_time(&loc_tm, "%Y%m%d, %H:%M:%S");
client.reqHistoricalData(3, con, ostr.str(), "2 w", "1 day",
    "MIDPOINT", 1, 1, FALSE, TagValueListSPtr());
std::this_thread::sleep_for(std::chrono::seconds(2));
client.signal.waitForSignal();
client.reader->processMsgs();

// Request fundamental data
client.reqFundamentalData(4, con, "ReportSnapshot",
    TagValueListSPtr());
std::this_thread::sleep_for(std::chrono::seconds(2));
client.signal.waitForSignal();
client.reader->processMsgs();

// Disconnect
client.eDisconnect();
return 0;
}
```

The third argument of `reqTickByTickData` is set to `MidPoint`, which means the `tickBytickMidPoint` callback will provide the average of the bid and ask prices. The fourth argument of `reqTickByTickData` is 10, which means the application is only looking for ten ticks.

The application wants historical data for the preceding two weeks, so it calls `reqHistoricalData` and sets the fourth argument to `2 w`. The historical data should end with the current date, so the `main` function creates a `time_t` structure for the present day and converts it into a string by calling `put_time`.

The `MarketReader` class extends `EClientSocket` and `EWrapper`, which means it provides request functions and callback functions. The code for the class is contained in the MarketReader.cpp file, and Listing 8.3 presents its content.

Listing 8.3: Ch08_MarketReader/MarketReader.cpp

```cpp
MarketReader::MarketReader(const char *host, int port,
  int clientId) : signal(1000), orderId(-1),
  EClientSocket(this, &signal) {

  // Connect to TWS
  bool conn = eConnect(host, port, clientId, false);
  if (conn) {

    // Launch the reader thread
    reader = new EReader(this, &signal);
    reader->start();
  }
  else
    std::cout << "Failed to connect" << std::endl;
}

// Called in response to reqTickByTickData
void MarketReader::tickByTickMidPoint(int reqId, time_t time,
double midPoint) {
  std::cout << "tickByTickMidPoint - Midpoint tick: "
    << midPoint << std::endl;
}

// Called in response to reqMktData
void MarketReader::tickPrice(TickerId tickerId, TickType field,
  double price, const TickAttrib& attrib) {
  std::cout << "tickPrice - field: " << field << ", price: "
    << price << std::endl;
}

// Called in response to reqMktData
void MarketReader::tickSize(TickerId tickerId, TickType field,
  int size) {
  std::cout << "tickSize - field: " << field << ", size: "
    << size << std::endl;
}

// Called in response to reqRealTimeBars
void MarketReader::realtimeBar(TickerId reqId, long time,
  double open, double high, double low, double close,
  long volume, double wap, int count) {
  std::cout << "realtimeBar - Opening price: " << open
    << std::endl;
}
```

Listing 8.3: Ch08_MarketReader/MarketReader.cpp (Continued)

```
// Called in response to reqHistoricalData
void MarketReader::historicalData(TickerId reqId, const Bar& bar)
{
  std::cout << "historicalData - Close price: "
    << bar.close << std::endl;
}

// Called in response to reqFundamentalData
void MarketReader::fundamentalData(TickerId reqId,
  const std::string& data) {
  std::cout << "Fundamental data: " << data << std::endl;
}

void MarketReader::error(int id, int code,
  const std::string& msg) {
  std::cout << "Error: " << code << ": " << msg << std::endl;
}
```

The `tickPrice` and `tickSize` callbacks are invoked in response to `reqMktData`, with `tickPrice` providing floating-point values and `tickSize` providing integer values. Both callbacks have a `TickType` value named `field` that identifies precisely what the output values represent,

Judging by its signature, you might think that the `realTimeBar` callback provides the `volume`, `wap` (weighted average price), and `count` of the IBM stock trades. But these values are only available if the sixth argument of `reqRealTimeBars` is set to `TRADES`. The `main` function sets this argument to `MIDPOINT`, so the only arguments that provide helpful values are `time`, `open`, `high`, `low`, and `close`.

The `data` argument of the `fundamentalData` callback provides XML-formatted text. In this example, the `main` function set the third argument of `reqFundamentalData` to `ReportSnapshot`, so the XML contains information related to IBM's recent financial reports. Reading XML is beyond the scope of this book, but I like to use TinyXML-2 (www.grinninglizard.com/tinyxml2). It's fast, free, and easy to code with.

8.5 Summary

The TWS API provides several functions for accessing financial data, and each has different strengths and weaknesses. For example, `reqTickByTickData` is faster than `reqMktData`, but `reqMktData` can provide more types of information.

When using these functions, it's vital to remember the limitations. For example, the TWS API supports a maximum of 50 messages per second. For Level I data, the maximum number of simultaneous subscriptions is determined by the number of market lines, which is 100 for most users. For Level II data, the maximum number of subscriptions drops to 3 for most users.

The timing statistics presented in the TWS API documentation are impressive, but you should always take network latency into account. Lag affects online traders as well as online gamers, and if your trading algorithm requires split-second precision, you may run into difficulty.

Chapter 9

Scanning for Securities

Each function presented in the preceding chapter requires a contract that identifies a specific financial instrument. But what if you don't know which contract you're interested in? What if you want IB to give you a list of interesting securities? In this case, you can take advantage of IB's Advanced Market Scanner, which accepts financial criteria and returns up to fifty suitable contracts.

Chapter 2 explained how to launch the scanner in TWS. This chapter explains how to access the scanner programmatically. The good news is that the functions are easy to work with. The bad news is there are a bewildering number of barely-documented search parameters. In addition, an application can only perform ten scans at a time.

Using the market scanner involves four steps:

1. Create a `ScannerSubscription`.
2. Request a scanner subscription by calling `reqScannerSubscription`.
3. Access the scan results through the `scannerData` callback.
4. Terminate the subscription by calling `cancelScannerSubscription`.

As the term *subscription* implies, IB provides scan results periodically after an application calls `reqScannerSubscription`. The application can halt the scanner by calling `cancelScannerSubscription`.

This chapter walks through the steps of using IB's scanner and presents the code needed to set up a subscription. At the end of the chapter, I'll present an application that uses the scanner to search for stocks according to price, trading volume, and market capitalization.

9.1 Creating a Scanner Subscription

To access the market scanner in code, the first step is to create an instance of the `ScannerSubscription` structure. This contains fields that tell the scanner about the types of contracts and selection criteria that you're interested in. Table 9.1 lists the different fields that can be set.

Table 9.1
Fields of the ScannerSubscription Structure

Report Identifier	Type	Description
`instrument`	`string`	Type of instrument to be searched
`locationCode`	`string`	The request's location
`scanCode`	`string`	Scanner criteria code
`numberOfRows`	`int`	Number of rows returned by the query
`abovePrice`	`double`	Filters out contracts whose price is below this value
`belowPrice`	`double`	Filters out contracts whose price is above this value
`aboveVolume`	`int`	Filters out contracts whose volume is below
`averageOptionVolumeAbove`	`int`	Filters out contracts whose average option volume is below this value
`marketCapAbove`	`double`	Filters out contracts whose market capitalization is below this value
`marketCapBelow`	`double`	Filters out contracts whose market capitalization is above this value
`moodyRatingAbove`	`string`	Filters out contracts whose Moody's rating is below this value
`moodyRatingBelow`	`string`	Filters out contracts whose Moody's rating is above this value
`spRatingAbove`	`string`	Filters out contracts whose S&P rating is below this value
`spRatingBelow`	`string`	Filters out contracts whose S&P rating is above this value
`maturityDateAbove`	`string`	Filters out contracts whose maturity date is earlier than the given date
`maturityDateBelow`	`string`	Filters out contracts whose maturity date is older than the given date

couponRateAbove	double	Filters out contracts whose coupon rate is below this value
couponRateBelow	double	Filters out contracts whose coupon rate is above this value
excludeConvertible	bool	Filters out convertible bonds
scannerSettingPairs	string	Provide pair values for parameters
stockTypeFilter	string	Filters stocks according to their types

The first three fields are the most important, and in many cases, they're the only fields you need to know. The `instrument` field identifies the type of securities to be scanned, and you can set it to any of the fields listed in Table 9.2.

Table 9.2
Instrument Values in the ScannerSubscription Structure

STK	FUT_EU	IND_EU	SLB_US
STOCK_EU	FUT_HK	IND_HK	WAR_EU
STOCK_HK	FUT_NA	IND_US	PMONITOR
STOCK_NA	FUT_US	EFP	PMONITORM
BOND			

The `locationCode` field sets the geographic location of the desired contracts. As listed in Table 9.3, location codes usually start with the desired security type.

Table 9.3
LocationCode Values in the ScannerSubscription Structure

STK.US	STK.EU.IBIS-ETF	FUT.HK.HKFE	FUT.EU.FTA
STK.NASDAQ	STK.EU.SBVM	FUT.HK.JAPAN	FUT.EU.IDEM
STK.NYSE	STK.EU.IBIS-NEWX	FUT.HK.KSE	FUT.EU.LIFFE
STK.AMEX	STK.EU.IBIS-EUSTARS	FUT.NYSELIFFE	FUT.EU.MEFFRV
STK.ARCA	STK.EU.IBIS-XETRA	FUT.HK.OSE.JPN	IND.HK.OSE.JPN
STK.NASDAQ.NMS	STK.EU.LSE	FUT.HK.SGX	FUT.EU.BELFOX
STK.NASDAQ.SCM	STK.EU.SBF	FUT.HK.SNFE	IND.US
STK.US.MAJOR	STK.EU.IBIS-USSTARS	FUT.HK.TSE.JPN	IND.HK.TSE.JPN

STK.US.MINOR	STK.EU.SFB	FUT.HK	IND.EU.DTB
STK.OTCBB	STK.EU.SWISS	FUT.IPE	IND.EU.FTA
STK.NA	STK.EU.VIRTX	FUT.NA.CDE	IND.EU.LIFFE
STK.NA.CANADA	STK.HK.ASX	FUT.NA	IND.EU.MONEP
STK.NA.TSE	STK.HK.NSE	FUT.NYBOT	IND.EU
STK.NA.VENTURE	STK.HK.SEHK	FUT.US	IND.HK.HKFE
STK.PINK	STK.HK.SGX	FUT.GLOBEX	IND.HK.JAPAN
STK.EU	STK.HK.TSE.JPN	FUT.NYMEX	IND.HK.KSE
STK.EU.AEB	STK.HK	FUT.HK.NSE	IND.HK.NSE
STK.EU.BM	WAR.EU.ALL	FUT.EU	FUT.EU.MONEP
STK.EU.BVME	SLB.AQS	FUT.ECBOT	IND.HK.SGX
STK.EU.EBS	BOND.US	FUT.EU.DTB	IND.HK.SNFE
STK.EU.IBIS	EFP	IND.HK	IND.EU.BELFOX

The third important field of the ScannerSubscription structure is scanCode. This identifies the main security criteria that you're interested in. Applications can (theoretically) set this to any of the values listed in Table 9.4.

Table 9.4
ScanCode Values in the ScannerSubscription Structure

TOP_PERC_GAIN	HIGH_RETURN_ON_EQUITY	LOW_SYNTH_ASK_REV_NAT_YIELD
TOP_PERC_LOSE	HIGH_VS_52W_HL	LOW_VS_13W_HL
MOST_ACTIVE	HIGH_VS_13W_HL	LOW_VS_26W_HL
ALL_SYMBOLS_ASC	HIGH_VS_26W_HL	LOW_VS_52W_HL
HIGH_BOND_ASK_CURRENT_YIELD_ALL	HIGH_SYNTH_BID_REV_NAT_YIELD	LOW_WAR_REL_IMP_VOLAT
BOND_CUSIP_AZ	HOT_BY_OPT_VOLUME	MARKET_CAP_USD_ASC
BOND_CUSIP_ZA	HOT_BY_PRICE	MARKET_CAP_USD_DESC
FAR_MATURITY_DATE	HOT_BY_PRICE_RANGE	MOST_ACTIVE_AVG_USD
HALTED	HOT_BY_VOLUME	MOST_ACTIVE_USD
ALL_SYMBOLS_DESC	LIMIT_UP_DOWN	NEAR_MATURITY_DATE
HIGH_BOND_ASK_YIELD_ALL	LOW_BOND_BID_CURRENT_YIELD_ALL	NOT_OPEN
HIGH_BOND_DEBT_2_BOOK_RATIO	LOW_BOND_BID_YIELD_ALL	OPT_OPEN_INTEREST_MOST_ACTIVE

HIGH_BOND_DEBT_2_EQUITY_RATIO	LOW_BOND_DEBT_2_BOOK_RATIO	OPT_VOLUME_MOST_ACTIVE
HIGH_BOND_DEBT_2_TAN_BOOK_RATIO	LOW_BOND_DEBT_2_EQUITY_RATIO	PMONITOR_AVAIL_CONTRACTS
HIGH_BOND_EQUITY_2_BOOK_RATIO	LOW_BOND_DEBT_2_TAN_BOOK_RATIO	PMONITOR_CTT
HIGH_BOND_EQUITY_2_TAN_BOOK_RATIO	LOW_BOND_EQUITY_2_BOOK_RATIO	PMONITOR_IBOND
HIGH_BOND_NET_ASK_CURRENT_YIELD_ALL	LOW_BOND_EQUITY_2_TAN_BOOK_RATIO	PMONITOR_RFQ
HIGH_BOND_NET_ASK_YIELD_ALL	LOW_BOND_NET_BID_CURRENT_YIELD_ALL	TOP_STOCK_BUY_IMBALANCE_ADV_RATIO
HIGH_BOND_NET_SPREAD_ALL	LOW_BOND_NET_BID_YIELD_ALL	TOP_OPT_IMP_VOLAT_LOSE
HIGH_MOODY_RATING_ALL	LOW_BOND_NET_SPREAD_ALL	TOP_OPT_IMP_VOLAT_GAIN
HIGH_COUPON_RATE	LOW_BOND_SPREAD_ALL	TOP_OPEN_PERC_LOSE
HIGH_DIVIDEND_YIELD	LOW_COUPON_RATE	TOP_PRICE_RANGE
HIGH_DIVIDEND_YIELD_IB	LOWEST_SLB_ASK	TOP_STOCK_SELL_IMBALANCE_ADV_RATIO
HIGHEST_SLB_BID	LOW_GROWTH_RATE	TOP_OPEN_PERC_GAIN
HIGH_GROWTH_RATE	LOW_MOODY_RATING_ALL	TOP_TRADE_COUNT
HIGH_BOND_SPREAD_ALL	LOW_OPEN_GAP	TOP_TRADE_RATE
HIGH_OPEN_GAP	LOW_OPT_IMP_VOLAT	TOP_VOLUME_RATE
HIGH_OPT_IMP_VOLAT	LOW_OPT_IMP_VOLAT_OVER_HIST	WSH_NEXT_ANALYST_MEETING
HIGH_OPT_OPEN_INTEREST_PUT_CALL_RATIO	LOW_OPT_OPEN_INTEREST_PUT_CALL_RATIO	WSH_NEXT_EARNINGS
HIGH_OPT_IMP_VOLAT_OVER_HIST	LOW_OPT_VOLUME_PUT_CALL_RATIO	WSH_NEXT_EVENT
HIGH_PE_RATIO	LOW_PE_RATIO	WSH_NEXT_MAJOR_EVENT
HIGH_OPT_VOLUME_PUT_CALL_RATIO	LOW_PRICE_2_BOOK_RATIO	WSH_PREV_ANALYST_MEETING
HIGH_PRICE_2_BOOK_RATIO	LOW_PRICE_2_TAN_BOOK_RATIO	WSH_PREV_EARNINGS
HIGH_PRICE_2_TAN_BOOK_RATIO	LOW_QUICK_RATIO	WSH_PREV_EVENT
HIGH_QUICK_RATIO	LOW_RETURN_ON_EQUITY	

For example, the following Python code creates a `ScannerSubscription` to return symbols of major U.S. stocks based on volume. Only stocks with share prices above 200 dollars should be considered.

```
ss = ScannerSubscription()
ss.instrument = 'STK'
ss.locationCode = 'STK.US.MAJOR'
ss.scanCode = 'HOT_BY_VOLUME'
ss.abovePrice = 200.0
```

The following C++ code creates a `ScannerSubscription` to search for European futures based on activity. Only contracts with a trading volume above 1,000,000 should be considered.

```
ScannerSubscription ss;
ss.instrument = "FUT.EU";
ss.locationCode = "FUT.EU.SOFFEX";
ss.scanCode = "MOST_ACTIVE";
ss.aboveVolume = 1000000;
```

The `ScannerSubscription` class doesn't have any methods of its own. Its only purpose is to hold data related to the desired subscription. An application passes this data to IB by calling `reqScannerSubscription`.

9.2 Requesting the Subscription

After you've created a `ScannerSubscription`, you can launch the scanning process by requesting a subscription. This is accomplished by calling the client's `reqScannerSubscription` function:

```
reqScannerSubscription(reqId, ScannerSubscription,
    scannerSubscriptionOptions,
    scannerSubscriptionFilterOptions)
```

The first two arguments are self-explanatory and the third is reserved for internal use. The last argument makes it possible to assign additional filter options. This section explains how to set these options and how to access scanning results through the `scannerData` callback.

9.2.1 Configuring Additional Filters

The scanner provides a maximum of fifty securities at a time, so it's important to set criteria that filters its results. The simplest way of doing this is by setting fields of the `ScannerSubscription` instance. For example, you can filter out stocks with prices below 100 by setting the `ScannerSubscription`'s `abovePrice` field to `100`.

You can set additional filter criteria through the fourth argument of `reqScannerSubscription`. This accepts a container of *name=value* pairs in which *name* identifies the nature of the filter and *value* sets the value that the criteria is checked against.

IB's documentation doesn't provide a great deal of information about these additional filter settings. But you can obtain information in code by calling `reqScannerParameters`. In response, the `scannerParameters` callback returns an XML-formatted string containing a vast amount of data.

If you look through this data, you'll find a number of `<AbstractField>` tags whose `<code>` tags contain filter names. Table 9.5 lists thirty-five of the available filter names and provides a description of each.

Table 9.5

Additional Filter Configuration

Filter Name	Description
`avgVolumeAbove`	Filters out securities whose average daily volume is below the given value
`avgVolumeBelow`	Filters out securities whose average daily volume is above the given value
`avgUsdVolumeAbove`	Filters out securities whose average daily volume (in USD) is below the given value
`avgUsdVolumeBelow`	Filters out securities whose average daily volume (in USD) is above the given value
`marketCapAbove1e6`	Filters out securities whose market capitalization falls below the given value (in millions)
`marketCapBelow1e6`	Filters out securities whose market capitalization falls above the given value (in millions)
`dividendFrdAbove`	Filters out securities whose dividend is less than the given value (percentage)
`dividendFrdBelow`	Filters out securities whose dividend is greater than the given value (percentage)

`dividendYieldFrdAbove`	Filters out securities whose dividend yield is less than the given value
`dividendYieldFrdBelow`	Filters out securities whose dividend yield is greater than the given value
`minGrowthRate`	Filters out securities whose growth rate is less than the given value
`maxGrowthRate`	Filters out securities whose growth rate is greater than the given value
`minPeRatio`	Filters out securities whose price/earnings ratio is less than the given value
`maxPeRatio`	Filters out securities whose price/earnings ratio is greater than the given value
`minRetnOnEq`	Filters out securities whose return on equity ratio is less than the given value
`maxRetnOnEq`	Filters out securities whose return on equity ratio is greater than the given value
`imbalanceAbove`	Filters out securities whose order imbalance (number of unmatched shares) is below the given value
`imbalanceBelow`	Filters out securities whose order imbalance (number of unmatched shares) is above the given value
`optVolumeAbove`	Filters out securities whose options trade at a volume below the given value
`optVolumeBelow`	Filters out securities whose options trade at a volume above the given value
`avgOptVolumeAbove`	Filters out securities whose options trade at an average volume below the given value
`optVolumePCRatioAbove`	Filters out options whose put-call ratio is below the given value
`optVolumePCRatioBelow`	Filters out options whose put-call ratio is above the given value
`impVolatAbove`	Filters out options whose implied volatility is below the given value
`impVolatBelow`	Filters out options whose implied volatility is above the given value
`impVolatOverHistAbove`	Filters out options whose implied volatility exceeds historical volatility by less than the given value

`impVolatOverHistBelow`	Filters out options whose implied volatility exceeds historical volatility by more than the given value
`ihNumSharesInsiderAbove`	Filters out stocks whose number of shares held by insiders falls below the given value
`ihNumSharesInsiderBelow`	Filters out stocks whose number of shares held by insiders exceeds the given value
`ihInsiderOfFloat` `    PercAbove`	Filters out stocks whose shares held by insiders as a percentage of float falls below the given value
`ihInsiderOfFloat` `    PercBelow`	Filters out stocks whose shares held by insiders as a percentage of float exceeds the given value
`iiNumShares` `    InstitutionalAbove`	Filters out stocks whose number of shares held by institutions falls below the given value
`iiNumShares` `    InstitutionalBelow`	Filters out stocks whose number of shares held by institutions exceeds the given value
`numRatingsAbove`	Filters out stocks whose number of analyst ratings falls below the given value
`numRatingsBelow`	Filters out stocks whose number of analyst ratings exceeds the given value

To use one of these filters, you need to set the last argument of `reqScannerSubscription` to an appropriate container. In Python, this container must be provided as a list of `TagValue` instances. The `TagValue` constructor accepts two strings: the filter name and the filter value.

The following code shows how this works. After creating a `ScannerSubscription`, it creates a list containing two `TagValues` and makes it the final argument of the client's `reqScannerSubscription` method.

```
ss = ScannerSubscription()
tagvalues = []
tagvalues.append(TagValue("avgVolumeAbove", "100000"))
client.reqScannerSubscription(0, ss, [], tagvalues)
```

In C++, the last argument of `reqScannerSubscription` must be set to a `TagValueListSPtr`. To understand this, you need to know about three type definitions:

```
typedef std::shared_ptr<TagValueList> TagValueListSPtr;
typedef std::vector<TagValueSPtr> TagValueList;
typedef std::shared_ptr<TagValue> TagValueSPtr;
```

Put simply, a `TagValueListSPtr` points to a `TagValueList`, which is a vector containing `TagValueSPtr` instances. A `TagValueSPtr` points to a `TagValue`, whose constructor accepts two `std::strings`: one that identifies the filter's name and one that sets the value used for comparison.

The following code shows how these types work together. It creates a `ScannerSubscription` and a `TagValueListSPtr` whose list contains one tag value. Then it passes both to the `reqScannerSubscription` function:

```
// Create the ScannerSubscription
ScannerSubscription ss;

// Create a pointer to a new TagValue
TagValueSPtr tag(new TagValue("avgVolumeAbove", "1000"));

// Create a pointer to a TagValueList and push the TagValue
TagValueListSPtr tagList(new TagValueList());
tagList->push_back(tag);

// Submit a request for a scanner subscription
client->reqScannerSubscription(0, ss,
    TagValueListSPtr(), tagList);
```

The API provides a wide range of filters, but many of them may not be accessible. For example, if you want to access fundamental data, such as P/E ratios, you'll need to configure your account with an appropriate market data subscription.

9.2.2 Receiving Subscription Data

After an application calls `reqScannerSubscription`, TWS will transfer the request to IB and the application can access the scanner results through the `scannerData` callback. Its signature is given as follows:

```
scannerData(reqId, rank, contractDetails, distance, benchmark,
    projection, legsStr)
```

The `rank` argument gives the ranking of the contract identified by the `contractDetails` argument. The `distance`, `benchmark`, and `projection` arguments depend on the security type. The last argument, `legsStr`, describes the legs of a combination when the scanner returns Exhange-For-Physical (EFP) results.

The `scannerData` callback will be called once for each desired result up to a maximum of 50. When the data transmission is complete, the `scannerDataEnd` callback function will be called.

9.3 Security Scanning in Code

Now that you understand the data structures and methods/functions involved with scanning, let's look at a simple practical example. In this section, the goal is to scan for stocks that meet three criteria:

1. Price below 100.
2. Average trading volume above 500,000.
3. Market capitalization above 10,000,000.

For the first criterion, we'll set the `abovePrice` criterion of the `ScannerSubscription`. For the second and third, we'll add tags to the last argument of `reqScannerSubscription`. This section explains how to scan for these stocks in Python and C++.

9.3.1 Scanning for Securities in Python

The code in Listing 9.1 shows how applications can scan for stocks using Python. The stock_scanner.py module starts by defining a `StockScanner` class that provides code for the `scannerData` and `scannerDataEnd` callbacks. Then it creates an instance of the class, configures a `ScannerSubscription`, and calls `reqScannerSubscription` to access stock data.

Listing 9.1: ch9/stock_scanner.py

```python
class StockScanner(EWrapper, EClient):
    ''' Serves as the client and the wrapper '''

    def __init__(self, addr, port, client_id):
        EWrapper.__init__(self)
        EClient.__init__(self, self)

        # Connect to TWS
        self.connect(addr, port, client_id)
        self.count = 0

        # Launch the client thread
        thread = Thread(target=self.run)
        thread.start()
```

Listing 9.1: ch9/stock_scanner.py (Continued)

```python
    @iswrapper
    def scannerData(self, reqId, rank, details,
        distance, benchmark, projection, legsStr):

        # Print the symbols in the returned results
        print('{}: {}'.format(rank, details.contract.symbol))
        self.count += 1

    @iswrapper
    def scannerDataEnd(self, reqId):

        # Print the number of results
        print('Number of results: {}'.format(self.count))

    @iswrapper
    def error(self, reqId, code, msg):
        print('Error {}: {}'.format(code, msg))

def main():

    # Create the client and connect to TWS
    client = StockScanner('127.0.0.1', 7497, 0)
    time.sleep(0.5)

    # Create the ScannerSubscription object
    ss = ScannerSubscription()
    ss.instrument = 'STK'
    ss.locationCode = 'STK.US.MAJOR'
    ss.scanCode = 'HOT_BY_VOLUME'

    # Set additional filter criteria
    tagvalues = []
    tagvalues.append(TagValue('avgVolumeAbove', '500000'))
    tagvalues.append(TagValue('marketCapAbove1e6', '10'))

    # Request the scanner subscription
    client.reqScannerSubscription(0, ss, [], tagvalues)

     # Sleep while the request is processed
    time.sleep(5)
    client.disconnect()
```

The subscription provides a maximum of 50 results for each scan. The `scannerData` callback is invoked as each result is received, and it prints the security's rank and symbol. When all of the results have been received, the `scannerDataEnd` callback prints the number of results.

9.3.2 Scanning for Securities in C++

The code in the Ch09_StockScanner project demonstrates how IB's stock scanner can be accessed in C++. The `main` function creates a `StockScanner` and a `ScannerSubscription`, and then calls `reqScannerSubscription` to obtain a subscription. Listing 9.2 presents the code for the `main` function.

Listing 9.2: Ch09_StockScanner/Main.cpp

```cpp
int main() {

  int reqId = 0;

  // Connect to TWS or IB Gateway
  StockScanner client("127.0.0.1", 7497, 0);

  // Create scanner subscription
  ScannerSubscription ss;
  ss.instrument = "STK";
  ss.locationCode = "STK.US.MAJOR";
  ss.scanCode = "HOT_BY_VOLUME";

  // Create a pointer to a new TagValue
  TagValueSPtr tag1(new TagValue("avgVolumeAbove", "500000"));
  TagValueSPtr tag2(new TagValue("marketCapAbove1e6", "10"));

  // Create a pointer to a TagValueList and push the TagValue
  TagValueListSPtr tagList(new TagValueList());
  tagList->push_back(tag1);
  tagList->push_back(tag2);

  // Submit a request for a scanner subscription
  client.reqScannerSubscription(0, ss,
    TagValueListSPtr(), tagList);
  std::this_thread::sleep_for(std::chrono::seconds(5));
  client.signal.waitForSignal();
  client.reader->processMsgs();
```

Listing 9.2: Ch09_StockScanner/Main.cpp (continued)

```
    // Disconnect
    client.eDisconnect();
    return 0;
}
```

When the `main` function creates a `StockScanner` instance, the constructor connects to TWS. The `StockScanner` class also provides code for two callbacks. `scannerData` prints each security symbol as it's received and `scannerDataEnd` prints a message after the last symbol is received. Listing 9.3 presents the code.

Listing 9.3: Ch09_StockScanner/StockScanner.cpp

```
StockScanner::StockScanner(const char *host,
  int port, int clientId) :
  signal(1000),
  count(0),
  EClientSocket(this, &signal) {

  // Connect to TWS
  bool conn = eConnect(host, port, clientId, false);
  if (conn) {

    // Launch the reader thread
    reader = new EReader(this, &signal);
    reader->start();
  }
  else
    std::cout << "Failed to connect" << std::endl;
}

StockScanner::~StockScanner() { delete reader; }

// Obtain contract ID
void StockScanner::scannerData(int reqId, int rank,
  const ContractDetails& details, const std::string& distance,
  const std::string& benchmark, const std::string& proj,
  const std::string& legsStr) {

  std::cout << rank << ": " << details.contract.symbol
    << std::endl;
  count += 1;
}
```

Listing 9.3: Ch09_StockScanner/StockScanner.cpp (Continued)

```
void StockScanner::scannerDataEnd(int reqId) {
  std::cout << "Number of results: " << count << std::endl;
}

void StockScanner::error(int id, int code,
  const std::string& msg) {

  std::cout << "Error: " << code << ": " << msg << std::endl;
}
```

The `StockScanner` constructor sets the member variable `count` to 0. Each time the scanner provides a new security, the `scannerData` callback prints the security's rank and symbol, and increments `count`. After the last security is received, the `scannerDataEnd` callback prints `count` to standard output.

9.4 Summary

In my opinion, scanning is one of the most impressive capabilities in the TWS API, but I've encountered few developers who use it regularly. It's not hard to see why. There are a vast number of configuration fields and the documentation is lousy.

Thankfully, the overall process of obtaining scanning data is straightforward. First, you need to create a `ScannerSubscription` and set its fields to filter out contracts. Then call `reqScannerSubscription` from the client and access the contracts of interest in the wrapper's `scannerData` callback.

Dealing with all the configuration fields is a pain, but the TWS API scanner makes it possible to discover contracts that may have escaped the notice of most investors. Scanning plays an important role in Chapter 14, which presents a simple but practical application for algorithmic trading.

Chapter 10

Advanced Order Configuration

Chapter 7 introduced the `Contract` and `Order` data structures, which play fundamental roles in algotrading applications. Given the vast number of configuration fields discussed in that chapter, you may be surprised to learn that there are advanced order configuration capabilities that haven't been mentioned. The goal of this chapter is to present these capabilities and show how they can be accessed in code.

The first capability involves parent-child orders. Most applications create and submit `Order` structures independently. But the TWS API makes it possible to define child `Orders` that depend on the execution of a parent `Order`. By taking advantage of this, applications can create bracket orders, adjust existing stop orders, or submit hedging orders.

The next topic deals with submitting orders for large numbers of securities. The TWS API makes it possible to submit block orders that take advantage of IB's ability to split orders into trades that won't disrupt the market. The API also supports scale orders, which allow developers to customize how the order is divided.

The third topic discusses the subject of order algorithms. As with block orders and scale orders, the goal is to break a large order into smaller orders that will have minimal impact on the security's price. Researchers have devised countless algorithms for this purpose, but this chapter only focuses on six: adaptive, percentage of volume, arrival price, dark ice, time weighted average price (TWAP), and volume weighted average price (VWAP).

The last part of the chapter explores the fascinating topic of dynamic conditions. Market conditions may change between the time an order is submitted and the time it's filled. Dynamic conditions make it possible to allow or disallow orders from being filled when specific criteria (price, volume, time) are met.

10.1 Parent-Child Orders

The TWS API makes it possible to configure `Order` structures as children of a central `Order` structure. These dependent orders won't become active until after the parent order is executed. This parent-child relationship becomes useful in three main instances:

- The application wants to associate a main order with two additional orders: a limit order if prices move favorably and a stop order if prices move unfavorably. This type of combination order is called a *bracket order*.

- The application wants to update the characteristics of a stop order that has already been submitted. This is called a *stop order adjustment* and it can only be performed once per stop order.

- The application wants to create an order opposite to the parent that reduces the risk. These secondary orders are called *hedging orders*.

Configuring an `Order` as a child is easy—just set the `parentId` field equal to the ID of the parent order. This section explains how this parent-child relationship can be used to create bracket orders, stop order adjustments, and hedging orders.

10.1.1 Bracket Orders

Suppose you want to submit a buy order, and you'd like to reduce the possible loss with an associated stop order. You also want to associate the order with a limit order at a higher price so you can take profit if the price surges.

The combination of an order with a loss-reducing stop order and a profit-taking limit order is called a *bracket order*. Setting up a bracket order requires three steps:

1. Create the parent order with the `transmit` field set to a false value. This ensures that the main order won't execute before its children.

2. Create a stop order to offset the parent order if the price moves unfavorably. Set its `parentId` field to the `orderId` of the main order and set its `transmit` field to a false value.

3. Create a limit order to offset the parent order if the price moves favorably. Set its `parentId` field to the `orderId` of the main order and set its `transmit` field to a true value.

In the following code, the main order is called `mainOrder`, the lower-price stop order is called `stopChild`, and the higher-price limit order is called `lmtChild`.

```
mainOrder = Order()
mainOrder.orderId = mainId
mainOrder.action = "BUY"
mainOrder.orderType = "LMT"
mainOrder.totalQuantity = 1000
mainOrder.lmtPrice = mainPrice
mainOrder.transmit = False

stopChild = Order()
stopChild.orderId = mainOrder.orderId + 1
stopChild.action = "SELL"
stopChild.orderType = "STP"
stopChild.totalQuantity = 1000
stopChild.auxPrice = lowPrice
stopChild.parentId = mainId
stopChild.transmit = False

lmtChild = Order()
lmtChild.orderId = mainId.orderId + 2
lmtChild.action = "SELL"
lmtChild.orderType = "LMT"
lmtChild.totalQuantity = 1000
lmtChild.lmtPrice = highPrice
lmtChild.parentId = mainId
lmtChild.transmit = True
```

In this example, the ID of the main order is `mainId`. To configure the bracket order, the `parentId` field of the child orders must be set to `mainId`. Because of this relationship, the child orders won't become active until the parent order is filled.

The `transmit` field of the first two orders is set to `False` and the `transmit` field of the last order is set to `True`. When submitting a bracket order, call `placeOrder` once for the parent and once for each child. The child whose `transmit` field is `True` should be submitted last.

10.1.2 Stop Order Adjustments

An earlier discussion explained how investors limit their losses by placing stop orders (`STP`), stop limit orders (`STP LMT`), trailing stop orders (`TRAIL`), and trailing stop limit orders (`TRAIL LIMIT`). After you've placed one of these orders, IB allows you to change it once without submitting a new order. This one-time modification is called an *adjustment* and it takes effect when the security reaches a trigger price.

To create a stop order adjustment in code, you need to create a new `Order` for the same quantity. To associate the new order with the order to be adjusted, set its `parentId` field to the parent's `orderId` field.

After the initial settings, you can further configure the stop order adjustment with the following fields:

- `triggerPrice` — the price at which the adjusted stop order should become active
- `adjustedOrderType` — the updated type of the parent order
- `adjustedStopPrice` — the price at which the new stop order becomes active
- `adjustedStopLimitPrice` — the price of the limit order that becomes active when the new stop order executes
- `adjustableTrailingUnit` — identifies whether the trailing amount identifies an amount (0) or a percentage (1)
- `adjustedTrailingAmount` — the amount/percentage by which the trailing stop order price trails the contract's price

For example, suppose you want to create an adjustment that increases the price of a stop order from 75 to 85 if the contract's price rises above 90. If the ID of the original stop order was `stopId`, you could create the adjustment with the following code:

```
Order order;
order.action = "SELL";
order.orderType = "STP";
order.totalQuantity = 1000;
order.auxPrice = 75;
order.parentId = stopId;
order.triggerPrice = 90;
order.adjustedStopPrice = 85;
```

Stop order adjustments can be extremely useful when you want to take advantage of shifts in the market. But keep in mind that these adjustments can only be made once.

10.1.3 Hedging

The goal of hedging is to reduce loss by using one investment to offset another. In stock trading, investors frequently hedge a long position in one stock by establishing a short position in a similar stock or exchange traded fund.

TWS API applications can attach a hedging order to an order by making it a child order. As in a bracket order, this involves two steps:

1. Create the main order and set its `transmit` field to a false value.
2. Create the hedging order with the `parentId` field set to the `orderId` of the main order and its `transmit` field set to a true value.

IB supports many types of hedging orders, and you can configure a hedging order by setting two fields

- **hedgeType** — Sets the hedge type: D (delta), B (beta), F (FX), or P (pair)
- **hedgeParams** — Value whose purpose depends on the hedge type

When setting hedgeType, a value of B implies a beta hedge, which uses one stock/ETF purchase to offset another. If the main stock follows the market with a ratio called beta, the hedging stock/ETF should follow the market with a ratio of approximately negative beta. For beta hedges, hedgeParams identifies the desired beta value, which IB uses to set the quantity of the hedge order.

Setting hedgeType to D indicates a delta hedge, which is used for options. As discussed in Chapter 3, delta measures how much an option's price changes with each single-dollar rise of the underlying asset. If the main option's delta value is d, delta hedging involves purchasing an option with delta equal to –d.

If you set hedgeType to F, IB will assume that you're making an FX, or foreign-exchange hedge. This usually involves purchasing a contract to offset the risk associated with a foreign currency. In theory, the contract's value will rise if the currency value falls, and vice-versa.

The last value of hedgeType is P, which stands for Pair. A pair hedge is used to offset one contract against another, usually in the same industry. For this type of hedge, you should set hedgeParams to the desired hedging ratio. IB will use this value to set the quantity of the hedging order.

10.2 Submitting Large Orders

When traders want to buy or sell a large quantity of contracts, they don't submit a single order for the entire quantity. This is because large orders can dramatically alter the security's price, causing portions of the order to be filled at successively worse prices. For this reason, dealers split large orders into smaller orders whose effect on the price will be minimal.

This section discusses two mechanisms for handling these types of orders. If an order is configured as a block order, IB will manage the process of splitting it into smaller orders. If an order is configured as a scale order, the application controls the size of the smaller orders and the times at which they should be submitted. These mechanisms are poorly documented, but in this section, I'll do my best to explain how they work.

10.2.1 Block Orders

If you want to submit an order for more than 50 contracts, you can submit it as a block order by setting the `blockOrder` field of the `Order` structure to a true value and by setting the `exchange` field to `ISE`. ISE stands for the International Securities Exchange, which defines a methodology for handling block orders.

To be specific, ISE Rule 716 governs the submission of block orders. One capability discussed in the rule is the Solicited Order Mechanism, which is available for orders of 500 contracts or more. This allows a dealer to ask other parties to execute portions of a block trade to reduce the impact of the order on the security's price.

10.2.2 Scale Orders

If you want greater control over the order-splitting process, you can configure an order as a scale order by setting fields of the `Order` structure. Table 10.1 lists ten of these fields.

Table 10.1
Scale Order Fields

Field	Type	Description
`scaleInitLevelSize`	int	Size of the initial order
`scaleInitPosition`	int	Position of the initial order
`scaleInitFillQty`	int	Fill quantity of the initial order
`scaleSubsLevelSize`	int	Size of subsequent components
`scalePriceIncrement`	double	Price difference between components
`scalePriceAdjustValue`	double	Price adjustment value
`scalePriceAdjustInterval`	int	Price adjustment interval
`scaleProfitOffset`	double	Profit offset
`scaleAutoReset`	bool	Auto reset
`scaleRandomPercent`	bool	Random percentage

Every large order is split into an initial smaller order and several subsequent smaller orders. The size of the initial order is given by `scaleInitLevelSize` and the desired fill quantity is given by `scaleInitFillQty`.

After the initial order executes, subsequent orders are submitted with a size set by `scaleSubsLevelSize`. Each subsequent order is less than the one before it, and the difference between orders is given by the `scalePriceIncrement` field.

10.3 Order Submission Algorithms

Many traders set an order's exchange to SMART and let it figure out how to place the order. Others prefer to customize how SMART operates. For these traders, the Order class provides two important fields:

- **algoStrategy** — A string that identifies the submission algorithm that should be employed
- **algoParams** — Values that determine how the strategy is implemented

If you set the contract's exchange to SMART, you can set algoStrategy to one of the six strategy codes listed in Table 10.2.

Table 10.2
Algorithm Codes

Code	Name	Description
Adaptive	Adaptive	Uses priority to find the best price for a market or limit order
PctVol	Percentage of Volume	Splits an order into orders whose sizes are based on trading volume
ArrivalPx	Arrival Price	Splits an order to achieve
DarkIce	Dark Ice	Uses a proprietary algorithm to hide separate orders
Twap	Time Weighted Average Price (TWAP)	Splits an order into multiple orders whose prices target TWAP
Vwap	Volume Weighted Average Price (VWAP)	Splits an order into multiple orders whose prices target VWAP

This discussion looks at each of these strategies and the parameters that configure their operation. An algorithm's parameters must be provided in the algoParams field, which associates names with tag values.

In Python, algoParams is a list of TagValues. Each TagValue contains two strings: the parameter's name and the desired value. The following code gives an idea of how this works:

```
order.algoParams = []
order.algoParams.append(TagValue("paramName", "paramValue"))
```

In C++, `algoParams` accepts a `TagValueListSPtr`, which is a shared pointer to a vector of `TagValueSPtrs`. A `TagValueSPtr` is a shared pointer to a `TagValue`, which contains the parameter's name and the desired value. The following code shows how this is used:

```
TagValueSPtr tag(new TagValue("paramName", "paramValue"));
order.algoParams->push_back(tag);
```

IB supports third-party strategies in addition to those listed in the table. For more information, visit https://www.interactivebrokers.com/en/software/tws/algosTop.htm.

10.3.1 Adaptive

Of the six algorithms in the table, the adaptive algorithm is the most popular. This algorithm allows applications to set a priority that tells SMART how long to wait for an optimal order price.

When using the Adaptive algorithm, the `adaptivePriority` parameter must be set to one of three values. These values determine how long the algorithm should wait while seeking better execution prices:

- `Urgent` — Wait briefly for better prices
- `Normal` — Wait a normal amount of time
- `Patient` — Wait a lengthy amount of time

According to IB's documentation, this algorithm leads to "better execution prices on average than for regular limit or market orders."

10.3.2 Percentage of Volume

If `algoStrategy` is set to `PctVol`, the Percentage of Volume algorithm will submit orders whose size is given as a percentage of volume in a time interval. To set the percentage and the time interval, five parameters can be set:

- `pctVol` — Target percentage (0.1–0.5)
- `noTakeliq` — Whether to avoid taking liquidity
- `startTime` — Starting time (`hh:mm:ss TMZ` or `YYYYMMDD-hh:mm:ss TMZ`)
- `endTime` — Ending time (`hh:mm:ss TMZ` or `YYYYMMDD-hh:mm:ss TMZ`)
- `monetaryValue` — Cash quantity

For example, suppose you want to buy 100,000 shares of BGCP but you don't want to submit the purchase in a single order. If you set `pctVol` to 0.15, multiple orders will be submitted whose size equals 15 percent of the volume. The orders will continue to be placed until the full order is complete or the market closes.

10.3.3 Arrival Price

The Arrival Price algorithm splits a large order into smaller orders to be filled at the midpoint of the contract's bid and ask prices. An application can configure when and how quickly these orders are submitted by assigning values to the following parameters:

- `riskAversion` — Urgency (`Get Done`, `Aggressive`, `Neutral`, `Passive`)
- `maxPctVol` — Maximum percentage of daily volume (0.1 - 0.5)
- `startTime` — Starting time (`hh:mm:ss TMZ` or `YYYYMMDD-hh:mm:ss TMZ`)
- `endTime` — Ending time (`hh:mm:ss TMZ` or `YYYYMMDD-hh:mm:ss TMZ`)
- `allowPastEndTime` — Allow trading past end time
- `forceCompletion` — Require completion within the day
- `monetaryValue` — Cash quantity

The greater the urgency, the more orders the algorithm will seek to execute and the greater the impact will be on the daily volume. You can control the maximum affected volume with the `maxPctVol` parameter. For example, a value of 0.1 corresponds to 10% of the volume and a value of 0.5 corresponds to 50% of the volume.

10.3.4 Dark Ice

In common finance parlance, an iceberg order is a large order that gets divided into smaller orders to hide the order's size. Each smaller order is simply a tip of the iceberg.

The goal of the Dark Ice algorithm is to execute large orders as iceberg orders. The execution algorithm is proprietary, but applications can configure its operation with four parameters:

- `displaySize` — The size that will be displayed to the market
- `startTime` — Starting time (`hh:mm:ss TMZ` or `YYYYMMDD-hh:mm:ss TMZ`)
- `endTime` — Ending time (`hh:mm:ss TMZ` or `YYYYMMDD-hh:mm:ss TMZ`)
- `allowPastEndTime` — Allow trading past `endTime`

`displaySize` doesn't control the final order size. Instead, the algorithm randomly sets the size of each order to +/-50% of the given value. This makes the orders as undetectable as possible.

The algorithm checks the probability of the price moving in a favorable direction. If so, it decides whether to set the limit price to one tick lower for buy offers or one tick higher for sell orders.

10.3.5 TWAP

The term TWAP stands for *time weighted average price,* and it identifies the average price of a contract over a day. The TWAP algorithm splits a large order into smaller orders whose prices are based on the TWAP during a selected time interval.

The algorithm's splitting and execution can be controlled by setting five parameters:

- `strategyType` — Trade strategy (`Marketable`, `Matching Midpoint`, `Matching Last`, `Matching Same Side`)
- `startTime` — Starting time (`hh:mm:ss TMZ` or `YYYYMMDD-hh:mm:ss TMZ`)
- `endTime` — Ending time (`hh:mm:ss TMZ` or `YYYYMMDD-hh:mm:ss TMZ`)
- `allowPastEndTime` — Allow trading past `endTime`
- `monetaryValue` — Cash quantity

The `strategyType` parameter determines when the algorithm should submit orders. If this is set to `Marketable`, the algorithm will submit orders when the price reaches the limit price. If this is set to `Matching Midpoint`, the order will be submitted when the midpoint of the bid/ask equals the limit price. If `Matching Last` is set, the algorithm will submit orders when the last price reaches the limit price.

If `strategyType` is set to `Matching Same Side`, the algorithm will submit orders when the limit price equals the price on the same side as the order. In other words this price depends on whether the order involves buying or selling.

10.3.6 VWAP

VWAP stands for *volume weighted average price,* and it's computed by multiplying order prices by their volumes, and dividing by the total volume. The VWAP order algorithm makes its best effort to execute a large order at the VWAP price. As with the Percent of Volume algorithm, applications can set a maximum percentage of the daily volume for trading. This algorithm accepts seven parameters:

- **maxPctVol** — Maximum percentage of average daily volume (0.1 – 0.5)
- **noTakeliq** — Whether to avoid taking liquidity
- **speedUp** — Compensate for the decreased fill rate due to presence of limit price
- **startTime** — Starting time (hh:mm:ss TMZ or YYYYMMDD-hh:mm:ss TMZ)
- **endTime** — Ending time (hh:mm:ss TMZ or YYYYMMDD-hh:mm:ss TMZ)
- **allowPastEndTime** — Allow trading past endTime
- **monetaryValue** — Cash quantity

By default, the algorithm halts order submission at the end of the specified time interval. But if `allowPastEndTime` is set to a true value, the algorithm will continue submitting orders beyond that time.

10.4 Dynamic Conditions

The last order-related capability I'd like to discuss involves dynamic conditions. When IB receives an order with associated dynamic conditions, it checks whether the conditions are met before making the order active. This gives traders an extra level of safety when placing orders.

In code, an application can set dynamic conditions by assigning a value to the `conditions` field of an `Order` structure. The assigned value must be a container of `OrderCondition` instances. Each `OrderCondition` identifies criteria that must be met before the `Order` can be executed.

In Python, the container must be provided as a list of `OrderConditions`. In C++, the container must have the following type:

```
std::vector<std::shared_ptr<OrderCondition>> conditions;
```

The `OrderCondition` class plays a central role in this discussion. Its subclasses represent different types of conditions that can be set. For example, if you only want the order to be executed if the price stays below a given price, you can create and configure a `PriceCondition`. If you only want an order to be activated within a specific time interval, you can create and configure a `TimeCondition`.

IB supports nine types of order conditions, and each is represented by a subclass of `OrderCondition`. Figure 10.1 illustrates the full inheritance hierarchy.

Chapter 10 Advanced Order Configuration

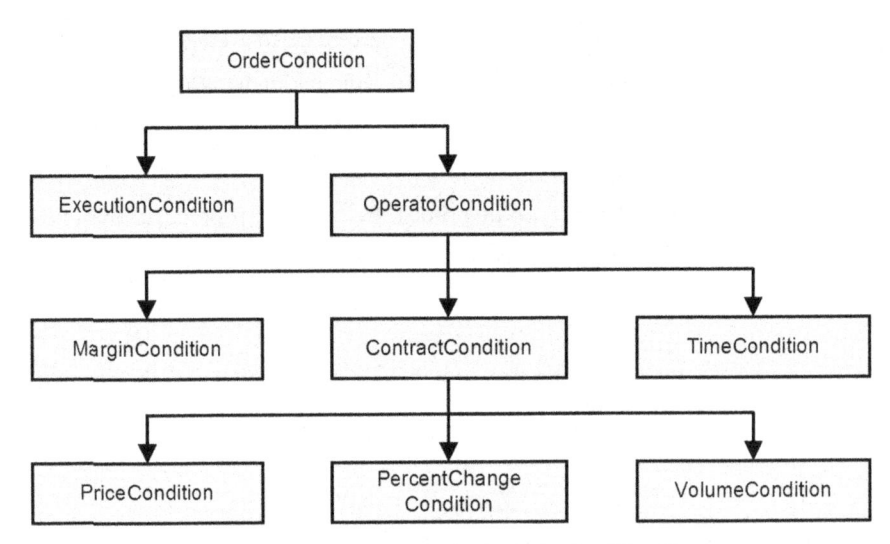

Figure 10.1 Inheritance Hierarchy for Order Condition Classes

This discussion looks at each of these classes, proceeding from top to bottom. But first, it's important to understand how these conditions can be created in code.

10.4.1 Creating Order Conditions

The process of defining an order condition depends on which language you use. In Python, this requires two steps:

1. Call the `Create` function of the `order_condition` module with a constant that identifies which subclass you want to instantiate. `Create` returns an instance of the desired subclass.
2. Set the fields of the instance to define the condition.

For example, the following Python code creates and configures a `TimeCondition` to ensure that the order is placed before 9:30 on October 1, 2019.

```
# Create an instance of the TimeCondition class
time_condition = order_condition.Create(OrderCondition.Time)

# Configure the condition's criteria
time_condition.isMore = false
time_condition.time = '20191001 09:30:00'
```

In C++, the process of defining an order condition is essentially similar, but requires C++ polymorphism. There are three steps involved:

1. Call the static `create` function of the `OrderCondition` class with a value of the `OrderConditionType` enumerated type. This returns a pointer to an instance of the `OrderCondition` class.
2. Using the `dynamic_cast` operator, cast the `OrderCondition` pointer into a pointer to an instance of the desired subclass.
3. Set the fields (Python) or call functions (C++) of the instance.

As an example, the following C++ code creates a `TimeCondition` similar to the one created in Python.

```
# Obtain a pointer to an OrderCondition instance
OrderCondition* orderCondition = OrderCondition::create(
  OrderCondition::OrderConditionType::Time);

# Obtain a pointer to a TimeCondition instance
TimeCondition* timeCondition =
  dynamic_cast<TimeCondition*>(orderCondition);

# Configure the condition's criteria
timeCondition->isMore(false);
timeCondition->time("20191001 09:30:00");
```

To invoke Python's `Create` or C++'s `create` function, you need to know which identifier is needed to instantiate the right subclass of `OrderCondition`. There are six identifiers in total (`Execution`, `Margin`, `PercentChange`, `Price`, `Time`, or `Volume`) and each corresponds to a different subclass (`ExecutionCondition`, `MarginCondition`, `PercentChangeCondition`, `PriceCondition`, `TimeCondition`, and `VolumeCondition`). The following discussion explores each of these subclasses and the different fields that can be set.

10.4.2 Order Condition Classes

Figure 10.1 illustrates eight subclasses of `OrderCondition`, but only six of them can be instantiated. For this reason, this discussion focuses on the `ExecutionCondition`, `TimeCondition`, `MarginCondition`, `PercentChangeCondition`, `VolumeCondition`, and `PriceCondition` classes.

These classes have the same names in Python and C++, but there's one major difference. Python classes accept data through instance variables and C++ classes accept data through functions.

ExecutionCondition

An execution condition allows an order to be fulfilled if its contract meets certain criteria. To be specific, the contract's symbol, exchange, and security type must have the same values as the corresponding variables of the `ExecutionCondition` class. You can configure this with the following fields (Python) or functions (C++):

- `symbol` — the contract's symbol
- `secType` — the contract's security type
- `exchange` — exchange where the symbol needs to be traded

For example, the following Python code creates an `ExecutionCondition` that only allows the order to be activated if its contract represents a bond.

```
exec_condition =
    order_condition.Create(OrderCondition.Execution)
time_condition.secType = 'BOND'
```

`ExecutionConditions` become helpful if an application wants to constrain the types of securities traded by an application or the exchanges used for trading.

TimeCondition

A `TimeCondition` allows an order to be submitted if the time is past a given time or before a given time. An application can set the condition's properties with the following fields (Python) or functions (C++):

- `time` — time reference
- `isMore` — identifies whether the time reference is the latest acceptable time (0) or the earliest possible time (1)

As an example, the following C++ code creates a `TimeCondition` that allows orders to be activated if the submission time is after November 1, 2019.

```
TimeCondition* timeCondition =
  dynamic_cast<TimeCondition*>(OrderCondition::create(
    OrderCondition::OrderConditionType::Time));
timeCondition->isMore(true);
timeCondition->time("20191101 09:30:00");
```

MarginCondition

Different contracts have different margin requirements, and requirements for futures contracts may change depending on volatility. By setting a `MarginRequirement`, you can disallow an order if the margin requirements are too high or too low.

- **percent** — the margin requirement to serve as a maximum or a minimum
- **isMore** — identifies whether the percent value is the maximum acceptable margin (0) or the minimum acceptable margin (1)

The following Python code creates a `MarginCondition` that only allows orders to be submitted if the margin requirement is less than forty percent.

```
margin_condition = order_condition.Create(OrderCondition.Margin)
margin_condition.isMore = false
margin_condition.percent = 40
```

PercentChangeCondition

A `PercentChangeCondition` makes it possible to disallow an order if the contract's price is too much higher or too much lower than the last closing price. To set this condition, you need to identify the maximum or minimum percent change. For this reason, the class provides the following fields (Python) or functions (C++):

- **changePercent** — The percent change to serve as the maximum or minimum
- **isMore** — If the `changePercent` value is a maximum (0) or a minimum (1)
- **conId** — The contract's ID
- **exch** — The contract's exchange

The `PercentChangeCondition` is the first of the `ContractConditions` discussed in this chapter. Because it's a subclass of `ContractCondition`, the application needs to set the contract's unique identifier (`conId`) and exchange (`exch`).

The following C++ code creates a `PercentChangeCondition` that only allows an order to be activated if its price has changed ten percent or less since the last closing price.

```
PercentChangeCondition* pcCondition =
  dynamic_cast<PercentChangeCondition*>(OrderCondition::create(
    OrderCondition::OrderConditionType::PercentChange));
pcCondition->isMore = false;
pcCondition->changePercent = 0.1;
```

VolumeCondition

A `VolumeCondition` is similar to a `PercentChangeCondition`, but it disallows orders based on the contract's current volume. By creating a `VolumeCondition`, applications can disallow an order if the current volume is too high or too low. A `VolumeCondition` provides access to the following fields (Python) or functions (C++):

- `volume` — The volume to serve as the maximum or minimum
- `isMore` — Whether the `volume` is a maximum (0) or a minimum (1)
- `conId` — The contract's ID
- `exch` — The contract's exchange

The following Python code creates a `VolumeCondition` that only allows orders to become active if the contract volume is greater than 20,000:

```
vol_condition = order_condition.Create(OrderCondition.Volume)
vol_condition.isMore = false
vol_condition.volume = 20000
```

Keep in mind that the `VolumeCondition` is concerned with the number of contracts that have been sold during the day, not the quantity of contracts traded in the order. None of the dynamic conditions are concerned with the order's quantity.

PriceCondition

The most complicated of the dynamic conditions is the `PriceCondition`, which makes it possible to allow or disallow orders if the contract's price has risen above a given price or fallen below a given price. To control how this works, an application can access five fields (Python) or functions (C++):

- `price` — The price to serve as the maximum or minimum
- `isMore` — Whether the price value is a maximum (0) or a minimum (1)
- `triggerMethod` — Determines how the contract's price is computed
- `conId` — The contract's ID
- `exch` — The contract's exchange

The `triggerMethod` field determine how the price is computed for the condition. This can be set to one of seven values: `Default`, `MidPoint`, `DoubleBidAsk`, `Last`, `DoubleLast`, `BidAsk`, or `LastBidAsk`.

The following C++ code shows how this works. It creates a `PriceCondition` that only allows contracts to be activated if the midpoint of the contract's bid and ask prices is less than 50.

```
PriceCondition* pcCondition =
  dynamic_cast<PriceCondition*>(OrderCondition::create(
    OrderCondition::OrderConditionType::Price));
pcCondition->isMore = false;
pcCondition->price = 50;
pcCondition->triggerMethod =
  PriceCondition::Method::MidPoint;
```

In Python, the values of `triggerMethod` are set by the `PriceCondition.TriggerMethodEnum` enumerated type. In C++, the `triggerMethod` values are defined in the `PriceCondition::Method` enumerated type.

10.5 Submitting Advanced Orders

At this point, you should be comfortable with order configuration, both the simple and advanced capabilities. In this section, I'll present an application that demonstrates how parent-child orders and dynamic order conditions can be used in practice. To be specific, this application performs six operations:

- Creates a contract for IBM stock
- Reads the unique identifier for the contract
- Creates a bracket order that associates a market order with a sell limit order and a sell stop order
- Creates a volume condition and associates it with the order
- Configures the order to use IB's Adaptive algorithm
- Places the order and prints the status

The code in this section demonstrates how these operations can be implemented in code. I'll start by explaining how they can be coded in Python and then show how they can be coded in C++.

10.5.1 Submitting Advanced Orders in Python

The code in the ch10/adv_order.py module shows how advanced ordering capabilities can be accessed in Python. The bracket order consists of a buy order to be submitted using IB's adaptive algorithm, a sell limit order to be executed if the price rises to 170 or beyond, and a sell stop order to be executed if the price falls to 120. Listing 10.1 presents the code.

Listing 10.1: ch10/adv_order.py

```python
class AdvOrder(EWrapper, EClient):
    ''' Serves as the client and the wrapper '''

    def __init__(self, addr, port, client_id):
        EWrapper.__init__(self)
        EClient.__init__(self, self)

        # Connect to TWS
        self.connect(addr, port, client_id)
        self.order_id = 0
        self.con_id = 0
        self.exch = ''

        # Launch the client thread
        thread = Thread(target=self.run)
        thread.start()

    @iswrapper
    def contractDetails(self, reqId, details):
        ''' Obtain details for the contract '''
        self.con_id = details.contract.conId
        self.exch = details.contract.exchange

    @iswrapper
    def nextValidId(self, order_id):
        ''' Obtain an ID for the order '''
        self.order_id = order_id

    @iswrapper
    def orderStatus(self, order_id, status, filled, remaining,
        avgFillPrice, permId, parentId, lastFillPrice, clientId,
        whyHeld, mktCapPrice):
        ''' Check the status of the submitted order '''

        print('Order status: {}'.format(status))
```

Listing 10.1: ch10/adv_order.py (Continued)

```python
    @iswrapper
    def error(self, req_id, code, msg):
        print('Error {}: {}'.format(code, msg))
def main():
    client = AdvOrder('127.0.0.1', 7497, 0)
    time.sleep(0.5)

    # Define the contract
    con = Contract()
    con.symbol = 'IBM'
    con.secType = 'STK'
    con.currency = 'USD'
    con.exchange = 'SMART'

    # Get unique ID for contract
    client.reqContractDetails(0, con)
    time.sleep(3)

    # Create a volume condition
    vol_condition = Create(OrderCondition.Volume)
    vol_condition.conId = client.con_id
    vol_condition.exchange = client.exch
    vol_condition.isMore = True
    vol_condition.volume = 20000

    # Obtain an ID for the main order
    client.reqIds(1000)
    time.sleep(2)

    # Create the bracket order
    main_order = Order()
    main_order.orderId = client.order_id
    main_order.action = 'BUY'
    main_order.orderType = 'MKT'
    main_order.totalQuantity = 100
    main_order.transmit = False
    main_order.conditions.append(vol_condition)

    # Set the algorithm for the order
    main_order.algoStrategy = 'Adaptive'
    main_order.algoParams = []
    main_order.algoParams.append(TagValue('adaptivePriority',
        'Patient'))
```

Listing 10.1: ch10/adv_order.py (Continued)

```
    # First child order - limit order
    first_child = Order()
    first_child.orderId = client.order_id + 1
    first_child.action = 'SELL'
    first_child.orderType = 'LMT'
    first_child.totalQuantity = 100
    first_child.lmtPrice = 170
    first_child.parentId = client.order_id
    first_child.transmit = False

    # Stop order child
    second_child = Order()
    second_child.orderId = client.order_id + 2
    second_child.action = 'SELL'
    second_child.orderType = 'STP'
    second_child.totalQuantity = 100
    second_child.auxPrice = 120
    second_child.parentId = client.order_id
    second_child.transmit = False

    # Submit each order
    client.placeOrder(client.order_id, con, main_order)
    client.placeOrder(client.order_id+1, con, first_child)
    client.placeOrder(client.order_id+2, con, second_child)

      # Sleep while the request is processed
    time.sleep(5)
    client.disconnect()

if __name__ == '__main__':
    main()
```

This code creates a `Contract` for IBM stock and then calls `reqContractDetails` to obtain the contract's unique ID and exchange. This information is needed to create the `VolumeCondition` associated with the order.

This module creates three `Order` structures—one parent order and two child orders. It's important to notice that each order has a different ID, but the `parentId` field of the child orders has the same value as the parent's order ID.

I've set the `transmit` field of each order to `False` to prevent readers from accidentally submitting an order that will affect their brokerage account. To make this code capable of real-world usage, set the transmit field of `second_child` to `True`.

10.5.2 Submitting Advanced Orders in C++

The code in the Ch10_AdvOrder project demonstrates how C++ developers can take advantage of IB's advanced ordering capabilities. This application creates and submits three orders: a market order, a sell limit order, and a sell stop order.

The `main` function creates a `Contract`, three `Orders`, and an instance of the `AdvOrder` class. Then it calls the `reqContractDetails`, `reqIds`, and `placeOrder` functions of the `AdvOrder` instance. Listing 10.2 presents its code.

Listing 10.2: Ch10_AdvOrder/Main.cpp

```
int main() {

  Order mainOrder, firstChild, secondChild;

  // Connect to TWS or IB Gateway
  AdvOrder client("127.0.0.1", 7497, 0);

  // Define the contract
  Contract con = Contract();
  con.symbol = "IBM";
  con.secType = "STK";
  con.currency = "USD";
  con.exchange = "SMART";

  // Access contract details
  client.reqContractDetails(0, con);
  std::this_thread::sleep_for(std::chrono::seconds(2));
  client.signal.waitForSignal();
  client.reader->processMsgs();

  // Create a volume condition
  VolumeCondition* volumeCondition =
    dynamic_cast<VolumeCondition*>(OrderCondition::create(
      OrderCondition::OrderConditionType::Volume));
  volumeCondition->isMore(true);
  volumeCondition->volume(20000);
  volumeCondition->conId(client.conId);
  volumeCondition->exchange(client.exch);
  std::shared_ptr<OrderCondition>
    condition(dynamic_cast<OrderCondition *>(volumeCondition));
```

Listing 10.2: Ch10_AdvOrder/Main.cpp (continued)

```cpp
// Create the bracket order
mainOrder.orderId = client.orderId;
mainOrder.action = "BUY";
mainOrder.orderType = "MKT";
mainOrder.totalQuantity = 100;
mainOrder.transmit = false;
mainOrder.conditions.push_back(condition);

// Define the algorithm for the order
mainOrder.algoStrategy = "Adaptive";
mainOrder.algoParams.reset(new TagValueList());
TagValueSPtr tag(new TagValue("adaptivePriority", "Patient"));
mainOrder.algoParams->push_back(tag);

// Limit order child
firstChild.orderId = client.orderId + 1;
firstChild.action = "SELL";
firstChild.orderType = "LMT";
firstChild.totalQuantity = 100;
firstChild.lmtPrice = 170;
firstChild.parentId = client.orderId;
firstChild.transmit = false;

// Stop order child
secondChild.orderId = client.orderId + 2;
secondChild.action = "SELL";
secondChild.orderType = "STP";
secondChild.totalQuantity = 100;
secondChild.auxPrice = 120;
secondChild.parentId = client.orderId;
secondChild.transmit = false;

// Get an order ID
client.reqIds(1000);
std::this_thread::sleep_for(std::chrono::seconds(1));
client.signal.waitForSignal();
client.reader->processMsgs();

// Place the order
client.placeOrder(client.orderId, con, mainOrder);
client.placeOrder(client.orderId+1, con, firstChild);
client.placeOrder(client.orderId+2, con, secondChild);
```

Listing 10.2: Ch10_AdvOrder/Main.cpp (continued)

```
std::this_thread::sleep_for(std::chrono::seconds(1));
client.signal.waitForSignal();
client.reader->processMsgs();

// Disconnect
client.eDisconnect();
return 0;
}
```

This code associates the parent order with a volume condition that allows the order to be executed if the volume exceeds 20,000. The `OrderCondition::create` function returns a pointer to an `OrderCondition`, so this must be dynamically cast to a `VolumeCondition` pointer.

Unfortunately, the `conditions` field of the `Order` structure contains only shared pointers to `OrderConditions`. So the `VolumeCondition` pointer must be converted into a shared pointer to an `OrderCondition`.

This code assigns a submission algorithm for the order by setting its `algoStrategy` field to `Adaptive`. Then it creates a `TagValue` that associates the `adaptivePriority` name to a value of `Patient`. Lastly, the `TagValue` is converted to a pointer (`TagValueSPtr`) and then pushed onto the order's `algoParams` field.

10.6 Summary

From what I've seen, the APIs of most brokerages are too simple, supporting too few languages and providing too few types of securities. But IB's API provides an overabundance of features, and this is nowhere more evident than when dealing with the fields of the `Contract` and `Order` structures.

This chapter has presented many, but not all, of the advanced ordering capabilities supported by IB. The first section explained how orders can be associated with one another using parent-child relationships. This is particularly important if you want to adjust a stop order or submit a bracket order. In my personal algorithmic trading, I *always* use bracket orders.

The second section presented methods for splitting large orders into small orders. If set to a true value, the `blockOrder` field tells IB to treat the order as a block order. For greater control, an application can create a scale order by assigning values to the many `scale-` fields of the `Order` structure.

In addition to supporting block orders and scale orders, IB makes it possible to associate orders with submission algorithms. Most of these algorithms are concerned with splitting large orders into smaller orders that won't impact the security's price.

If you're concerned about changing market conditions, you can associate orders with dynamic conditions. These conditions identify criteria related to an order, such as its price, volume, margin, and so on. When the order is submitted, IB will only execute the order if the condition's criteria is met. The code for setting dynamic conditions is complex, but this is a powerful capability.

Chapter 11

Technical Indicators

In 1962, Richard Hamming famously asserted that "The purpose of computing is insight, not numbers." This is particularly true in algorithmic trading. Functions like `reqMktData` provide prices and volume data, but if you want to understand what's happening to a security over time, you need technical indicators.

Analysts use indicators to judge a security's condition in the same way doctors check a patient's health by listening to the heartbeat. To be specific, analysts use indicators to draw conclusions about the security's price: the price's future direction and whether the price implies that the security is oversold or undersold.

Analysts have devised countless indicators for examining securities. This chapter looks at eight popular indicators and divides them into four categories:

- **trend indicators** — based on averages of a security's price over time, determine how the security's current price relates to past prices
- **momentum indicators** — based on the change in a security's closing price from day to day (momentum)
- **volume indicators** — based on a security's price and average daily volume
- **volatility indicators** — based on changes in a security's price over time

In each case, I'll present the theory behind the indicator and then show how it can be computed in Python and C++. Later chapters build on these indicators to form more advanced trading systems.

11.1 Trend Indicators

Trend indicators seek to predict future prices by comparing the current price to past prices. This section discusses two popular trend indicators: the moving average indicator and the moving average convergence/divergence (MACD) indicator. After presenting the theory, I'll present code that demonstrates both methods.

For the sake of simplicity, all of the example code in this chapter accesses data related to IBM stock. IBM is traded on the NYSE exchange, so you'll need to have a suitable subscription to execute the code.

11.1.1 Moving Average

A moving average is computed by adding the closing prices of a security over N trading days and dividing by N. Applications can obtain prices by calling `reqHistoricalData` or `reqHistoricalTicks`, which were discussed in Chapter 8.

`reqHistoricalTicks` is fine for minute to minute data, but I prefer `reqHistoricalData` for daily closing prices. As a reminder, its signature is given as follows:

```
reqhistoricalData(tickerid, contract, endDateTime, durationstring,
    barsizesetting, whatToShow, useRTH, formatDate, keepUpToDate,
    chartoptions)
```

After the server provides its response, the financial data will be provided by the `historicalData` callback function:

```
historicalData(reqId, bar)
```

The `bar` parameter is an instance of the `Bar` class, which provides fields like `open`, `high`, `low`, and `close`. If `whatToShow` is set to `TRADES`, three additional `Bar` fields are available: `count`, `volume`, and `wap`.

Many traders prefer to compute weighted moving averages by multiplying each price by a weight. The largest weight is applied to the most recent price and the smallest weight is applied to the oldest price. One popular weighted average is the exponential moving average (EMA), and I'll discuss it shortly.

A common time frame or *lookback period* for a moving average is 100 days. Therefore, the following discussion presents code that computes 100-day moving averages in Python and C++.

Computing the Moving Average in Python

The code in the ch11/moving_average.py module computes the 100-day moving average of IBM stock for the preceding six months. To be precise, the `main` function creates a `Contract` for IBM stock and then calls `reqHistoricalData`.

Afterward, the `historicalData` updates a deque (double-ended queue) and computes the average when the deque is full. When all the data has been received, `historicalDataEnd` prints the list of averages. Listing 11.1 presents the code in the `historicalData` function.

Listing 11.1: ch11/moving_average.py (callback functions)

```
@iswrapper
def historicalData(self, reqId, bar):

    # Append the closing price to the deque
    self.stock_vals.append(bar.close)

    # Compute the average if 100 values are available
    if len(self.stock_vals) == 100:
        avg = sum(self.stock_vals)/len(self.stock_vals)
        self.avg_vals.append(avg)

@iswrapper
def historicalDataEnd(self, reqId, start, end):
    print('Moving average: {}'.format(self.avg_vals))
```

The constructor creates the deque with a maximum size of 100. If the deque is full and `historicalData` appends a value, the oldest value on the deque will be popped from the front. This makes deques particularly useful for moving averages and other operations requiring collections with a maximum size.

Computing the Moving Average in C++

The code in the Ch11_MovingAverage application computes the 100-day moving average of IBM stock for the preceding six months. The `main` function creates an instance of the `MovingAverage` class and calls `reqHistoricalData` to obtain stock prices.

As each price is received, the `historicalData` callback pushes the price onto its double-ended queue (deque). When the size of the deque reaches 100, the callback computes the moving average and pops the first element. Listing 11.2 presents the code of the `historicalData` and `historicalDataEnd` functions.

Listing 11.2: Ch11_MovingAverage/MovingAverage.cpp (callback functions)

```cpp
// Called in response to reqHistoricalData
void MovingAverage::historicalData(TickerId reqId,
  const Bar& bar) {

  double avg;

  // Get the 100-day moving average
  priceVals.push_back(bar.close);
  if (priceVals.size() == 100) {
    avg = std::accumulate(priceVals.begin(),
      priceVals.end(), 0.0) / priceVals.size();
    averageVals.push_back(avg);
    priceVals.pop_front();
  }
}

// Called after all data has been processed
void MovingAverage::historicalDataEnd(int reqId,
  const std::string& startDate, const std::string& endDate) {
  std::cout << "Moving Average: ";
  for (double val: averageVals) {
    std::cout << val << " ";
  }
  std::cout << std::endl;
}
```

The `historicalData` callback computes the moving average by invoking `std::accumulate` and dividing the result by the number of elements (100). Then it pushes the average onto a vector named `averageVals`.

The `historicalDataEnd` callback executes after all of the historical data has been received. This iterates through `averageVals` and prints each value to the console.

11.1.2 Moving Average Convergence/Divergence (MACD)

The moving average convergence/diverence (MACD) indicator is popular among analysts, but it's not easy to compute. To compute this indicator, you need to obtain three exponential moving averages, or EMAs. An EMA is a weighted moving average whose weights are determined by an exponentially decreasing series.

The EMA is computed by multiplying each closing price by an element of this series and adding the products together. Figure 11.1 illustrates a set of weights that could be used to obtain a 20-day EMA.

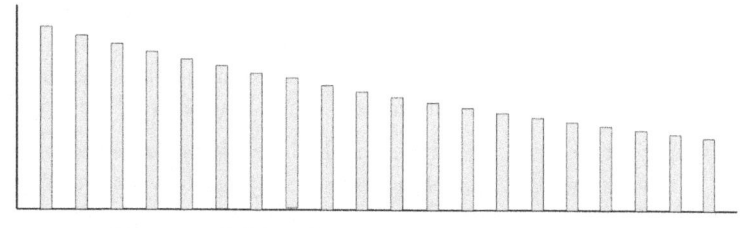

Figure 11.1 Weights of an Exponential Moving Average (EMA)

To compute the EMA, the first step is to determine how much the most recent price should be weighted. This value, denoted α, is usually set to 2/(N + 1), where N is the length of the desired series. Once this is computed, the N-day EMA for a series of prices p_i (p_0 through p_{N-1}) can be computed with the following equation:

$$EMA = \alpha p_0 + \alpha(1-\alpha)p_1 + \alpha(1-\alpha)^2 p_2 + \cdots + \alpha(1-\alpha)^{N-1} p_{N-1}$$

Traders apply the MACD indicator by comparing two series: the MACD series and the MACD signal line series. These can be computed with the following steps:

1. Compute the EMA of the prices over a 26-day period (the slow EMA).
2. Compute the EMA of the prices over a 12-day period (the fast EMA).
3. Take the difference between the slow and fast EMA. This is the MACD.
4. Compute the EMA of the MACD series over a 9-day period. This is the MACD signal line.

Analysts monitor the relationship between the MACD and the signal line to detect subtle changes to the security's price. If the two are close to one another (convergent), it implies that no sudden changes are expected to the price. But if the MACD crosses above the signal line, it implies that a rise in the security's price is significant. If the MACD crosses below the signal line, it implies that a fall in the security's price is significant.

Computing the MACD in Python

The code in ch11/macd.py demonstrates how the MACD indicator can be computed in Python. It starts by creating three deques:

- `slow_ema` — A 26-element deque that holds slow EMA values
- `fast_ema` — A 12-element deque that holds fast EMA values
- `macd_ema` — A 9-element deque that holds the differences between the slow EMA and fast EMA values

As new prices are received, `historicalData` multiplies each closing price by a suitable value of α and inserts it into the `slow_ema` and `fast_ema` deques. Then it computes the average of both deques and inserts the difference into `macd_ema`. Finally, the function updates the value of α using the relationship described earlier.

If the `macd_ema` deque is full, the callback computes the value of the MACD series and the MACD Signal Line series, and stores the values in separate lists. After all the data values have been received, the `historicalDataEnd` callback prints both lists to the console. Listing 11.3 shows how the callback functions are implemented.

Listing 11.3: macd.py (callback functions)

```
def historicalData(self, reqId, bar):

    # Append the closing price to the deques
    self.slow_ema.append(self.slow_alpha * bar.close)
    self.fast_ema.append(self.fast_alpha * bar.close)

    # Compute the averages if the slow deque is full
    if len(self.slow_ema) == SLOW_PERIOD:
        slow_avg = sum(self.slow_ema)/len(self.slow_ema)
        fast_avg = sum(self.fast_ema)/len(self.fast_ema)
        self.macd_ema.append(self.macd_alpha *
            (fast_avg - slow_avg))

    # Compute MACD and the signal line if the MACD deque is full
    if len(self.macd_ema) == MACD_PERIOD:
        self.macd_vals.append(self.macd_ema[-1])
        self.signal_vals.append(sum(self.macd_ema)/
            len(self.macd_ema))

    # Update exponential weights
    self.slow_alpha *= 1 - 2/(SLOW_PERIOD + 1)
    self.fast_alpha *= 1 - 2/(FAST_PERIOD + 1)
    self.macd_alpha *= 1 - 2/(MACD_PERIOD + 1)
def historicalDataEnd(self, reqId, start, end):
    print('MACD: {}'.format(self.macd_vals))
    print('Signal Line: {}'.format(self.signal_vals))
```

Each of the three deques has a corresponding value of α used to compute the series of exponential weights. For each deque, the initial value of α is set to 2/(N+1), where N is the maximum size of the deque. As new values are received, the new weight is obtained by multiplying the old weight by 1 − α.

Computing the MACD in C++

The Ch11_Macd project contains code that demonstrates how the MACD indicator can be computed in C++. Listing 11.4 presents the two callback functions that receive and process historical data to compute the indicator.

Listing 11.4: Ch11_Macd/Macd.cpp (callback functions)

```
// Called in response to reqHistoricalData
void Macd::historicalData(TickerId reqId, const Bar& bar) {

  double slowAvg, fastAvg, macdAvg;

  // Append the closing price to the deques
  slowEma.push_back(slowAlpha * bar.close);
  fastEma.push_back(fastAlpha * bar.close);

  // Compute the fast, slow, and MACD averages
  if (fastEma.size() == FAST_PERIOD + 1) {
    fastEma.pop_front();
  }
  if (slowEma.size() == SLOW_PERIOD) {
    fastAvg = std::accumulate(fastEma.begin(),
      fastEma.end(), 0.0) / fastEma.size();
    slowAvg = std::accumulate(slowEma.begin(),
      slowEma.end(), 0.0) / slowEma.size();
    macdEma.push_back(macdAlpha * (fastAvg - slowAvg));
    slowEma.pop_front();
  }

  // Compute MACD and the signal line if the MACD deque is full
  if (macdEma.size() == MACD_PERIOD) {
    macdVals.push_back(macdEma.back());
    macdAvg = std::accumulate(macdEma.begin(),
      macdEma.end(), 0.0) / macdEma.size();
    signalVals.push_back(macdAvg);
    macdEma.pop_front();
  }

  // Update exponential weights
  slowAlpha *= 1.0 - 2.0 / (SLOW_PERIOD + 1);
  fastAlpha *= 1.0 - 2.0 / (FAST_PERIOD + 1);
  macdAlpha *= 1.0 - 2.0 / (MACD_PERIOD + 1);
}
```

Listing 11.4: Ch11_Macd/Macd.cpp (callback functions continued)

```cpp
// Called after all historical data has been received/processed
void Macd::historicalDataEnd(int reqId, const std::string& startDate,
  const std::string& endDate) {

  std::cout << "MACD: ";
  for (double val: macdVals) {
    std::cout << val << " ";
  }
  std::cout << std::endl << "MACD Signal Line: ";
  for (double val : signalVals) {
    std::cout << val << " ";
  }
  std::cout << std::endl;
}
```

When a new closing price becomes available, `historicalData` multiplies it by `slowAlpha` and stores the product in the `slowEma` deque. It also multiplies the closing price by `fastAlpha` and stores the product in the `fastEma` deque. If the size of the `fastEma` deque exceeds the maximum, the callback pops the front value.

If the `slowEma` deque reaches its maximum size, the callback computes the average of both deques and inserts the difference into the `macdEma` deque. Then the function pops the front value from `slowEma` to ensure that the size never exceeds the maximum.

If the `macdEma` deque reaches its maximum value, the callback pushes the back value of the deque into the MACD series. Then it computes the average of `macdEma` and uses this to update the MACD signal line. After all the data values have been received, `historicalDataEnd` prints both lists to the console.

11.2 Momentum Indicators

Momentum indicators are similar to trend indicators, but in addition to paying attention to a security's price trend, they pay attention to its momentum. Momentum takes two important phenomena into account: rising asset prices tend to keep rising and falling prices tend to keep falling.

In practice, momentum is the difference between one day's closing price and the preceding day's closing price. By keeping track of momentum over several days, analysts can gauge whether investors are becoming more or less interested in trading the security.

This section focuses on two indicators that use momentum to gauge a security's price change. The first is the True Strength Index (TSI) and the second is the Relative Strength Index (RSI). Despite their similar names, the process of computing these indicators is quite different.

11.2.1 True Strength Index (TSI)

The True Strength Index, or TSI, assigns a value to the change in momentum over time. A high value indicates high buying momentum, which indicates that the security may be overbought. A low (negative) value indicates high selling momentum, which implies that the security may be oversold.

Computing the TSI requires six steps:

1. Compute the momentum by subtracting the previous day's closing price from today's closing price.
2. Compute the EMA of momentum over 25 days. I'll refer to this EMA as the *numerator base*.
3. Compute the EMA of the numerator base over 13 days. I'll refer to this EMA as the *numerator*.
4. Compute the EMA of the absolute value of momentum over 25 days. I'll refer to this EMA as the *denominator base*.
5. Compute the EMA of the denominator base over 13 days. I'll refer to this EMA as the *denominator*.
6. Divide the numerator by the denominator and multiply the quotient by 100. The result is the TSI.

Denoting momentum as m and the EMA of momentum over n days as EMA(m, n), the formula of the TSI can be expressed in the following way:

$$TSI = 100 \cdot \frac{EMA(EMA(m, 25), 13)}{EMA(EMA(|m|, 25), 13)}$$

The following discussion explains how to compute this indicator in Python and C++. In both cases, the applications rely on double-ended queues (deques) similar to those used in preceding indicators.

Computing TSI in Python

If you grasped how the deques were used in preceding discussions, you'll have no trouble understanding how the TSI indicator is computed in ch11/true_strength.py. This application creates four deques:

- num_base — Holds EMA values in the numerator base
- numerator — Holds EMA values in the numerator
- den_base — Holds EMA values in the denominator base
- denominator — Holds EMA values in the denominator

The historicalData callback updates these deques and the historicalDataEnd callback displays the final TSI values. Listing 11.5 presents the code.

Listing 11.5: ch11/true_strength.py (callback functions)

```python
def historicalData(self, reqId, bar):

    if self.old_close == -1:
        self.old_close = bar.close
        return

    # Compute momentum and absolute momentum
    m = bar.close - self.old_close
    abs_m = abs(m)
    self.old_close = bar.close

    # Update the numerator base and denominator base
    self.num_base.append(self.slow_alpha * m)
    self.den_base.append(self.slow_alpha * abs_m)

    # Compute the averages if the slow deque is full
    if len(self.num_base) == SLOW_PERIOD:
        num_base_avg = sum(self.num_base)/len(self.num_base)
        den_base_avg = sum(self.den_base)/len(self.den_base)
        self.numerator.append(self.fast_alpha * num_base_avg)
        self.denominator.append(self.fast_alpha * den_base_avg)

    # Compute MACD and the signal line if the MACD deque is full
    if len(self.numerator) == FAST_PERIOD:
        num_avg = sum(self.numerator)/len(self.numerator)
        den_avg = sum(self.denominator)/len(self.denominator)
        self.tsi_vals.append(100.0 * num_avg/den_avg)
```

Listing 11.5: ch11/true_strength.py (callback functions continued)

```
    # Update exponential weights
    self.slow_alpha *= 1 - 2/(SLOW_PERIOD + 1)
    self.fast_alpha *= 1 - 2/(FAST_PERIOD + 1)

@iswrapper
def historicalDataEnd(self, reqId, start, end):
    print('TSI: {}'.format(self.tsi_vals))
```

This module creates four deques, but there are only two different sizes. Therefore, only two different alpha values need to be computed, `slow_alpha` and `fast_alpha`. As each new closing price is received, `historicalData` multiplies it by `slow_alpha` and stores it in the numerator base deque (`num_base`) or the denominator base deque (`den_base`).

Both deques become full at the same time. When this happens, the application computes the average of the numerator base and denominator base, and uses this to update the deques containing the numerator and denominator.

When the numerator/denominator deques become full, the code computes their averages and divides them. Then it appends the result to the `tsi_vals` list and updates the alpha values. When all the close prices have been processed, `historicalDataEnd` prints the list to the console.

Computing TSI in C++

The code in the Ch11_TrueStrength project demonstrates how the TSI can be computed in C++. It processes closing prices as they're received, and stores processed values using four deques:

- `numBase` — Stores EMA values in the numerator base
- `num` — Stores EMA values in the numerator
- `denBase` — Stores EMA values in the denominator base
- `den` — Stores EMA values in the denominator

Each deque stores the result of the exponential moving average, EMA. The first and third deques have a maximum size of 25, so the corresponding alpha value (`slowAlpha`) is initialized to 1/26. The second and fourth deques have a maximum size of 13, so the corresponding alpha value (`fastAlpha`) is initialized to 1/14. The code in Listing 11.6 presents the `historicalData` callback, which updates the deques and alpha values.

Listing 11.6: Ch11_TrueStrength/TrueStrength.cpp (historicalData callback)

```cpp
void TrueStrength::historicalData(TickerId reqId, const Bar& bar)
{
  double m, absM, numBaseAvg, numAvg, denBaseAvg, denAvg;
  if (oldClose == -1.0) {
    oldClose = bar.close;
    return;
  }

  // Compute momentum and absolute momentum
  m = bar.close - oldClose;
  absM = abs(m);
  oldClose = bar.close;

  // Add momentum values to the deques
  numBase.push_back(slowAlpha * m);
  denBase.push_back(slowAlpha * absM);

  // Compute the nun/den base averages
  if (numBase.size() == SLOW_PERIOD) {
    numBaseAvg = std::accumulate(numBase.begin(),
      numBase.end(), 0.0) / numBase.size();
    num.push_back(fastAlpha * numBaseAvg);
    denBaseAvg = std::accumulate(denBase.begin(),
      denBase.end(), 0.0) / denBase.size();
    den.push_back(fastAlpha * denBaseAvg);
    numBase.pop_front();
    denBase.pop_front();
  }

  // Compute TSI values
  if (num.size() == FAST_PERIOD) {
    numAvg = std::accumulate(num.begin(),
      num.end(), 0.0) / num.size();
    denAvg = std::accumulate(den.begin(),
      den.end(), 0.0) / den.size();
    tsiVals.push_back(numAvg/denAvg);
    num.pop_front();
    den.pop_front();
  }

  // Update exponential weights
  slowAlpha *= 1.0 - 2.0 / (SLOW_PERIOD + 1);
  fastAlpha *= 1.0 - 2.0 / (FAST_PERIOD + 1);
}
```

After `historicalData` computes the average of each deque, it calls `pop_front` to remove the front value. This ensures that the length of each deque remains below its maximum.

After the averages are computed for the numerator and denominator, the quotient is pushed onto the `tsiVals` vector. The `historicalDataEnd` callback iterates through the vector and prints each TSI to the console.

11.2.2 Relative Strength Index (RSI)

Like the TSI, the Relative Strength Index (RSI) uses momentum to predict a security's future price. But the RSI uses a different type of moving average and computes the averages of different values.

As with the TSI, the RSI is based on the difference of the current closing price minus yesterday's closing price. A higher current price implies upward movement and a lower current price implies downward movement. The RSI stores upward movements and downward movements separately, and computes the average of each. The ratio of the two averages is called the *relative strength*, or RS.

To compute these averages, RSI relies on a new method called the smoothed moving average, or SMMA. If the current value of the series is p_i, the SMMA over N values is given by the following equation:

$$avg_i = \frac{(N-1)avg_{i-1} + p_i}{N} = \frac{p_i}{N} + \frac{(N-1)}{N}avg_{i-1}$$

Before the RSI can be determined, an application needs to determine the relative strength. This involves five steps:

1. Create a container of up periods. If the day's close is greater than the preceding day's, store the difference in the container. If not, store 0.
2. Create a container of down periods. If the preceding day's close is greater than the current close, store the difference in the container. If not, store 0.
3. Compute the SMMA of the container of up periods over 14 days. This is the *average gain*.
4. Compute the SMMA of the container of down periods over 14 days. This is the *average loss*.
5. Divide the average gain into the average loss. This is the current relative strength, or RS.

After the relative strength has been computed, the relative strength index (RSI) can be determined. Denoting relative strength as RS, RSI can be computed with the following equation:

$$RSI = 100 - \frac{100}{1+RS}$$

As shown, the result always lies between 0 and 100. According to RSI's inventor, J. Welles Wilder, a value of 70 indicates that the stock's price is reaching a high and a value of 30 indicates that the price is reaching a low.

Computing RSI in Python

The code in the ch11/relative_strength.py module demonstrates how the RSI can be computed in Python. This code receives closing prices through the `historicalData` callback and stores processed values in two deques:

- `up_periods` — Holds momentum when the current price is higher
- `down_periods` — Holds momentum when the current price is lower

The module computes the SMMA of both deques for the last 14 periods, and then divides the average to obtain the relative strength. Listing 11.7 presents the code that accomplishes this.

Listing 11.7: ch11/relative_strength.py (callback functions)

```
@iswrapper
def historicalData(self, reqId, bar):

    if self.old_close == -1:
        self.old_close = bar.close
        return

    # Append values to up/down periods
    if bar.close > self.old_close:
        self.up_periods.append(bar.close - self.old_close)
        self.down_periods.append(0.0)
    else:
        self.up_periods.append(0.0)
        self.down_periods.append(self.old_close - bar.close)
    self.old_close = bar.close
```

Listing 11.7: ch11/relative_strength.py (callback functions continued)

```python
        # Compute the SMMA of the up/down periods
        if len(self.up_periods) == RSI_PERIOD:
            up_avg = sum(self.up_periods)/RSI_PERIOD
            down_avg = sum(self.down_periods)/RSI_PERIOD
            if self.old_up_avg != -1:
                up_avg += (RSI_PERIOD-1) * self.old_up_avg/RSI_PERIOD
                down_avg += (RSI_PERIOD-1) *
                    self.old_down_avg/RSI_PERIOD
            self.old_up_avg = up_avg
            self.old_down_avg = down_avg

            # Compute the RS and the RSI
            rs = up_avg/down_avg
            self.rsi_vals.append(100 - 100/(1 + rs))

@iswrapper
def historicalDataEnd(self, reqId, start, end):
    print('RSI: {}'.format(self.rsi_vals))
```

The SMMA is easier to compute than the EMA because there are no alpha values to update and multiply. However, the application needs to store old values of the average (`old_up_avg` and `old_down_avg`) in order to compute the SMMA.

After computing the averages of the up periods and down periods, the module obtains the relative strength by dividing the two. Then it determines the RSI by computing 100 – 100/(1 + RS). The module stores each RSI value in a list, and the `historicalDataEnd` callback prints the list after all the prices have been processed.

Computing RSI in C++

The code in the Ch11_RelativeStrength project demonstrates how the RSI can be computed in C++. The `main` function calls `reqHistoricalData` to request six months of price data for IBM stock.

The data is provided by the `historicalData` callback, which subtracts the previous close from the current close. The result is pushed into one of two deques:

- `upPeriods` — Stores the difference when the current close is higher
- `downPeriods` — Stores the difference when the current close is lower

After computing the SMMAs of both deques, `historicalData` computes the relative strength and the RSI. Listing 11.8 presents the code.

Listing 11.8: Ch11_RelativeStrength/RelativeStrength.cpp (historicalData callback)

```cpp
void RelativeStrength::historicalData(TickerId reqId,
  const Bar& bar) {

  double m, upAvg, downAvg, rs;

  if (oldClose == -1.0) {
    oldClose = bar.close;
    return;
  }

  // Store momentum according to sign
  m = bar.close - oldClose;
  if (m > 0) {
    upPeriods.push_back(m);
    downPeriods.push_back(0.0);
  }
  else {
    upPeriods.push_back(0.0);
    downPeriods.push_back(-1.0 * m);
  }
  oldClose = bar.close;

   // Compute the SMMA of the up / down periods
  if (upPeriods.size() == RSI_PERIOD) {
    upAvg = std::accumulate(upPeriods.begin(),
      upPeriods.end(), 0.0) / upPeriods.size();
    downAvg = std::accumulate(downPeriods.begin(),
      downPeriods.end(), 0.0) / downPeriods.size();
    if (oldUpAvg != -1.0) {
      upAvg += (RSI_PERIOD - 1) * oldUpAvg / RSI_PERIOD;
      downAvg += (RSI_PERIOD - 1) *
        oldDownAvg / RSI_PERIOD;
    }
    oldUpAvg = upAvg;
    oldDownAvg = downAvg;

    // Compute the RS and the RSI
    rs = upAvg / downAvg;
    rsiVals.push_back(100.0 - 100.0 / (1.0 + rs));

    upPeriods.pop_front();
    downPeriods.pop_front();
  }
}
```

This code computes the SMMA of each deque by calling `std::accumulate` and dividing the sum by the deque's size. The result is added to the preceding average multiplied by 13/14.

After computing the SMMAs for the `upPeriods` and `downPeriods` deques, the callback divides the averages to obtain the relative strength (rs). Then it computes the RSI as 100 − 100/(1 + rs) and pushes the value onto the `rsiVals` vector. The `historicalDataEnd` callback prints the vector's content to the console.

11.3 Volume Indicators

Unlike the preceding indicators, volume indicators take both price and volume into account. A major increase in volume implies a new trend and a major decrease in volume implies an end to the current trend.

This section discusses two helpful volume indicators:

- **on-balance volume** — confirms price trends by monitoring whether volume is increasing or decreasing
- **accumulation/distribution line** — weights price changes by volume to confirm price movements

This section discusses both indicators and shows how they can be implemented in Python and C++.

11.3.1 On-Balance Volume

The on-balance volume, or OBV, is one of the oldest technical indicators, but many analysts continue to use it to confirm price movements. This indicator keeps a running sum of a security's daily volume, and the volume's sign is set to a negative value if the closing price is less than the previous closing price.

Denoting the current on-balance volume as OBV_i, the formula for on-balance volume is given as follows:

$$OBV_i = OBV_{i-1} + \begin{cases} volume & \text{if close}_i > \text{close}_{i-1} \\ 0 & \text{if close}_i = \text{close}_{i-1} \\ -volume & \text{if close}_i < \text{close}_{i-1} \end{cases}$$

As shown, the volume has a positive influence on OBV when the momentum (current close minus previous close) is positive. The volume has a negative influence on OBV when the momentum is negative. The following discussion explains how to implement this algorithm in Python and C++.

Computing On-Balance Volume in Python

The code in the ch11/on_balance_volume.py module shows how simple it is to implement the on-balance volume indicator. There are no deques to manage or moving averages to compute.

As `historicalData` receives a new price, it checks the sign of the momentum to determine how to update the preceding value. Then it computes the current value and appends it to a list named `obv_vals`. Listing 11.9 presents the code.

Listing 11.9: ch11/on_balance_volume.py (callback functions)

```python
@iswrapper
def historicalData(self, reqId, bar):

    if self.old_close == -1:
        self.old_close = bar.close
        return

    # Append values to up/down periods
    if bar.close > self.old_close:
        update = bar.volume
    elif bar.close < self.old_close:
        update = -1 * bar.volume
    else:
        update = 0
    self.old_close = bar.close

    # Update container of OBV values
    if not self.obv_vals:
        self.obv_vals.append(update)
    else:
        self.obv_vals.append(self.obv_vals[-1] + update)

@iswrapper
def historicalDataEnd(self, reqId, start, end):
    print('OBV: {}'.format(self.obv_vals))
```

This callback computes the current OBV value by adding `update` to the preceding OBV value. If the current close is greater than the preceding close, `update` is set to the current volume. If the current close is less than the preceding close, `update` is set to the negative of the current volume.

Computing On-Balance Volume in C++

The code in the Ch11_OnBalanceVolume project uses C++ to compute the on-balance volume indicator for six months of IBM stock. Instead of creating deques and computing their averages, it creates a single vector named `obvVals` to hold the final result.

The application receives new prices through `historicalData`, which compares each new price to the old price. Depending on the comparison, the application increases or decreases the current on-balance volume value. Listing 11.10 presents the code.

Listing 11.10: Ch11_OnBoardVolume/OnBoardVolume.cpp (callback functions)

```
void OnBalanceVolume::historicalData(TickerId reqId,
  const Bar& bar) {

  long long update, obv;

  if (oldClose == -1.0) {
    oldClose = bar.close;
    return;
  }

  // Append values to up / down periods
  if (bar.close > oldClose) {
    update = bar.volume;
  }
  else if (bar.close < oldClose) {
    update = -1 * bar.volume;
  }
  else {
    update = 0;
  }
  oldClose = bar.close;

  // Update container of OBV values
  if (obvVals.empty()) {
    obvVals.push_back(update);
  }
```

Listing 11.10: Ch11_OnBoardVolume/OnBoardVolume.cpp (callback functions continued)

```
    else {
      obv = obvVals.back() + update;
      obvVals.push_back(obv);
    }
}

// Called after all data has been processed
void OnBalanceVolume::historicalDataEnd(int reqId,
  const std::string& startDate, const std::string& endDate) {
  std::cout << "On-balance volume: ";
  for (long long val: obvVals) {
    std::cout << val << " ";
  }
  std::cout << std::endl;
}
```

If the preceding day's close is less than the current close, the callback sets `update` equal to the current volume. If the preceding day's close is greater than the current close, the callback sets `update` equal to the negative current volume.

If `obvVals` is empty, the callback pushes `update` onto the vector. Otherwise, it adds `update` to the last value in `obvVals`. The `historicalDataEnd` callback iterates through `obvVals` and prints its values to the console.

11.3.2 Accumulation/Distribution Line

Like a momentum indicator, the accumulation/distribution line monitors day-to-day price differences. Unlike momentum indicators, it multiplies each of these differences by the daily volume.

To derive the accumulation/distribution, this indicator relies on the *close location value*, or CLV. This identifies the day's closing price relative to the high and low prices, and it can be computed with the following equation:

$$CLV = \frac{(Close - Low) - (High - Close)}{High - Low}$$

The CLV ranges from +1 to −1. A positive value indicates that the closing price was closer to the high than the low. A negative value indicates that the closing price was closer to the low than the high.

To obtain points on the accumulation/distribution line, this indicator weights the CLV by the day's volume and adds it to the preceding day's value. Denoting the indicator as AD, this relationship can be expressed with the following equation:

$$AD_i = AD_{i-1} + volume \cdot CLV$$

A large value of AD implies that the stock is in accumulation (traders are buying) and a low value implies that the stock is in distribution (traders are selling). If AD is rising but the price is falling, it indicates that the price may start to rise. If AD is falling but the price is rising, it indicates that the price may start to decline.

Computing the Accumulation/Distribution Line in Python

The accumulation/distribution line is straightforward to compute, and this is made clear by the ch11/acc_dist.py module. As the `historicalData` callback receives a new price, it computes a new CLV. Then it multiplies the CLV by the current volume and updates the `acc_dist_vals` list. Listing 11.11 presents the code of the `historicalData` and `historicalDataEnd` callbacks.

Listing 11.11: ch11/acc_dist.py (callback functions)

```
@iswrapper
def historicalData(self, reqId, bar):

    # Compute the close location value(CLV)
    # and multiply it by volume
    clv = ((bar.close - bar.low) -
        (bar.high - bar.close))/(bar.high - bar.low)
    clv *= bar.volume

    # Update container of results
    if not self.acc_dist_vals:
        self.acc_dist_vals.append(clv)
    else:
        self.acc_dist_vals.append(self.acc_dist_vals[-1] + clv)

@iswrapper
def historicalDataEnd(self, reqId, start, end):
    print('Accumulation/Distribution:
        {}'.format(self.acc_dist_vals))
```

When a new price is received, `historicalData` computes the CLV using the close, high, and low prices. Then it multiplies the CLV by the current volume.

If the `acc_dist_vals` list is empty, the callback appends the CLV to the list. Otheriwse, it adds the CLV to the last element of `acc_dist_vals` and appends the sum to the list. Once all the data has been processed, the `historicalDataEnd` callback prints the list to the console.

Computing the Accumulation/Distribution Line in C++

The code in the Ch11_AccDist project shows how the accumulation/distribution line can be computed in C++. As each price is received, the `historicalData` callback computes the CLV and updates the `accDistVals` vector. Listing 11.12 presents the code for the `historicalData` and `historicalDataEnd` callbacks.

Listing 11.12: Ch11_AccDist/AccDist.cpp (callback functions)

```cpp
void AccDist::historicalData(TickerId reqId, const Bar& bar) {

  double ad;

  // Compute the CLV and multiply it by volume
  double clv = ((bar.close - bar.low) -
    (bar.high - bar.close)) / (bar.high - bar.low);
  clv *= bar.volume;

  // Update container of results
  if (accDistVals.empty()) {
    accDistVals.push_back(clv);
  }
  else {
    ad = accDistVals.back() + clv;
    accDistVals.push_back(ad);
  }
}

void AccDist::historicalDataEnd(int reqId, const std::string& startDate, const std::string& endDate) {
  std::cout << "Accumulation/Distribution: ";
  for (double val: accDistVals) {
    std::cout << val << " ";
  }
  std::cout << std::endl;
}
```

After computing the CLV, `historicalData` checks if the `accDistVals` vector is empty. If it is, the callback pushes the CLV onto the vector. If not, the callback adds the CLV to the last value in the vector and pushes the sum onto the vector. The `historicalDataEnd` callback prints the elements of `accDistVals` after all the prices have been received and processed.

11.4 Volatility Indicators

The preceding indicators have taken price and volume into account, but none of them have considered volatility. This may be acceptable for long-term investors, but in the short-term, volatility plays a major role in determining a security's price. This section looks at two volatility indicators: the Average True Range (ATR) and Bollinger Bands.

11.4.1 Average True Range (ATR)

A security's Average True Range (ATR) provides insight into a security's volatility by measuring *true ranges*. Normally, a security's range is just the difference between its daily high and low. The concept of true range extends this to include prices from the preceding day. A security's true range is the largest of three values:

- the normal range (high minus low)
- absolute value of the high minus the previous close
- absolute value of the low minus the previous close

The goal of the true range is to measure the level of interest in trading a security. Increasing ranges indicate that traders will continue trading with equal or greater enthusiasm. Decreasing ranges indicates that traders are growing disinterested.

The usual timeframe for true range measurement is 14 days. After the true ranges have been computed for 14 days, the first Average True Range (ATR) is computed using the smoothed moving average (SMMA) discussed earlier. Denoting the current true range as TR_i, the Average True Range (ATR) can be computed with the following equation:

$$ATR_i = \frac{13 \cdot ATR_{i-1} + TR_i}{14} = \frac{TR_i}{14} + \frac{13}{14} ATR_{i-1}$$

The first average, ATR_0, is obtained by taking the average of the N true ranges.

Computing the Average True Range in Python

The code in the ch11/average_true_range.py module demonstrates how to compute the ATR in Python. As the `historicalData` callback receives new prices, it computes the true range and then applies the SMMA to determine the Average True Range. Listing 11.13 presents the code.

Listing 11.13: ch11/average_true_range.py (callback functions)

```
@iswrapper
def historicalData(self, reqId, bar):

    if self.old_close == -1:
        self.old_close = bar.close
        return

    # Compute the true range
    true_range = max(bar.high - bar.low,
        abs(bar.high - self.old_close),
        abs(bar.low - self.old_close))
    self.true_ranges.append(true_range)
    self.old_close = bar.close

    # Compute the SMMA of the true range
        if len(self.true_ranges) == ATR_PERIOD:
            if not self.atr_vals:
                atr = sum(self.true_ranges)/ATR_PERIOD
            else:
                atr = ((ATR_PERIOD-1) * self.atr_vals[-1] +
                    true_range)/ATR_PERIOD
            self.atr_vals.append(atr)

@iswrapper
def historicalDataEnd(self, reqId, start, end):
    print('ATR: {}'.format(self.atr_vals))
```

The callback starts by computing the true range, which is the maximum of the difference between the high and low, the absolute value of the difference between the high and yesterday's close, and the absolute value of the difference between the low and yesterday's close. The result is appended to a deque named `true_ranges`.

When the deque is full, the callback computes the smoothed moving average of its values. Then it appends the result to a list named `atr_vals`. The `historicalDataEnd` callback prints the content of the list to the console.

Computing the Average True Range in C++

The Ch11_AverageTrueRange project contains code that computes the ATR in C++. When a new price is received, `historicalData` computes the true range and then pushes it onto a deque named `trueRanges`. Then the callback finds the Average True Range by computing the smoothed moving average of the deque's values. Listing 11.14 presents the code of the `historicalData` function.

Listing 11.14: Ch11_AverageTrueRange/AverageTrueRange.cpp (historicalData callback)

```cpp
// Called in response to reqHistoricalData
void AverageTrueRange::historicalData(TickerId reqId,
  const Bar& bar) {
  double trueRange, atrAvg;
  if (oldClose == -1.0) {
    oldClose = bar.close;
    return;
  }

  // Compute the true range
  trueRange = std::max({ bar.high - bar.low,
    abs(bar.high - oldClose), abs(bar.low - oldClose) });
  trueRanges.push_back(trueRange);
  oldClose = bar.close;

  // Compute the SMMA of the true range
  if (trueRanges.size() == ATR_PERIOD) {
    if (atrVals.empty()) {
      atrAvg = std::accumulate(trueRanges.begin(),
        trueRanges.end(), 0.0) / trueRanges.size();
    }
    else {
      atrAvg = ((ATR_PERIOD - 1) * atrVals.back() +
        trueRange) / ATR_PERIOD;
    }
    atrVals.push_back(atrAvg);
    trueRanges.pop_front();
  }
}
```

This code computes the SMMA by computing the average of the true ranges and adding this to the previous ATR multiplied by 13/14. The result is pushed onto the `atrVals` vector. The `historicalDataEnd` callback iterates through this vector and prints each ATR value to the console.

11.4.2 Bollinger Bands

Devised by John Bollinger in the 1980s, Bollinger Bands combine trend analysis and volatility analysis. Short-term investors frequently employ them to predict highs and lows in a security's pricing. To use this indicator, an application needs to compute three series:

- A 20-day simple moving average
- The 20-day moving average plus twice the standard deviation (upper band)
- The 20-day moving average minus twice the standard deviation (lower band)

The upper band represents high prices for the security and the lower band represents low prices. Many traders use these bands to set stop loss orders. Chapter 13 introduces a full trading system based on Bollinger Bands.

To compute values in the upper and lower bands, you need to be familiar with standard deviation. Standard deviation measures how far a variable moves away from its mean, and it's usually denoted σ (sigma). If a series contains N prices, denoted p_i, and the average price is μ, the following equation shows how σ can be computed:

$$\sigma = \sqrt{\frac{\sum_i (x_i - \mu)^2}{N}}$$

The following discussion explains how Bollinger Bands can be computed in Python and C++.

Computing Bollinger Bands in Python

The code in the ch11/bollinger.py module demonstrates how Bollinger Bands can be computed in Python. As new prices are received, `historicalData` stores them in a deque named `prices`.

When the deque's length reaches 20, the callback processes its values and stores the results in three lists:

- `avg_vals` — Contains the 20-day moving average
- `upper_band` — Contains the values in the upper band
- `lower_band` — Contains the values in the lower band

Listing 11.15 presents the callbacks that compute the Bollinger Bands in Python.

Listing 11.15: ch11/bollinger.py (callback functions)

```python
@iswrapper
def historicalData(self, reqId, bar):

    # Append the closing price to the deque
    self.prices.append(bar.close)

    # Compute the average if 100 values are available
    if len(self.prices) == AVERAGE_LENGTH:
        avg = sum(self.prices)/len(self.prices)

        # Compute the standard deviation
        avg_array = np.array(self.prices)
        sigma = np.std(avg_array)

        # Update the containers
        self.avg_vals.append(avg)
        self.upper_band.append(avg + 2*sigma)
        self.lower_band.append(avg - 2*sigma)

@iswrapper
def historicalDataEnd(self, reqId, start, end):
    print('Moving average: {}'.format(self.avg_vals))
    print('Upper band: {}'.format(self.upper_band))
    print('Lower band: {}'.format(self.lower_band))
```

In Python, the standard deviation can be computed with NumPy's `std` function. This code converts the `prices` deque to a NumPy array, and then calls `std` to obtain `sigma`. Then it uses `sigma` to compute values in the `upper_band` and `lower_band` lists. The `historicalDataEnd` callback prints all of the output lists to the console.

Computing Bollinger Bands in C++

The code in the Ch11_Bollinger project demonstrates how Bollinger Bands can be computed in C++. As `historicalData` receives new prices, it stores them in a deque named `prices`. When the size of `prices` reaches 20, the callback computes the average and standard deviation of the deque's values.

After computing the average and standard deviation, the callback stores the results in three vectors: `avgVals`, `upperVals`, and `lowerVals`. Listing 11.16 presents the code of the `historicalData` callback.

Listing 11.16: Ch11_Bollinger/Bollinger.cpp (callback functions)

```cpp
// Called in response to reqHistoricalData
void Bollinger::historicalData(TickerId reqId, const Bar& bar) {

  double avg, stdDev;

  // Compute the moving average
  prices.push_back(bar.close);
  if (prices.size() == BOLLINGER_PERIOD) {

    // Compute the average
    avg = std::accumulate(prices.begin(),
      prices.end(), 0.0) / prices.size();
    avgVals.push_back(avg);

    // Compute the standard deviation
    auto devFunc = [&avg](double acc, const double& p) {
      return acc + (p - avg)*(p - avg);
    };
    stdDev = std::accumulate(prices.begin(), prices.end(),
      0.0, devFunc);
    stdDev = std::sqrt(stdDev / BOLLINGER_PERIOD);

    // Compute the upper and lower bands
    upperVals.push_back(avg + 2 * stdDev);
    lowerVals.push_back(avg - 2 * stdDev);

    prices.pop_front();
  }
}
```

The most difficult aspect of this code involves finding the standard deviation. The C++ language doesn't provide a built-in function, so I've coded a simple operation named devFunc. This captures the moving average (avg), subtracts it from the incoming value, and returns the product of the difference with itself. The standard deviation is found by finding the mean of devFunc's return value and taking the square root.

When the second call to std::accumulate executes, it calls devFunc for each price in the prices deque. After computing the standard deviation, the callback computes the upper band value by adding twice the standard deviation to the current moving average. Then it computes the low band value by subtracting twice the standard deviation from the current moving average. The results are pushed onto the upperVals and lowerVals vectors, respectively.

11.5 Summary

Indicators play a central role in the field of technical analysis, and every analyst has a favorite set of indicators that they rely on. This chapter hasn't made any recommendations, but has introduced several indicators and demonstrated how they can be computed in code.

Trend indicators gauge a security's future direction by examining its past prices. Moving averages are particularly popular, and this chapter has looked at a few different ways of computing them. A simple moving average computes the average of past prices over a look-back period. An exponential moving average (EMA) weights each price by a value raised to an exponent. The moving average convergence/divergence (MACD) indicator judges a security's price by combining three EMAs: a 26-day EMA, a 12-day EMA, and a 9-day EMA.

Like trend indicators, momentum indicators form judgements based on a security's price. The difference is that momentum indicators focus on the price's momentum—the difference between the current closing price and the preceding closing price. The True Strength Index (TSI) judges whether a security is undersold or oversold by comparing the momentum to the absolute value of the momentum. The Relative Strength Index (RSI) reaches a similar decision by comparing the smoothed moving average of up periods (positive momentum) to the smoothed moving average of down periods (negative momentum).

Volume indicators take price and volume data into account. The on-balance volume (OBV) indicator judges the strength of price trends by checking whether volume is increasing or decreasing. The accumulation-distribution line multiplies the close location value by volume to determine whether a security is being accumulated (purchased) or distributed (sold).

Volatility indicators measure how much a security's price changes over time. The Average True Range (ATR) measures how far the security's price has moved within a day compared to the preceding day. Bollinger Bands measure the average and standard deviation of a security's price to predict a security's highs and lows.

Many traders rely on indicators to form a full decision-making process, or a trading system. Chapter 13 presents two trading systems based on indicators. The Turtle trading system relies on the Average True Range (ATR) discussed in this chapter, and the Bollinger-MFI system relies on Bollinger Bands.

Chapter 12

Implementing Option Combinations

Until this chapter, almost all of the code examples have focused on stocks. This chapter puts aside stocks and bonds and focuses solely on options and their combinations. This chapter walks through the process of selecting a directional strategy (credit spread) and a delta neutral strategy (straddle/strangle).

Before jumping into the code, the first section presents four functions that perform operations specific to options. Using these functions, applications can exercise options, read an option chain, or compute an option's volatility and price. These functions are particularly helpful when deciding when to execute a trade.

The second section explains how to select a credit spread and execute the order. As discussed in Chapter 4, a credit spread consists of two trades: the sale of an option for a large premium and the purchase of an option of the same type for a smaller premium. The second section presents a methodology for choosing the spread's strike prices and premiums, and then explains how to implement the method in code.

The third section walks through the process of selecting straddles and strangles. These strategies make a profit if the stock's price moves in either direction, so they're called delta neutral strategies. Both strategies consist of a put and call. The difference is that a straddle's put and call have the same strike price (at the money), while a strangle's put and call have different strike prices (out of the money). Strangles require larger price movements to make money, but are less expensive than straddles.

Keep in mind that I'm not a financial advisor and the methods discussed in this chapter shouldn't be construed as professional advice. My goal is simply to show how the TWS API can be used to read option chains and analyze them to decide on different option combinations.

12.1 Option-Specific Functions

Most of the functions in the TWS API apply to several types of securities, but four functions are specific to options trading. These haven't been discussed in preceding chapters, but they play an important role in this one. Table 12.1 lists each of them.

Table 12.1
Options-Specific Functions

Function	Description

`exerciseOptions(int tickerId,`
`    Contract contract, int exerciseAction,`
`    int exerciseQuantity, string account,`
`    int ovrd)`
	Exercise the specified option or allow it to lapse

`reqSecDefOptParams(int reqId,`
`    string underlyingSymbol,`
`    string futFopExchange,`
`    string underlyingSecType,`
`    int underlyingConId)`
	Request option chain data (strike prices and expirations)

`calculateImpliedVolatility(`
`    int reqId, Contract contract,`
`    double optionPrice, double underPrice,`
`    List<TagValue> impliedVolatilityOptions)`
	Computes implied volatility based on the price of the option and its underlying security

`calculateOptionPrice(int reqId,`
`    Contract contract, double volatility,`
`    double underPrice,`
`    List<TagValue> optionPriceOptions)`
	Computes an option's price based on the price and volatility of the underlying security

All of these functions except `exerciseOptions` are request functions. That is, they all belong to the client class and they all ask IB for information. After the response is received, applications can access the data through the wrapper's callback functions.

12.1.1 Exercising Options

An application can cancel orders by calling `cancelOrder` or `reqGlobalCancel`, but the only way to exercise an option is to call `exerciseOptions`. This accepts a contract that identifies the option and a parameter called `exerciseAction`. If this is set to 1, the function will exercise the option. If it's set to 2, the option will lapse.

By default, IB exercises ITM options and allows OTM options to lapse. If you're calling `exerciseOptions` to perform a contrasting operation, your application needs to set the `ovrd` parameter (override) to 1.

For example, the following code tells IB to exercise the option corresponding to the `goodCall` contract. Because `ovrd` is set to 1, IB will exercise the option even if it's out of the money.

```
exerciseOptions(0, goodCall, 1, 1, '...', 1)
```

Unlike most of the functions provided by the client, `exerciseOptions` doesn't have an associated callback function. This means the only way to find out whether your options have been exercised is to call `reqPositions` or one of the other account information functions discussed in Chapter 7.

12.1.2 Reading an Option Chain

Chapter 3 explained how to access option chains for a security in TWS. Accessing the same information in code isn't as easy. Calling `reqContractDetails` without a strike price provides some information, but it can be slow depending on how much data needs to be sent.

For this reason, IB recommends calling `reqSecDefOptParams`. This function accepts information about the underlying contract, such as its symbol, security type, and ID. It also accepts a parameter named `futFopExchange`, which only needs to be set if the underlying contract is a futures contract.

After calling `reqSecDefOptParams`, applications receive data through the `securityDefinitionOptionParameter` callback. Its signature is given as follows:

```
securityDefinitionOptionParameter(reqId, exchange,
    underlyingConId, tradingClass, multiplier, expirations,
    strikes)
```

The most important parameters of the callback are the last two. `expirations` contains expiration dates and `strikes` contains strike prices. With this information, an application can access option prices by calling one of the data request functions presented in Chapter 8.

Many option chains provide statistics such as volume, open interest, and implied volatility. Applications can obtain this in code by calling `reqMktData`, and I'll demonstrate this later in the chapter.

12.1.3 Computing Volatility, Greeks, and Options Pricing

Chapter 3 provided an overview of implied volatility (IV) and briefly mentioned the Black-Scholes equation that makes it possible to compute it. Many options traders use custom-coded Black-Scholes functions to determine theoretical options prices, but IB developers don't need to do this. The last two functions in Table 12.1, `calculateImpliedVolatility` and `calculateOptionPrice`, handle the heavy math for us.

The `calculateImpliedVolatility` function computes IV for a particular contract given the option's price and the price of the underlying security. For example, suppose `con` is a `Contract` for an option, `conPrice` is the option's price, and `undPrice` is the price of the underlying security. The option's IV can be obtained in Python using the following code:

```
calculateImpliedVolatility(0, con, conPrice, undPrice, [])
```

After calling `calculateImpliedVolatility`, an application can access the server's response through the `tickOptionComputation` callback. Its signature is given as follows:

```
tickOptionComputation(tickerId, field, impliedVolatility, delta,
    optPrice, pvDividend, gamma, vega, theta, undPrice)
```

This callback provides much more information than just the implied volatility. Chapter 3 discussed the `delta`, `gamma`, `vega`, and `theta` parameters, collectively called the Greeks. The `pvDividend` parameter identifies the present value of the dividend of the underlying security.

If you already know the IV, you can call `calculateOptionPrice` to obtain the theoretical price of an option. As an example, suppose `con` is a `Contract` for an option, `vol` is the option's volatility, and `undPrice` is the price of the underlying security. The option's theoretical price can be obtained in Python using the following code:

```
calculateOptionPrice(0, con, vol, undPrice, [])
```

Applications can access the option's price through the `tickOptionComputation` callback, which is the same callback associated with `calculateImpliedVolatility`. The computed option price is provided in the `optPrice` parameter.

12.1.4 Reading Option Chains in Code

The strategy-selection algorithms discussed in this chapter are based on option chain data. This makes it important to understand how option chains can be accessed in code. The process involves four steps:

1. Call `reqContractDetails` to obtain the ID of the underlying contract.
2. Call `reqTickByTickData` to obtain the current price of the underlying contract.
3. Call `reqSecDefOptParams` to obtain the option's strike prices and expirations.
4. Call `reqMktData` to access statistics like ask/bid prices, and ask/bid sizes.

Of these steps, the last is the most complex. This is because `reqMktData` requires a special code to request particular option data. Then the data returned by `tickPrice` and `tickSize` needs to be identified by tick ID.

This discussion explains how to implement these operations in Python and C++. In both cases, the goal is to read the chain for an option based on IBM stock.

Reading Option Chains in Python

In this chapter, option chains are represented by a nested map that associates strike prices with option types and statistics. The first key identifies the strike price and the second key identifies the option type (C for call or P).

The chain associates these keys with statistic names, which are mapped to values. For example, suppose a call with a strike price of 120 has an ask price of 80, an ask size of 150, a bid price of 75, and a bid size of 220. If the name of the option chain is chain, these values can be set with the following code:

```
chain[120]['C']['ask_price'] = 80
chain[120]['C']['ask_size'] = 150
chain[120]['C']['bid_price'] = 75
chain[120]['C']['bid_size'] = 220
```

The example application is only concerned with the earliest valid date over 21 days away. It's only concerned with strike prices at most seven units away from the current price of the underlying stock.

The code in ch12/chain_reader.py demonstrates how option chain data can be accessed in code. Listing 12.1 presents the read_option_chain function, which calls the four functions (reqContractDetails, reqTickByTickData, reqSecDefOptParams, and reqMktData) that request data.

Listing 12.1: ch12/chain_reader.py (read_option_chain function)

```
def read_option_chain(client, ticker):

    # Define a contract for the underlying stock
    contract = Contract()
    contract.symbol = ticker
    contract.secType = 'STK'
    contract.exchange = 'SMART'
    contract.currency = 'USD'
    client.reqContractDetails(0, contract)
    time.sleep(2)

    # Get the current price of the stock
    client.reqTickByTickData(1, contract, "MidPoint", 1, True)
    time.sleep(4)

    # Request strike prices and expirations
    if client.conid:
        client.reqSecDefOptParams(2, ticker, '',
            'STK', client.conid)
        time.sleep(2)
    else:
        print('Failed to obtain contract identifier.')
        exit()

    # Create contract for stock option
    req_id = 3
    if client.strikes:
        for strike in client.strikes:
            client.chain[strike] = {}
            for right in ['C', 'P']:

                # Add to the option chain
                client.chain[strike][right] = {}

                # Define the option contract
                contract.secType = 'OPT'
                contract.right = right
                contract.strike = strike
                contract.exchange = client.exchange
                contract.lastTradeDateOrContractMonth =
                    client.expiration
```

Listing 12.1: ch12/chain_reader.py (read_option_chain function continued)

```
                # Request option data
                client.reqMktData(req_id, contract,
                    '100', False, False, [])
                req_id += 1
                time.sleep(1)
    else:
        print('Failed to access strike prices')
        exit()
    time.sleep(5)

    # Remove empty elements
    for strike in client.chain:
        if client.chain[strike]['C'] == {} or
            client.chain[strike]['P'] == {}:
            client.chain.pop(strike)
    return client.chain, client.atm_price
```

This function accepts the client to use for communication and the ticker of the option's underlying stock. The function starts by creating a contract for the stock and calling `reqContractDetails` to obtain the contract's ID. Then it calls `reqTickByTickData` to obtain the current price of the stock.

Next, the function calls `reqSecDefOptParams` to obtain the different strike prices and expirations for the stock option. For each strike price and option type, the function creates a contract representing the option and calls `reqMktData` to obtain the option's bid size, ask size, bid price, and bid size.

After the server sends its response, the application can access it through its callback functions. Listing 12.2 presents the callback functions in the chain_reader.py module.

Listing 12.2: ch12/chain_reader.py (callback functions)

```
@iswrapper
def contractDetails(self, reqId, desc):
    ''' Obtain contract ID '''
    self.conid = desc.contract.conId

@iswrapper
def tickByTickMidPoint(self, reqId, time, midpoint):
    ''' Obtain current price '''
    self.current_price = midpoint
```

Listing 12.2: ch12/chain_reader.py (callback functions continued)

```python
@iswrapper
def securityDefinitionOptionParameter(self, reqId, exchange,
underlyingConId, tradingClass, multiplier, expirations, strikes):
    ''' Provide strike prices and expiration dates '''

    # Save expiration dates and strike prices
    self.exchange = exchange
    self.expirations = expirations
    self.strikes = strikes

@iswrapper
def securityDefinitionOptionParameterEnd(self, reqId):
    ''' Process data after receiving strikes/expirations '''

    # Find strike price closest to current price
    self.strikes = sorted(self.strikes)
    min_dist = 99999.0
    for i, strike in enumerate(self.strikes):
        if strike - self.current_price < min_dist:
            min_dist = abs(strike - self.current_price)
            self.atm_index = i
    self.atm_price = self.strikes[self.atm_index]

    # Limit strike prices to +7/-7 around ATM
    front = self.atm_index - 7
    back = len(self.strikes) - (self.atm_index + 7)
    if front > 0:
        del self.strikes[:front]
    if back > 0:
        del self.strikes[-(back-1):]

    # Find an expiration date just over a month away
    self.expirations = sorted(self.expirations)
    for date in self.expirations:
        exp_date = datetime.strptime(date, '%Y%m%d')
        current_date = datetime.now()
        interval = exp_date - current_date
        if interval.days > 21:
            self.expiration = date
            print('Expiration: {}'.format(self.expiration))
            break
```

Listing 12.2: ch12/chain_reader.py (callback functions continued)

```python
@iswrapper
def tickPrice(self, req_id, field, price, attribs):
    ''' Provide option's ask price/bid price '''

    if (field != 1 and field != 2) or price == -1.0:
        return

    # Determine the strike price and right
    strike = self.strikes[(req_id - 3)//2]
    right = 'C' if req_id & 1 else 'P'

    # Update the option chain
    if field == 1:
        self.chain[strike][right]['bid_price'] = price
    elif field == 2:
        self.chain[strike][right]['ask_price'] = price

@iswrapper
def tickSize(self, req_id, field, size):
    ''' Provide option's ask size/bid size '''

    if (field != 0 and field != 3) or size == 0:
        return

    # Determine the strike price and right
    strike = self.strikes[(req_id - 3)//2]
    right = 'C' if req_id & 1 else 'P'

    # Update the option chain
    if field == 0:
        self.chain[strike][right]['bid_size'] = size
    elif field == 3:
        self.chain[strike][right]['ask_size'] = size
```

As discussed earlier, the `securityDefinitionOptionParameter` and `securityDefinitionOptionParameterEnd` callbacks are called in response to `reqSecDefOptParam`. The first callback provides strike prices and expiration dates for a given exchange and the second callback is called when all of the data has been provided.

The `securityDefinitionOptionParameterEnd` iterates through the strike prices to find the one closest to the current stock price. If necessary, the callback reduces the list of prices to seven entries on either side of the ATM price.

After receiving the strike prices, the application calls `reqMktData` to request option chain data for a specific strike price. The application accesses the data through the `tickSize` and `tickPrice` callbacks. To be specific, `tickSize` provides the bid size (`field` equals 0) and ask size (`field` equals 3). `tickPrice` provides the bid price (`field` equals 1) and ask price (`field` equals 2).

`tickSize` and `tickPrice` may be called out of order. For this reason, the application checks the callback's request ID to determine which strike price and type corresponds to the provided data. An odd ID value indicates that the data corresponds to a call and an even ID indicates that the data corresponds to a put.

Reading Option Chains in C++

The code in the Ch12_ChainReader project demonstrates how to read an option chain in C++. The `main` function starts by creating an instance of the `ChainReader` class, and once the connection is established, it requests data by calling the `ChainReader`'s functions. After the data has been received and processed, `main` prints the option chain and disconnects.

The `ChainReader` class is declared in the ChainReader.h header file and its functions are defined in ChainReader.cpp. More precisely, ChainReader.cpp defines the callback functions invoked in response to the data requests.

As the callback functions are called, the `ChainReader` stores the processed data in three containers:

- `expirations` — a `std::set` of strings identifying expiration dates
- `strikes` — a `std::set` of double-precision values identifying strike prices
- `chain` — a `std::map` that associates each strike price with a second `std::map` that associates rights with an `Option` structure

Each right is identified by a character: C for a call option, P for a put option. In case the `chain` container sounds confusing, its declaration in the ChainReader.h header file is given as follows:

```
std::map<double, std::map<char, Option>> chain;
```

An `Option` structure stores the price and volume data for an option. This has four fields, and each is a `double`: `bidSize`, `askSize`, `bidPrice`, and `askPrice`. These values are set in the `ChainReader`'s `tickSize` and `tickPrice` callbacks. Listing 12.3 presents these and other callback functions of ChainReader.cpp.

Listing 12.3: Ch12_ChainReader/ChainReader.cpp (callback functions)

```cpp
// Obtain contract ID
void ChainReader::contractDetails(int reqId,
    const ContractDetails& details) {
    conId = details.contract.conId;
}

// Obtain current price
void ChainReader::tickByTickMidPoint(int reqId, time_t time,
    double midPoint) {
    currentPrice = midPoint;
}

// Read strike prices and expiration dates
void ChainReader::securityDefinitionOptionalParameter(int reqId,
    const std::string& exch, int underlyingConId,
    const std::string& tradingClass,
    const std::string& multiplier,
    const std::set<std::string>& exp,
    const std::set<double>& optStrikes) {

    exchange = exch;
    expirations = exp;
    strikes = optStrikes;
}

// Process data after receiving strikes/expirations
void ChainReader::securityDefinitionOptionalParameterEnd(
    int reqId) {

    double minDist = 99999.0;
    int atmIndex, i = 0;
    std::set<double>::iterator strikeIter;
    struct std::tm tmpTime = { 0 };
    long int expTime;
    int year, month, day;

    // Find the index of the strike nearest ATM
    for (double strike : strikes) {
        if (strike - currentPrice < minDist) {
            minDist = abs(strike - currentPrice);
            atmIndex = i;
        }
        i++;
    }
```

Chapter 12 Implementing Options Combinations

Listing 12.3: Ch12_ChainReader/ChainReader.cpp (callback functions continued)

```cpp
    // Limit strike prices to +7/-7 around ATM
    int front = atmIndex - 7;
    int back = -1 * (strikes.size() - (atmIndex + 7));

    // Update strike prices
    if (front > 0) {
        strikeIter = strikes.begin();
        std::advance(strikeIter, front);
        strikes.erase(strikes.begin(), strikeIter);
    }
    if (back < 0) {
        strikeIter = strikes.end();
        std::advance(strikeIter, back);
        strikes.erase(strikeIter, strikes.end());
    }

    // Initialize structures in option chain
    for (double strike : strikes) {
        chain[strike]['C'].bidSize = -99;
        chain[strike]['P'].bidSize = -99;
    }

    // Find the nearest expiration date over 21 days away
    long int monthTime = static_cast<long int>
        (std::time(nullptr)) + 60 * 60 * 24 * 21;
    for (std::string exp : expirations) {

      // Can't use std::get_line because of Visual Studio issues
      sscanf(exp.c_str(), "%4d%2d%2d", &year, &month, &day);
      tmpTime.tm_sec = 0;
      tmpTime.tm_min = 0;
      tmpTime.tm_hour = 0;
      tmpTime.tm_year = year - 1900;
      tmpTime.tm_mon = month - 1;
      tmpTime.tm_mday = day;
      expTime = static_cast<long int>(std::mktime(&tmpTime));

      // Compare expiration date to three weeks away
      if (expTime > monthTime) {
          expiration = exp;
          break;
      }
   }
}
```

The `contractDetails` callback provides the unique identifier associated with the IBM stock. The `main` function needs this to call `reqSecDefOptParams`, which requests parameters related to the stock option.

When `reqSecDefOptParams` is called, the response data is provided in the `securityDefinitionOptionalParameter` callback. In this application, the only parameters needed are the option's exchange, strike prices, and expiration dates.

Once this data becomes available, `securityDefinitionOptionalParameterEnd` determines which expiration date and strike prices should be stored in the option chain. To select strike prices, it finds the difference between each strike price and the stock's current price. It limits the prices to seven above the current price and seven below the current price.

Next, the callback selects one of the many available expiration dates. In particular, it's interested in the nearest option that expires over three weeks away. To make this selection, it converts each expiration date to a `std::tm` and converts this to the number of seconds since the epoch. Using epoch values, it checks whether the expiration date is greater than three weeks past the current date.

The callback also iterates through the strike prices and sets the `bidSize` field of each option to -99. This may seem confusing, but it's necessary to ensure that the `main` function can distinguish between uninitialized option structures and option structures whose fields have been set to zero.

12.2 Constructing Vertical Spreads

Many books have been written on options trading and they all provide advice regarding which type of combination to trade when different conditions arise. But I've never encountered a book that presents a mathematical method for picking strike prices and premiums of options in a combination. This is a shame, because algorithmic trading requires precise instructions.

To make up for this shortcoming, I've devised an algorithm for trading vertical spreads consisting of monthly options. As discussed in Chapter 4, a vertical spread consists of selling and buying two options with the same type, expiration, and underlying security. I'll refer to the option trade with the higher premium as the *major trade* and the option trade with the lower premium as the *minor trade*.

Keep in mind that this is a book on programming, not strategy development. I won't defend this algorithm or make any claims regarding its performance or reliability. But I am certain that it can be implemented in Python and C++, and I'll present the code after I explain how the algorithm works.

12.2.1 A Spread Selection Algorithm

To understand this algorithm, it's important to be familiar with probability and expected profit. If a trade has N possible profits r_i and each outcome has probability p_i, the expected profit, R, is given as follows:

$$R = \sum_{i=0}^{N} p_i r_i$$

An example will make this clear. Suppose your algorithm picks good trades 70% of the time and bad trades 30% of the time. Suppose further that each good trade has an averge profit of 5 and each bad trade has an average profit of −8. Then each trade picked by the algorithm has an expected profit of 0.7(5) + 0.3(−8) = 1.1.

The expected profit of a vertical spread can be obtained by multiplying the profit at each stock price by the probability of the stock reaching that price. Finding the spread's profit at a stock price is easy, as illustrated in Figure 12.1, which depicts a bear call spread.

In this figure, the stock's price is represented by S, the major trade has premium P1 and strike price K1, and the minor trade has premium P2 and strike price K2.

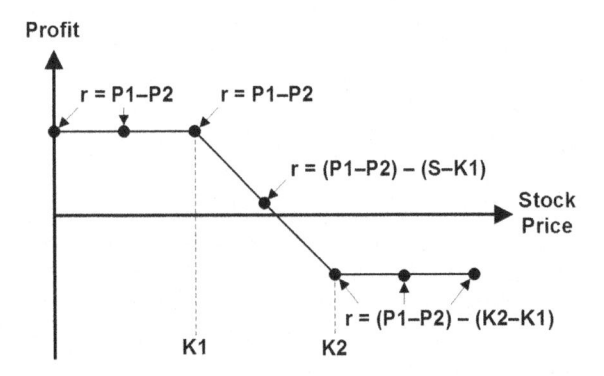

Figure 12.1 Computing the Profit of a Vertical Spread

The difficulty involves obtaining the probabilities of the different stock prices. Countless methods have been devised for this purpose, and I'm going to present one more. The algorithm discussed here computes probabilities according to the behavior of options sellers, particularly sellers of OTM options. The focus is on sellers instead of buyers because sellers have much more to lose.

To explain how this algorithm determines price probability from seller behavior, I need to explain how an option trade conveys the seller's *belief*. If a trader offers to sell an option with strike price K at a premium P, the algorithm assigns a level of belief using the following method:

- If the option is a call, the seller makes a profit if the stock price stays below the breakeven point, K + P. If the ask size for this option is N, the algorithm assigns a belief level of N that the stock's price is going to equal K + P or stay below.
- If the option is a put, the seller makes a profit if the stock price stays above the breakeven point, K − P. If the ask size for this option is N, the algorithm assigns a belief level of N that the stock's price is going to equal K − P or stay above.

After obtaining belief levels for different options in an option chain, the algorithm computes probabilities for the stock's future price. The computation process consists of five steps:

1. Form an array of sorted prices, one for each OTM option in the chain. For each OTM put, set the price to K − P. For each OTM call, set the price to K + P.
2. Associate each price with a belief whose initial value is 0.
3. Find the ask size of the put corresponding to the lowest price and add this to the belief level of all prices. Find the ask size of the put corresponding to the second lowest price (K, P) and add this to the belief level of all prices equaling K − P or greater. Repeat this for all puts in the chain.
4. Do the reverse for the calls. That is, find the ask size of the call corresponding to the highest price and add this to the belief level of all prices. Find the ask size of the call corresponding to the second highest price (K, P) and add this to the belief level of all prices equaling K + P or less. Repeat this for all calls in the chain.
5. Compute the sum of all the belief levels. For each price, divide the belief level into the sum. The result is the predicted probability for the price.

To see how this works, it helps to walk through an example. Consider the abridged option chain in Figure 12.2. The algorithm is only interested in the OTM ask prices, which are colored in gray.

To the right of the option chain, a column lists the prices, beliefs, and probabilities for each option. For calls, the prices equal the strike price plus the premium. For puts, the prices equal the strike price minus the premium.

Chapter 12 Implementing Options Combinations

| CALLS | | Strike | PUTS | | Price | Belief | Probability |
Ask Price	Ask Size	Price	Ask Price	Ask Size			
4.40	402	49	0.08	441	49.08	1813	0.098
3.45	474	50	0.12	292	50.12	2105	0.113
2.52	10	51	0.21	316	51.21	2421	0.130
1.71	229	52	0.40	379	52.40	2800	0.151
--	--	53	--	--	--	--	--
0.54	96	54	1.24	53	53.46	2800	0.151
0.25	415	55	1.97	132	54.75	2704	0.146
0.11	652	56	2.92	119	55.89	2289	0.123
0.05	209	57	3.85	26	56.95	1637	0.088
						Expected Price:	52.995

Figure 12.2 Abridged Option Chain and Beliefs

After computing probabilities, the algorithm determines the expected value of the stock price by multiplying each belief by its probability. As shown in the lower right of the figure, the result is 52.995.

We can also compute the projected profit of vertical spreads. To see how this works, consider a bear call spread in which the trader sells a call with a strike price of K1 for P1 and buys a call at a strike price of K2 for P2. Figure 12.3 shows what this looks like.

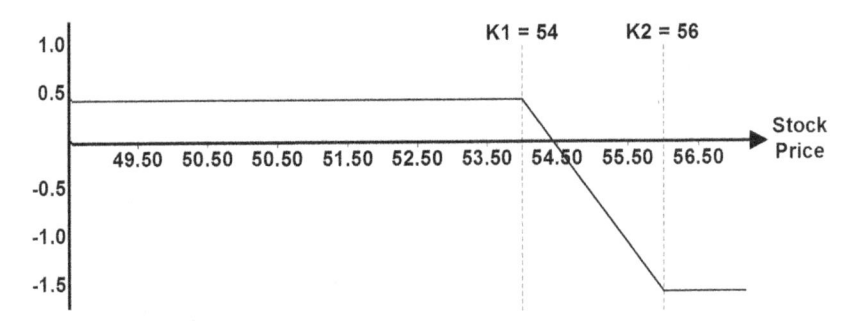

Figure 12.3 Profit of a Vertical Spread

The profit obtained by the trader depends on the stock price (S):

- If S is less than K1, the profit is (P1 − P2).
- If S is greater than K1 but less than K2, the profit is (P1 − P2) − (S − K1)
- If S is greater than K2, the profit is (P1 − P2) − (K2 − K1)

The expected profit of this spread can be obtained by multiplying the profit of each belief by the associated probability. Table 12.2 presents the results.

Table 12.2
Computing Expected Profit

Belief	Expression for Profit	Result
49.08	(0.54 - 0.11) * 0.098	0.042
50.12	(0.54 - 0.11) * 0.113	0.049
51.21	(0.54 - 0.11) * 0.130	0.056
52.40	(0.54 - 0.11) * 0.151	0.065
53.46	(0.54 - 0.11) * 0.151	0.065
54.75	[(0.54 - 0.11) - (54.75 - 54)] * 0.146	-0.047
55.89	[(0.54 - 0.11) - (55.89 - 54)] * 0.123	-0.180
56.95	[(0.54 - 0.11) - (56 - 54)] * 0.088	-0.138
		-0.088

As stated on the last row, the expected profit for this spread is −0.088. This indicates that the spread isn't worth considering.

Having derived a process for computing the expected return of one spread, it's straightforward to determine the best vertical spread for a given option chain. Just iterate through each vertical spread and choose the one with the highest expected profit.

For the option chain in Figure 12.2, there are 24 possible vertical spreads that involve OTM trades. Table 12.3 lists their types, strike prices, and expected profit.

Table 12.3
Comparing Returns of Vertical Spreads

Spread Type	K1	K2	Expected Profit
Bull call	54	55	0.031
Bull call	55	56	0.058
Bull call	56	57	0.024
Bull call	54	56	0.089
Bull call	55	57	0.082
Bull call	54	57	0.112
Bear call	54	55	-0.031
Bear call	55	56	-0.058
Bear call	56	57	-0.024
Bear call	54	56	-0.089

Bear call	55	57	-0.082
Bear call	54	57	-0.112
Bull put	52	51	-0.048
Bull put	51	50	-0.021
Bull put	50	49	0.032
Bull put	52	50	-0.087
Bull put	51	49	-0.004
Bull put	52	49	-0.103
Bear put	52	51	0.048
Bear put	51	50	0.021
Bear put	50	49	-0.032
Bear put	52	50	0.087
Bear put	51	49	0.004
Bear put	52	49	0.103

As shown, this algorithm recommends a bull call spread. To be specific, it recommends selling a call at strike price of 54 and buying a call at 57. The expected profit is 0.112.

Before I explain how to implement this algorithm in code, I'd like to present four important shortcomings:

- The practice of computing price probability based on ask sizes of OTM options is highly questionable.
- The algorithm doesn't take into account bid sizes, ATM/ITM options, or the price of the underlying security.
- The algorithm assumes that the stock won't move outside the price range contained in the option chain.
- The algorithm computes profit, not return. That is, it doesn't express the profit relative to the cost of the combination. As a result, it frequently chooses to sell the most expensive option and purchase the least expensive options

This algorithm can be improved in a number of ways. Applications can obtain price probabilities using more information, such as the trend of the underlying security. It's also a good idea to compare the current option price with the price provided by the `calculateOptionPrice` function discussed earlier. It would also be a good idea to update the algorithm so that it's concerned with return instead of profit.

12.2.2 Coding the Algorithm in Python

The ch12/best_spread.py module reads the option chain and current price by calling the read_option_chain method of the chain_reader.py module discussed earlier in the chapter. Then it determines the beliefs associated with the option chain and computes their probabilities. Using these probabilities, the module iterates through vertical spreads and selects the one with the highest profit. Listing 12.4 presents the code.

Listing 12.4: ch12/best_spread.py

```python
def compute_probabilities(chain, current_price):

    # Initialize beliefs
    beliefs = {}
    for strike in chain:
        if strike < current_price:
            price = chain[strike]['P']['ask_price']
            beliefs[strike + price] = 0.0
        elif strike > current_price:
            price = chain[strike]['C']['ask_price']
            beliefs[strike - price] = 0.0

    # Update probabilities
    prob_len = len(beliefs)
    prob_keys = list(beliefs.keys())
    for i, strike in enumerate(chain):

        # Process OTM puts
        if strike < current_price:
            size = chain[strike]['P']['ask_size']
            for j in range(i, prob_len):
                beliefs[prob_keys[j]] += size

        # Process OTM calls
        elif strike > current_price:
            size = chain[strike]['C']['ask_size']
            for j in range(0, i):
                beliefs[prob_keys[j]] += size

    # Replace beliefs with probabilities
    total = sum(list(beliefs.values()))
    for key in beliefs:
        beliefs[key] /= total
    return beliefs
```

Listing 12.4: ch12/best_spread.py (continued)

```
def best_spread(probs, chain, spreads):

    profits = []
    max_profit = -1000.0
    max_index = -1
    for i, spread in enumerate(spreads):

        # Strike prices: K1 for buy, K2 for sell
        K1 = spread[1]
        K2 = spread[2]

        # Premiums
        right = 'C' if spread[0] == 'bear call'
            or spread[0] == 'bull call' else 'P'
        P1 = chain[K1][right]['ask_price']
        P2 = chain[K2][right]['ask_price']

        # Iterate through probabilities
        profit = 0.0
        for j, belief in enumerate(probs):

            if spread[0] == 'bull call':
                if belief < K1:
                    profit += -(P1 - P2) * probs[belief]
                elif belief > K1 and belief < K2:
                    profit += ((belief - K1) -
                        (P1 - P2)) * probs[belief]
                else:
                    profit += ((K2 - K1) -
                        (P1 - P2)) * probs[belief]

            elif spread[0] == 'bear call':
                if belief < K1:
                    profit += (P1 - P2) * probs[belief]
                elif belief > K1 and belief < K2:
                    profit += ((P1 - P2) -
                        (belief - K1)) * probs[belief]
                else:
                    profit += ((P1 - P2) -
                        (K2 - K1)) * probs[belief]
```

Listing 12.4: ch12/best_spread.py (continued)

```
            elif spread[0] == 'bull put':
                if belief < K2:
                    profit += ((P1 - P2) -
                        (K1 - K2)) * probs[belief]
                elif belief > K2 and belief < K1:
                    profit += ((P1 - P2) -
                        (belief - K2)) * probs[belief]
                else:
                    profit += (P1 - P2) * probs[belief]

            elif spread[0] == 'bear put':
                if belief < K2:
                    profit += ((K1 - K2) -
                        (P1 - P2)) * probs[belief]
                elif belief > K2 and belief < K1:
                    profit += ((belief - K2) -
                        (P1 - P2)) * probs[belief]
                else:
                    profit += -(P1 - P2) * probs[belief]

        print('{} with K1 = {}, K2 = {}:
            profit = {}'.format(spread[0], K1, K2, profit))
        profits.append(profit)
        if profit > max_profit:
            max_profit = profit
            max_index = i

    return max_profit, max_index

def main():

    # Create the client and connect to TWS
    client = ChainReader('127.0.0.1', 7497, 0)
    chain, atm_price = read_option_chain(client, 'FDX')
    client.disconnect()

    # Compute probabilities at different prices
    probs = compute_probabilities(chain, atm_price)

    # Create and process vertical spreads
    strikes = list(chain.keys())
    rev = strikes[::-1]
    atm_index = strikes.index(atm_price)
```

Listing 12.4: ch12/best_spread.py (continued)

```python
    spreads = []
    for type in ['bull call', 'bear call',
        'bull put', 'bear put']:

        for i in range(0, atm_index):
            for j in range(i+1, atm_index):
                if type == 'bull put' or type == 'bear put':
                    spreads.append([type, strikes[j],
                        strikes[i]])
                else:
                    spreads.append([type, rev[j], rev[i]])

    # Find the best spread
    max_profit, max_index = best_spread(probs, chain, spreads)
    print('Maximum profit: {} for {}'.format(max_profit,
        spreads[max_index]))
```

The `compute_probabilities` function accepts the option chain and current price, and creates a dict named `beliefs`. This matches each belief price (strike price plus premium for puts, strike price minus premium for calls) to a probability. The function computes probabilities by iterating through the option chain and using ask sizes to determine the likelihood of the stock reaching the belief price.

After receiving the `beliefs` list, the `main` function creates another list called `spreads`. Each element identifies a vertical spread using three values: a string identifying the spread's type (e.g. `bull put`), the strike price of the major trade (K1), and the strike price of the minor trade (K2).

`main` passes the `spreads` list to the `best_spread` function, which iterates through the list and computes the profit associated with each spread. `best_spread` returns the index of the spread with the maximum profit and its profit.

12.2.3 Coding the Algorithm in C++

The code in the Ch12_BestSpread project demonstrates how the spread selection algorithm can be implemented in C++. The `main` function creates a `Contract` for IBM stock, calls `reqTickByTickData` to obtain the current price, and then calls `reqSecDefOptParams` to obtain the option's expiration dates and strike prices. Listing 12.5 presents its code.

Listing 12.5: Ch12_BestSpread/Main.cpp (main function)

```cpp
int main() {

  int maxIndex, reqId = 0;
  std::array<char, 2> rights{ {'C', 'P'} };
  std::pair <double, int> result;
  std::vector<Spread> spreads;
  std::string spreadTypes[4] =
    {"bull call", "bear call", "bull put", "bear put"};

  // Connect to TWS or IB Gateway
  BestSpread client("127.0.0.1", 7497, 0);

  // Create contract
  Contract con = Contract();
  con.symbol = "IBM";
  con.secType = "STK";
  con.exchange = "SMART";
  con.currency = "USD";
  client.reqContractDetails(reqId++, con);
  std::this_thread::sleep_for(std::chrono::seconds(3));
  client.signal.waitForSignal();
  client.reader->processMsgs();

  // Get the current price of the stock
  client.reqTickByTickData(reqId++, con, "MidPoint", 1, true);
  std::this_thread::sleep_for(std::chrono::seconds(4));
  client.signal.waitForSignal();
  client.reader->processMsgs();

  // Request strike prices and expirations
  if (client.conId != -1) {
    client.reqSecDefOptParams(reqId++, con.symbol, "",
      "STK", client.conId);
    std::this_thread::sleep_for(std::chrono::seconds(2));
    client.signal.waitForSignal();
    client.reader->processMsgs();
  }
  else {
    std::cout << "Failed to obtain contract identfiier" <<
      std::endl;
    exit(-1);
  }
```

Listing 12.5: Ch12_BestSpread/Main.cpp (main function continued)

```cpp
// Create contract for stock option
if (!client.strikes.empty()) {
  for (double strike : client.strikes) {
    for (char right : rights) {
      con.secType = "OPT"; con.right = right;
      con.strike = strike; con.exchange = client.exchange;
      con.lastTradeDateOrContractMonth = client.expiration;
      client.reqMktData(reqId++, con, "100", false,
        false, TagValueListSPtr());
    }
  }
  std::this_thread::sleep_for(std::chrono::seconds(5));
  client.signal.waitForSignal();
  client.reader->processMsgs();
}
else {
  std::cout << "Failed to access strike prices" << std::endl;
  exit(-1);
}

// Remove empty elements
for (auto const& opt : client.chain) {
  if (client.chain[opt.first]['C'].bidSize == -99 &&
    client.chain[opt.first]['P'].bidSize == -99) {
    client.chain.erase(opt.first);
  }
}

// Compute stock probabilities
computeProbabilities(client);

// Create and process vertical spreads
int n = client.strikes.size() - 1;
std::vector<double> strikeVec(client.strikes.begin(),
  client.strikes.end());
for (std::string type: spreadTypes) {
  for (int i=0; i<client.atmIndex; i++) {
    for (int j=i+1; j<client.atmIndex; j++) {
      if (type == "bull put" || type == "bear put")
        spreads.push_back({type, strikeVec[j], strikeVec[i]});
      else
        spreads.push_back({type, strikeVec[n-j],
          strikeVec[n-i]});
}}}
```

Listing 12.5: Ch12_BestSpread/Main.cpp (main function continued)

```
    result = bestSpread(client, spreads);
    maxIndex = result.second;
    std::cout << "Maximum profit of " << result.first << " for a "
        << spreads[maxIndex].type << " with strikes " <<
        spreads[maxIndex].k1
        << " and " << spreads[maxIndex].k2 << std::endl;

    // Disconnect
    client.eDisconnect();
    return 0;
}
```

After obtaining the option chain, the `main` function calls `computeProbabilities` to estimate the probabilities associated with the different stock prices. The stock prices and probabilities are stored in a `std::map` called `beliefs`.

When the probabilities are available, the `main` function creates a series of `Spread` structures and stores them in a vector called `spreads`. The `Spread` structure is defined in BestSpread.h with the following code:

```
typedef struct {
  std::string type;
  double k1;
  double k2;
} Spread;
```

The `type` field identifies the spread's type and can be set to `bull call`, `bull put`, `bear call`, and `bear put`. The `k1` and `k2` fields identify the strike prices.

After creating the spreads, the `main` function calls the `bestSpread` function to determine which spread provides the highest profit. As an example, the following code computes the profit of a bull call spread.

```
if (spread.type == "bull call") {
  if (belief < k1)
    profit += -(p1 - p2) * prob;
  else if (belief > k1 && belief < k2)
    profit += ((belief - k1) - (p1 - p2)) * prob;
  else
    profit += ((k2 - k1) - (p1 - p2)) * prob;
```

After computing the profits for each of the strike prices, `main` displays the spread that provides maximum profit.

12.3 Constructing Delta Neutral Strategies

If you're confident that a security is going to move significantly but you don't know which direction, you should consider a delta neutral strategy. Chapter 4 presented a number of these strategies, including straddles, strangles, butterfly spreads, and condor spreads. In this section, I'm going to present a method for choosing the best delta neutral strategy for a given option chain.

This algorithm is based in large part on the spread selection algorithm discussed earlier. There are four steps involved:

1. Compute beliefs according to OTM ask sizes.
2. Compute price probabilities according to beliefs.
3. Using price probabilities, find the straddle/strangle with the highest expected return.
4. Of the different delta neutral strategies, choose the one with the highest expected return.

This section presents a process for finding the best straddle or strangle for an option chain. Then it shows how the method can be implemented in Python and C++.

12.3.1 Straddles and Strangles

Chapter 4 introduced the straddle and strangle, which involve buying a put and a call for the same underlying security at the same expiration date. The difference between them is that straddles are more expensive because the put and call are both ATM. In contrast, the put and call in a strangle are both OTM. As a review, Figure 12.4 presents the risk graphs associated with straddles and strangles.

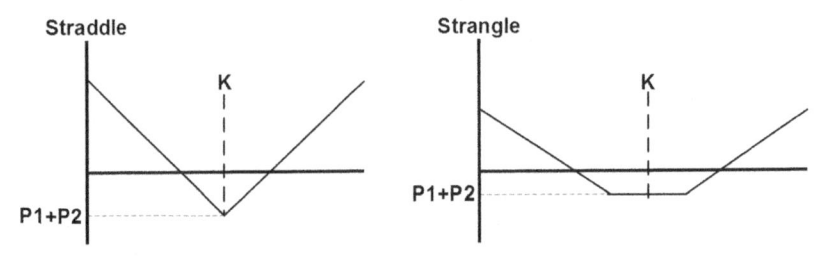

Figure 12.4 Risk Graphs for Straddles and Strangles

In both cases, the maximum loss is the sum of the options' premiums. Straddles are expensive because both options are at the money. Strangles are less expensive because the options are out of the money.

Now let's look at the returns of these strategies. Suppose a trader executes a strangle whose put has a strike price of K1 and a premium of P1. The call has a strike price of K2 and a premium of P2. The return of the strangle depends on the relationship of the stock price (S) to K1 and K2:

- If S is less than K1, the return is (K1 − S) − (P1 + P2)
- If S is greater than K2, the return is (S − K2) − (P1 + P2)
- If S is between K1 and K2, the return is −(P1 + P2).

To get an idea of how a strangle's return can be computed, consider Figure 12.5. This presents an option chain whose strike prices range from 133 to 145.

\multicolumn{4}{c}{CALLS}	Strike	\multicolumn{4}{c}{PUTS}
Bid Price	Bid Size	Ask Price	Ask Size	Price	Bid Price	Bid Size	Ask Price	Ask Size
5.95	419	6.90	162	133	0.35	210	0.41	226
5.75	295	6.00	150	134	0.46	214	0.51	226
4.90	349	5.15	237	135	0.60	178	0.67	220
4.10	228	4.35	807	136	0.79	121	0.85	296
3.35	515	3.60	479	137	1.02	180	1.09	76
2.70	170	2.88	143	138	1.33	28	1.42	226
--	--	--	--	139	--	--	--	--
1.55	189	1.65	2	140	2.08	395	2.37	404
1.11	357	1.20	77	141	2.70	131	2.85	267
0.76	237	0.85	2	142	3.15	540	3.55	258
0.50	281	0.56	168	143	4.05	169	4.30	190
0.31	218	0.36	133	144	4.75	255	5.25	604
0.18	279	0.27	315	145	3.70	35	7.90	28

Figure 12.5 Example Option Chain

The section in gray identifies out of the money options. Now suppose a trader buys a strangle composed of the following options:

- The put's strike price is 138 and its premium is 1.09.
- The call's strike price is 140 and its premium is 1.11.

To determine the expected return of this strangle, the first step is to determine the beliefs and probabilities associated with the different stock prices. Figure 12.6 shows what this looks like.

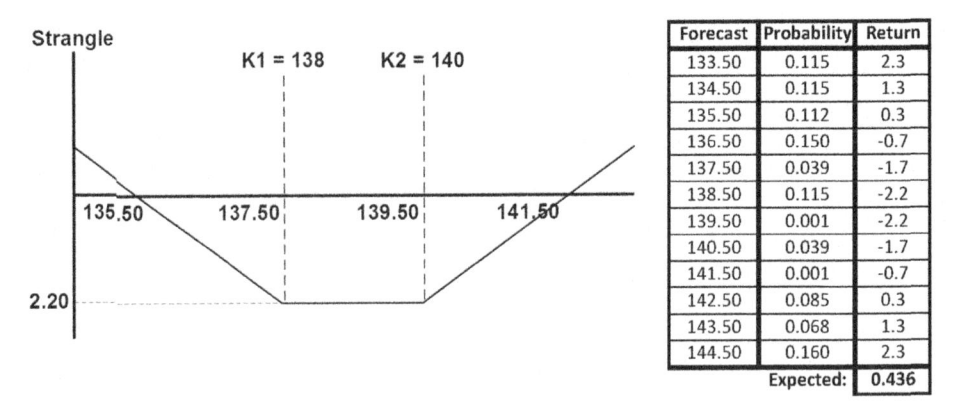

286   Chapter 12 Implementing Options Combinations

Figure 12.6 Expected Return of the Example Strangle

Forecast	Probability	Return
133.50	0.115	2.3
134.50	0.115	1.3
135.50	0.112	0.3
136.50	0.150	-0.7
137.50	0.039	-1.7
138.50	0.115	-2.2
139.50	0.001	-2.2
140.50	0.039	-1.7
141.50	0.001	-0.7
142.50	0.085	0.3
143.50	0.068	1.3
144.50	0.160	2.3
Expected:		0.436

The table to the right of the figure lists the probabilities and returns of the different forecasts. Multiplying the returns by the probabilities and adding the products leads to an expected return of 0.436.

12.3.2 Finding the Best Straddle/Strangle

For a given option chain, the process of finding the best straddle/strangle is simpler than finding the best vertical spread. For one thing, there can only be one delta neutral straddle because there's only one ATM call and only one ATM put.

There can be several strangles for an option chain. To be specific, if an option chain has N strikes above/below the current stock price, N-1 strangles can be constructed. Each strangle has a different cost and return. This is illustrated in Figure 12.7, which shows three strangles for the same option chain.

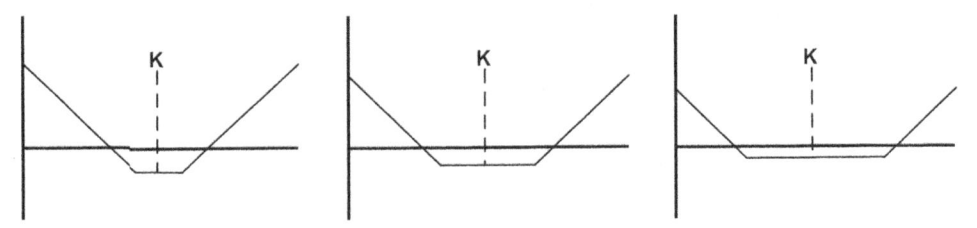

Figure 12.7 Different Strangles for an Option Chain

In this figure, the leftmost strangle makes money over a longer range of stock prices, but has the most expensive net premium. The rightmost strangle makes money over a smaller range of stock prices, but costs the least. This is because the options that make up the strangle are so far out of the money.

If the figure illustrated a straddle, it would be positioned further to the left. This is because both options are at the money. This provides the widest range of money-making stock prices, but costs more than any strangle.

To estimate the return for an option chain's straddle and strangles, the example code follows a process similar to that of finding the return of a vertical spread. That is, it multiplies the profit at each stock price by the probability and adds the products together.

For this application, the example code computes return as the difference between the profit and cost divided by the cost. In this case, the cost is determined as the sum of the premiums of the options that make up the spread. For example, if the put's premium is denoted P1 and the call's premium is given as P2, the return is computed in the following way:

$$return = \frac{profit - (P1 + P2)}{P1 + P2}$$

The following discussion shows how to implement this method for computing the optimal straddle/strangle in Python and C++.

12.3.3 Finding the Best Straddle/Strangle in Python

The code in the ch12/best_neutral.py module shows how an application can select an optimal straddle/strangle for trading. As in the ch12/best_spread.py module, it starts by creating an instance of the `ChainReader` class and calling its `read_option_chain` method. This provides the current option chain for IBM stock.

Next, `main` calls `compute_probabilities`, which populates a dict named `beliefs`. When `compute_probabilities` is finished, `beliefs` will associate stock prices with their estimated probabilities.

Once the probabilities have been computed, `main` populates a list called `spreads` with the straddle and strangles that can be purchased for the option chain. Each element of this list is a tuple containing the strike price of the put and the strike price of the option. After all of the spreads have been generated, `main` calls the `best_neutral` function.

`best_neutral` consists of two loops. The first iterates through the spreads provided by `main` and the second iterates through the stock prices in the `beliefs` dictionary. The code in Listing 12.6 presents the code for the `best_neutral` function.

Listing 12.6: ch12/best_neutral.py (best_neutral function)

```
def best_neutral(probs, chain, spreads):

    profits = []
    max_profit = -1000.0
    max_index = -1
    for i, spread in enumerate(spreads):

        # Strike prices and premiums
        K1 = spread[0]
        K2 = spread[1]
        P1 = chain[K1]['P']['ask_price']
        P2 = chain[K2]['C']['ask_price']

        # Iterate through probabilities
        profit = 0.0
        for belief in probs:

            if belief < K1:
                profit += ((K1 - belief) - (P1 + P2)) *
                    probs[belief]/(P1 + P2)
            elif belief > K2:
                profit += ((belief - K2) - (P1 + P2)) *
                    probs[belief]/(P1 + P2)
            else:
                profit += -(P1 + P2) * probs[belief]/(P1 + P2)

        # Check for spread with maximum profit
        profits.append(profit)
        if profit > max_profit:
            max_profit = profit
            max_index = i

    return max_profit, max_index
```

For each spread, `best_neutral` starts by determining the strike prices (K1 and K2) and premiums (P1 and P2) of the two options that make up the straddle/strangle. The strike price of the put, K1, should always be less than or equal to the strike price of the call, K2. The only time they're equal is when the application processes a straddle.

Then the function iterates through the `probs` dict, whose elements associate stock prices with estimated probabilities. After finding the spread that produces the maximum profit, the function returns the estimated profit and the index of the spread. Then the `main` function prints the information to standard output.

12.3.4 Finding the Best Straddle/Strangle in C++

The code in the Ch12_BestNeutral project demonstrates how an application can compute returns of straddles and strangles in C++. In Main.cpp, the `main` function creates an instance of the `BestNeutral` class and a `Contract` representing IBM stock. Then it calls four functions to request information:

- `reqContractDetails` requests the contract's ID
- `reqTickByTickData` requests the current price of the stock
- `reqSecDefOptParams` requests the option's strike prices and expiration dates
- `reqMktData` requests the option's ask/bid price and ask/bid size

After requesting this information, `main` initializes the fields of the option chain structure, estimates probabilities of stock prices, and decides on the straddle or strangle that provides the highest return. Listing 12.7 presents the code that makes up the `main` function.

Listing 12.7: Ch12_BestNeutral/Main.cpp (main function)

```cpp
int main() {

  int maxIndex, reqId = 0;
  std::array<char, 2> rights{ {'C', 'P'} };
  std::pair <double, int> result;
  std::vector<Spread> spreads;
  std::string spreadTypes[4] =
    {"bull call", "bear call", "bull put", "bear put"};

  // Connect to TWS or IB Gateway
  BestNeutral client("127.0.0.1", 7497, 0);

  // Create contract
  Contract con = Contract();
  con.symbol = "IBM";
  con.secType = "STK";
  con.exchange = "SMART";
  con.currency = "USD";
  client.reqContractDetails(reqId++, con);
  std::this_thread::sleep_for(std::chrono::seconds(3));
  client.signal.waitForSignal();
  client.reader->processMsgs();
```

Listing 12.7: Ch12_BestNeutral/Main.cpp (main function continued)

```cpp
// Get the current price of the stock
client.reqTickByTickData(reqId++, con, "MidPoint", 1, true);
std::this_thread::sleep_for(std::chrono::seconds(4));
client.signal.waitForSignal();
client.reader->processMsgs();

// Request strike prices and expirations
if (client.conId != -1) {
  client.reqSecDefOptParams(reqId++, con.symbol, "",
    "STK", client.conId);
  std::this_thread::sleep_for(std::chrono::seconds(2));
  client.signal.waitForSignal();
  client.reader->processMsgs();
} else {
  std::cout << "Failed to obtain contract identfiier" <<
    std::endl;
  exit(-1);
}

// Create contract for stock option
if (!client.strikes.empty()) {
  for (double strike : client.strikes) {
    for (char right : rights) {

      // Define the option contract
      con.secType = "OPT";
      con.right = right;
      con.strike = strike;
      con.exchange = client.exchange;
      con.lastTradeDateOrContractMonth = client.expiration;

      // Request option data
      client.reqMktData(reqId++, con, "100", false,
        false, TagValueListSPtr());
    }
  }
  std::this_thread::sleep_for(std::chrono::seconds(5));
  client.signal.waitForSignal();
  client.reader->processMsgs();
} else {
  std::cout << "Failed to access strike prices" << std::endl;
  exit(-1);
}
```

Listing 12.7: Ch12_BestNeutral/Main.cpp (main function continued)

```cpp
  // Remove empty elements
  for (auto const& opt : client.chain) {
    if (client.chain[opt.first]['C'].bidSize == -99 &&
      client.chain[opt.first]['P'].bidSize == -99) {
      client.chain.erase(opt.first);
    }
  }

  // Compute stock probabilities
  computeProbabilities(client);

  // Create and process vertical spreads
  std::vector<double> strikeVec(client.strikes.begin(),
    client.strikes.end());
  for (int i=0; i<client.atmIndex-1; i++) {
    spreads.push_back({strikeVec[client.atmIndex-i],
      strikeVec[client.atmIndex+i]});
  }

  // Find the best straddle/strangle
  result = bestNeutral(client, spreads);
  maxIndex = result.second;
  std::cout << "Maximum profit of " << result.first
    << " for a straddle/strangle " << " has strikes "
    << spreads[maxIndex].k1 << " and "
    << spreads[maxIndex].k2 << std::endl;

  // Disconnect
  client.eDisconnect();
  return 0;
}
```

After all of the contract information has been received, `main` calls `computeProbabilities`. This populates a map that associates stock prices with estimated probabilities.

Next, `main` iterates through the strike prices and populates a vector called `spreads`. Each element is a pair that combines the strike price of the spread's put and the strike price of the spread's call. The first element represents a straddle and the rest are strangles.

`main` passes spreads to the `bestNeutral` function, which iterates through each spread to determine its profit. The goal is to find the straddle or strangle that provides the maximum return, and Listing 12.8 presents its code.

Chapter 12 Implementing Options Combinations

Listing 12.8: Ch12_BestNeutral/Main.cpp (bestNeutral function)

```cpp
std::pair <double, int> bestNeutral(BestNeutral& client,
  std::vector<Spread>& spreads) {

  std::vector<double> profits;
  double k1, k2, p1, p2, profit, maxProfit = -1000.0;
  double belief, prob;
  int count = 0, maxIndex = -1;
  char right;

  // Iterate through straddle and strangles
  for (Spread spread: spreads) {

    // Premiums and strike prices
    p1 = client.chain[k1]['P'].askPrice;
    p2 = client.chain[k2]['C'].askPrice;
    k1 = spread.k1;
    k2 = spread.k2;

    // Iterate through probabilities
    profit = 0.0;
    for (auto el: client.beliefs) {
      belief = el.first;
      prob = el.second;

      if (belief < k1)
        profit += ((k1 - belief) - (p1 + p2)) * prob/(p1 + p2);
      else if (belief > k2)
        profit += ((belief - k2) - (p1 + p2)) * prob/(p1 + p2);
      else
        profit += -(p1 + p2) * prob/(p1 + p2);
    }

    // Store profit
    profits.push_back(profit);
    if (profit > maxProfit) {
      maxProfit = profit;
      maxIndex = count;
    }
    count++;
  }
  return std::make_pair(maxProfit, maxIndex);
}
```

This function starts by iterating through the elements of the `spreads` vector. Each element has two values: the strike price of the put associated with the straddle/strangle and the strike price of the call. As the `bestNeutral` function iterates, it sets the values of `k1` and `k2` (the strike prices) and `p1` and `p2` (the premiums of the two options).

Next, `bestNeutral` iterates through the elements of the `beliefs` map. Each element associates a stock price with an estimated probability. This inner loop determines the profit of the straddle/strangle at the given strike price, multiplies it by the probability, and divides by the cost, which equals the sum of the options' premiums.

`bestNeutral` returns its result in a pair that combines the maximum estimated profit and the index of the spread that yields the maximum profit. After completion, the `main` function displays the results.

12.4 Summary

To make money from options, traders need to keep track of a vast number of variables: bid/ask prices, Greeks, expiration dates, and many others. This chapter has explained how these variables can be accessed programmatically and how they can be used to select option spreads.

The first part of the chapter presented a handful of functions that request option data or perform operations related to options. For analysts, the most important of these is `reqSecDefOptParams`, which provides an option's exchange, strike prices, and expirations. Other important functions include `calculateImpliedVolatility`, which computes IV, and `exerciseOptions`, which exercises an option-based contract.

The next part of the chapter showed how the TWS API's functions make it possible to read an option chain. This requires bid/ask prices and bid/ask sizes for each of the option's strike prices. The remainder of the chapter uses this option chain to select vertical spreads, straddles, and strangles.

Chapter 13

The Turtle Trading and Bollinger-MFI Systems

A trading system is a complete decision-making process for buying and selling securities. At minimum, a system needs to identify when to enter a long or short position and when to exit the position. It should also identify the number of securities to be bought or sold with each order and the type of order to be submitted (market, limit, stop, and so on).

Trading systems base their decisions on technical indicators. As discussed in Chapter 11, indicators enable analysts to draw conclusions about a security by analyzing prices and volume data. Professional traders employ many different types of indicators, including trend indicators, momentum indicators, volume indicators, and volatility indicators.

Trading systems are essential for algorithmic trading, and for this reason, this chapter looks at two popular systems: the Turtle trading system developed by Richard Dennis and the Bollinger-MFI (Money Flow Index) system developed by John Bollinger. The first employs the Average True Range (ATR) indicator to trade futures contracts. The second relies on Bollinger Bands and Money Flow Index indicators.

This chapter shows how both systems work and explains how they use indicators to generate entry signals (when to enter a position) and exit signals (when to exit the position). This discussion presents Python and C++ code that demonstrates how the two systems can be implemented with the TWS API. At the end, I'll test both systems and compare their performance.

When comparing trading systems, testing plays a central role. It's important to find financial data that resembles the real-world data to be processed. Therefore, before I discuss the two systems in depth, I'd like to explain how I obtained the data that will be used throughout this chapter.

13.1 Obtaining Test Data

This chapter discusses and compares two popular trading systems:

- The Turtle trading system developed by Richard Dennis
- The Bollinger-MFI system developed by John Bollinger

The first system focuses on futures contracts, while the second can be applied to any type of security. For the sake of simplicity, this chapter focuses on futures contracts. To be specific, the tests will be based on a year's worth of data on nine contracts: Eurodollars (GE), E-mini S&P futures (ES), Swiss francs (CHF), British pounds (GBP), Canadian dollars (CAD), gold (GC), silver (SI), copper (HG), and unleaded gas (RB).

As discussed in Chapter 5, a futures contract doesn't last an entire year, so we need a way to combine successive contracts into a single contract. The TWS API makes this possible by providing continuous futures contracts, represented by the CONTFUT security type. I've provided code to read continuous contracts in the read_futures.py module (Python) and the Ch13_ReadFutures project (C++).

In both cases, the code performs four steps:

1. Create a continuous futures (CONTFUT) contract for each of the nine contracts.
2. Call reqContractDetails to obtain information about the contract, such as its local symbol and multiplier.
3. Call reqHistoricalData to request a year's worth of price/volume data for the contract.
4. Store the data to a comma-separated value (CSV) file named after the symbol (GE.csv, ES.csv, and so on).

Both applications generate nine CSV files in the working directory. I've split the data into separate files to enable general-purpose testing and because I usually encounter errors when I try to load data for nine contracts at once. This section presents the code that makes this possible.

13.1.1 Obtaining Test Data in Python

Listing 13.1 presents the code of the read_futures.py module, which can be found in the ch13 folder of the Python example code. This obtains information for nine contracts and produces nine CSV files. Keep in mind that different contracts are traded on different exchanges (GE is traded on GLOBEX, GC is traded on NYMEX, and so on.)

Listing 13.1: ch13/read_futures.py

```python
class ReadFutures(EWrapper, EClient):
    ''' Serves as the client and the wrapper '''

    def __init__(self, addr, port, client_id):
        EWrapper.__init__(self)
        EClient.__init__(self, self)

        # Initialize properties
        self.local_symbol = None
        self.multiplier = None
        self.symbols = {'GE':'GLOBEX', 'ES':'GLOBEX',
            'CHF':'GLOBEX', 'GBP':'GLOBEX', 'CAD':'GLOBEX',
            'GC':'NYMEX', 'SI':'NYMEX', 'HG':'NYMEX', 'RB':'NYMEX'}
        self.price_dict = {}

        # Connect to TWS
        self.connect(addr, port, client_id)

        # Launch the client thread
        thread = Thread(target=self.run)
        thread.start()

    @iswrapper
    def contractDetails(self, req_id, details):
        ''' Called in response to reqContractDetails '''

        # Obtain data for the contract
        self.local_symbol = details.contract.localSymbol
        self.multiplier = details.contract.multiplier

    @iswrapper
    def historicalData(self, req_id, bar):
        ''' Called in response to reqHistoricalData '''

        # Add the futures prices to the dictionary
        self.price_dict['CLOSE'].append(bar.close)
        self.price_dict['LOW'].append(bar.low)
        self.price_dict['HIGH'].append(bar.high)
        self.price_dict['VOL'].append(bar.volume)

    def error(self, req_id, code, msg):
        print('Error {}: {}'.format(code, msg))
```

Listing 13.1: ch13/read_futures.py (continued)

```python
def main():

    # Create the client and connect to TWS
    client = ReadFutures('127.0.0.1', 7497, 0)

    # Get expiration dates for contracts
    for symbol in client.symbols:

        # Define contract of interest
        con = Contract()
        con.symbol = symbol
        con.secType = "CONTFUT"
        con.exchange = client.symbols[symbol]
        con.currency = "USD"
        con.includeExpired = True
        client.reqContractDetails(0, con)
        time.sleep(3)

        # Request historical data for each contract
        if client.local_symbol:

            # Initialize price dict
            for v in ['CLOSE', 'LOW', 'HIGH', 'VOL']:
                client.price_dict[v] = []

            # Set additional contract data
            con.localSymbol = client.local_symbol
            con.multiplier = client.multiplier

            # Request historical data
            end_date = datetime.today().date() -
                timedelta(days=1)
            client.reqHistoricalData(1, con,
                end_date.strftime("%Y%m%d %H:%M:%S"),
                '1 Y', '1 day', 'TRADES', 1, 1, False, [])
            time.sleep(3)

            # Write data to a CSV file
            if client.price_dict['CLOSE']:
                df = pd.DataFrame(data=client.price_dict)
                df.to_csv(symbol + '.csv', encoding='utf-8',
                    index=False)
                client.price_dict.clear()
```

Listing 13.1: ch13/read_futures.py (continued)

```
        else:
            print('Could not access contract data')
            exit()

    # Disconnect from TWS
    client.disconnect()

if __name__ == '__main__':
    main()
```

After creating an instance of the `ReadFutures` class, the `main` function iterates through the nine symbols and creates a `Contract` for each. The security type is set to `CONTFUT` because we want continuous futures data. That is, we want data for successive futures contracts to be spliced together into a single series.

Next, the application calls `reqContractDetails` to obtain the contract's local symbol and multiplier. When this information is available, the `main` function updates the `Contract` and calls `reqHistoricalData` to request a year's worth of data, ending with yesterday's date. The third argument is set to `1 day`, so each bar will contain information for a single day.

The fourth argument is set to `TRADES`. This is important because we want each bar to provide the day's volume as well as its high/low/open/close prices. If the fourth argument is set to anything except `TRADES`, each bar's volume will be set to –1.

As each bar is received, the `historicalData` callback stores four fields to a dictionary: `bar.close`, `bar.low`, `bar.high`, and `bar.volume`. When all of the data has been read, the `main` function writes the dictionary to a pandas dataframe named `df`. Then it writes the dataframe to a CSV file named after the current symbol.

13.1.2 Obtaining Test Data in C++

The process of reading futures data in C++ is essentially similar to that described above. The code in the Ch13_ReadFutures project creates a contract for each symbol, requests contract details, and then requests a year's worth of historical bars.

The main difference between the C++ code and Python code is that C++ doesn't have dictionaries. The `ReadFutures` class stores bar data in four vectors: `closeVec` contains closing prices, `highVec` contains high prices, `lowVec` contains low prices, and `volVec` contains trading volumes. Listing 13.2 presents the code of the `ReadFutures` class.

Listing 13.2: Ch13_ReadFutures/ReadFutures.cpp

```cpp
ReadFutures::ReadFutures(const char *host, int port,
  int clientId) :
  signal(1000),
  symbols({{"GE", "GLOBEX"}, {"ES" , "GLOBEX"},
    {"CHF", "GLOBEX"}, {"GBP" , "GLOBEX"},
    {"CAD" , "GLOBEX"}, {"GC" , "NYMEX"},
    {"SI" , "NYMEX"}, {"HG" , "NYMEX"}, {"RB" , "NYMEX"}}),
  EClientSocket(this, &signal) {

  // Connect to TWS
  bool conn = eConnect(host, port, clientId, false);
  if (conn) {

    // Launch the reader thread
    reader = new EReader(this, &signal);
    reader->start();
  }
  else
    std::cout << "Failed to connect" << std::endl;
}

// Called in response to reqContractDetails
void ReadFutures::contractDetails(int reqId,
  const ContractDetails& details) {
  localSymbol = details.contract.localSymbol;
  multiplier = details.contract.multiplier;
}

// Called in response to reqHistoricalData
void ReadFutures::historicalData(TickerId reqId,
  const Bar& bar) {

  // Update the price dictionary
  closeVec.push_back(bar.close);
  lowVec.push_back(bar.low);
  highVec.push_back(bar.high);
  volVec.push_back(bar.volume);
}

void ReadFutures::error(int id, int code, const std::string& msg)
{
  std::cout << "Error: " << code << ": " << msg << std::endl;
}
```

As shown, the class provides code for two callback functions: `contractDetails` and `historicalData`. The `contractDetails` callback provides the contract's local symbol and multiplier. The `main` function uses this data to precisely specify which futures contract is being analyzed.

The `historicalData` callback provides bars containing historical data. The `ReadFutures` class stores this data in its four vectors, and the `main` function iterates through the bars and writes their data to a CSV file. Listing 13.3 presents the code of the `main` function.

Listing 13.3: Ch13_ReadFutures/Main.cpp

```
int main() {

  // Connect to TWS or IB Gateway
  ReadFutures client("127.0.0.1", 7497, 0);

  for (const auto &symbol : client.symbols) {

    // Create contract
    Contract con = Contract();
    con.symbol = symbol.first;
    con.secType = "CONTFUT";
    con.exchange = symbol.second;
    con.currency = "USD";
    con.includeExpired = TRUE;
    client.reqContractDetails(0, con);
    std::this_thread::sleep_for(std::chrono::seconds(3));
    client.signal.waitForSignal();
    client.reader->processMsgs();

    // Request historical bars
    if (!client.localSymbol.empty()) {

      // Clear vectors
      client.closeVec.clear();
      client.lowVec.clear();
      client.highVec.clear();
      client.volVec.clear();

      // Set additional contract data
      con.localSymbol = client.localSymbol;
      con.multiplier = client.multiplier;
```

Listing 13.3: Ch13_ReadFutures/main.cpp (Continued)

```cpp
      // Request historical data
      time_t tm = std::time(nullptr);
      std::tm loc_tm = *std::localtime(&tm);
      std::ostringstream ostr;
      ostr << std::put_time(&loc_tm, "%Y%m%d, %H:%M:%S");
      client.reqHistoricalData(1, con, ostr.str(),
        "1 Y", "1 day", "TRADES", 1, 1, FALSE,
        TagValueListSPtr());
      std::this_thread::sleep_for(std::chrono::seconds(3));
      client.signal.waitForSignal();
      client.reader->processMsgs();

      // Write data to file
      std::ofstream csvFile(symbol.first + ".csv");
      csvFile << "CLOSE,LOW,HIGH,VOL" << std::endl;
      for (unsigned int i = 0; i < client.closeVec.size(); i++) {
        csvFile << client.closeVec[i] << ","
           << client.lowVec[i] << ","
           << client.highVec[i] << ","
           << client.volVec[i] << std::endl;
      }
      csvFile.close();
    }
  }

  // Disconnect
  client.eDisconnect();
  return 0;
}
```

Inside the `main` function, the outer loop iterates once for each symbol and creates a new `Contract` with each iteration. The `setType` field is set to `CONTFUT` because we want data about multiple futures contracts to be combined into a continuous array. The `main` function calls `reqContractDetails` to obtain the contract's local symbol and multiplier.

After defining the `Contract`, the `main` function calls `reqHistoricalData` to obtain a year's worth of bars. The duration of each bar is one day. After waiting for the callback, the `main` function creates an output file stream named after the symbol (ES.csv, GE.csv, and so on), and then writes each day's closing price, low price, high price, and volume to the file.

13.2 The Turtle System

After making hundreds of millions of dollars in the 1970s, a commodity trader named Richard Dennis wanted to settle a debate regarding whether successful trading could be taught. To this end, he recruited 23 people with no trading experience and gave them two weeks of training and $100,000. Five years later, his students made profits in excess of $175 million.

Dennis referred to his students as Turtles and his trading methodology as the Turtle system. His system can be boiled down to a set of rules that specify when to make trades and how much capital to allocate for each trade. In this section, I'll present the rules of the Turtle system and implement them in code.

13.2.1 Rules of the Turtle System

The Turtle system deals with trading futures contracts, which were discussed in Chapter 5. To be specific, the Turtles traded Treasuries (30-year, 10-year, and 90-day), Eurodollars, French and Swiss francs, British pounds, Canadian dollars, Japanese yen, the S&P 500 stock index, coffee, cocoa, sugar, cotton, gold, silver, copper, crude oil, heating oil, and unleaded gas.

The Turtles considered making a new trade when the contract's price reached one of two conditions:

- The contract's price rose above its 20-day high or fell below its 20-day low, unless the last 20-day breakout would have led to a successful trade.
- The contract's price rose above its 55-day high or fell below its 55-day low.

When making trades, the Turtles purchased one unit at a time. The concept of a unit is determined in the following way:

$$unit = \frac{1\% \text{ of account}}{N \cdot dollars \text{ per point}}$$

In this equation, N is the 20-day exponential moving average (EMA) of the security's Average True Range, or ATR. Chapter 11 discussed the ATR and explained how it can be implemented in code.

For example, suppose a trader has $1M and wants to buy a gold (GC) contract, which costs $100 per point. If the ATR is 25, each unit size is (1,000,000 * 0.01)/(25 * 100), or four contracts.

After purchasing or short selling a unit, the system allows purchasing or short selling additional units if the security's price rises or falls by N/2. The maximum number of units that can be traded is determined by the following rules:

- Maximum of four units for a single contract
- Maximum of six units for closely-correlated markets
- Maximum of ten units for loosely-correlated markets
- Maximum of four units in a single market

Each trade was required to have an associated stop at 2N. For example, if a trader entered a long position, he/she would set the stop price at the trade price minus 2N. If entering a short position, he/she would set the stop price at the trade price plus 2N.

In addition, traders had to fully exit a position if the security's price reached a 10-day low for long positions. For short positions, traders exited the position if the price reached a 10-day high.

The code in this section implements a slightly simplified version of the Turtle system. To be specific, the code follows four rules:

1. If the price reaches a 20-day high, the trader buys a unit. If the price reaches a 20-day low, the trader short sells a unit.
2. If the trader is long and the price rises N/2 over the last buy price, the trader buys another unit. If the trader is short and the price falls N/2 below the last sell price, the trader shorts another unit.
3. If the trader is long and the price falls 2N below the last buy price, the trader exits the long position. If the trader is short and the price rises 2N above the last sell price, the trader exits the short position.
4. If the trader is long and the price reaches a 10-day low, the trader exits the long position. If the trader is short and the price reaches a 10-day high, the trader exits the short position.

To store prices, the application creates three containers. One stores the true ranges needed to compute the Average True Range (ATR). The second container stores the last twenty prices so that the 20-day highs and lows can be computed. The last container stores the last ten prices so that the 10-day highs and lows can be computed.

An application can make multiple trades for a given security at different prices. To keep track of these trades, the application creates a map (`dict` in Python, `std::map` in C++) that associates trade prices with the number of securities traded.

13.2.2 Implementing the Turtle System in Python

The code in the ch13/turtle_trading.py module demonstrates how the Turtle system can be coded in Python. This module reads the CSV files generated by the read_futures.py module discussed earlier. Listing 13.4 presents the code.

Listing 13.4: ch13/turtle_trading.py

```python
InvState = Enum('InvState', 'OUT LONG SHORT')
init_funds = 10000000.00

def main():

    # Define symbols and price/point
    symbols = {'GE': 2500, 'ES': 50, 'CHF': 125000,
        'GBP': 62500, 'CAD': 100000, 'GC': 100, 'SI': 5000,
        'HG': 25000, 'RB': 42000}

    # Create containers
    true_ranges = deque(maxlen=ATR_PERIOD)
    enter_deque = deque(maxlen=ENTER_PERIOD)
    exit_deque = deque(maxlen=EXIT_PERIOD)
    positions = {}

    csv_files = [f for f in os.listdir('.')
        if f.endswith('.csv')]
    for csv_file in csv_files:

        # Initialize values
        inv_state = InvState.OUT
        funds = init_funds
        last_price = 0.0
        old_close = -1
        old_atr = -1.0
        true_ranges.clear()
        enter_deque.clear()
        exit_deque.clear()
        positions.clear()

        # Contract-specific information
        symbol = csv_file.split('.')[0]
        contract_size = symbols[symbol]
        df = pd.read_csv(csv_file)
```

Listing 13.4: ch13/turtle_trading.py (continued)

```python
            # Iterate through bars
            for i, bar in df.iterrows():

                # Find true range
                if old_close != -1:
                    true_range = max(bar['HIGH'] - bar['LOW'],
                        abs(bar['HIGH'] - old_close),
                        abs(bar['LOW'] - old_close))
                    true_ranges.append(true_range)
                    old_close = bar['CLOSE']
                else:
                    old_close = bar['CLOSE']
                    continue

                # Compute the Average True Range (ATR)
                if len(true_ranges) == ATR_PERIOD:
                    N=((ATR_PERIOD-1)*old_atr+true_range)/ATR_PERIOD
                    old_atr = N
                else:
                    N = sum(true_ranges)/len(true_ranges)
                    old_atr = N
                    continue

                # Initialize parameters
                price = bar['CLOSE']
                unit_size = int(0.01 * funds/(N * contract_size))

                # Check for entry
                if inv_state == InvState.OUT and \
                    len(enter_deque) == ENTER_PERIOD:

                    # Buy 1 unit at 20-day high
                    if price > max(enter_deque):
                        positions[price] = unit_size
                        last_price = price
                        inv_state = InvState.LONG

                    # Short 1 unit at 20-day low
                    elif price < min(enter_deque):
                        positions[price] = unit_size
                        last_price = price
                        inv_state = InvState.SHORT
```

Listing 13.4: ch13/turtle_trading.py (continued)

```python
            # Exit position if 10-day low/high
            elif (inv_state == InvState.LONG and \
                price < min(exit_deque)) or \
                (inv_state == InvState.SHORT and \
                price > max(exit_deque)):
                
                # Exit the position
                for p in positions:
                    if inv_state == InvState.LONG:
                        change = positions[p] * \
                            contract_size * (price - p)
                    else:
                        change = positions[p] * \
                            contract_size * (p - price)
                    funds += change
                
                positions.clear()
                last_price = 0.0
                inv_state = InvState.OUT
            
            # Exit position if the price falls/rises by 2N
            elif (inv_state == InvState.LONG and \
                price < last_price - 2*N) or \
                (inv_state == InvState.SHORT and \
                price > last_price + 2*N):
                
                # Apply stop condition
                price = last_price - 2*N \
                    if inv_state == InvState.LONG \
                    else last_price + 2*N
                
                # Exit the position
                for p in positions:
                    if inv_state == InvState.LONG:
                        change = positions[p] * \
                            contract_size * (price - p)
                    elif inv_state == InvState.SHORT:
                        change = positions[p] * \
                            contract_size * (p - price)
                    funds += change
                
                positions.clear()
                last_price = 0.0
                inv_state = InvState.OUT
```

Listing 13.4: ch13/turtle_trading.py (continued)

```
            # Increase position if the price rises/falls by N/2
            elif ((inv_state == InvState.LONG and \
                price > last_price + N/2) or \
                (inv_state == InvState.SHORT and \
                price < last_price - N/2)):

                # Make sure position doesn't exceed 4 units
                tot_position = sum(positions.values())
                if tot_position + unit_size < 4 * unit_size:
                    if price in positions:
                        positions[price] += unit_size
                    else:
                        positions[price] = unit_size
                    last_price = price

        enter_deque.append(price)
        exit_deque.append(price)

    # Determine return
    for p in positions:
        if inv_state == InvState.LONG:
            funds += positions[p] * \
                contract_size * (price - p)
        elif inv_state == InvState.SHORT:
            funds += positions[p] * \
                contract_size * (p - price)
    ret = funds/init_funds
    print('Return for {0}: {1:.4f}'.format(symbol, ret))
```

The `main` function creates two loops: one for each symbol and one for each bar read from the symbol's CSV file. When a new bar is processed, the function computes the true range and the Average True Range (ATR). The ATR serves as N, which traders use to determine unit sizes and buy/sell signals.

The trader's position is represented by an enumerated type (`InvState`) that can take three values: `OUT`, `LONG`, and `SHORT`. The initial position is `OUT`, and this remains until the security reaches a 20-day high or a 20-day low.

The application exits positions when one of two conditions are met. First, it exits the position when the price reaches a 10-day low (long position) or a 10-day high (short position). The application will also exit its position if the price falls by 2N (long position) or rises by 2N (short position). In each case, `funds` is updated by the position times the contract size and the difference between the current price and position price.

13.2.3 Implementing the Turtle System in C++

The code in the Ch13_TurtleTrading project demonstrates how the Turtle system can be written in C++. The `main` function reads CSV files in the current directory and iterates through their rows. Listing 13.5 presents the code.

Listing 13.5: Ch13_TurtleTrading/Main.cpp (main function)

```
int main() {

  // Iterate through files
  for (const auto &f :
    std::filesystem::directory_iterator(".")) {

    // Find CSV files
    fileName = f.path().string();
    if(fileName.compare(fileName.length()-4,4,".csv") != 0) {
      continue;
    }

    // Initialize values and containers
    funds = initFunds;
    oldAtr = -1.0;
    oldClose = -1.0;
    invState = InvState::outPos;
    trueRanges.clear();
    enters.clear();
    exits.clear();
    positions.clear();

    // Open file and read lines
    csvFile.open(fileName, std::ios::in);
    std::getline(csvFile, line);
    while (std::getline(csvFile, line)) {

      // Read values
      ss << line;
      std::getline(ss, str, ',');
      close = std::stod(str);
      std::getline(ss, str, ',');
      low = std::stod(str);
      std::getline(ss, str, ',');
      high = std::stod(str);
      ss.str("");
```

Listing 13.5: Ch13_TurtleTrading/Main.cpp (continued)

```cpp
      // Find true range
      if (oldClose != -1.0) {
        trueRange = std::max({high - low,
          abs(high - oldClose),
          abs(low - oldClose)});
        trueRanges.push_back(trueRange);
        oldClose = close;
      }
      else {
        oldClose = close;
        continue;
      }

      // Compute Average True Range
      if (trueRanges.size() == ATR_PERIOD) {
        N = ((ATR_PERIOD - 1) * oldAtr +
          trueRange) / ATR_PERIOD;
        oldAtr = N;
        trueRanges.pop_front();
      }
      else {
        oldAtr = std::accumulate(trueRanges.begin(),
          trueRanges.end(), 0.0) / trueRanges.size();
        continue;
      }

      // Compute unit size and contract size
      str = fileName.substr(2, fileName.length()-6);
      contractSize = symbols[str];
      unitSize = static_cast<int>(0.01 *
        funds/(N * contractSize));

      // Check for entry
      if ((invState == InvState::outPos)
        && (enters.size() == ENTER_PERIOD)) {

        // Buy 1 unit at 20-day high
        if (close > *std::max_element(enters.begin(),
          enters.end())) {
          positions[close] = unitSize;
          lastPrice = close;
          invState = InvState::longPos;
        }
```

Listing 13.5: Ch13_TurtleTrading/Main.cpp (continued)

```cpp
      // Short 1 unit at 20-day low
      else if (close < *std::min_element(
        enters.begin(), enters.end())) {
        positions[close] = unitSize;
        lastPrice = close;
        invState = InvState::shortPos;
      }
    }

    // Exit position if price at 10-day low/high
    else if (((invState == InvState::longPos) &&
   (close < *std::min_element(exits.begin(), exits.end()))) ||
   ((invState == InvState::shortPos) &&
   (close > *std::max_element(exits.begin(), exits.end())))) {

      for (const auto &pos : positions) {
        if (invState == InvState::longPos) {
          funds += pos.second * contractSize *
            (close - pos.first);
        }
        else {
          funds += pos.second * contractSize *
            (pos.first - close);
        }
      }
      positions.clear();
      lastPrice = 0.0;
      invState = InvState::outPos;
    }

    // Exit position if price falls/rises by 2N
    else if (((invState == InvState::longPos) &&
       (close < lastPrice - 2*N)) ||
       ((invState == InvState::shortPos) &&
       (close > lastPrice + 2*N))) {

      // Apply stop condition
      if (invState == InvState::longPos) {
        close = lastPrice - 2 * N;
      }
      else {
        close = lastPrice + 2 * N;
      }
```

Listing 13.5: Ch13_TurtleTrading/Main.cpp (continued)

```cpp
      // Exit position
      for (const auto &pos : positions) {
        if (invState == InvState::longPos) {
          funds += pos.second * contractSize *
            (close - pos.first);
        }
        else {
          funds += pos.second * contractSize *
            (pos.first - close);
        }
      }
      positions.clear();
      lastPrice = 0.0;
      invState = InvState::outPos;
    }

    // Increase position if price rises/falls by N/2
    else if (((invState == InvState::longPos) &&
      (close > lastPrice + N / 2)) ||
      ((invState == InvState::shortPos) &&
      (close < lastPrice - N / 2))) {

      // Make sure position doesn't exceed 4 units
      totPosition = 0.0;
      for (const auto &pos : positions) {
        totPosition += pos.second;
      }
      if (totPosition + unitSize < 4 * unitSize) {

        if (positions.count(close) > 0) {
          positions[close] += unitSize;
        }
        else {
          positions[close] = unitSize;
        }
        lastPrice = close;
      }
    }

    // Update containers
    if (enters.size() == ENTER_PERIOD) {
      enters.pop_front();
    }
```

Listing 13.5: Ch13_TurtleTrading/Main.cpp (continued)

```
      enters.push_back(close);
      if (exits.size() == EXIT_PERIOD) {
        exits.pop_front();
      }
      exits.push_back(close);
    }

    // Exit position and print result
    for (const auto &pos : positions) {
      if (invState == InvState::longPos) {
        funds += pos.second * contractSize *
          (close - pos.first);
      }
      else {
        funds += pos.second * contractSize *
          (pos.first - close);
      }
    }
    ret = funds / initFunds;
    std::cout << "Return for " << str << ": " <<
      std::setprecision(4) << ret << std::endl;
    csvFile.close();
  }
  return 0;
}
```

After computing the ATR for each bar, `main` checks the `enters` deque to see if a 20-day minimum/maximum has been reached. If it has, and the current state is `InvState::outPos`, the function establishes a long or short position.

After checking the 20-day high/low, `main` checks the `exits` deque check for a 10-day high or low, depending on the position. If this condition is met, the function exits the position. It will also exit the position if the price is 2N less than or greater than the previous trade price, depending on the position.

Once all the checks have been made, the function updates the `enters` and `exits` deques. If either deque has reached its maximum size (`ENTER_PERIOD` and `EXIT_PERIOD`), the `pop_front` function discards its oldest value.

For each bar, `main` makes four checks to see if a trade should be made. It's important to note that multiple conditions may be met in a single iteration. For this reason, it's important to order the conditions from most important to least important. This is why the two exit conditions are checked before the increase condition.

13.2.4 Analyzing the Turtle System

When I run the Turtle trading application on my system, it prints the following results:

```
Return for CAD: 0.9554
Return for CHF: 0.8850
Return for ES:  1.0962
Return for GBP: 0.9945
Return for GC:  1.1135
Return for GE:  1.0648
Return for HG:  1.1388
Return for RB:  1.1366
Return for SI:  0.9553
```

The average return for these futures contracts is approximately 1.0388, which isn't quite as impressive as the legend would suggest. There are many possible reasons for this, including the lack of human intervention, lack of intra-day information, and lack of trades that decrease the position without exiting.

It's instructive to look at the futures contract at which it performed worst. Figure 13.1 illustrates the prices of the CHF (Swiss franc) futures contract over the course of a year. The system produced a return of 0.8850, which is the lowest of the computed returns.

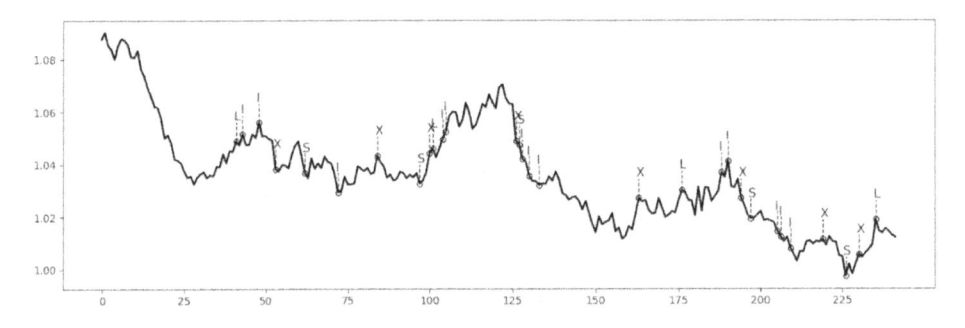

Figure 13.1 Trading Swiss Franc Futures (CHF) with the Turtle System

Each dashed line identifies an event that resulted in a trade, and each has a letter that identifies the type of trade:

- **L** — Enter a long position
- **S** — Enter a short position
- **I** — Increase the long or short position
- **X** — Exit the position

The fundamental problem with the Turtle system, like that of trend following systems in general, is that it exits the position too long after the trend has reversed. This issue is more pronounced for the illustrated CHF futures contract, which never establishes a long-term upward or downward trend.

To see what I mean, consider the trades starting around Day 40. The system enters a long position at a 20-day high and increases the position twice as the price rises. But the prices reverse around Day 55, and the system exits at a price lower than the initial price.

This money-losing pattern continues throughout the year, and many trend following systems have the same problem. One possible solution is to make the system more responsive to reverses. The current system exits the position when the price reverses by 2N, but it may be a good idea to reduce that to 1.5N or N.

Another possible solution is to make the system less greedy—instead of following a trend to its end, the system should exit before the trend reverses. That is, the system should exit the position on the second or third increase, depending on volatility. This reduces the amount of profit from a lengthy trend, but also reduces the loss associated with steep reversals.

As discussed, the Turtle system enters positions on 20-day highs and lows and exits positions on 10-day highs and lows. It may be worthwhile to adapt the length of the entry and exit periods to the contract's volatility. For example, if the contract is highly volatile, it may be better to enter positions on 10-day highs/lows and exit on 5-day highs/lows. The length of these periods can be determined by computing the average duration of the contract's trends and its reversals.

The fundamental question is this: How do we distinguish between significant trend reversals and minor fluctuations in price? One solution involves taking volume into account. Many trend reversals are accompanied by major spikes in volume, while minor fluctuations have only minor changes in volume. The Turtle system doesn't look at a contract's volume, but the Bollinger-MFI system does.

13.3 The Bollinger-MFI System

In the 1980s, a technical analyst named John Bollinger developed the idea of Bollinger Bands, which measure how much a security's price deviates from a running average. Chapter 11 discussed how to compute Bollinger Bands in Python and C++.

In 2001, Bollinger presented his methodology in a book entitled *Bollinger on Bollinger Bands*. Chapter 19 of this book describes a trading system that combines Bollinger Bands with a volume indicator called the money flow index (MFI). In this chapter, I'll refer to the system as the *Bollinger-MFI system*.

This section presents the theory behind this system and explains how it can be implemented in code. The last part of the section analyzes its performance.

13.3.1 Computing Bollinger Bands and the MFI

As discussed in Chapter 11, the Bollinger Band indicator requires three calculations:

- A 20-day simple moving average
- The 20-day moving average plus twice the standard deviation (upper band)
- The 20-day moving average minus twice the standard deviation (lower band)

The upper and lower bands serve as boundaries that distinguish regular price behavior from irregular price behavior. That is, a price is considered irregular if it exceeds the upper band or falls below the lower band.

Using these bands, analysts compute a value called %b, which identifies how close a security's price is to the two bands. %b is 0 when the price intersects the lower band and %b is 100 when the price intersects the upper band. If %b is 50, the price is exactly at its average value.

Bollinger suggests a handful of indicators to use in conjunction with Bollinger Bands, and a popular indicator is the money flow index, or MFI. This measures how much money flows into and out of a security over an interval. Like the relative strength index (RSI) discussed in Chapter 11, it measures how many bullish days and bearish days have transpired. Unlike the RSI, the MFI takes volume into account.

The process of computing the MFI consists of five steps:

1. For each day, compute the security's typical price, which is the average of the day's high, low, and closing prices: (high + low + close)/3.
2. For each day, compute the money flow, which is the product of the typical price and the daily volume.
3. Compute the positive money flow, which is the sum of the money flows of the days where the typical price exceeded the previous day's typical price.
4. Compute the negative money flow, which is the sum of the money flows of the days where the typical price is lower than the typical price of the preceding day.
5. Compute the money flow index (MFI) using the following equation:

$$MFI = \frac{100 \cdot positive\ money\ flow}{positive\ money\ flow\ +\ negative\ money\ flow}$$

As shown, the MFI ranges from 0 to 100. A value of 0 implies that all of the trading days have had negative money flow (decreasing prices day after day). A value of 100 implies that all of the days have had positive money flow (increasing prices day after day).

Once %b and MFI have been computed, Bollinger's system consists of two simple rules:

- Buy when %b is greater than 0.8 and MFI is greater than 80.
- Sell when %b is less than 0.2 and MFI is less than 20.

These rules leave a number of questions unanswered, such as how much should be bought or sold in each trade. The system also doesn't identify when to increase, decrease, or exit a position.

To implement the Bollinger-MFI system in an algorithm, these rules need to be extended. The code discussed in this section adds some aspects of the Turtle system (unit size and exits) to the Bollinger-MFI system. The resulting algorithm has three steps:

1. Determine the unit size, which is 1% of the available funds divided by the contract size.
2. If %b rises above 80 and MFI rises above 80, purchase one unit if the algorithm has a long position or no position. If the algorithm is in a short position, exit the position.
3. If %b falls below 20 and MFI falls below 20, short one unit if the algorithm has a short position or no position. If the algorithm is in a long position, exit the position.

As with the Turtle system, I'll present code that implements the Bollinger-MFI system in Python and C++. Then I'll discuss the results.

13.3.2 Implementing the Bollinger-MFI System in Python

The code for the Bollinger-MFI system is simpler than that of the Turtle system. There are three primary containers:

- `prices` — a deque containing each day's closing price
- `money_flows` — a deque containing each day's money flow, needed to compute the money flow index (MFI)
- `positions` — a dictionary associating trade prices with the number of contracts traded

The full code for the system is in the ch13/bollinger_mfi.py module. Listing 13.6 presents the code in its `main` function.

Listing 13.6: ch13/bollinger_mfi.py

```
def main():

    # Define symbols of interest
    symbols = {'GE': 2500, 'ES': 50, 'CHF': 125000,
        'GBP': 62500, 'CAD': 100000, 'GC': 100, 'SI': 5000,
        'HG': 25000, 'RB': 42000}

    # Load data
    prices = deque(maxlen=BOLLINGER_PERIOD)
    money_flows = deque(maxlen=MFI_PERIOD)
    positions = {}

    csv_files = [f for f in os.listdir('.')
        if f.endswith('.csv')]
    for csv_file in csv_files:

        # Initialize values
        old_typical = -1.0
        prices.clear()
        money_flows.clear()
        funds = init_funds
        inv_state = InvState.OUT
        positions.clear()

        # Contract-specific information
        symbol = csv_file.split('.')[0]
        contract_size = symbols[symbol]
        unit_size = int(0.01 * funds/contract_size)
        df = pd.read_csv(csv_file)

        # Iterate through prices
        for i, bar in df.iterrows():

            # Compute the money flow
            typical = (bar['HIGH'] + bar['LOW'] +
                bar['CLOSE'])/3.0
            if old_typical > typical:
                old_typical = typical
                typical *= -1.0
            else:
                old_typical = typical
            money_flow = bar['VOL'] * typical
```

Listing 13.6: ch13/bollinger_mfi.py (Continued)

```python
            money_flows.append(money_flow)
            if len(money_flows) == MFI_PERIOD:
                mf_array = np.array(money_flows)
                pos_flow = np.sum(mf_array[mf_array > 0])
                neg_flow = -1.0 * np.sum(mf_array[mf_array < 0])
                mfi = 100.0 * pos_flow/(pos_flow + neg_flow)
            else:
                continue

            # Compute the upper/lower bands
            prices.append(bar['CLOSE'])
            if len(prices) == BOLLINGER_PERIOD:
                avg = sum(prices)/len(prices)

                # Compute the standard deviation, bands, and %b
                price_array = np.array(prices)
                sigma = np.std(price_array)
                upper = avg + 2*sigma
                lower = avg - 2*sigma
                percent_b = 100.0 * \
                    (bar['CLOSE'] - lower)/(upper - lower)

                # Check buy signal
                price = bar['CLOSE']
                if percent_b > 80 and mfi > 80:

                    if inv_state == InvState.OUT:
                        positions[price] = unit_size
                        inv_state = InvState.LONG

                    elif inv_state == InvState.LONG:
                        if price in positions:
                            positions[price] += unit_size
                        else:
                            positions[price] = unit_size

                    elif inv_state == InvState.SHORT:
                        for p in positions:
                            funds += positions[p] * \
                                contract_size * (p - price)
                        positions.clear()
                        inv_state = InvState.OUT
```

Listing 13.6: ch13/bollinger_mfi.py (Continued)

```python
            # Check sell signal
            elif percent_b < 20 and mfi < 20:

                # If out, enter short position
                if inv_state == InvState.OUT:
                    positions[price] = unit_size
                    inv_state = InvState.SHORT

                # If long, exit position
                elif inv_state == InvState.LONG:
                    for p in positions:
                        funds += positions[p] * contract_size
                            * (price - p)
                    positions.clear()
                    inv_state = InvState.OUT

                # If short, increase short position
                elif inv_state == InvState.SHORT:
                    if price in positions:
                        positions[price] += unit_size
                    else:
                        positions[price] = unit_size

    # Compute return
    for p in positions:
        if inv_state == InvState.LONG:
            funds += positions[p] * contract_size *
                (price - p)
        elif inv_state == InvState.SHORT:
            funds += positions[p] * contract_size *
                (p - price)
    ret = funds/init_funds
    print('Return for {0}: {1:.4f}'.format(symbol, ret))
```

The `main` function iterates through each bar of each CSV file in the current directory. For each bar, it computes the money flow, and once enough values are available, the function computes the MFI.

Afterward, `main` computes the moving average and standard deviation of each day's closing price. Once the upper and lower bands have been computed, the function uses %b and MFI to determine which trades to make. A high %b/MFI implies that the algorithm should go long. Low values imply that the algorithm should go short.

13.3.3 Implementing the Bollinger-MFI System in C++

The Ch13_BollingerMFI project contains code that implements the Bollinger-MFI project in C++. There's no need to access the TWS API, so the only source file is Main.cpp, which defines the `main` function. Listing 13.7 presents its code.

Listing 13.7: Ch13_BollingerMFI/Main.cpp

```
int main() {
  double avg, stdDev;

  // Iterate through files
  for (const auto &f :
    std::filesystem::directory_iterator(".")) {

    // Find CSV files
    fileName = f.path().string();
    if (fileName.compare(fileName.length()-4,4,".csv") != 0) {
      continue;
    }

    // Initialize values and containers
    funds = initFunds;
    oldTypical = -1.0;
    invState = InvState::outPos;
    moneyFlows.clear();
    prices.clear();
    positions.clear();

    // Compute unit size
    symbol = fileName.substr(2, fileName.length() - 6);
    contractSize = symbols[symbol];
    unitSize = static_cast<int>(0.01 * funds / contractSize);

    // Open file and read lines
    csvFile.open(fileName, std::ios::in);
    std::getline(csvFile, line);
    while (std::getline(csvFile, line)) {

      // Read values
      std::stringstream ss(line);
      std::getline(ss, str, ',');
      close = std::stod(str);
      std::getline(ss, str, ',');
      low = std::stod(str);
```

Listing 13.7: Ch13_BollingerMFI/Main.cpp (continued)

```cpp
      std::getline(ss, str, ',');
      high = std::stod(str);
      std::getline(ss, str);
      vol = std::stoi(str);

      // Compute the money flow
      typical = (high + low + close) / 3.0;
      if (oldTypical > typical) {
        oldTypical = typical;
        typical *= -1.0;
      }
      else {
        oldTypical = typical;
      }
      moneyFlow = typical * vol;

      // Compute the money flow index
      moneyFlows.push_back(moneyFlow);
      if (moneyFlows.size() == MFI_PERIOD) {

        // Compute positive/negative money flows
        posFlow = 0.0;
        negFlow = 0.0;
        for (double flow : moneyFlows) {
          if (flow > 0) {
            posFlow += flow;
          }
          else {
            negFlow += -1.0 * flow;
          }
        }
        mfi = 100.0 * posFlow / (posFlow + negFlow);
        moneyFlows.pop_front();
      }
      else { continue; }

      // Compute upper, lower, and %b
      prices.push_back(close);
      if (prices.size() == BOLLINGER_PERIOD) {

        // Compute the average
        avg = std::accumulate(prices.begin(),
          prices.end(), 0.0) / prices.size();
```

Listing 13.7: Ch13_BollingerMFI/Main.cpp (continued)

```cpp
        // Compute the standard deviation
        auto devFunc=[&avg](double acc,const double& p) {
          return acc + (p - avg)*(p - avg);
        };
        stdDev = std::accumulate(prices.begin(),
          prices.end(), 0.0, devFunc);
        stdDev = std::sqrt(stdDev / BOLLINGER_PERIOD);

        // Compute %b
        upper = avg + 2 * stdDev;
        lower = avg - 2 * stdDev;
        percentB = 100.0 * (close - lower) /
          (upper - lower);

        // Check for buy signal
        if ((percentB > 80.0) && (mfi > 80.0)) {

          // If out, enter long position
          if (invState == InvState::outPos) {
            positions[close] = unitSize;
            invState = InvState::longPos;
          }

          // If long, increase position
          else if (invState == InvState::longPos) {
            if (positions.count(close) > 0) {
              positions[close] += unitSize;
            }
            else {
              positions[close] = unitSize;
            }
          }

          // If short, exit position
          else if (invState == InvState::shortPos) {
            for (const auto &pos : positions) {
              funds += pos.second * contractSize *
                (pos.first - close);
            }
            positions.clear();
            invState = InvState::outPos;
          }
        }
```

Listing 13.7: Ch13_BollingerMFI/Main.cpp (continued)

```cpp
      // Check for sell signal
      else if ((percentB < 20.0) && (mfi < 20.0)) {

        // If out, enter long position
        if (invState == InvState::outPos) {
          positions[close] = unitSize;
          invState = InvState::shortPos;
        }

        // If long, exit position
        else if (invState == InvState::longPos) {
          for (const auto &pos : positions) {
            funds += pos.second * contractSize *
              (close - pos.first);
          }
          positions.clear();
          invState = InvState::outPos;
        }

        // If short, increase position
        else if (invState == InvState::shortPos) {
          if (positions.count(close) > 0) {
            positions[close] += unitSize;
          }
          else {
            positions[close] = unitSize;
          }
        }
      }
      prices.pop_front();
    }
  }

  // Exit position and print result
  for (const auto &pos : positions) {
    if (invState == InvState::longPos) {
      funds += pos.second * contractSize *
        (close - pos.first);
    }
    else if (invState == InvState::shortPos) {
      funds += pos.second * contractSize *
        (pos.first - close);
    }
  }
```

Listing 13.7: Ch13_BollingerMFI/Main.cpp (continued)

```
    ret = funds / initFunds;
    std::cout << "Return for " << symbol << ": " <<
      std::setprecision(4) << ret << std::endl;
    csvFile.close();
  }
  return 0;
}
```

As the application executes, it updates three important containers:

- `moneyFlows` — stores the money flows needed to compute the money flow index (MFI)
- `prices` — stores the closing prices needed to compute the moving average and the Bollinger Bands
- `positions` — associates each trade price with the number of contracts traded

For each line in a CSV file, the application computes the money flow and the money flow index. Then it computes the average of the last 20 prices and standard deviation by calling the `std::accumulate` function. Using these values, the application finds the values of the upper Bollinger Band, the lower Bollinger Band, and %b.

After computing %b and the MFI, the application checks their values for buy/sell signals. Values above 80 tell the application to buy and values below 20 tell the application to sell.

13.3.4 Analyzing the Bollinger-MFI System

When I execute the Bollinger-MFI algorithm with nine CSV files in the working directory, it prints the following results:

```
Return for CAD: 0.9989
Return for CHF: 1
Return for ES: -15.65
Return for GBP: 1.001
Return for GC: 0.1435
Return for GE: 1
Return for HG: 1.021
Return for RB: 1.018
Return for SI: 0.9989
```

These results aren't impressive, and this may be caused by multiple factors. One possibility is that, while Bollinger's rules identify how to generate entry/exit signals, it's insufficient to serve as a trading system. For example, the algorithm only exits a position when the opposite signal is received.

The system's return for E-mini S&P 500 futures (ES) is −15, which means the trader loses fifteen times his/her initial investment. To see how this is possible, consider the graphs displayed in Figure 13.2. The upper graph illustrates the ES prices over a year, and denotes each trade by a letter (L for long entry, S for short entry, I for position increase, and X for exiting the position).

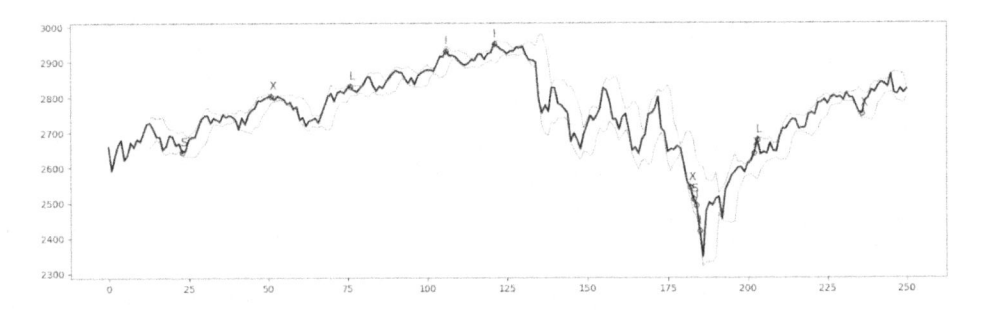

Figure 13.2 Trading E-Mini S&P 500 Futures (CHF) with the Bollinger-MFI System

On Day 24, the algorithm short sells the contract at a local minimum. On Day 203, it enters a long position at a local maximum. This is the opposite of how a trading system is supposed to behave, and it may be worthwhile to test the system with reversed rules (sell when %b/MFI are greater than 80, buy when %b/MFI are less than 20).

The fundamental problem is that the Bollinger rules don't identify when the algorithm should reduce or exit a position. For example, the prices near Day 180 intersect the lower band repeatedly. With each intersection, the algorithm increases its short position. Then the prices increase abruptly, and the Bollinger rules don't identify when the algorithm should exit the short position.

13.4 Summary

This chapter has explored the theory and implementation of the Turtle trading system and the Bollinger-MFI system. As shown by the testing results, both have significant strengths and drawbacks.

The Turtle trading system focuses on a security's price relative to its 20-day high/low and 55-day high/low. This is a trend-following strategy, and only enters a position when the trend is clearly established. The size of each trade is determined by the available funds and the Average True Range, which was discussed in Chapter 11.

According to my tests, the Turtle trading system makes a relatively small profit. This is because the system waits too long to exit a position. In addition, it fails to take into account the security's volume when analyzing trends.

When it comes to establishing trading rules, the Bollinger-MFI system isn't as thorough as the Turtle trading system. It provides broad rules regarding when to enter positions, but fails to clearly identify when to reduce and exit positions. As a result, the average return is significantly worse than that of the Turtle trading system.

Chapter 14

Practical Algorithmic Trading

The preceding chapter explained how to implement existing trading systems using the TWS API. This chapter focuses on helping you implement a custom system using Python and C++.

To be specific, this chapter introduces a simple but practical trading application named SimpleAlgo. I don't endorse SimpleAlgo and I make no promise that it will make anyone money. In presenting this application, my goal is to demonstrate how algorithmic trading can be implemented in code. The application checks the market sentiment, searches for securities, analyzes financial data, creates a bracket order, and submits it to IB for execution.

To select stocks, SimpleAlgo relies on a breakout strategy. That is, it computes support or resistance levels for each candidate stock and checks if the price has broken through. A stock is interesting if its price has just risen above the resistance level or has just fallen below the support level. After selecting the most interesting stock, SimpleAlgo places the order.

This chapter doesn't introduce any new classes, or functions. Its only purpose is to show how SimpleAlgo can be coded in Python and C++. I've written the application to be modular, so you shouldn't have any trouble modifying it and extending it for your own use.

As a professional programmer, I always prefer to modify working applications instead of writing code from scratch. This reduces development time and decreases the potential for error. And if there's ever been a branch of programming that punishes errors, it's algorithmic trading.

14.1 Introducing SimpleAlgo

At a high level, SimpleAlgo evaluates a set of stocks and submits a bracket order for the stock that it finds most suitable. Its operation consists of six stages:

1. Evaluate investor sentiment (bullish or bearish) by checking the S&P 500 index and the volatility index.
2. Use a market scanner to obtain a set of suitable stocks whose prices are near their 13-week high or 13-week low.
3. For each stock, compute support and resistance levels to determine whether a breakout has occurred. Filter out stocks that haven't moved above or below resistance and support.
4. Use quadratic regression to estimate the trajectory of each stock of interest.
5. Select a target stock and place a bracket order.
6. Display the order's status.

In preceding chapters, example applications were sufficiently short that all of the request code could be placed in the `main` function. But SimpleAlgo is larger than other applications, so I've split the code into five functions:

- `checkSentiment` — gauges market sentiment by looking at securities based on the S&P 500 and the volatility index
- `assembleStockList` — scans for candidate stocks based on criteria involving prices, volume, and proximity to 13-week high or 13-week low
- `computeSupportResistance` — compute support/resistance levels for each stock in the list
- `selectTargetStock` — access market data to estimate whether stock will break and its future price
- `placeOrder` — submit a bracket order for the most suitable stock and access the order's status

The rest of this chapter explores each of these functions, starting with evaluating investor sentiment. Instead of presenting all the code at the end, I'll provide the code for each function as it's encountered.

14.2 Evaluating Investor Sentiment

To get an idea of what investors are thinking, analysts look at market indexes. In the United States, two are particularly popular:

- S&P 500 stock index — Combines the prices of (approximately) 500 U.S. stocks
- Volatility index — Measures volatility of the stocks in the S&P 500

Both indexes have securities that track their values. The SPDR S&P 500 Trust ETF (SPY) tracks the S&P 500 index and the iPath Series B S&P 500 VIX Short-Term ETN (VXX) tracks the volatility index. Applications can't access the indexes directly, but they can access the prices of the corresponding securities.

When following SPY and VXX, the exact prices aren't fundamentally important. The main concern is how their prices change over time. This section discusses both securities and explains how to interpret their price changes. At the end of the section, I'll present code that demonstrates how to access these prices programmatically.

14.2.1 SPDR S&P 500 Trust ETF (SPY)

In 1923, Standard & Poors (S&P) combined the prices of a select number of U.S. stocks into a single value to serve as a bellwether of America's corporate performance. In 1957, the S&P index expanded to 500 stocks, and today, the S&P 500 is one of the most popular market indexes available.

In 1993, the Standard and Poors Depository Receipts (SPDR) was created as America's first exchange-traded fund (ETF). This contains the stocks in the S&P 500 and its price is determined by the market capitalization weighting method used by the S&P 500. This method multiplies the price of each stock by its company's market capitalization and adds the prices together. At the time of this writing, the two highest-weighted stocks are Apple (market cap: $939.68B) and Microsoft (market cap: $1.050T).

SPY starts trading at 8:00 am on trading days, and the trading volume is high even early in the morning. For this reason, many investors start their day by checking SPY. A rising price implies a bullish market and a decreasing price implies a bearish market.

14.2.2 iPath Series B S&P 500 VIX Short-Term ETN (VXX)

Just as the S&P index measures corporate performance, the CBOE Volatility Index (VIX) measures the index's expected volatility. VIX is frequently referred to as the *fear index* and it's based on the prices of options on the stocks in the S&P 500. The more expensive the options, the more investors expect the S&P index to rise or fall.

The VIX is given as a percentage that identifies how much the S&P 500 index is expected to change in the upcoming year. As I write this, VIX equals 14.09, which implies that the S&P 500 will rise or fall 14.09% in the next year.

TWS applications can't read VIX directly, but they can access VIX through one of the securities whose prices are based on VIX. The most popular VIX-based security is the iPath Series B S&P 500 VIX short-term ETN, whose ticker is VXX.

Like an ETF, an ETN (exchange-traded note) can be traded on major exchanges and its price tracks underlying assets. The main difference is that, while ETFs resemble stocks, ETNs resemble bonds. An ETN represents unsecured debt and may end up worthless if the issuer defaults. Thankfully, the issuer of the VXX ETN is Barclays plc, a bank that has remained solvent since the seventeenth century.

The price of VXX is determined by CBOE futures contracts based on the VIX. To be specific, VXX is based on the two nearest VX contracts, whose value is based on options on the S&P 500 stocks. Because VXX is based on futures contracts, its value usually decreases as the contracts come close to expiring.

In theory, a rise in VXX would only imply greater changes in the prices of the S&P 500. In practice, a rise in VXX usually implies a drop in the S&P 500. Similarly, a fall in VXX implies a rise in the S&P 500. Therefore, investors frequently look at VXX to predict what may happen to the stock market.

SimpleAlgo reads the prices of SPY and VXX, and if SPY is rising and VXX is falling, SimpleAlgo decides that the market is bullish. If VXX is rising and SPY is falling, the market is bearish. If SPY and VXX move in the same direction, SimpleAlgo doesn't trade.

14.2.3 Evaluating Investor Sentiment in Python

The ch14 directory contains two files: simplealgo.py and main.py. simplealgo.py defines the `SimpleAlgo` class and its callback methods. The `main` function in main.py creates an instance of `SimpleAlgo` and calls its request methods.

Listing 14.1 presents the code for the `check_sentiment` function. This creates two contracts and calls `reqHistoricalData` to obtain data for the preceding day.

Listing 14.1: ch14/main.py (check_sentiment function)

```
# Check SPY and VXX to determine sentiment
def check_sentiment(client):

    # Create a contract for the SPY ETF
    spy_con = Contract()
    spy_con.symbol = 'SPY'
    spy_con.secType = 'STK'
    spy_con.exchange = 'SMART'
    spy_con.currency = 'USD'

    # Access SPY data
    now = datetime.now().strftime('%Y%m%d, %H:%M:%S')
    client.reqHistoricalData(2, spy_con, now, '1 d', '1 day',
        'MIDPOINT', False, 1, False, [])

    # Access the SPY ETF
    vxx_con = Contract()
    vxx_con.symbol = 'VXX'
    vxx_con.secType = 'STK'
    vxx_con.exchange = 'SMART'
    vxx_con.currency = 'USD'

    # Create a contract for the VXX ETN
    client.reqHistoricalData(3, vxx_con, now, '1 d', '1 day',
        'MIDPOINT', False, 1, False, [])
    time.sleep(5)

    # Determine market sentiment
    return client.sentiment
```

The `historicalData` callback is called twice—once for SPY and once for VXX. The callback's code is given as follows.

```
def historicalData(self, req_id, bar):
    if req_id == 2:
        self.spy_bullish = (bar.close > bar.open)
    elif req_id == 3:
        vxx_bullish = (bar.close < bar.open)
        if self.spy_bullish and vxx_bullish:
            self.sentiment = Sentiment.BULLISH
        elif not self.spy_bullish and not vxx_bullish:
            self.sentiment = Sentiment.BEARISH
        else:
            self.sentiment = Sentiment.MIXED
```

This callback computes two values, `spy_bullish` and `vxx_bullish`. If both are true, SimpleAlgo decides that the market is bullish. If both are false, SimpleAlgo decides that the market is bearish.

14.2.4 Evaluating Investor Sentiment in C++

In the Ch14_SimpleAlgo project, the `main` function creates an instance of the `SimpleAlgo` class and then calls a series of functions to implement algorithmic trading. The first of these functions is `checkSentiment` and Listing 14.2 presents its code.

Listing 14.2: Ch14_SimpleAlgo/Main.cpp (checkSentiment function)

```
Sentiment checkSentiment(SimpleAlgo& client) {

  // Get the current time
  time_t tm = std::time(nullptr);
  std::tm loc_tm = *std::localtime(&tm);
  std::ostringstream ostr;
  ostr << std::put_time(&loc_tm, "%Y%m%d, %H:%M:%S");

  // Contract for the SPY ETF
  Contract spyCon = Contract();
  spyCon.symbol = "SPY";
  spyCon.secType = "STK";
  spyCon.exchange = "SMART";
  spyCon.currency = "USD";

  // Access SPY data
  client.reqHistoricalData(2, spyCon, ostr.str(), "1 d",
    "1 day", "MIDPOINT", 1, 1, false, TagValueListSPtr());

  // Contract for the VXX ETN
  Contract vxxCon = Contract();
  vxxCon.symbol = "VXX";
  vxxCon.secType = "STK";
  vxxCon.exchange = "SMART";
  vxxCon.currency = "USD";

  // Access VXX data and wait
  client.reqHistoricalData(3, vxxCon, ostr.str(), "1 d",
    "1 day", "MIDPOINT", 1, 1, false, TagValueListSPtr());
  std::this_thread::sleep_for(std::chrono::seconds(2));
  client.signal.waitForSignal();
  client.reader->processMsgs();
```

Listing 14.2: Ch14_SimpleAlgo/Main.cpp (checkSentiment function continued)

```
  // Determine market sentiment
  return client.sentiment
}
```

The `checkSentiment` function creates a contract for SPY and calls `reqHistoricalData` to obtain market data for the preceding day. Then it does the same for VXX. As a result, the `historicalData` callback is invoked once with a request ID of 2 and once with a request ID of 3.

```
void SimpleAlgo::historicalData(TickerId reqId, const Bar& bar) {

  bool vxxBullish;
  if (reqId == 2) {

    // Check if SPY is bullish or bearish
    spyBullish = (bar.close > bar.open);
  }

  else if (reqId == 3) {

    // Estimate market sentiment
    vxxBullish = (bar.open > bar.close);

    if (vxxBullish && spyBullish)
      sentiment = Sentiment::BULLISH;

    else if (!vxxBullish && !spyBullish)
      sentiment = Sentiment::BEARISH;

    else
      sentiment = Sentiment::MIXED;
  }
}
```

The operation performed by the callback depends on the request ID. If the ID is 2, the callback computes `spyBullish`, which is true if SPY's closing price is greater than its opening price.

If the request ID is 3, the callback computes `vxxBullish`, which is true if VXX's closing price is less than its opening price. If `spyBullish` and `vxxBullish` are true, SimpleAlgo decides the market is bullish. If both are false, SimpleAlgo decides the market is bearish. Otherwise, it assumes the market's sentiment is mixed.

14.3 Selecting Candidate Stocks

SimpleAlgo uses the estimated sentiment to determine which stocks it should examine. If the market appears to be bullish, SimpleAlgo searches for stocks trading near their 13-week high to see if any have risen above their resistance level. If the market appears to be bearish, SimpleAlgo looks at stocks trading near their 13-week low to see if any have fallen below their support level.

To perform the search, SimpleAlgo relies on the market scanner discussed in Chapter 9. In code, SimpleAlgo creates a `ScannerSubscription` and sets four criteria:

- Share price must be greater than 10 USD.
- Share price must be less than available funds/200. This ensures that a round lot (100 shares) will cost less than half of available funds.
- Average volume must be greater than 20,000.
- Price must be trading at the 13-week high (bullish market) or the 13-week low (bearish market).

The rest of this section explains how this stock selection can be coded in Python and C++. The `main` function selects candidate stocks by calling the `assemble_stock_list` function (Python) or the `assembleStockList` function (C++).

14.3.1 Selecting Candidate Stocks in Python

After estimating the market sentiment, SimpleAlgo calls `assemble_stock_list` to acquire a list of stocks that meet the given criteria. The process is simple: create a `ScannerSubscription`, configure its criteria, and call `reqScannerSubscription`. Listing 14.3 presents the Python code that makes this possible.

Listing 14.3: ch14/simplealgo/main.py (assemble_stock_list function)

```
def assemble_stock_list(client, sentiment):

    # Define scanner subscription
    ss = ScannerSubscription()
    ss.instrument = 'STK'
    ss.locationCode = 'STK.US.MAJOR'
    ss.abovePrice = 10.0
    ss.belowPrice = client.funds/200.0
    ss.aboveVolume = 20000
```

Listing 14.3: ch14/simplealgo.py (assemble_stock_list function continued)

```
    # Set scan code according to sentiment
    if sentiment == Sentiment.bullish:
        ss.scanCode = 'HIGH_VS_13W_HL'
    else:
        ss.scanCode = 'LOW_VS_13W_HL'

    # Request securities
    client.reqScannerSubscription(4, ss, [], [])
    time.sleep(3)
```

The fields of the `ScannerSubscription` determine what stocks will be returned by the scanner. The `instrument` field is set to `STK`, so only stocks and ETFs will be returned. The `abovePrice` field is set to `10.0` and the `locationCode` is set to `STK.US.MAJOR`, so each stock will have a price greater than 10 USD.

SimpleAlgo intends to trade a round lot (100 shares) of the final stock, and this shouldn't require more than half of the available funds. For this reason, the `belowPrice` field is set to `client.funds/200.0`.

The `scanCode` field depends on the sentiment obtained earlier. If the sentiment is bullish, SimpleAlgo wants stocks that have penetrated the resistance level, so `scanCode` is set to `HIGH_VS_13W_HL`. If the sentiment is bearish, SimpleAlgo wants stocks that have fallen through the support level, so the field is set to `LOW_VS_13W_HL`.

After configuring the `ScannerSubscription`, the function requests scanner results by calling `reqScannerSubscription`. After the response is received, the results are provided by the `scannerData` callback:

```
def scannerData(self, reqId, rank, details, distance,
    benchmark, projection, legsStr):

    # Append scanned stock to list
    self.scan_results.append(details.contract)
```

As shown, the callback simply adds each contract to the `scan_results` list. SimpleAlgo will iterate through this list to determine which stock is most suitable for trading.

After the last contract is received from the scanner, the `scannerDataEnd` callback will be invoked. At this point, the application can determine the number of scanned securities by obtaining the length of `scan_results`. This is a convenient place to initialize containers whose size depends on the number of scanned contracts.

```python
def scannerDataEnd(self, req_id):
    self.num_stocks = len(self.scan_results)
    self.rs_levels = np.zeros(self.num_stocks)
    self.prices = np.zeros([self.num_stocks, 20])
```

This callback sets `num_stocks` to the number of scanned securities and initializes two NumPy arrays. The first, `rs_levels`, stores the resistance/support levels computed for each security. The second, `prices`, stores the 20 most recent prices of each security.

14.3.2 Selecting Candidate Stocks in C++

In the Ch14_SimpleAlgo project, the `main` function obtains the set of candidate stocks by calling `assembleStockList`. This function starts by creating and configuring a `ScannerSubscription`. Then it requests stocks from the scanner by calling `reqScannerSubscription`. Listing 14.4 presents the code.

Listing 14.4: Ch14_SimpleAlgo/Main.cpp (assembleStockList function)

```cpp
void assembleStockList(SimpleAlgo& client, Sentiment sent) {

  // Create scanner subscription
  ScannerSubscription ss;
  ss.instrument = "STK";
  ss.locationCode = "STK.US.MAJOR";
  ss.scanCode = "HOT_BY_VOLUME";
  ss.abovePrice = 10.0;
  ss.belowPrice = client.funds/200.0;
  ss.aboveVolume = 20000;

  // Set scan code according to sentiment
  if (sent == Sentiment::BULLISH)
    ss.scanCode = "HIGH_VS_13W_HL";
  else if (sent == Sentiment::BEARISH)
    ss.scanCode = "LOW_VS_13W_HL";

  // Submit a request for a scanner subscription
  client.reqScannerSubscription(4, ss,
    TagValueListSPtr(), TagValueListSPtr());
  std::this_thread::sleep_for(std::chrono::seconds(5));
  client.signal.waitForSignal();
  client.reader->processMsgs();
}
```

Most of the code in `assembleStockList` is concerned with setting fields of the `ScannerSubscription`. The `abovePrice` field is set to `10.0`, so every returned contract must have a price greater than 10.0. The `aboveVolume` field is set to `20000`, so every returned contract must have an average volume greater than 20,000.

The `belowPrice` field is set to `client.funds/200`, so a round lot will always cost less than half of the available funds. For example, if the client has 15,000 USD, the maximum price of the returned contracts will be 15000/200 = 75 USD.

The last configuration field is `scanCode`. If the market is expected to be bullish, this is set to `HIGH_VS_13W_HL` to find stocks that have risen above the resistance level. If the market is expected to be bearish, `scanCode` is set to `HIGH_VS_13W_HL` to find stocks that may have fallen below the support level.

After configuring the `ScannerSubscription`, the function makes it the second argument of `reqScannerSubscription`. This function requests results from the market scanner, and when the response is received, the results are provided through the `scannerData` callback, given as follows:

```
void SimpleAlgo::scannerData(int reqId, int rank,
  const ContractDetails& details,
  const std::string& distance,
  const std::string& benchmark,
  const std::string& projection,
  const std::string& legsStr) {

  // Append scanned stock to vector
  scanResults.push_back(details.contract);
}
```

As each result is received from the scanner, the callback pushes the corresponding contract to the back of `scanResults`. This is a vector that holds `Contract`s. SimpleAlgo iterates through this vector to find a stock suitable for trading.

When the last result is received from the scanner, the application can allocate data structures whose sizes depend on the number of returned securities. For this reason, the application allocates memory for variables in the `scannerDataEnd` callback.

```
void SimpleAlgo::scannerDataEnd(int reqId) {

  numStocks = scanResults.size();
  rsLevels = new double[numStocks];
  prices = new double*[numStocks];
  for (int i = 0; i < numStocks; i++) {
    prices[i] = new double[20];
  }
}
```

This code sets `numStocks` equal to the number of candidate stocks and then allocates memory for two important arrays. The `rsLevels` array contains a resistance or support value for each candidate stock. `prices` is a two-dimensional array that contains 20 prices for each candidate stock.

14.4 Implementing a Breakout Strategy

One of the oldest and most popular investing strategies involves buying a security if it rises above its typical high and selling a security if it falls below its typical low. A price movement that goes beyond typical limits is called a *breakout*. An investing strategy based on breakouts is called a *breakout strategy*.

Analysts refer to a security's typical high as its *resistance* and its typical low as its *support*. Many investors (and algotrading applications) take support and resistance into account when placing trades.

On the following page, Figure 14.1 gives an idea of what these levels look like for E-Mini S&P futures quotes. The upper-right corner of the figure illustrates a positive breakout, in which the price rises above the resistance level.

After obtaining a set of suitable stocks, SimpleAlgo computes the support and resistance of each. The ideal time to trade is immediately after the stock breaks out. Therefore, SimpleAlgo is concerned with stocks that are just above the resistance level and rising (bullish market) or just below the support level and falling (bearish market).

Many traders know how to use resistance and support levels, but few know how to calculate them from a security's prices. Therefore, before I present the SimpleAlgo code, I'll start this discussion by presenting a method for computing a security's support and resistance levels.

14.4.1 Computing Support and Resistance

Despite the popularity of support and resistance levels, there's no consensus on how they should be calculated. Many analysts simply draw lines between prominent high values and low values. Others use Andrew's Pitchfork, which obtains support and resistance according to a median line drawn between the midpoints of highs and lows.

A popular approach to computing support and resistances involves *pivot points*, which identify stable past prices. The value of a pivot point is denoted P, and is computed by taking the average of the preceding day's high (H), low (L), and closing (C) prices. Put mathematically, $P = (H + L + C)/3$.

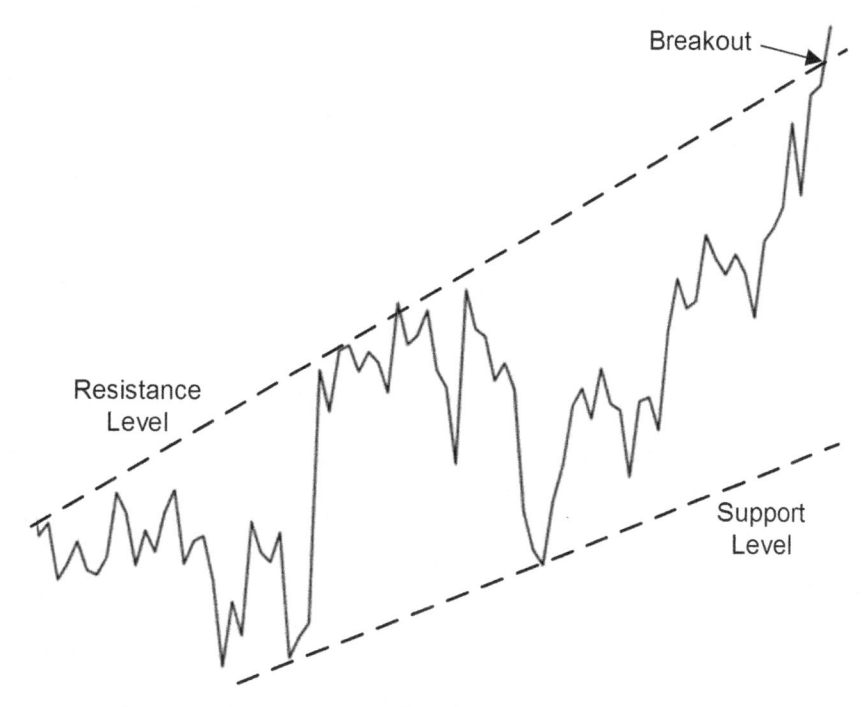

Figure 14.1 Futures Contract Prices with Support, Resistance, and Breakout

Once a pivot point is computed, the resistance level, R, can be determined by multiplying P by 2 and subtracting the preceding day's lowest price, L. Similarly, the support level S can be determined by multiplying P by 2 and subtracting the preceding high price, H. In equation form, $R = 2P - L$ and $H = 2P - H$.

It's important to see that these support/resistance levels change from day to day, and remain constant throughout a day. To obtain price data, SimpleAlgo calls `reqHistoricalData` for each candidate stock. Then the `historicalData` callback computes support and resistance levels. The rest of this section explains how this can be accomplished in Python and C++.

14.4.2 Computing Support and Resistance in Python

To compute the support or resistance level for a given stock, SimpleAlgo needs the high, low, and opening prices of the preceding day. The `main` function accomplishes this by calling `compute_support_resistance`. Listing 14.5 presents its code.

Listing 14.5: ch14/simplealgo/main.py (compute_support_resistance function)

```
def compute_support_resistance(client):
    ''' Compute support/resistance for each stock '''

    # Create string for the date/time at midnight
    midnight = datetime.now().strftime('%Y%m%d, 00:00:00')

    # Request five minutes of price data for all stocks
    for i, contract in enumerate(client.scan_results):
        client.reqHistoricalData(i + 10, contract, midnight,
            '1 d', '1 day', 'MIDPOINT', False, 1, False, [])
        time.sleep(1)
```

The function starts by obtaining a string identifying the time at midnight. Then it iterates through each contract provided by the scanner (`scan_results`) and calls `reqHistoricalData` to obtain prices from the preceding day. For the ith iteration, the request ID is set to i + 10 to ensure separate requests for different contracts.

After the response is received, the price data is provided by the `historicalData` callback. The following code shows how the callback processes data when the request ID is between 10 and 100.

```
def historicalData(self, reqId, bar):
    ...
    elif req_id > 9 and req_id < 100:

        # Compute pivot point and resistance/support
        p = (bar.high + bar.low + bar.close)/3.0

        if self.sentiment == Sentiment.BULLISH:
            self.rs_levels[req_id - 10] = 2.0 * p - bar.low

        elif self.sentiment == Sentiment.BEARISH:
            self.rs_levels[req_id - 10] = 2.0 * p - bar.high
```

The callback starts by computing the pivot point P = (H + L + C)/3.0. If the market sentiment is bullish, the callback computes the stock's resistance level, R = 2P − L. If the sentiment is bearish, the callback determines the support level, R = 2P − H.

After calculating the resistance/support value, the callback stores it in a list named `rs_levels`. This will be accessed later to select the best of the candidate stocks.

14.4.3 Computing Support and Resistance in C++

In the Ch14_SimpleAlgo project, the `main` function calls `computeSupportResistance` to determine support or resistance level for a given stock. Listing 14.6 presents the code.

Listing 14.6: Ch14_SimpleAlgo/Main.cpp (computeSupportResistance function)

```
// Compute a stock's support level or resistance
void computeSupportResistance(SimpleAlgo& client) {

  // Get the time at midnight
  time_t tm = std::time(nullptr);
  std::tm loc_tm = *std::localtime(&tm);
  std::ostringstream ostr;
  ostr << std::put_time(&loc_tm, "%Y%m%d, 00:00:00");

  // Find support or resistance for each stock
  int i = 10;
  for (Contract con: client.scanResults) {
    client.reqHistoricalData(i++, con, ostr.str(), "1 d",
      "1 day", "MIDPOINT", 1, 1, false, TagValueListSPtr());
    std::this_thread::sleep_for(std::chrono::seconds(1));
    client.signal.waitForSignal();
    client.reader->processMsgs();
  }
}
```

The function starts by constructing a string that identifies the date and time at the preceding midnight. Then it calls `reqHistoricalData` to obtain prices for the period up to midnight. For the ith contract, the request ID is set to i + 10 so the callback will know which candidate stock corresponds to the request.

When `historicalData` executes, it checks the request ID to determine how it should process the data. The following code shows how it operates when the ID is between 10 and 100.

```
void SimpleAlgo::historicalData(TickerId reqId, const Bar& bar) {
  ...
  else if (reqId > 10 && reqId < 100) {

    // Set resistance/support levels
    p = (bar.high + bar.low + bar.close)/3.0;
```

```
      if (sentiment == Sentiment::BULLISH)
         rsLevels[reqId - 10] = 2.0 * p - bar.low;

      else if (sentiment == Sentiment::BEARISH)
         rsLevels[reqId - 10] = 2.0 * p - bar.high;
   }
}
```

The callback computes the pivot point by taking the average of the preceding day's high, low, and opening prices. Then, depending on the perceived market sentiment, it computes the resistance or support level.

14.5 Selecting the Target Stock

For SimpleAlgo, the ideal stock has just broken through its resistance level and is rising like a rocket, or has just fallen through its support level and is dropping like a stone. To determine which stock best meets this ideal, SimpleAlgo performs six steps:

1. For each stock, get prices every 30 seconds for the last ten minutes.
2. For each stock, compare the most recent price to its support/resistance level.
3. Discard stocks that haven't broken through support/resistance.
4. For remaining stocks, sort by magnitude of breakout.
5. For ten stocks with the least breakout, use quadratic regression to fit a parabola to the prices.
6. Of the remaining stocks, choose the stock with the most favorable regression results.

Most of these steps should look familiar, but quadratic regression may be new to many readers. For this reason, the section starts by explaining why quadratic regression is useful and how it can be computed. Then I'll show how SimpleAlgo's stock selection can be performed in Python and C++.

14.5.1 Quadratic Regression

If you've worked with data analysis for any length of time, you're probably famliar with linear regression, which fits a straight line to a set of points. Quadratic regression is similar, but fits a parabola instead of a straight line. To see why quadratic regression might be preferable, consider the graphs in Figure 14.2.

```
                  Linear Regression: y = 3.22x + 11.43
```

```
                  Quadratic Regression: y = -0.5x² + 9.76x - 2.73
```

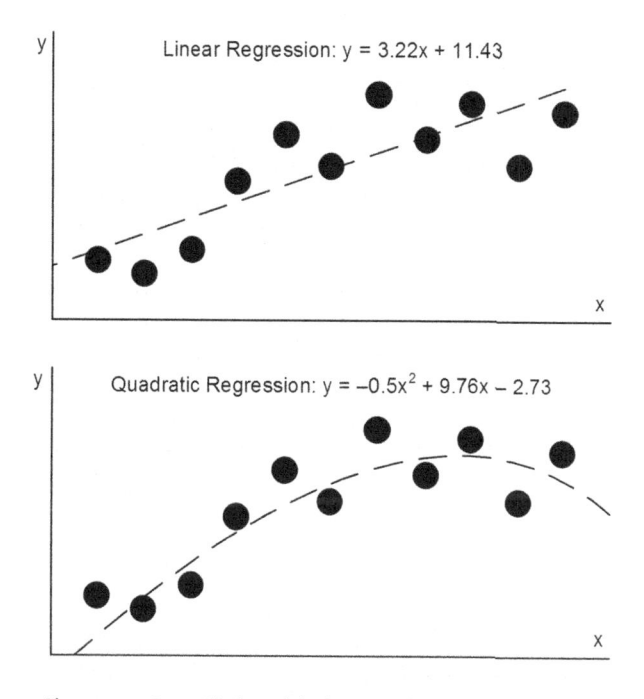

Figure 14.2 Curve Fitting with Linear and Quadratic Regression

Both graphs illustrate the same points that represent stock prices over time. In the upper graph, the straight line obtained through linear regression has a positive slope, which implies that the price is rising. But in the lower graph, the parabola obtained through quadratic regression implies that the price has already reached its peak, and is currently falling.

The equation of a parabola in the x-y plane is $y = ax^2 + bx + c$. Of the three coefficients, the only one SimpleAlgo needs to compute is a. A positive value indicates that the curve is rising over time. A negative value means that the curve is falling over time. In the figure's bottom graph, a equals –0.5, which indicates that the stock's prices indicate a falling trend.

In addition to the sign of a, the magnitude of a identifies whether the parabola is narrow or wide. A large magnitude implies a narrow parabola and a small magnitude implies a wide parabola. This is made clear in the figure, where the small magnitude of a (0.5) corresponds to the wide parabola.

The value of a helps SimpleAlgo estimate the trajectory of the stock price, but it's not easy to compute. Denoting the stock prices as y_i, the corresponding times as x_i, and the number of points as N, the process of finding a requires computing five intermediate values s_0 through s_4. The following equations show how this is accomplished.

$$a = \frac{s_0 s_3 - s_1 s_2}{s_0 s_4 - s_2^2}$$

$$s_0 = \sum x_i^2 - \frac{(\sum x_i)^2}{N}$$

$$s_1 = \sum x_i y_i - \frac{\sum x_i \sum y_i}{N}$$

$$s_2 = \sum x_i^3 - \frac{\sum x_i^2 \sum x_i}{N}$$

$$s_3 = \sum x_i^2 y_i - \frac{\sum x_i^2 \sum y_i}{N}$$

$$s_4 = \sum x_i^4 - \frac{(\sum x_i^2)^2}{N}$$

The time values, x_i, are known in advance, so the computation isn't as complex as it looks. The measurements are taken at equal intervals, so SimpleAlgo sets x_i to i. That is, x_0 equals 0, x_1 equals 1, x_2 equals 2, and so on. This allows us to compute s_0, s_2, and s_4 in advance (s_0 equals 665, s_2 equals 12,635, and s_4 equals 257,621).

After performing quadratic regression, SimpleAlgo can select a target stock. This selection process involves choosing the stock with the highest value of a (bullish market) or the stock with the lowest value of a (bearish market). The following discussion shows how this can be accomplished in Python and C++.

14.5.2 Selecting the Target Stock in Python

In main.py, the `select_target_stock` function requests the price data needed to perform quadratic regression. As in preceding functions, this consists of creating a date string and calling `reqHistoricalData`.

The difference is that the function requests prices every thirty seconds for the preceding ten minutes. In addition, the function calls `reqHistoricalData` for every stock returned by the scanner. Listing 14.7 presents the full code.

Listing 14.7: ch14/simplealgo/main.py (select_target_stock function)

```python
def select_target_stock(client):
    ''' Choose the stock based on recent prices '''

    # Create string for the current date/time
    now = datetime.now().strftime('%Y%m%d, %H:%M:%S')

    # Create string for the current date/time
    for i, contract in enumerate(client.scan_results):
        client.reqHistoricalData(i + 100, contract, now,
            '600 S', '30 secs', 'MIDPOINT', False, 1, False, [])
        time.sleep(1)

    # Sort remaining stocks by diff, remove all but 10
    if client.short_list:
        client.short_list.sort(key=lambda rec: rec[1])
        if len(client.short_list) > 10:
            client.short_list = client.short_list[0:10]

        # Find stock with best quadratic regression coefficient
        con = None
        if client.sentiment == Sentiment.BULLISH:
            index = max(client.short_list,
                key=lambda rec: rec[2])[0]
        elif client.sentiment == Sentiment.BEARISH:
            index = min(client.short_list,
                key=lambda rec: rec[2])[0]

        con = client.scan_results[index]
        print('Selected stock: {}'.format(con.symbol))
        return con
    else:
        print('No stocks fit the criteria')
        return None
```

The function increments the request ID for each stock, starting from 100. Each time `reqHistoricalData` is called, the `historicalData` callback stores price values in a list called `prices`. After all of the prices have been received, the `historicalDataEnd` callback performs three operations:

- Computes each stock's proximity to its resistance/support level
- Uses quadratic regression to compute a in the equation $y = ax^2 + bx + c$.
- Stores results of computation in a list called `short_list`.

Listing 14.8 presents the code in `historicalData` and `historicalDataEnd`.

Listing 14.8: ch14/simplealgo/simplealgo.py (callback functions)

```python
// Called in response to reqHistoricalData
def historicalData(self, req_id, bar):

    ...

    // Check the request ID
    elif req_id > 99:

        # Store recent price for later processing
        self.prices[req_id - 100, self.index] = bar.close
        self.index += 1
        self.index %= 20

// Called after all historical data has been received
def historicalDataEnd(self, req_id, start, end):

    // Check the request ID
    if req_id > 99:
        i = req_id - 100
        if self.prices[i][0] == 0.0 or self.rs_levels[i] == 0.0:
            return

        # Compute diff between price and support/resistance
        level_diff = self.prices[i][-1] - self.rs_levels[i]

        # Perform quadratic regression
        if self.sentiment == Sentiment.BULLISH and
            level_diff > 0:

            // Compute value of a
            yi = np.array(self.prices[i])
            yi_sum = np.sum(yi)
            s1 = np.dot(self.xi, yi) - self.xi_sum * yi_sum/20
            s3 = np.dot(self.xi_sqr, yi) -
                self.xi_sqr_sum * yi_sum/20
            a_val = (665.0 * s3 - 12635.0 * s1)/11674740.0

            // If a is suitable, add index to short list
            if a_val > 0:
                self.short_list.append((i, level_diff, a_val))
```

Listing 14.8: ch14/simplealgo/simplealgo.py (callback functions continued)

```
        elif self.sentiment == Sentiment.BEARISH and
            level_diff < 0:

            yi = np.array(self.prices[i])
            yi_sum = np.sum(yi)
            s1 = np.dot(self.xi, yi) - self.xi_sum * yi_sum/20
            s3 = np.dot(self.xi_sqr, yi) -
                self.xi_sqr_sum * yi_sum/20
            a_val = (665.0 * s3 - 12635.0 * s1)/11674740.0
            print('a: {}'.format(a_val))

            if a_val < 0:
                self.short_list.append((i, level_diff, a_val))
```

The `level_diff` variable is set to the difference between the stock's most recent price and its computed resistance/support level. The callback performs quadratic regression on the stock's prices if the market is bullish and `level_diff` is positive, or the market is bearish and `level_diff` is negative.

The time values (0-19) are known in advance and the constructor has already computed the regression terms that involve time, such as `xi`, `xi_sum`, and `xi_sqr`. Therefore, the only terms needed for regression are those that involve time and the stock's prices. For this reason, the callback computes `s1` and `s3` and then solves an equation for the value of `a_val`.

If `a_val`'s sign implies a favorable trajectory, the stock is added to `short_list`. The `select_target_stock` function sorts this list by distance to support/resistance and keeps at most ten stocks with the lowest difference. Of the remaining stocks, the function selects the contract with the most favorable regression value.

14.5.3 Selecting the Target Stock in C++

In the Ch14_SimpleAlgo project, the `main` function invokes `selectTargetStock` to choose the contract that appears most likely to continue breaking away. `selectTargetStock` starts by requesting prices for each stock. After the callbacks execute, the function selects one of the remaining stocks for trading.

To obtain price data, the function loops through the candidate stocks and calls `reqHistoricalData` for each. This requests stock prices for the last ten minutes at intervals of thirty seconds. Listing 14.9 presents the code.

Listing 14.9: Ch14_SimpleAlgo/main.cpp (selectTargetStock function)

```cpp
// Choose the stock based on recent prices
std::pair<Contract, double> selectTargetStock(SimpleAlgo& client)
{
  int index;
  double price;
  Contract con;

  // Get the current time
  time_t tm = std::time(nullptr);
  std::tm loc_tm = *std::localtime(&tm);
  std::ostringstream ostr;
  ostr << std::put_time(&loc_tm, "%Y%m%d, %H:%M:%S");

  // Read recent prices for all contracts
  int i = 100;
  for (Contract con: client.scanResults) {
    client.reqHistoricalData(i++, con, ostr.str(), "600 S",
      "30 secs", "MIDPOINT", 1, 1, false, TagValueListSPtr());
    std::this_thread::sleep_for(std::chrono::seconds(1));
    client.signal.waitForSignal();
    client.reader->processMsgs();
  }

  // Sort remaining stocks by diff
  if (!client.shortList.empty()) {
    std::sort(client.shortList.begin(), client.shortList.end(),
      []( std::tuple<int, double, double> x,
        std::tuple<int, double, double> y ) {
        return std::get<1>(x) < std::get<1>(y); });

    // Remove all elements but ten
    if (client.shortList.size() > 10)
      client.shortList.erase(client.shortList.begin() + 9,
      client.shortList.end() - 1);

    // Find stock with best quadratic regression coefficient
    std::tuple<int, double, double> result;
    if (client.sentiment == Sentiment::BULLISH) {
        result = *std::max_element(client.shortList.begin(),
        client.shortList.end(),
        []( const std::tuple<int, double, double>& x,
          const std::tuple<int, double, double>& y ) {
          return std::get<2>(x) > std::get<2>(y); });
    }
```

Listing 14.9: Ch14_SimpleAlgo/main.cpp (selectTargetStock function continued)

```cpp
    else if (client.sentiment == Sentiment::BEARISH) {
        result = *std::min_element(client.shortList.begin(),
        client.shortList.end(),
        []( const std::tuple<int, double, double>& x,
           const std::tuple<int, double, double>& y ) {
           return std::get<2>(x) < std::get<2>(y); });
    }
    index = std::get<0>(result);
    con = client.scanResults[index];
    price = client.prices[index][19];
    return std::make_pair(con, price);
  }

  // No stocks could be found
  else {
    std::cout << "No stocks fit the criteria" << std::endl;
    return std::make_pair(con, 0.0);
  }
}
```

As each result is received, the `historicalData` callback stores the closing price in an array named `prices`. After the last price for a stock is received, `historicalDataEnd` uses the `prices` array and the `rsLevels` array to update a vector of final candidate stocks named `shortList`. Listing 14.10 presents code in both callbacks.

Listing 14.10: Ch14_SimpleAlgo/SimpleAlgo.cpp (callback functions)

```cpp
// Access historical data
void SimpleAlgo::historicalData(TickerId reqId, const Bar& bar) {
  ...
  else if (reqId > 99) {

    // Store recent price for later processing
    prices[reqId - 100][index++] = bar.close;
    index %= 20;
  }
}

void SimpleAlgo::historicalDataEnd(int reqId,
  const std::string& startDateStr,
  const std::string& endDateStr) {

  double levelDiff, priceSum, s1, s3, aVal;
```

Listing 14.10: Ch14_SimpleAlgo/SimpleAlgo.cpp (callback functions continued)

```cpp
  if (reqId > 99) {
    int i = reqId - 100;
    if (prices[i][0] == 0.0 || rsLevels[i] == 0.0)
      return;

    // Compute diff between price and support/resistance
    levelDiff = prices[i][19] - rsLevels[i];
    if (sentiment == Sentiment::BULLISH && levelDiff > 0) {
      priceSum = std::accumulate(prices[i],
        prices[i]+20, 0.0);
      s1 = std::inner_product(xi, xi+20, prices[i], 0.0)
        - xiSum * priceSum/20;
      s3 = std::inner_product(xiSqr, xiSqr+20, prices[i], 0.0)
        - xiSqrSum * priceSum/20;
      aVal = (665.0 * s3 - 12635.0 * s1)/11674740.0;
      if (aVal > 0)
        shortList.push_back(std::make_tuple(i, levelDiff, aVal));
    }
    else if (sentiment == Sentiment::BEARISH and levelDiff < 0) {
      priceSum = std::accumulate(prices[i], prices[i]+20, 0.0);
      s1 = std::inner_product(xi, xi+20, prices[i], 0.0)
        - xiSum * priceSum/20;
      s3 = std::inner_product(xiSqr, xiSqr+20, prices[i], 0.0)
        - xiSqrSum * priceSum/20;
      aVal = (665.0 * s3 - 12635.0 * s1)/11674740.0;
      if (aVal < 0)
        shortList.push_back(std::make_tuple(i, levelDiff, aVal));
    }
  }
}
```

To determine if the stock has already broken out, `historicalDataEnd` computes the difference between the resistance/support level and the most recent price. If this is favorable, the callback uses quadratic regression to get an idea of the price's trajectory. The constructor computes many of the required values (`xi`, `xiSqr`, `xiSum`, `xiSqrSum`), so all the callback needs to do to determine the value of a is compute `s1` and `s3`.

If the sign of a is favorable, the callback combines the contract's index, distance to support/resistance, and regression value into a tuple and appends the tuple to a vector named `shortList`. After all the stocks have been processed, `selectTargetStock` sorts `shortList` according to the distance to support/resistance and discards all but the ten most favorable contracts. The final selection is performed by choosing the contract with the most favorable regression value.

14.6 Placing the Order

After the target stock is selected, the next step is to create an order and submit it to IB. To keep potential loss to a minimum, SimpleAlgo creates a bracket order. As discussed in Chapter 10, a bracket order combines a regular order with two opposite-side child orders: one child executes if the stock moves favorably, the other child executes if the stock moves unfavorably.

An example will clarify how bracket orders work. Suppose you want to buy 100 shares of BGCP at 100. If the price rises, you want to lock in profit by selling when the price reaches 150. If the price falls, you want to cut your losses by selling at 80.

The TWS API makes it possible to combine these orders into a single bracket order. The buy limit order at 100 is a parent order with two children. The first child order is a sell limit order at 150 and the second child order is a sell stop order at 80.

The selected stock is (presumably) rising or falling quickly, so SimpleAlgo submits a market order to ensure rapid execution. The first child is a limit order whose price is set to 125% of the current price (bullish) or 75% of the current price (bearish). The second child is a stop order whose price is set to 90% of the current price (bullish) or 110% of the current price (bearish).

14.6.1 Placing the Order in Python

After the stock has been selected, the main function in ch14/main.py places a bracket order by calling the place_order function. place_order creates three Order structures: a parent order and two children. The first child is a limit order to be activated if the price moves favorably. The second child is a stop order to be activated if the price moves unfavorably.

After creating the orders, place_order submits them by calling placeOrder. Then it calls reqPositions to get a list of the current positions. Listing 14.11 presents the code.

Listing 14.11: ch14/main.py (place_order function)

```
# Place an order for the selected stock
def place_order(client, con):

    # Get an order ID
    client.reqIds(1000)
    time.sleep(2)
```

Listing 14.11: ch14/main.py (place_order function continued)

```python
    # Calculate prices
    qty = 100
    if client.sentiment == Sentiment.BULLISH:
        action = 'BUY'
        lmt_price = client.prices[-1] * 1.25
        lmt_action = 'SELL'
        stop_price = client.prices[-1] * 0.90
        stop_action = 'SELL'
    elif client.sentiment == Sentiment.BEARISH:
        action = 'SELL'
        lmt_price = client.prices[-1] * 0.75
        lmt_action = 'BUY'
        stop_price = client.prices[-1] * 1.10
        stop_action = 'BUY'

    # Create the bracket order
    main_order = Order()
    main_order.orderId = client.order_id
    main_order.action = action
    main_order.orderType = 'MKT'
    main_order.totalQuantity = qty
    main_order.transmit = False

    # Limit order child
    lmt_child = Order()
    lmt_child.orderId = client.order_id + 1
    lmt_child.action = lmt_action
    lmt_child.orderType = 'LMT'
    lmt_child.totalQuantity = qty
    lmt_child.lmtPrice = lmt_price
    lmt_child.parentId = client.order_id
    lmt_child.transmit = False

    # Stop order child
    stop_child = Order()
    stop_child.orderId = client.order_id + 2
    stop_child.action = stop_action
    stop_child.orderType = 'STP'
    stop_child.totalQuantity = qty
    stop_child.auxPrice = stop_price
    stop_child.parentId = client.order_id
    stop_child.transmit = False
```

Listing 14.11: ch14/main.py (place_order function continued)

```
# Place the order
client.placeOrder(client.order_id, con, main_order)
time.sleep(2)

# Request positions
client.reqPositions()
time.sleep(2)
```

This code is straightforward to understand but it can be hard to keep track of the fields of the `Order` structure. As a quick review, here are the order configuration fields set in this application:

- **orderId** — Unique ID for the order (obtained with `reqIds`)
- **parentId** — ID of the parent order
- **action** — side (buy or sell)
- **orderType** — nature of the order (MKT, LMT, STP, and so on)
- **totalQty** — number of contracts traded in the order
- **lmtPrice** — the limit price for limit orders and stop limit orders
- **auxPrice** — auxiliary (stop) price
- **transmit** — whether the order should be transmitted by TWS

In a regular bracket order, the `transmit` field of the parent and first child are set to false and the `transmit` field of the second child is set to true. But in this code, all of the `transmit` fields are set to false to ensure that no one submits any real-world orders accidentally.

After configuring the three `Order` structures, the function calls the client's `placeOrder` function to submit the order. After the order has been processed, the `openOrder` callback prints the order's status:

```
def openOrder(order_id, contract, order, state):
    print('Status of {} order: {}'.format(contract.symbol,
        state.status))
```

The `place_order` function also calls the client's `reqPositions` function. The `position` callback prints the open positions, but by default, the client's positions won't change because all of the `transmit` fields are set to false.

14.6.2 Placing the Order in C++

After the most suitable stock has been selected, the `main` function calls `placeOrder` to create an order and submit it to IB. This entails creating three `Order` structures and configuring them as a bracket order. Listing 14.12 presents the code.

Listing 14.12: Ch14_SimpleAlgo/main.cpp (placeOrder function)

```cpp
void placeOrder(SimpleAlgo& client, Contract target,
  double price) {

  Order mainOrder, lmtChild, stopChild;
  std::string action, lmtAction, stopAction;
  double lmtPrice, stopPrice;

  // Get an order ID
  client.reqIds(1000);
  std::this_thread::sleep_for(std::chrono::seconds(1));
  client.signal.waitForSignal();
  client.reader->processMsgs();

  // Calculate prices
  int qty = 100;
  if (client.sentiment == Sentiment::BULLISH) {
    action = "BUY";
    lmtPrice = price * 1.25;
    lmtAction = "SELL";
    stopPrice = price * 0.90;
    stopAction = "SELL";
  }
  else if (client.sentiment == Sentiment::BEARISH) {
    action = "SELL";
    lmtPrice = price * 0.75;
    lmtAction = "BUY";
    stopPrice = price * 1.10;
    stopAction = "BUY";
  }

  // Create the bracket order
  mainOrder.orderId = client.orderId;
  mainOrder.action = action;
  mainOrder.orderType = "MKT";
  mainOrder.totalQuantity = qty;
  mainOrder.transmit = false;
```

Listing 14.12: Ch14_SimpleAlgo/main.cpp (placeOrder function continued)

```cpp
    // Limit order child
    lmtChild.orderId = client.orderId + 1;
    lmtChild.action = lmtAction;
    lmtChild.orderType = "LMT";
    lmtChild.totalQuantity = qty;
    lmtChild.lmtPrice = lmtPrice;
    lmtChild.parentId = client.orderId;
    lmtChild.transmit = false;

    // Stop order child
    stopChild.orderId = client.orderId + 2;
    stopChild.action = stopAction;
    stopChild.orderType = "STP";
    stopChild.totalQuantity = qty;
    stopChild.auxPrice = stopPrice;
    stopChild.parentId = client.orderId;
    stopChild.transmit = false;

    // Place the order
    client.placeOrder(client.orderId, target, mainOrder);
    std::this_thread::sleep_for(std::chrono::seconds(1));
    client.signal.waitForSignal();
    client.reader->processMsgs();

    // Request positions
    client.reqPositions();
    std::this_thread::sleep_for(std::chrono::seconds(1));
    client.signal.waitForSignal();
    client.reader->processMsgs();
}
```

The function starts by calling `reqIds` to obtain a unique ID for the order. This is provided by the `nextValidId` callback and set equal to the `orderId` field of the first `Order` structure. This structure, named `mainOrder`, is a market order to trade 100 shares of the selected stock.

After creating `mainOrder`, the function creates `lmtChild`, a limit order to offset the market order if the price rises to 125% (bullish market) or falls to 75% (bearish market). Finally, the function creates `stopChild`, which represents a stop order to offset the market order if the price falls to 90% (bullish market) or rises to 110% (bearish market). These percentages are completely arbitrary and shouldn't be construed as recommended investment advice.

It's important to see that the `transmit` field of all three `Order` structures is set to false. This prevents the bracket order from being submitted accidentally. If you want to submit a real bracket order, set the `transmit` field of the second child order to true. This ensures that the three orders will be processed together.

After creating the orders, the function submits them to IB by calling the client's `placeOrder` method. After the order is processed, the `openOrder` callback prints the status.

The function completes its operation by calling `reqPositions`, which requests all open positions associated with the current account. As a result, the `position` callback prints output related to each open position.

14.7 Summary

This chapter has presented SimpleAlgo, a basic but non-trivial algorithmic trading application. SimpleAlgo focuses only on stocks, and buys or sells stocks depending on trends related to the S&P 500 and volatility index. If the market is perceived to be bullish, SimpleAlgo searches for stocks near their 13-week high. If the market is perceived to be bearish, SimpleAlgo searches for stocks near their 13-week low.

After using the scanner to find candidate stocks, SimpleAlgo implements a breakout strategy to find stocks of interest. To be specific, it uses pivot points to determine support levels or resistance levels, depending on the market sentiment. The goal is to find stocks that have recently risen through the support level or below the resistance level.

In addition to checking support/resistance levels, SimpleAlgo uses quadratic regression to gauge the trajectory of a stock's price. After computing the regression results and support/resistance levels, SimpleAlgo decides on a final stock and places an order. This is given as a bracket order, which consists of a parent order and two child orders.

Appendix A

The FIX Protocol

IB algotraders are familiar with the TWS API, but IB supports a lesser-known communication mechanism called the FIX CTCI (Financial Information eXchange Computer-To-Computer Interface). A major advantage is that clients don't have to send messages through the Internet. FIX CTCI supports high-speed dedicated lines, extranet connections, and virtual private network (VPN) communication.

The major disadvantage is cost. When you use the TWS API, the minimum commission is $10 per month. When you use the FIX CTCI (Computer-To-Computer Interface), the minimum commission is $1,500 per month. Most individual investors can't afford that, so this book has focused on the TWS API.

IB is far from the only brokerage/exchange to allow access through FIX. The Chicago Mercantile Exchange allows traders to submit orders through its FIX-based iLink platform. The Boston Options Exchange lets clients submit trades through its FIX-based SOLA platform.

FIX is an open-source protocol that enables applications to send requests and read financial data. In essence, FIX enables the same type of communication supported by the TWS API. From an algotrader's point of view, the primary advantage of FIX is that you don't have to place orders through IB. If you want to submit an order on an exchange that supports FIX, your application can send messages directly.

Given the breadth of FIX's usage, I believe that this is an important topic for algorithmic trading. This appendix starts with a high-level overview of FIX and then presents an open-source toolset called QuickFIX, which enables applications to send and receive FIX messages.

A.1 Overview of FIX

The best way to explain FIX is to compare FIX-based applications to TWS API applications. API applications call client functions like `placeOrder` and `reqHistoricalData` to send requests to TWS. These functions send requests using network sockets, and after an application receives a response, it can access response data through wrapper functions like `openOrder` and `historicalData`.

FIX applications work in essentially the same way. They send messages to a server using network sockets and receive messages in response. But instead of defining functions for sending/receiving messages, the FIX standard defines the structure of the messages. To be precise, FIX defines a series of message types and specifies what each byte in a message represents.

FIX message types include order cancellation messages, margin inquiry messages, and quote request messages. FIX defines how these messages are structured, but doesn't define any functions for sending or receiving them.

A.1.1 Specifications

The first FIX specification was written in 1992, and as I write this in 2019, the current version is 5.0. Most applications use version 4.2 or 4.4.

The main site for the FIX specification is https://www.fixtrading.org/standards. If you visit this site, you'll find a number of standards related to the FIX protocol. Table A.1 lists eight of them and provides a description of each.

Table A.1
FIX Protocol Standards (Abridged)

FIX Standard	Description
Version 5.0 SP 2	Primary standard, describes FIX message types and content
FIXML	Defines XML encoding for FIX messages
SBE	Simple Binary Encoding, defines high-performance binary encoding
FAST	FIX Adapted for Streaming, supports high-speed market data transmission
FIXT	FIX transport session protocol
FIXP	FIX high-performance session layer
SOFH	FIX simple open framing header
FIXS	FIX-over-TLS, secures FIX communication

Most of the FIX standards on the main site present different methods of structuring message bytes for improved speed, security, or readability. From what I've seen, most applications use the basic encoding method defined in the main standard.

A.1.2 Messages, Fields, and Tags

In a FIX session, a client and server communicate by sending messages back and forth. Every message is composed of fields and every field assigns a value to a tag. Fields in a FIX message have the same format:

```
tag=value | ...
```

tag is an integer that identifies the field's type, *value* contains the field's data, and | is a delimiter that separates fields. These characters are encoded with 8-bit ASCII.

For example, suppose a field is given by 9=192. This indicates that the tag whose ID is 9 is assigned to the value of 192. FIX supports hundreds and hundreds of tag IDs, and Table A.2 lists the first sixty.

Table A.2
FIX Message Tags (Abridged)

Tag ID	Tag Name	Description
1	Account	Account identifier
2	AdvId	Advertisement identifier
3	AdvRefID	Identifier used with Replace/Cancel transactions
4	AdvSide	Broker's side of advertised trade
5	AdvTransType	Advertisement message transaction type
6	AvgPx	Average price of order's fills
7	BeginSeqNo	Index of first message to be resent
8	BeginString	String that identifies the FIX version
9	BodyLength	Number of bytes in the message's body
10	CheckSum	Checksum used to validate message
11	ClOrdID	Identifier for the client's order
12	Commission	Commission charged in transaction
13	CommType	Commission type identifier
14	CumQty	Total quantity filled by order

Appendix A The FIX Protocol

15	Currency	Identifier of currency used in transaction
16	EndSeqNo	Index of last message to be resent
17	ExecID	Identifier of execution report
18	ExecInst	Instructions for executing the order
19	ExecRefID	Identifier used in Cancel/Correct messages
20	ExecTransType	Transaction type (no longer used)
21	HandlInst	Instructions for handling the order
22	SecurityIDSource	Identifies source of Security ID
23	IOIID	Identifier of the Indication of Interest (IOI) message
24	IOIOthSvc	Identifies if indication was advertised (no longer used)
25	IOIQltyInd	Quality of indication of interest
26	IOIRefID	Reference ID of IOI Replace/Cancel messages
27	IOIQty	Quantity associated with indication of interest
28	IOITransType	Transaction type of indication of interest
29	LastCapacity	Broker capacity in order execution
30	LastMkt	Market where the last fill was executed
31	LastPx	Price of the order's last fill
32	LastQty	Quantity purchased in last fill
33	NoLinesOfText	Number of lines of text body
34	MsgSeqNum	Index of the message in a sequence
35	MsgType	Identifies the purpose of the message
36	NewSeqNo	New sequence number
37	OrderID	ID of order (assigned by sell-side)
38	OrderQty	Quantity ordered
39	OrdStatus	Current status of order
40	OrdType	Type of order
41	OrigClOrdID	Original client order ID
42	OrigTime	Time that message originated
43	PossDupFlag	Required for retransmitted messages
44	Price	Price per quantity (per share)
45	RefSeqNum	Reference message sequence number
46	RelatdSym	Symbol of issue related to story (no longer used)
47	Rule80A	Order capacity (no longer used)
48	SecurityID	Identifier for security

49	SenderCompID	Component ID of sending party
50	SenderSubID	ID assigned to message originator (trader or desk)
51	SendingDate	Date of transmission (no longer used)
52	SendingTime	Time of transmission
53	Quantity	Overall total quantity
54	Side	Order side (buy/sell)
55	Symbol	Ticker symbol
56	TargetCompID	Component ID of receiving party
57	TargetSubID	ID assigned to message recipient (trader or desk)
58	Text	User-configurable text string
59	TimeInForce	How long the order should remain in effect
60	TransactTime	Time of order execution

This appendix won't discuss all of these tags in depth. Instead, I'll focus on the general structure of FIX messages. Later on, I'll explain how these fields are combined into different types of messages.

The fields in a FIX message can be divided into three main sections:

- **header** — provides metadata, such as the message's type and body length
- **body** — the content of the message
- **trailer** — a single field used for error-checking

The header of a FIX message always begins with three tags: BeginString (Tag 8), BodyLength (Tag 9), and MsgType (35). BeginString identifies the version of FIX used by the message. BodyLength identifies the number of bytes in the body, and MsgType identifies the type of the message.

For example, suppose a message is based on FIX 4.4 and its body contains 120 bytes. If the message is a bid request, its header will start with the following fields:

```
8=FIX.4.4 | 9=120 | 35=k | ...
```

In the third field, k is the identifier used for bid request messages. I'll discuss message types later in the appendix. Keep in mind that a message's type applies to the entire message and a tag's type applies only to a field in the message.

Every message ends with a CheckSum (10) field, also known as the trailer. This identifies a value that can be used to check for errors.

A.2 QuickFIX

Rather than present the byte-level details of the FIX protocol, this appendix presents FIX through the open-source QuickFIX toolset. If you can write applications with QuickFIX, you'll have a solid grasp of what FIX is all about. You'll also be able to transfer messages to and from FIX-compatible recipients.

To understand QuickFIX development, you should be familiar with the four operations that all QuickFIX applications need to accomplish:

1. Create a subclass of the `Application` class to manage the application
2. Configure and establish the connection
3. Access the current session
4. Send and receive messages

The following discussion presents these steps. You can find the official documentation for QuickFix at http://www.quickfixengine.org/quickfix/doc/html/?quickfix/doc/html.

A.2.1 Creating the Application

The central class of the QuickFIX API is the `Application` class. This provides seven methods that are called at various times in the application's lifecycle. As developers, our job is to code a subclass of `Application` and customize these methods to perform our operations. Table A.3 lists the signatures of each `Application` method.

Table A.3
Lifecycle Methods of the Application Class

Method	Description
`onCreate(sessionID)`	Called when a new session is created
`onLogon(sessionID)`	Called when the application logs in
`onLogout(sessionID)`	Called when the session is no longer online
`toAdmin(message, sessionID)`	Called when admin messages are sent
`toApp(message, sessionID)`	Called when application messages are sent
`fromAdmin(message, sessionID)`	Called when admin messages are received
`fromApp(message, sessionID)`	Called when application messages are received

When you launch a browser and access a web site, you're creating a session composed of HTTP requests and the server's HTTP responses. FIX sessions are similar, and consist of FIX messages sent back and forth between the application and another party. An application may take part in multiple sessions at once, and each FIX session is identified by a numerical ID that each function accepts as a parameter.

The last four methods are the most important: `toAdmin`, `toApp`, `fromAdmin`, and `fromApp`. To understand their purpose, you need to be familiar with the two main categories of QuickFIX messages:

- **administrative (admin) messages** — messages related to the overall session
- **application messages** — messages containing financial information

When an application receives a message, `toAdmin` or `toApp` will be called, depending on the nature of the message. When the application sends messages, `fromAdmin` or `fromApp` will be called, depending on the message type.

The `Application` constructor doesn't accept any parameters. After creating an instance of your subclass, you'll use it to create a `SocketInitiator`, which I'll discuss next.

A.2.2 Configure and Establish the Connection

As discussed in Chapter 6, TWS API applications establish socket communication by calling methods of an `EClient`. In QuickFIX, socket communication is managed by an instance of the `SocketInitiator` class. The constructor is given as follows:

```
SocketInitiator(application: Application,
    factory: FileStoreFactory, settings: SessionSettings,
    logFactory: FileLogFactory)
```

The `Application` class has already been discussed, but the `FileStoreFactory`, `SessionSettings`, and `FileLogFactory` classes are new. Of these, the `SessionSettings` class is particularly important because it provides information needed to initiate communication.

The `SessionSettings` constructor accepts a parameter that identifies a text file called the *settings file*. There are three points to know about settings files:

- Configuration settings are provided in *key=value* pairs, with one pair per line
- All settings are listed under a heading, which can be [DEFAULT] or [SESSION]
- Comments are preceded with a #, just as in Python

The following text gives an idea of what the content of a settings file looks like:

```
[DEFAULT]
ConnectionType=initiator
ReconnectInterval=60
SenderCompID=APP

[SESSION]
BeginString=FIX.4.2
TargetCompID=TARGET
StartTime=12:30:00
EndTime=20:30:00
```

Applications may need to communicate using different versions of FIX, and for each supported version, the settings file should have a different `[SESSION]` block. Settings in the `[DEFAULT]` block apply to all sessions.

FIX supports a vast number of configuration settings, and you can view the full list at http://www.quickfixengine.org/quickfix/doc/html/configuration.html. Table A.4 lists 15 of the configuration keys and the values they accept.

Table A.4
QuickFix Configuration Settings

Key	Type	Description
`ConnectionType`	string	Whether application will serve as initiator or acceptor
`ReconnectInterval`	integer	The application's ID for the session
`BeginString`	string	FIX version for the current session
`SenderCompID`	string	The application's ID for the session
`TargetCompID`	string	The application's ID for the session
`StartTime`	time	Time that the session becomes active
`EndTime`	time	Time that the session becomes inactive
`HeartBtInt`	integer	Heartbeat interval in seconds
`SocketConnectHost`	IP addr	Target host for the session
`SocketConnectPort`	integer	Socket port for the given session
`DataDictionary`	path	File to validate incoming FIX messages
`AppDataDictionary`	path	File to validate incoming application messages
`FileLogPath`	path	Directory to store log data
`MaxLatency`	integer	The maximum number of seconds allowed for the message to be processed

After you've created a `SessionSettings` object, you can use it to create instances of the `FileStoreFactory` and `FileLogFactory`, and use these instances to create a `SocketInitiator`. The following code shows how this works in Python:

```
# Create an instance of an Application subclass
application = CustomApplication()

# Create a SessionSettings object with the configuration file
settings = fix.SessionSettings('config.txt')

# Create a FileStoreFactory to store messages
factory = fix.FileStoreFactory(settings)

# Create a FileLogFactory to store log messages
logFactory = fix.ScreenLogFactory(settings)

# Create a SocketInitiator
socketInit = fix.SocketInitiator(application, factory, settings, logFactory)
```

After creating the `SocketInitiator`, an application can call its methods to manage communication. Table A.5 lists seven important methods of the `SocketInitiator` class.

Table A.5
SocketInitiator Methods (Abridged)

Method	Description
start()	Initiates communication over a network socket
stop()	Halts communication
isLoggedOn()	Identifies if any sessions are active
isStopped()	Identifies if communication has been halted
getSession(sessionId)	Access the Session with the given ID
getApplication()	Access the current Application instance
getLog()	Access the log associated with the application

Of these, `start` is the most important. This reads the configuration settings and connects to a server using a network socket. After the socket is created, the application will be able to manage ommunication through its `toAdmin/toApp/fromAdmin/fromApp` methods. The communication channel remains available until the application terminates or the application calls the `SocketInitiator`'s `stop` method.

A.2.3 Understanding Sessions

If the `SocketInitiator`'s `start` method executes without error, the application has established a session to the FIX server. In code, this connection is represented by an instance of the `Session` class. The methods of this class make it possible to access properties of the communication and configure aspects of the channel.

To be specific, the `Session` instance provides methods like `getMaxLatency`, `getLogonTimeOut`, and `getLogoutTimeout`. Applications can also call `getLog` to access the log, `getStore` to access the `MessageStore`, and disconnect to terminate the session.

The most important method of the `Session` class is a static method named `sendToTarget`, which has the following signature:

```
Session.sendToTarget(message, sessionID)
```

This method delivers a `Message` to the session identified by `sessionId`. The session ID can be obtained from any of the `Application` lifecycle methods discussed earlier (`onCreate`, `onLogon`, `onLogout`, `toAdmin`, `fromAdmin`, `toApp`, and `fromApp`).

A.2.4 Messages and Fields

The hardest part of developing FIX-based applications is dealing with the many different types of messages and their many fields. Messages in QuickFIX are represented by the `Message` class and Table A.6 lists six of its methods.

Table A.6

Message Methods (Abridged)

Method	Description
`getField(fieldID)`	Convert message field to string
`setField(fieldID, string)`	Assign string (ASCII) to given field
`setField(FieldBase)`	Assign field with FieldBase
`getHeader()`	Returns the Header instance associated with the message
`getTrailer()`	Returns the message's trailer field
`toXML()`	Returns an XML representation of the message

For most applications, the primary `Message` functions to know are `setField`, `getField`, and `getHeader`. The following code gives an idea of how `getHeader` and `setField` work together.

```
msg = quickfix.Message()
...
msg.getHeader().setField(quickfix.StringField(56, "TARGET"))
msg.getHeader().setField(quickfix.CharField(35, 'F'))
...
msg.setField(quickfix.StringField(11, "221"))
msg.setField(quickfix.StringField(55, "XYZ"))
```

The `StringField`, `CharField`, and `IntField` classes are subclasses of `FieldBase`. Other subclasses include `BoolField`, `DoubleField`, and `UtcDateField`. The constructors of these classes accept a field ID (integer) and a value to be assigned to the field. In the preceding code, the second line creates a `StringField` that assigns Tag 56 to the string `XYZ` and sets this as a field in the message's header.

To simplify development further, QuickFIX provides tag-specific subclasses of `StringField`, `IntField`, and so on. These classes have the same names as the corresponding tags and their constructors only accept the value to be assigned to the tag.

For example, suppose you want to set a message's client order ID, whose tag name is ClOrdID. Instead of creating a `StringField` as in the preceding code, you can call the `clOrdID` function, as shown:

```
msg.setField(fix.clOrdID('987'))
```

The next discussion explains how to use similar tag-specific subclasses to set fields in a message's header.

A.2.5 Setting a Message's Header

Every FIX message has a header, a body, and a trailer. QuickFIX sets the trailer automatically, but applications must define the content of the header and body.

A message's header is represented by a `Header`, which can be accessed through the `getHeader` method of a `Message` instance. Like the `Message` class, the `Header` class has a `setField` method that accepts a `FieldBase`.

A header's purpose is to provide metadata about the message, such as its type, body size, and destination. A header is like a mailing label on a package and the body is the package itself.

FIX fields can be divided into two classes: those used in the header and those used in the message's body. Table A.7 lists 13 of the fields that can be included in a QuickFIX message's header.

Table A.7

Header Fields

Tag ID	Tag Name	Description
8	**BeginString**	String that identifies the FIX version
9	**BodyLength**	Number of bytes in the message's body
35	**MsgType**	Identifies the purpose of the message
49	SenderCompId	Component ID of sending party
56	TargetCompID	Component ID of receiving party
34	MsgSeqNum	Position of the message in a sequence
50	SenderSubID	ID assigned to message originator (trader or desk)
57	TargetSubId	ID assigned to message target (trader or desk)
52	SendingTime	Time of transmission
142	SendingLocationID	ID of the sender's location
143	TargetLocationID	ID of the target's location
43	PossDupFlag	Required for retransmitted messages
97	PossResend	Required when message may be duplicate of another message

The first three fields are printed in bold because these must be the first three fields of every message header. That is, every FIX message must start with a begin string, body length, and message type.

The BeginString field identifies which FIX version the message uses. An application can set this field by calling the BeginString function. The following code shows how this works.

```
msg = quickfix.Message()
msg.getHeader().setField(quickfix.BeginString())
```

To set a message's type, you need to be aware of the many different message types supported by the FIX standard. I'll discuss this next.

A.2.6 Message Types

The third field of every message is the MsgType field, which identifies the message's purpose. When an application receives a message through `toApp`, it can call `MsgType` to determine the type of the received message. When an application creates a new message, it sets the MsgType field by calling `MsgType` with an identifier for the type.

The FIX specification defines a wide range of message types. Like TWS API functions, some messages request information, others provide responses, and some cancel requests. The left column of Table A.8 lists QuickFIX IDs of message types that request information and the right column lists IDs of messages that respond with information (like callbacks in the `EWrapper` class).

Table A.8
Message Type Identifiers (Abridged)

Request Message Type ID	Response Message Type ID
`ApplicationMessageRequest`	`ApplicationMessageReport`
`BidRequest`	`BidResponse`
`CollateralRequest`	`CollateralResponse`
`ConfirmationRequest`	`Confirmation`
`DerivativeSecurityListRequest`	`DerivativeSecurityList` `DerivativeSecurityListUpdateReport`
`ListStatusRequest`	`ListStatus`
`MarketDataRequest`	`MarketDataIncrementalRefresh` `MarketDataSnapshotFullRefresh`
`MarketDefinitionRequest`	`MarketDefinition` `MarketDefinitionUpdateReport`
`OrderCancelRequest`	`OrderCancelReject`
`OrderMassActionRequest`	`OrderMassActionReport`
`OrderMassCancelRequest`	`OrderMassCancelReport`
`PositionMaintenanceRequest`	`PositionMaintenanceReport`
`QuoteRequest`	`Quote, QuoteResponse` `QuoteRequestReject`
`QuoteStatusRequest`	`QuoteStatusReport`
`RequestForPositions`	`PositionReport`
`SecurityDefinitionRequest`	`SecurityDefinition`

`SecurityListRequest`	`SecurityList` `SecurityListUpdateReport`
`SecurityStatusRequest`	`SecurityStatus`
`SecurityTypeRequest`	`SecurityTypes`
`TradeCaptureReportRequest`	`TradeCaptureReport`
`TradingSessionStatusRequest`	`TradingSessionStatus`
`UserRequest`	`UserResponse`

In code, each of the identifiers in Table A.8 must be preceded with the `MsgType_` prefix. For example, the following code creates a message named `msg` and configures it as a bid request message.

```
msg = quickfix.Message()
msg.getHeader().setField(quickfix.MsgType(
    quickfix.MsgType_BidRequest))
```

Setting fields of a message's header is simple. The difficult part of FIX development involves setting fields in the body. The next section will make this clear.

A.3 Common Messages

At this point, you should have a solid understanding of message fields and the contents of a message's header. But how does an application set the fields of the message's body? This is a difficult question because the body's content depends on the message's type. For example, a `BidRequest` message will contain a different set of fields than a `QuoteResponse` message.

It would take an entire book to present the fields required for every message type. Therefore, this section explores four message types that are commonly used:

- **MarketDataRequest** — Requests market data (similar to `reqMktData`)
- **NewOrderSingle** — Submits a single order (similar to `placeOrder`)
- **ExecutionReport** — Provides a report after an order has been executed, rejected or cancelled (similar to `executionReport`)
- **QuoteResponse** — Responds to a request for a quote for a given security

This section presents the fields that may be included in the body of these message types. The vast number of fields may seem daunting, but in general, only a small number of fields are required for each type.

A.3.1 Market Data Request Messages

Like the `reqMktData` function in the TWS API, a MarketDataRequest message requests financial information. Each requested item is called a market data entry, and a message can request several market data entries. Every market data entry must identify the symbols of the requested instruments and the number of trading sessions.

The body of a MarketDataRequest message starts by defining characteristics of the overall request, such as whether the request is looking for a subscription or a snapshot. Then the body presents the fields of each market data entry in sequence. Table A.9 lists the different fields that make up the body.

Table A.9
Fields in the MarketDataRequest Message Body

Tag ID	Tag Name	Description
262	MDReqID	Identifier for the market data request
263	**SubscriptionRequestType**	Indicates whether the response should be a snapshot or subscription
264	MarketDepth	Indicates the market depth level
265	MDUpdateType	Identifies whether snapshots should be full refresh or incremental refresh
266	AggregatedBook	Identifies whether data entries should be aggregated
286	OpenCloseSettlFlag	Clarifies price in market data entry
546	Scope	Identifies whether the data's scope is local, national, or global
547	MDImplicitDelete	Identifies how bids/offers outside the market depth should be handled
267	NoMDEntryTypes	Number of market data entries requested
269	**MDEntryType**	Sets the type of a market data entry
146	NoRelatedSym	Number of symbols (instruments) requested
--	<Component Block>	The primary financial instrument

711	`NoUnderlyings`	Number of underlyings
555	`NoLegs`	Number of legs in a multi-leg quote
--	`<Component Block>`	The financial instrument for each leg
386	`NoTradingSessions`	Number of trading sessions for which the request is valid
336	`TradingSessionID`	Identifier for the trading session
625	`TradingSessionSubID`	Market-assigned subidentifier for the trading session
815	`ApplQueueAction`	Action to take in response to level queuing
812	`ApplQueueMax`	Maximum queue depth before queuing action starts

Most of these fields are optional but the entries in bold are required. The SubscriptionRequestType field must be set to one of three values: snapshot (0), snapshot and updates (1), and disable snapshot/updates (2).

Every MarketDataRequest message must provide at least one market data entry and each entry has a type that specifies the nature of its data. This is set by the MDEntryType field, which can be set to bid (0), offer (1), trade (2), index value (3), opening price (4), closing price (5), settlement price (6), session high (7), session low (8), volume-weighted average price (9), imbalance (A), trade volume (B), or open interest (C).

Each financial instrument is identified with a component block, and as shown in the table, a complex MarketDataRequest message may have several component blocks. Each block defines a set of fields that identify financial instruments, such as a Symbol field, SecurityID field, and SecurityType field. In essence, these component blocks are similar to `Contract` structures in the TWS API.

A.3.2 Single Order Messages

FIX supports a handful of message types for placing orders and the simplest is the NewOrderSingle type. This message makes it possible to transmit many different types of orders, and they can be submitted with special instructions for handling or execution.

As in TWS API applications, order IDs are very important. A NewOrderSingle message may have many different IDs associated with it, each with a different purpose.

Table A.10 lists all the possible fields that may be found in a NewOrderSingle message. Required fields are in bold.

Table A.10
Fields in the NewOrderSingle Message Body

Tag ID	Tag Name	Description
11	**ClOrdID**	Client order identifier
526	SecondaryClOrdID	Secondary client order ID
583	ClOrdLinkID	Identifies groups of orders
--	<Component Block>	Entities involved in the financial transaction
229	TradeOriginationDate	Date trade was initiated
75	TradeDate	Date of trade
1	Account	Account ID
660	AcctIDSource	Identifies the source of the account ID
581	AccountType	Type of account associated with the order
589	DayBookingInst	Identifies whether automatic booking is allowed
590	BookingUnit	Identifies how executions form a bookable unit
591	PreallocMethod	Preallocation method (pro-rata or not)
70	AllocID	Unique identifier for allocation message
78	NoAllocs	Number of allocation accounts/prices
79	AllocAccount	Sub-account identifier
661	AllocAcctIDSource	Identifies the source of the allocation account ID
736	AllocSettlCurrency	Currency of the allocation account
467	IndividualAllocID	Identifier for allocation group
--	<Component Block>	Identifies nested parties
80	AllocQty	Quantity allocated for sub-account
63	SettlType	Order settlement period
64	SettlDate	Date of trade settlement
544	CashMargin	Identifies whether an order is a margin order
635	ClearingFeeIndicator	Type of fee needed at the exchange
21	HandlInst	Order handling instructions
18	ExecInst	Trading floor handling instructions
110	MinQty	Minimum quantity of an order to be executed
111	MaxFloor	Maximum quantity to be displayed

100	ExDestination	Order's execution destination
386	NoTradingSessions	Number of trading session IDs
336	TradingSessionID	Trading session identifier
625	TradingSessionSubID	Market-assigned trading session sub-identifier
81	ProcessCode	Processing code for sub-account
--	\<Component Block\>	Financial instruments
--	\<Component Block\>	Financing details
711	NoUnderlyings	Number of underlyings
--	\<Component Block\>	Underlying financial instruments
140	PrevClosePx	Previous closing price
54	**Side**	Order side (buy/sell)
114	LocateReqd	Indicates whether broker is required to locate stock for a short order
60	**TransactTime**	Time order request was initiated/released
--	\<Component Block\>	Fixed income stipulations
854	QtyType	Quantity type (units or contracts)
--	\<Component Block\>	Order quantity data
40	**OrdType**	Type of order (market, limit, stop, and so on)
423	PriceType	Value represented by price (per unit, discount, ...)
44	Price	Order price
99	StopPx	Stop price for stop/stop limit orders
--	\<Component Block\>	Spread or benchmark curve data
--	\<Component Block\>	Yield data
15	Currency	Currency used for price
376	ComplianceID	Transaction ID for compliance purposes
377	SolicitedFlag	Identifies if the order was solicited
23	IOIID	ID of the Indication of Interest message
117	QuoteID	Unique identifier of quote
59	TimeInForce	How long the order remains in effect
168	EffectiveTime	Time the order should take effect

432	ExpireDate	Order expiration date
126	ExpireTime	Order expiration time
427	GTBookingInst	Identifies whether to book executions of a partly filled GT order on the day of execution
--	<Component Block>	Commission data
528	OrderCapacity	Capacity of the firm placing the order
529	OrderRestrictions	Restrictions associated with an order
582	CustOrderCapacity	Capacity of the customer placing the order
121	ForexReq	Whether to execute a forex trade after the security trade
120	SettlCurrency	Currency of the settlement denomination
775	BookingType	Method for booking this order
58	Text	Free format text string
354	EncodedTextLen	Byte length of encoded text field
355	EncodedText	Encoded representation of text field
193	SettlDate2	Settlement date of the future part of an F/X swap order
192	OrderQty2	Order quantity of the future part of an F/X swap order
640	Price2	Price of the future part of an F/X swap order
77	PositionEffect	Whether the resulting position should be an opening position or closing position
203	CoveredOrUncovered	Identifies whether the derivative trade is covered or uncovered
210	MaxShow	Maximum displayed quantity for an order
--	<Component Block>	Peg instructions
--	<Component Block>	Discretion instructions
847	TargetStrategy	Order's target strategy (submission algorithm)
848	TargetStrategyParameters	Parameters to constrain target strategy
849	ParticipationRate	Identifies participation rate used for strategy
480	CancellationRights	Identifies whether cancellation rights or cooling off period applies

481	MoneyLaunderingStatus	Identifies status of money laundering check
513	RegistID	Identifier for registration details
494	Designation	Identifies assets of an underlying investor using a common registration

The first required component block identifies the financial instruments to be traded. These blocks accept the same fields as the similar component blocks from the MarketDataRequest message.

The ordType field plays a central role because it identifies the type of order to be executed. For example, market orders set ordType to 1 while limit orders set ordType to 2 and stop orders set ordType to 3. For the full list, open a web browser and visit the web site http://fixwiki.org/fixwiki/OrdType.

FIX orders can be configured with pre-trade allocation, which allocates block trades to multiple client accounts. The characteristics of this allocation are set with the AllocID, AllocAccount, AllocAcctIDSource, and AllocSettlCurrency fields.

A.3.3 Execution Reports

After a broker receives and processes a NewOrderSingle message, it will respond with an ExecutionReport message. This is one of the most important message types defined in the FIX standard, and every client application should be able to read them.

An ExecutionReport message may serve one of six roles:

- Confirm the receipt of an order
- Confirm changes to an existing order
- Provide order status
- Specify how orders were filled
- Reject orders
- Report trading fees

Because an execution report can serve so many purposes, its body may contain a wide range of fields. Table A.11 lists these fields and provides a description of each. Required fields are in bold.

Table A.11
Fields in the ExecutionReport Message Body

Tag ID	Tag Name	Description
37	**OrderID**	Unique identifier for the order
198	SecondaryOrderID	Exchange-provided order ID
526	SecondaryClOrderID	Client order ID assigned by originating party
527	SecondaryExecID	Execution ID assigned by the accepting party
11	ClOrdID	Client order ID
41	OrigClOrdID	Client order ID of the previous order
583	ClOrdLinkID	ID for a group of client orders
693	QuoteRespID	Reference for the quote response
790	OrdStatusReqID	Identifies an order status request message
584	MassStatusReqID	ID assigned by the mass status request issuer
911	TotNumReports	Total number of reports returned
912	LastRptRequested	Identifies if this is the last report message
--	<Component Block>	Firm identication fields
229	TradeOriginationDate	Date that counter-parties agreed to trade
382	NoContraBrokers	Number of contra brokers
375	ContraBroker	Identifies a contra broker
337	ContraTrader	Identifies the contra broker's trader
437	ContraTradeQty	Quantity traded with the contra broker
438	ContraTradeTime	Time of the trade with the contra broker
655	ContraLegRefID	Identifies a leg of a contract broker
66	ListID	Identifies a list containing orders
548	CrossID	Identifies a cross order
551	OrigCrossID	Original ID of the cross order
549	CrossType	Type of cross trade
17	**ExecID**	Unique ID for execution report
19	ExecRefID	Reference ID in Trade Cancel/Trade Correct messages
150	**ExecType**	Identifies the report's purpose

39	**OrdStatus**	Describes the state of an order chain
636	WorkingIndicator	Identifies if a new order is being worked
103	OrdRejReason	Reason for order rejection
378	ExecRestatementReason	Reason for report restatement
1	Account	Account identifier
660	AcctIDSource	Identifies the source of the account ID
581	AccountType	Specifies type of account
589	DayBookingInst	Identifies whether automatic booking is allowed
590	BookingUnit	Identifies how executions form a bookable unit
591	PreallocMethod	Preallocation method (pro-rata or not)
63	SettlType	Order settlement period
64	SettlDate	Date of trade settlement
544	CashMargin	Identifies whether an order is a margin order
635	ClearingFeeIndicator	Type of fee needed at the exchange
--	**<Component Block>**	Identifies one or more financial instruments
--	<Component Block>	Financing details
711	NoUnderlyings	Number of underlyings
--	<Component Block>	Underlying financial instruments
54	**Side**	Order side (buy or sell)
--	<Component Block>	Fixed income stipulations
854	QtyType	Type of quantity (units or contracts)
--	<Component Block>	Order quantity data
40	OrdType	Type of order (market, limit, stop, and so on)
423	PriceType	Value represented by price (unit, discount, …)
44	Price	Order price
99	StopPx	Stop price for stop/stop limit orders
--	<Component Block>	Peg instructions
--	<Component Block>	Discretion instructions
839	PeggedPrice	Current price the order is pegged at

Appendix A The FIX Protocol

845	DiscretionPrice	Current discretionary price of the order
847	TargetStrategy	Target strategy of the order
848	TargetStrategyParameters	Further specification of the target strategy
849	ParticipationRate	The target participation rate
850	TargetStrategyPerformance	Order performance versus the target strategy
15	Currency	Currency used for price
376	ComplianceID	Transaction ID for compliance purposes
377	SolicitedFlag	Identifies if the order was solicited
59	TimeInForce	Indicates how long the order is active
168	EffectiveTime	Time at which the order is considered valid
432	ExpireDate	Order expiration date
126	ExpireTime	Order expiration time
18	ExecInst	Trading floor handling instructions
528	OrderCapacity	Capacity of the firm placing the order
529	OrderRestrictions	Restrictions associated with an order
582	CustOrderCapacity	Capacity of the customer placing the order
32	LastQty	Quantity bought/sold in the last fill
652	UnderlyingLastQty	Traded quantity of the underlying instrument
31	LastPx	Price of the last fill
651	UnderlyingLastPx	Traded price of the underlying instrument
669	LastParPx	Last price expressed in percent-of-par
194	LastSpotRate	F/X spot rate
195	LastForwardPoints	F/X forward points added to last spot rate
30	LastMkt	The market where the trade was executed
336	TradingSessionID	Trading session identifier
625	TradingSessionSubID	Market-assigned trading session sub-identifier
943	TimeBracket	Time interval in which a fill/trade occurred
29	LastCapacity	Broker capacity in order execution
151	**LeavesQty**	Quantity open for further execution

Tag	Field	Description
14	`CumQty`	Executed quantity for chain of orders
6	`AvgPx`	Average price of all fills in order
424	`DayOrderQty`	Order quantity of GT orders minus quantity traded on previous days
425	`DayCumQty`	Quantity on a GT order that has traded today
426	`DayAvgPx`	Average price for quantity on a GT order that has traded today
427	`GTBookingInst`	Identifies whether to book executions of a partly filled GT order on the day of execution
75	`TradeDate`	Date of trade
60	`TransactTime`	Time of execution/order creation
113	`ReportToExch`	Identifies party for exchange reporting
--	`<Component Block>`	Commission data
--	`<Component Block>`	Spread or benchmark curve data
--	`<Component Block>`	Yield data
381	`GrossTradeAmt`	Total amount traded
157	`NumDaysInterest`	Number of days of interest for convertible bonds and fixed income
230	`ExDate`	Date when a distribution of interest is deducted
158	`AccruedInterestRate`	Amount the buyer compensates the seller for the portion of the next coupon payment
159	`AccruedInterestAmt`	Amount of accrued interest for convertible bonds and fixed income
738	`InterestAtMaturity`	Amount of interest at maturity
920	`EndAccruedInterestAmt`	Accrued interest applicable to transaction
921	`StartCash`	Initial dirty cash consideration
922	`EndCash`	Final dirty cash consideration
258	`TradedFlatSwitch`	Identifies driver and part of trade
259	`BasisFeatureDate`	Request date for alternative fixed income calls
260	`BasisFeaturePrice`	Price for basis feature date
238	`Concession`	Reduction in price for secondary municipal market

237	TotalTakedown	Price at which securities are distributed to the underwriting group
118	NetMoney	Amount due as a result of the transaction
119	SettlCurrAmt	Total amount due expressed in settlement currency
120	SettlCurrency	Currency of settlement denomination
155	SettlCurrFxRate	Foreign exchange rate used to compute settlement current amount
156	SettlCurrFxRateCalc	Identifies if settlement foreign exchange rate should be multiplied or divided
21	HandlInst	Instructions for order handling on the trading floor
110	MinQty	Minimum quantity of an order to be executed
111	MaxFloor	Maximum quantity of an order to be shown on the exchange floor
77	PositionEffect	Identifies whether the position after a trade should be opening or closing
210	MaxShow	Maximum quantity of an order to be displayed to other customers
775	BookingType	Method for booking the order
58	Text	Free format text string
354	EncodedTextLen	Byte length of encoded text field
355	EncodedText	Encoded representation of text field
193	SettlDate2	Settlement date of the future part of an F/X swap order
192	OrderQty2	Order quantity of the future part of an F/X swap order
641	LastForwardPoints2	F/X forward points of the future part of an F/X swap order
442	MultilegReportingType	Identifies whether the report represents a single security, a leg, or a multi-leg security
480	CancellationRights	Identifies whether cancellation rights or cooling off period applies
481	MoneyLaunderingStatus	Identifies status of money laundering check
513	RegistID	Identifier for registration details

Appendix A The FIX Protocol

494	Designation	Identifies assets of an underlying investor using a common registration
483	TransBkdTime	Date/time stamp to indicate the time a CIV order was booked
515	ExecValuationPoint	Date/time stamp to indicate the fund valuation point with respect to an order
484	ExecPriceType	Identifies how the execution price was calculated from the fund unit/share price
485	ExecPriceAdjustment	Amount or percentage by which the fund unit or share price was adjusted
638	PriorityIndicator	Indicates if a cancel/replace has caused an order to lose book priority
639	PriceImprovement	Amount of price improvement
851	LastLiquidityInd	Indicator to identify whether this fill was a result of a liquidity provider or taker
518	NoContAmts	Number of contract details in this message
519	ContAmtType	Type of the contract amount value
520	ContAmtValue	Value of the contract amount
521	ContAmtCurr	Currency for the contract amount
555	NoLegs	Number of legs
---	<Component Block>	Financial instrument legs
687	LegQty	Quantity of the given leg
690	LegSwapType	Identifies how fixed income swap is determined
---	<Component Block>	Financial leg stipulations
564	LegPositionEffect	Indicates whether the resulting position after a leg should be opening or closing
565	LegCoveredOrUncovered	Indicates whether the leg trade is covered or uncovered
566	LegPrice	Price associated with a leg
587	LegSettlType	Leg settlement period
588	LegSettlDate	Date of leg settlement
637	LegLastPx	Execution price assigned to a leg of a multi-leg instrument

797	`CopyMsgIndicator`	Indicates whether this message is a drop copy of another message
136	`NoMiscFees`	Number of groups representing miscellaneous fees
137	`MiscFeeAmt`	Miscellaneous fee value
138	`MiscFeeCurr`	Currency used in miscellaneous fee value
139	`MiscFeeType`	Type of miscellaneous fee
891	`MiscFeeBasis`	Units for miscellaneous fee

Of the required fields in an ExecReport message, the most important to know are ExecType and OrdStatus. Both provide similar information, but ExecType describes the specific report and OrdStatus identifies the status of the current order.

Both fields take the same values. For example, a value of 0 implies that the report is in response to a new order. A value of 1 implies a partial fill, 2 implies a complete fill, 3 indicates that the trade is done for the day, 4 implies cancellation, and 5 implies replacement.

The ExecTransType field identifies the type of transaction described by the report. This can take one of four values: New (0), Cancel (1), Correct (2), and Status (3).

A.3.4 Quote Responses

The FIX standard provides two different ways of requesting information about a security: quote requests and indication of interest (IOI) messages. In both cases, the broker provides a response using the QuoteResponse type. Table A.12 lists the possible fields that can make up this message. Required fields are printed in bold.

Table A.12
Fields in the QuoteResponse Message Body

Tag ID	Tag Name	Description
693	**`QuoteRespID`**	**Unique ID of the response**
117	`QuoteID`	ID of the quote request
694	**`QuoteRespType`**	**Type of the quote response**
11	`ClOrdID`	ID of the order assigned by the buyer
528	`OrderCapacity`	Capacity of the firm placing the order
23	`IOIID`	ID of the indication of interest (IOI)

Appendix A The FIX Protocol

537	QuoteType	Type of the quote
735	NoQuoteQualifiers	Number of quote qualifiers
695	QuoteQualifier	Code to qualify quote use
---	<Component Block>	Parties involved in communication
336	TradingSessionID	ID of the trading session
625	TradingSessionSubID	Market-assigned identifier for a trading session
---	**<Component Block>**	**Instruments for which the quote was requested**
---	<Component Block>	Financing details involved in the quote
711	NoUnderlyings	Number of underlying contracts
---	<Component Block>	Describes underlying instruments
54	Side	Side of the trade (buy, sell, and so on)
---	<Component Block>	Information related to order quantity
63	SettlType	Order settlement period
64	SettlDate	Date of trade settlement
193	SettlDate2	Settlement date of the future part of an FX swap order
192	OrderQty2	Order quantity of the future part of an FX swap order
15	Currency	Currency of the quoted prices
---	<Component Block>	Stipulations associated with the quote response
1	Account	Account ID
660	AcctIDSource	Identifies the source of the account ID
581	AccountType	Type of account associated with the order
555	NoLegs	Number of legs for the quote
---	<Component Block>	Describes each leg involved in the quote
687	LegQty	Quantity of the given leg
690	LegSwapType	Identifies how fixed income swap is determined
587	LegSettlType	Leg settlement period
588	LegSettlDate	Date of leg settlement
---	<Component Block>	Leg stipulations
---	<Component Block>	Nested parties
686	LegPriceType	Type of price used in the leg

681	LegBidPx	Bid price of the leg
684	LegOfferPx	Offer price of the leg
---	<Component Block>	Benchmark curve data
132	BidPx	Quote's bid price
133	OfferPx	Quote's offer price
645	MktBidPx	Market's bid price
646	MktOfferPx	Market's offer price
647	MinBidSize	Minimum bid size
134	BidSize	Quote's bid size
648	MinOfferSize	Minimum offer size
135	OfferSize	Quote's offer size
62	ValidUntilTime	TIme when the quote will expire
188	BidSpotRate	Bid FX spot rate
190	OfferSpotRate	Offer FX spot rate
189	BidForwardPoints	Bid FX forward points added to spot rate
191	OfferForwardPoints	Offer FX forward points added to spot rate
631	MidPx	Mid price/rate
632	BidYield	Bid yield
633	MidYield	Mid yield
634	OfferYield	Offer yield
60	TransactTime	Time of order execution
40	OrdType	Specify the quote's order type
642	BidForwardPoints2	Bid FX forward points of the future portion of an FX quote added to the spot rate
643	OfferForwardPoints2	Offer FX forward points of the future portion of an FX quote added to the spot rate
656	SettlCurrBidFxRate	Foreign exchange rate used to compute the bid price
657	SettlCurrOfferFxRate	Foreign exchange rate used to compute the offer price
156	SettlCurrFxRateCalc	Specifies whether SettlCurrFxRate should be multiplied or divided

12	`Commission`	Commission charged in transaction
13	`CommType`	Commission type identifier
582	`CustOrderCapacity`	Capacity of the customer placing the order
100	`ExDestination`	Execution destination as defined by institution when order is entered
58	`Text`	Free format text string
354	`EncodedTextLen`	Length of encoded text
355	`EncodedText`	Encoded representation of the Text field
44	`PriceType`	Value represented by price (per unit, discount, ...)
423	`Price`	Order price
---	`<Component Block>`	Spread or benchmark curve data
---	`<Component Block>`	Yield data

As shown, a QuoteResponse message has three required tags: QuoteRespID, QuoteRespType, and a component block listing the instruments for which the quote was requested. The QuoteRespType tag can be set to one of six values: Hit/Lift, Counter, Expired, Cover, Done Away, and Pass.

A.4 Summary

While the TWS API is specific to Interactive Brokers, the FIX protocol makes it possible to communicate with many different brokerages and exchanges. The protocol defines a series of messages sent back and forth between a client and a broker. Each message is made up of a header, body, and trailer, and each of these three parts is a sequence of fields. Each field assigns a value to a tag.

In my opinion, the chief drawback of the FIX protocol is the vastness of the different configuration options. The protocol supports hundreds of different tags and hundreds of different message types. A message type may require hundreds of fields to convey its information.

Thankfully, projects like QuickFIX provide a way to write programs that communicate using FIX. The chief class of QuickFIX is the `Application` class, whose methods are called when the application sends or receives messages. Other important classes include `SocketInitiator`, `Session`, and `Message`.

Every FIX message type contains a different set of fields, and the last section of this chapter presented the fields in four message types: MarketDataRequest, NewOrderSingle, ExecutionReport, and QuoteResponse. As shown, these types of messages contain a bewildering number of fields. Thankfully, brokerages and exchanges provide their own FIX-based protocols, which only require a subset of these fields.

Appendix B

The Kelly Criterion

In 2016, researchers Victor Haghani and Richard Dewey conducted an experiment to see how people make decisions in the face of uncertainty. They invited test subjects to bet on an imaginary coin that was guaranteed to come up heads 60% of the time. Each subject started with $25 and could place up to 300 bets. Subjects received a dollar each time they guessed correctly and lost a dollar each time they guessed incorrectly.

Given that the test subjects knew the odds in advance, you'd think that many of them made money. But the test results were surprising:

- The average test subject ended up with only $91.
- 28% of the subjects lost all their money
- 29.5% of the subjects bet everything on one toss
- 66% of the subjects bet on tails at some point

These results show how awful humans are at making decisions in uncertain situations. To improve on human failings, a researcher named J. L. Kelly devised a formula for determining how much to wager when faced with uncertainty. This is called the Kelly criterion, and if any of the test subjects had known about it, they would have bet 20% of their capital on each guess, and would have won much more money.

The Kelly criterion is important for algorithmic trading because it provides a systematic method for determining how much capital should be risked in a trade. This appendix starts by explaining how the Kelly criterion works and then derives the formula using the principles of probability and the Law of Large Numbers.

B.1 Using the Kelly Criterion

The Kelly criterion tells us how much of our resources to allocate when trading. This discussion presents the equation and the next section walks through the process of deriving the equation.

Suppose your trading algorithm is correct p percent of the time. This can be expressed as the success probability, p, by dividing the percentage by 100. That is, if your algorithm is correct 80% of the time, p is 0.8.

The probability of failure, denoted q, is found by subtracting p from 1. If your algorithm makes correct decisions 90% of the time, p equals 0.9 and q equals 1 − 0.9, which equals 0.1.

Now suppose that you make a profit, denoted b, if the algorithm succeeds. If the algorithm fails, your loss is given by a. With this information, the Kelly criterion says that the optimal fraction to risk with each trade is given as follows:

$$f = \frac{pb - qa}{ab}$$

An example will demonstrate how this is used. Suppose a trading algorithm is correct 75% of the time, which means p equals 0.75 and q equals 0.25. Further suppose that each successful trade makes a profit of 5 and each failed trade results in a loss of 6. Therefore, b equals 5 and a equals 6.

According to the Kelly criterion, f equals (0.75*5 − 0.25*6)/6*5, which equals 2.25/30 or 0.075. Therefore the criterion recommends risking at most 7.5% of your available capital per trade.

Returning to the example at the start of the chapter, suppose that a coin comes up heads 60% of the time. If a player gets a dollar every time the coin comes up heads and loses a dollar each time it comes up tails, the player should risk 20% of his/her capital with each flip. This is because (0.6 − 0.4)/1.0 = 0.2.

B.2 Derivation

The Kelly criterion is easy to use but hard to prove. Therefore, before I present the derivation, I need to introduce two important topics: the fundamentals of probability and the Law of Large Numbers.

B.2.1 Brief Review of Probability

To understand the Kelly criterion, you need to have a basic grasp of probability theory, which is concerned with events and their outcomes. For example, if an event is the toss of a coin, probability is concerned with the likelihood of each of the event's outcomes: heads and tails.

To analyze probability, mathematicians assign events to random variables, such as x, and assign each outcome of an event to a value, such as x_i. If x is an event with N possible outcomes, mathematicians want to know the likelihood of each outcome x_i, where i runs from 0 to N-1.

To represent the likelihood of an event's outcomes, we pass the variable to a special function called p. p is called a *probability distribution* and $p(x_i)$ is called the probability of outcome x_i. For example, suppose that x is a coin toss, x_0 represents heads, and x_1 represents tails. If the coin is fair, $p(x_0) = p(x_1) = 1/2$.

The value of $p(x_i)$ always lies between 0.0 and 1.0, and greater values imply greater likelihood. If $p(x_i)$ equals 1, it means that x_i is certain to occur. If $p(x_i) = 0$, it means that x_i is certain not to occur.

Given an event, we know that one of the outcomes will occur. For example, suppose that d represents the roll of a six-sided die and the outcomes are denoted d_0, d_1, d_2, d_3, d_4, and d_5. Regardless of the die's fairness, we know that the sum of the probabilities, $p(d_0) + p(d_1) + p(d_2) + p(d_3) + p(d_4) + p(d_5)$, must equal 1. Therefore, if x is a random variable, we know that the sum of $p(x_i)$ for all x_i must equal 1.

B.2.2 Law of Large Numbers

In real world experiments, we rarely know the exact probability of an event. For example, we can approximate the probability of a coin coming up heads as 0.5, but real coins always have flaws that produce results slightly greater than or less than 0.5.

As the number of experiments grows very large, the Law of Large Numbers makes it possible to arrive at probabilities using experimental results. According to this law, the average of the results obtained from a large number of trials will approach the value expected from the given probability.

As an example, consider the tossing of six-sided dice. In theory, each face has a 1/6 chance of coming up, so the average value of a throw can be found by multiplying each face by its probability: $1(1/6) + 2(1/6) + 3(1/6) + 4(1/6) + 5(1/6) + 6(1/6) = 3.5$.

The Law of Large Numbers states that, as the number of throws increases, it becomes more likely that the average throw will approach 3.5. That is, if you throw the die N times, the result will be closer to 3.5 as N increases.

B.2.3 Obtaining the Kelly Criterion

To derive the formula for the Kelly criterion, let's review the notation established at the start of the chapter:

- **p** — Probability that the algorithm succeeds
- **q** — Probability that the algorithm fails (1 − p)
- **a** — Loss for each dollar traded
- **b** — Profit for each dollar traded
- **f** — Fraction of the total capital risked per trade

In this discussion, the trader's capital is denoted by C_j, where j identifies the number of trades that have executed. C_0 is the trader's initial capital, which means the trader will risk fC_0 on the first trade. If the first trade is successful, the resulting capital is given as follows:

$$C_1 = C_0 + fC_0 b = C_0(1+fb)$$

Looking at this equation, it should be clear that the result of every successful trade can be obtained by multiplying the original capital by 1 + fb. The situation is similar for failed trades. If the second trade fails, the resulting capital is given as follows:

$$C_2 = C_1(1-fa) = C_0(1+fb)(1-fa)$$

This multiplication of 1 + fb and 1 − fa can be expanded for any number of trades. Suppose that a trader executes N trades that result in S_N successes and F_N losses. The trader's final capital is given by this expression:

$$C_N = C_0(1+fb)^{S_N}(1-fa)^{F_N}$$

As N grows large, the Law of Large Numbers tells us that we can approximate p with S_N/N and approximate q with F_N/N. Replacing S_N with pN and F_N with qN produces the following result:

$$C_N = C_0(1+fb)^{pN}(1-fa)^{qN}$$

Appendix B The Kelly Criterion

Now the goal is to compute the value of f that leads to the largest possible value of C_N. It's easier to work with sums of terms instead of products of terms, so it helps to transform the equation using logarithms. For this discussion, there are four points to know:

- As a value increases, its logarithm will increase. Therefore, the maximum value of C_N will be reached when $\log(C_N)$ reaches its maximum value.
- The logarithm of a product equals the sum of the logarithms of the values that form the product. In equation form, $\log(ab) = \log(a) + \log(b)$.
- The logarithm of a value raised to an exponent equals the exponent times the logarithm of the value. In equation form, $\log(x^N) = N \log(x)$.
- The derivative of the logarithm of a function equals the reciprocal of the function. In equation form, the derivative with respect to x of $\log(x) \approx 1/x$.

With this in mind, we can transform the preceding equation by dividing both sides by C_0, taking the logarithm of both sides, and dividing by N. Here's the result:

$$\log\left(\frac{C_N}{C_0}\right) = \log\left[(1+fb)^{pN}(1-fa)^{qN}\right]$$

$$\log\left(\frac{C_N}{C_0}\right) = \log\left[(1+fb)^{pN}\right] + \log\left[(1-fa)^{qN}\right]$$

$$\log\left(\frac{C_N}{C_0}\right) = pN\log(1+fb) + qN\log(1-fa)$$

$$\frac{1}{N}\log\left(\frac{C_N}{C_0}\right) = p\log(1+fb) + q\log(1-fa)$$

The term on the left is called the *logarithm of wealth*. It should be clear that this reaches its maximum value when C_N reaches its maximum value. Therefore, the value of f that maximizes the logarithm of wealth will also maximize C_N.

We can determine which value of f maximizes C_N by finding the derivative of the right side with respect to f and setting it to zero. The values p, q, b, and a are all constant with respect to f, so the resulting relationship can be expressed in the following way:

$$\frac{d}{df}\{p\log(1+fb) + q\log(1-fa)\} = 0$$

$$\frac{pb}{1+fb} - \frac{qa}{1-fa} = 0$$

At this point, solving for f becomes a matter of algebraic manipulation:

$$\frac{pb}{1+fb} - \frac{qa}{1-fa} = 0$$
$$\frac{pb}{1+fb} = \frac{qa}{1-fa}$$
$$pb - pbfa = qa + qafb$$
$$pbfa + qafb = pb - qa$$
$$fab(p+q) = pb - qa$$
$$f = \frac{pb-qa}{ab(p+q)} = \frac{pb-qa}{ab}$$

As promised, the result is the Kelly criterion. The simplification in the last line is possible because q equals 1 − p. Therefore, the sum of p and q can be replaced with 1.

B.3 Criticism and Alternatives

While the Kelly criterion has been adopted by many gamblers and investors, a number of people have found fault with it. One issue is that the criterion recommends very large wagers when the probability of winning is high. For example, if an event has an 80% chance of success and equal payoff/loss, the criterion recommends risking 60%.

Rather than risk so much, many traders prefer the half Kelly system, which divides the criterion's result by two. Others prefer a fractional Kelly system, which divides the criterion's result by a number greater than two. These strategies produce suboptimal returns, but they ensure that the trader won't lose a substantial amount of money.

Another issue is that the criterion requires precise knowledge of the probability of success, which is hard to come by. To address this, three researchers at Simon Fraser University (Dani Chu, Yifan Wu and Tim B. Swartz) devised a modified criterion that takes uncertainty into account. To be specific, they replaced p with a density function $\pi(p)$ and used Bayesian reasoning to arrive at a new expression for the amount to be risked. Their modified criterion always recommends risking less than the Kelly criterion.

The math behind the modified Kelly criterion is beyond the scope of this book. But you can freely download the research paper at people.stat.sfu.ca/~tim/papers/kelly.pdf.

B.4 Summary

Journalists love to harp on the difficulty of financial trading, and countless articles have been written about the small percentage of day traders and futures traders who make money. The failure rates make it sound like the game is rigged, but people overlook how terrible humans are at making decisions in the face of risk. The game may not be completely fair, but in many cases, a trader's biggest obstacle is his or her own mindset.

To assist with the decision-making process, the Kelly criterion tells us how much an algorithm should risk on a given trade. As discussed in this chapter, the criterion can be derived by combining the basic laws of probability with the Law of Large Numbers.

Many successful investors, such as Warren Buffett and Bill Gross, rely on the Kelly criterion when making trades. Others are more skeptical. Rather than risk significant portions of their capital, they prefer the half Kelly or fractional Kelly strategies, which reduce the amount to be risked. Also, researchers have devised a modified Kelly criterion that accounts for the uncertainty in determining the probabilities of failure and success.

Index

A

accountSummary callback function 142, 150, 154
accumulation/distribution line 248, 249, 250, 251
adaptive algorithm 211, 222, 227
algorithms
  adaptive 211-212, 222, 227
  arrival price 211-213
  dark ice 211, 213-214
  percentage of volume 211-213
  Time Weighted Average Price (TWAP) 211, 214
  Volume Weighted Average Price (VWAP) 211, 214-215
Application class 364, 388
arrival price algorithm 211, 213
Average True Range (ATR) 251-253, 304, 308, 313

B

basic probability theory 393
bear call spreads 62-63
bear put spreads 62
Black-Scholes equation 52, 262
block orders 209-210, 228
Bollinger Bands 254-256, 317-326
Bollinger, John 315
Bollinger-MFI trading system 315-326

box spreads 72
bracket orders 26, 206-207, 222, 227, 353, 355
brokerage mode 16
bull call spreads 61
bull put spreads 62
butterfly spreads 69-71

C

calculateImpliedVolatility function 260, 262
calculateOptionPrice function 260, 262
calendar spreads 64, 86
callable bonds 32, 34
callback functions 97
cancelOrder function 260
candlestick charts 23-24
close location value (CLV) 248-251
ComboLeg structure 117-118
ComisssionReport structure 144
commissionReport callback function 142-143
CommissionReport structure 145
Computer-To-Computer Interface (CTCI) 359
condor spreads 71-72
connect function 96
connection state 101-102

continuous futures contracts 81
`ContractDescription` structure 123-127
`contractDetails` callback function 119-120, 127, 301
`ContractDetails` structure 119-125
`Contract` structure
  accessing data 123, 126
  accessing details 118-120
  derivative-specific fields 116-117
  fundamental fields 112-114
  introduction 111
  optional fields 115, 116
convertible bonds 32
corporate bonds 29-35
coupon payments 30
covered calls 58-59
credit quality 31
currency configuration 113
`currentTime` callback function 95-99, 107
CUSIP code 34

D

dark ice algorithm 211, 213-214
`Decoder` class 96
delta 52, 53, 54, 66
delta neutral strategies 66
Dennis, Richard 296, 303
derivatives 37

E

`EClient` class 91, 94-103, 118
`EClientSocket` class 102, 106-107, 185
`EClientSocketSSL` class 103
`EDecoder` class 105
EFP (exchange for physical) 85-88
`EMessage` class 105
`EReader` class 96, 104-108
error callback function 97, 107
`ESocketClient` class 100
`ESocketClientSSL` class 100
`EWrapper` class 91, 95-107, 139, 185

example code 9, 10
exchange for physical (EFP) 85-88
exchanges (supported by IB) 114-115
`execDetails` callback function 142-143
`ExecutionCondition` class 217-218
`ExecutionFilter` structure 143
`Execution` structure 143-144
`exerciseOptions` function 260, 261
exponential moving average (EMA) 230, 232-239, 243, 303

F

face value 30
`FieldBase` class 369
`FileLogFactory` class 367
`FileStoreFactory` class 367
Financial Information eXchange (FIX)
  introduction 359-360
  message tags 361-363
  specifications 360-361
FOK (fill or kill orders) 137-138
fundamental data analysis 157
`fundamentalData` callback function 177, 187
futures contracts
  cash settlement 81, 84
  continuous 81, 296-299, 302
  expiration 80-81, 86
  fees 6
  index futures 84
  introduction 78-80
  margin requirements 81-82, 84
  physical delivery 81, 84
  position limits 82
  single-stock futures (SSFs) 84
  trading limits 82
  underlying assets 79-80

G

gamma 52-54
generic ticks 164-165

H

Hamming, Richard 229
hedging orders 206-209
`histogramData` callback function 176
historical data access 158
`historicalData` callback 246, 301
`historicalData` callback function 173, 231-236, 239-243, 247, 249-255, 299-301, 342-343, 347, 351
`historicalDataEnd` callback function 231, 234, 238-241, 248-251, 255, 347, 351
`historicalDataUpdate` callback function 173
`historicalNews` callback function 181
`historicalTicksBidAsk` callback function 175
`historicalTicks` callback function 175
HTTP (Hypertext Transfer Protocol) 92-93, 103

I

IB Gateway 92
 downloading 35
 introduction 35
 usage 36
iceberg order 213
implied volatility 51-52, 262
initial margin 28
Interactive Brokers
 fees 4-6
 history 2-3
 starting an account 3
iron butterfly spreads 70
iron condor spreads 71

J

junk bonds 32

K

Kelly criterion
 criticism 396

derivation 392-396
introduction 391-392

L

Law of Large Numbers 393-394, 397
LEAPS (long-term equity anticipation securities) 48
Level II data 159-160, 171, 188
Lewis, Michael 1
limit orders 26, 39, 129, 131-134, 353
linear regression 344-345
logarithms 395-396

M

MACD (moving average convergence/diverence) 232-236
maintenance margin 28
margin 28-29
`MarginCondition` class 217-219
market data access 158
market data lines 160-161
market data request messages 373-374
market data subscriptions 159-160
market order 138
market orders 26, 128-131
market scanner 29, 33, 189-190
`Message` class 368-369, 388
message queues 94, 105
messages 94, 105
modified Kelly criterion 396, 397
momentum indicators 236-245
Money Flow Index (MFI) 316-325
moneyness 50, 53-55
moving averages 230-231
municipal bonds 29

N

NBBO (National Best Bid and Offer) 135-136, 160
`newsArticle` callback function 180
news feeds 179
`newsProviders` callback function 178

news sources 178
news subscriptions 178
`nextValidId` callback function 154, 357

O

OCA (one cancels all) 138, 139
official documentation 12
on-balance volume (OBV) 245-247
one cancels all (OCA) orders 26
`openOrder` callback function 97, 140-142, 150, 154, 355, 358
option chains 48-49, 263-270
options
  assignment 40
  bear call spreads 62
  bear put spreads 62
  bull put spreads 62
  butterfly spreads 69
  calls 40-44
  covered calls 58-59
  credit spreads 62-63
  diagonal spreads 66
  expiration 39-41, 46-47, 49
  Greeks 52-55
  horizontal spreads 64-66
  implied volatility 51-52
  introduction 38-47
  moneyness 50, 57
  premium 39-40
  protective puts 59
  puts 44-46
  risk graphs 39, 42-44, 58-59, 62-69
  spreads 62
  strike price 39-41
  value 50-51
  vertical spreads 60-63
  weekly 47
Options Clearing Corporation 5
`OrderCondition` class 215-217, 227
order status 27
`orderStatus` callback function 140-142, 154
`Order` structure

accessing data 144
dynamic conditions 215-221
fundamental fields 128-129
introduction 111, 128
obtaining valid ID 139-140
placing the order 139-141
requesting data 142-143
submission algorithms 211
submitting large orders 209-210
timing and visibility 136-138
types of orders 129-136
order types 25-26

P

paper-trading mode 16
parent-child orders 206-208, 224
pegged orders 129, 134-136
percentage of volume algorithm 211-213
`PercentChangeCondition` class 217-219
Peterffy, Thomas 1-2
pivot points 340-344
`placeOrder` function 140, 148-152, 225, 355-356
polymorphism 217
`position` callback function 142, 150, 154, 358
`PriceCondition` class 215, 217, 220-221
Price Improvement Period (PIP) 115
price-to-earnings ratio 23
probability distributions 393
protective puts 59
putable bonds 32-33
PYTHONPATH variable 95

Q

quadratic regression 344-346, 349, 352
QuickFIX
  `Application` class 364-365, 388
  execution report messages 379-385
  execution reports 378, 385
  `FieldBase` class 369
  `FileLogFactory` class 367
  `FileStoreFactory` class 367

introduction 364
market data request messages 373-374
`Message` class 368-369, 388
message types 371
`Session` class 368, 388
settings file 366
single order messages 374-378
`SocketInitiator` class 365-388

R

ratio spreads 72-73
`realTimeBar` callback function 184
Relative Strength Index (RSI) 241-245, 316
`reqAccountSummary` function 142-148, 150, 152
`reqAllOpenOrders` function 142, 143
`reqAutoOpenOrders` function 142, 143
`reqContractDetails` function 118-120, 123-127, 225, 261-263, 296, 299, 302
`reqCurrentTime` function 94-99, 107-108
`reqExecutions` function 142-143
`reqFundamentalData` function 176-177, 181-184
`reqGlobalCancel` function 260
`reqHistogramData` function 172, 176
`reqHistoricalData` function 172-176, 181-185, 230-231, 243, 296-302, 341-347
`reqHistoricalNews` function 180
`reqHistoricalTicks` function 172-175, 230
`reqIds` function 148, 152, 225, 357
`reqMatchingSymbols` function 118, 122, 123-127
`reqMktData` function 164-165, 170, 179-182, 184, 261, 263
`reqMktDepth` function 171
`reqNewsArticle` function 180
`reqNewsBulletins` function 179
`reqNewsProviders` function 178
`reqOpenOrders` function 97, 142-143
`reqPositions` function 142-145, 148-152, 261, 358
`reqRealTimeBars` function 170, 181, 182, 184, 187
`reqScannerSubscription` function 189, 194-199, 201-203, 336-339
`reqSecDefOptParams` function 260-265, 271
`reqTickByTickData` function 161-163, 181-185, 263
resistance level 340-344, 347, 349, 352

S

scale orders 209-210, 228
`scannerData` callback function 189, 194-203, 337, 339
`scannerDataEnd` callback function 337, 339
`scannerParameters` callback function 195
`ScannerSubscription` structure 189, 190-195, 198, 199, 336-339
Secure Sockets Layer (SSL) 18, 92, 93, 103
`securityDefinitionOptionalParameter` callback function 271
`securityDefinitionOptionParameter` callback function 261
`serverVersion` function 101
`Session` class 368, 388
short sales 27, 45
single-stock futures (SSFs) 84, 87
SMART routing 114, 129, 136-138

smoothed moving average (SMMA) 241-245, 251-252
snapshots 164-165
socket communication 92-97
`SocketInitiator` class 365-388
S&P 500 stock index 331
special memorandum accounts (SMAs) 147
spreads
  bear call spreads 63
  bear put spreads 62
  box spreads 72
  bull put spreads 62
  butterfly spreads 70-71
  calendar spreads 86
  condor spreads 71-72
  credit spreads 60, 63
  debit spreads 60-63

diagonal spreads 66
futures contracts 85
horizontal spreads 64-66, 85
iron butterfly spreads 70
iron condor spreads 71
ratio spreads 72-73
straddles 66-67
strangles 66-68
vertical spreads 60, 75
SSFs (single stock futures) 84, 87
SSL (secure sockets layer) 92-93, 103
standard deviation 254-256
stop order adjustments 206-208
stop orders 26, 129-133, 353
straddles 66-67, 259
strangles 66-68, 259
support 352
support level 340-344, 347-349
`symbolSamples` callback function 123-125

T

technical data 157
theta 52, 55
`tickByTickAllLast` callback function 162
`tickByTickBidAsk` callback function 162
`tickByTickMidpoint` callback function 162-163, 184
`tickEFP` callback function 166
`tickGeneric` callback function 166
`tickOptionComputation` callback function 166, 262
`tickPrice` callback function 166, 170, 187, 263
ticks (generic) 164-165
`tickSize` callback function 166, 187, 263
`tickString` callback function 166
ticks versus bars 158
tick types 162, 166
`TimeCondition` class 215-218
time in force 26, 137-138
Time Weighted Average Price (TWAP) algorithm 211, 214
Trader Workstation

bond trading 29-35
corporate bonds 33
downloading 15
futures trading 83-87
history 2
introduction 7-8, 15-16
main window 16-18
market scanner 29, 33
options trading 48-52
order placement process 19
spread trading 74
stock trading 19-27
watchlists 20-21
Trader Worsktation
spread trading 73
Trading Academy 12
trailing stop orders 129, 133-134
Treasury bonds 29
trend indicators 230-236
True Strength Index (TSI) 237-239
Turtle trading system 303-315
TWS API
downloading 8
file structure 9

U

`updateMktDepth2` callback function 172
`updateMktDepth` callback function 172
`updateNewsBulletin` callback function 179

V

vega 52-55
vertical spreads 60
virtual functions 104
volatility index 331-332
volatility indicators 251-256
volatility orders 129, 136
`VolumeCondition` class 217, 220, 224, 227
volume indicators 245-247, 250
Volume Weighted Average Price (VWAP) algorithm 211, 214-215

X

XML (eXtensible Markup Language) 177, 181, 187

Y

yield to maturity (YTM) 31

Made in the USA
Columbia, SC
01 March 2021